TAKING SIDES

Clashing Views on Controversial

Issues in Business Ethics and Society

EIGHTH EDITION

W9-BNU-499

TAKING SIDES

Clashing Views on Controversial

Issues in Business Ethics and Society

EIGHTH EDITION

Selected, Edited, and with Introductions by

Lisa H. Newton
Fairfield University

and

Maureen M. Ford
Fairfield University

McGraw-Hill/Dushkin
A Division of The McGraw-Hill Companies

To our husbands—Victor J. Newton, Jr.,
and James H. L. Ford, Jr.

Photo Acknowledgment
Cover image: © 2004 by PhotoDisc, Inc.

Cover Art Acknowledgment
Charles Vitelli

Copyright © 2004 by McGraw-Hill/Dushkin,
A Division of The McGraw-Hill Companies, Inc., Guilford, Connecticut 06437

Copyright law prohibits the reproduction, storage, or transmission in any form by any means of any portion of this publication without the express written permission of McGraw-Hill/Dushkin and of the copyright holder (if different) of the part of the publication to be reproduced. The Guidelines for Classroom Copying endorsed by Congress explicitly state that unauthorized copying may not be used to create, to replace, or to substitute for anthologies, compilations, or collective works.

Taking Sides ® is a registered trademark of McGraw-Hill/Dushkin

Manufactured in the United States of America

Eighth Edition

23456789BAHBAH7654

Library of Congress Cataloging-in-Publication Data
Main entry under title:
Taking sides: clashing views on controversial issues in business ethics and society/selected, edited, and with introductions by Lisa H. Newton and Maureen M. Ford.—8th ed.
Includes bibliographical references and index.
1. Business ethics. I. Newton, Lisa H., *comp.* II. Ford, Maureen M., *comp.*
174.4
0-07-291719·9
ISSN: 95-83859

Printed on Recycled Paper

Preface

*From the very beginning of critical thought, we find the distinction be-
tween topics susceptible of certain knowledge and topics about which
uncertain opinions are available. The dawn of this distinction, explicitly
entertained, is the dawn of modern mentality. It introduces criticism.*

— Alfred North Whitehead
Adventures of Ideas (1933)

This volume contains 38 selections, presented in a pro and con format,
that debate a total of 19 different controversial issues in business ethics. In this
book we ask you, the reader, to examine the accepted practices of business in
light of human needs, justice, rights, and dignity. We ask you to consider what
moral imperatives and values should be at work in the conduct of business.

This method of presenting opposing views on an issue grows out of the
ancient learning method of *dialogue*. Two presumptions lead us to seek the
truth in a dialogue between opposed positions: The first presumption is that
the truth is really out there and that it is important to find it. The second is
that no one of us has all of it (the truth). The way to reach the truth is to form
our initial opinions on a subject and give voice to them in public. Then we
let others with differing opinions reply, and while they are doing so, we listen
carefully. The truth that comes into being in the public space of the dialogue
becomes part of our opinion—now a more informed opinion, and now based
on the reasoning that emerged in the course of the airing of opposing views.

Each issue in this volume has an issue *introduction*, which sets the stage
for the debate as it is argued in the YES and NO selections. Each issue concludes
with a *postscript* that makes some final observations and points the way to other
questions related to the issue. The introductions and postscripts do not preempt
what is the reader's own task: to achieve a critical and informed view of the
issue at stake. In reading an issue and forming your own opinion, you should
not feel confined to adopt one or the other of the positions presented. There
are positions in between the given views, or totally outside of them, and the
suggestions for further reading that appear in each issue postscript should help
you to continue your study of the subject. At the back of the book is a listing
of all the *contributors to this volume*, which will give you information on the
philosophers, business professors, businesspeople, and business commentators
whose views are debated here.

Changes to this edition This edition represents a substantial revision. There
are four completely new issues: *Can Individual Virtue Survive Corporate Pressure?*
(Issue 2); *Should Corporations Adopt Policies of Corporate Social Responsibility?* (Issue 4); *Are Pharmaceutical Firms Obliged to Cut Their Prices for Poor AIDS Victims?*
(Issue 5); and *Does the Enron Collapse Show That We Need More Regulation of the*

Energy Industry? (Issue 8). The introductions and postscripts for all of the issues have been modified in minor ways to account for the changing of the century. However, they have also been updated to reflect more substantial changes that have taken place since the previous edition of the book, such as the magnitude of increase in CEO salaries. This has required new analysis and has been incorporated into the material.

A word to the instructor   An *Instructor's Manual With Test Questions* (multiple-choice and essay) is available through the publisher for the instructor using *Taking Sides* in the classroom. A general guidebook, *Using Taking Sides in the Classroom*, which discusses methods and techniques for integrating the pro-con approach into any classroom setting, is also available. An online version of *Using Taking Sides in the Classroom* and a correspondence service for *Taking Sides* adopters can be found at http://www.dushkin.com/usingts/.

Taking Sides: Clashing Views on Controversial Issues in Business Ethics and Society is only one title in the Taking Sides series. If you are interested in seeing the table of contents for any of the other titles, please visit the Taking Sides Web site at http://www.dushkin.com/takingsides/.

Acknowledgments   Praise and thanks are due to God and our families, without whose patience and support this volume would never have been completed.

Lisa H. Newton
Fairfield University

Maureen M. Ford
Fairfield University

Contents In Brief

Contents

Free-market economist Adam Smith (1723–1790) states that if self-interested people are left alone to seek their own economic advantage, the result will be greater advantage for all. German philosopher Karl Marx (1818–1883) and German sociologist Friedrich Engels (1820–1895) argue that if people are left to their own self-interested devices, those who own the means of production will rapidly reduce everyone else to virtual slaves.

Joining the long-standing debate on the possibility of free choice and moral agency in the business world, Quincy Lee Centennial Professor of Business and Philosophy at the University of Texas in Austin Robert C. Solomon argues that whatever the structures, the individual's choice is free, and therefore his character or virtue is of the utmost importance in creating a good moral tone in the life of a business. Stuart Professor of Philosophy at Princeton University Gilbert Harman employs determinist arguments to conclude that no individual can of his own free choice make a difference in a group enterprise.

Josef Wieland, director of the German Business Ethics Network's Centre for Business Ethics, concludes that one can only be a moral person at work when the workplace, too, is moral. Ian Maitland, professor of business, government, and society at the University of Minnesota's Carlson School of Management, counters that changing the rules will only succeed in impairing the corporation's efficiency.

Robert D. Hay, professor of management at the University of Arkansas, and Edmund R. Gray, professor and chair of the Department of Management at Loyola Marymount University, argue that in the long run, businesses will only be successful if they are directed to the needs of the society. If they choose to ignore that advice, government regulation is likely to fill the gap between business operations and the welfare of the people the government is sworn to protect. In this classic defense of *laissez-faire*, Paul Snowden Russell Distinguished Service Professor Emeritus of Economics at the University of Chicago Milton Friedman states that businesses have neither the right, in law or morals, nor the ability to meddle with "social responsibility." Customers, employees, and the general public, he concludes, are best served when the company simply does its job with maximum efficiency.

PART 2   CURRENT ISSUES IN BUSINESS   97

Writer Debra Watson argues that the greed of AIDS profiteers is killing impoverished people with AIDS all over the world—including in the United States. She concludes that only drastic price reductions will make necessary drugs available to the victims. Senior fellow at the Manhattan Institute

Robert Goldberg doubts that reducing pharmaceutical prices will make much of a difference to AIDS sufferers, since the education and health infrastructures remain inadequate to reach and teach the victims.

Political theorist William A. Galston and research scholar David Wasserman argue that there are significant moral objections to widespread casino gambling. Professor of economics William R. Eadington counters that gambling is a normal extension of commercial activity.

Frank Partnoy, former trader and salesman at Morgan Stanley, states that derivative instruments are generally good only for making large commissions for the salesmen who push them on unwary insurance companies and pension funds. Merton H. Miller, a Nobel Prize–winning economist, contends that derivatives allow financial players to hedge their bets more efficiently, and in doing so they make the world a safer place.

Writer Richard Rosen contends that the disastrous collapse of the Enron energy company—accompanied by soaring prices in California, disruptions of the market in the United States and abroad, and accusations of fraud all around—means that America needs more government oversight. Christopher L. Culp, adjunct professor of finance at the Graduate School of Business at the University of Chicago, and Steve H. Hanke, professor of applied economics at the Johns Hopkins University, maintain that it was unwise regulation that caused the Enron problem in the first place. They conclude that only deregulation will let the market clear up the problems with the industry.

corporations tend to deal with long-term customers and suppliers and must therefore adhere to moral standards or lose business.

Susan S. Black, publisher of *Bobbin*, argues that customers will not tolerate goods made by slave labor, children, or women working in inhumane conditions. Allen R. Myerson, a writer for the *New York Times*, looks at the economies of less developed countries and finds that allowing their citizens to work in sweatshops may be the only option these nations have.

Jeremy Rifkin, president of the Foundation on Economic Trends, fears that genetic engineering extends human power over the rest of nature in ways that are unprecedented and whose consequences cannot be known. William Domnarski, an intellectual property lawyer, finds the patenting of genes or genetic discoveries no different than patenting any other ideas.

PART 6   ENVIRONMENTAL POLICY AND CORPORATE RESPONSIBILITY   329

John Shanahan, vice president of the Alexis de Tocqueville Institution in Arlington, Virginia, concedes that environmental problems exist but denies that there is any environmental "crisis." Environmental scientists Paul R. Ehrlich and Anne H. Ehrlich contend that many objections to environmental protections are self-serving and based on bad or misused science.

Economics professors Thomas A. Carr and Sunder Ramaswamy and mathematics teacher Heather L. Pedersen state that sustainable use of rain forest products helps to preserve the forest and support the local economy. Investigative reporter Jon Entine asserts that most green marketing programs do nothing to slow forest destruction and frequently result in the mistreatment of employees, vendors, and customers.

Introduction

An Essay on the Background of Business Ethics: Ethics, Economics, Law, and the Corporation

Lisa H. Newton

Maureen M. Ford

All philosophy is a conversation, and the part of the philosophy known as *ethics* is no exception. Ethics is a conversation about conduct, the doing of good and the avoiding of evil. *Business ethics* is a conversation about right and wrong conduct in the business world.

This book is aimed at an audience of students who expect to be in business, who know that there are knotty ethical problems out there, and who want a chance to confront them ahead of time. The method of confronting them is an invitation to join in a debate, a contest of contrary facts and conflicting values in many of the major issues of the day. This introductory essay should make it easier to join in the arguments. Managing ethical policy problems in a company requires a wide background—in ethics, economics, law, and the social sciences—which this book cannot hope to provide. But since some background assumptions in these fields are relevant to several of the problems we examine in this volume, we will sketch out very briefly the major understandings that control them. There is ultimately no substitute for thorough study of the rules of the game and years of experience and practice; but an overview of the playing field may at least make it easier for you to understand the object and limitations of the standard plays.

"Business ethics" was generally known to be an oxymoron until the last twenty years. Then came the alarming newspaper headlines. Foreign bribes, scandals on Wall Street, exploding cars, and conflicts over whistle blowers and civil rights in the workplace suddenly appeared in the headlines and would not go away. Now value questions are never absent from business decisions, and moral responsibility is the first requirement of a manager in any business. Out of this has emerged a general consensus that a thorough grounding in ethical reasoning is essential preparation for a career in business.

This book will not supply the substance of a course in ethics. For that you are directed to any of several excellent texts in business ethics or to any general text in ethics. *Taking Sides: Clashing Views on Controversial Issues in Business Ethics and Society* teaches ethics from the issue upward, rather than from the

Table 1

Fundamental Duties

	Beneficence—promoting human welfare	Justice—acknowledging human equality	Respect for Persons—honoring individual freedom
Basic fact about human nature that grounds the duty	Humans are animals, with vulnerable bodies and urgent physical needs, capable of suffering.	Humans are social animals who must live in communities and therefore must adopt social structures to maintain communities.	Humans are rational, free—able to make their own choices, foresee the consequences, and take responsibility.
Value realized in performance of the duty	Human welfare; happiness.	Human equality.	Human dignity; autonomy.
Working out of the duty in ethical theory	Best modern example is utilitarianism, from Jeremy Bentham and John Stuart Mill, who saw morality as that which produced the greatest happiness for the greatest number. Reasoning is consequential, aimed at results.	Best modern example is John Rawls's theory of justice as "fairness"; maintaining equality unless inequality helps everyone. Reasoning is deontological: morality derived from duty, not consequences.	Best modern example is Immanuel Kant's formalism, where morality is seen as the working out of the categorical imperative. Reasoning is deontological.
Samples of implementation of the duty in business	Protecting safety of employees; maintaining pleasant working conditions; contributing funds to the local community.	Obedience to law; enforcing fair rules; nondiscrimination; no favoritism; giving credit where credit is due.	Respect for employee rights; treating employees as persons, not just as tools; respecting differences of opinion.

© 1988 Lisa Newton

principle downward. You will, however, come upon much of the terminology of ethical reasoning in the course of considering these cases. For your reference, a brief summary of the ethical principles and forms of reasoning most used in this book is found in Table 1.

Economics: The Capitalist Background

Capitalism as we know it is the product of the thought of Adam Smith (1723–1790), a Scottish philosopher and economist, and a small number of his European contemporaries. The fundamental capitalist act is the *voluntary exchange:* two adults of sound mind and clear purposes meet in the marketplace, to which each repairs in order to satisfy some felt need. To the participant in the free market, the *marginal utility* of the thing acquired must exceed that of the thing traded, or else why make the deal? So each party to the voluntary exchange walks away from it richer.

Adding to the value of the exchange is the *competition* of dealers and buyers; because there are many purveyors of each good in the marketplace, the customer is not forced to pay exorbitant prices for things needed. Conversely, competition among the customers (typified by an auction) makes sure that the available goods end up in the hands of those to whom they are worth the most. So at the end of the market day, everyone goes home not only richer (in real terms) than when they came—the voluntariness of the exchange ensures that— but also as rich as they could possibly be, since each had available all possible options of goods or services to buy and all possible purchasers of the goods or services brought to the marketplace for sale.

Sellers and buyers win the competition through *efficiency;* that is, through producing the best quality goods at the lowest possible price or through allotting their scarce resources toward the most valuable of the choices presented to them. It is to the advantage of all participants in the market, then, to strive for efficiency. Adam Smith's most memorable accomplishment was to recognize that the general effect of all this self-interested scrambling would be to make the most possible goods of the best possible quality available at the least possible price. Meanwhile, sellers and buyers alike must keep an eye on the market as a whole, adjusting production and purchasing to take advantage of fluctuations in *supply and demand*. Short supply will make goods more valuable, raising the price, and that will bring more suppliers into the market, whose competition will lower the price to just above the cost of manufacture for the most efficient producers. Increased demand for any reason will have the same effect. Should supply exceed demand, the price will fall to a point where the goods will be bought. Putting this all together, Smith realized that in a system of free enterprise, you have demonstrably the best possible chance of finding for sale what you want, in good quantity and quality and at a reasonable price. Forget benevolent monarchs ordering things for our own good, Smith suggested; in this system, we are led as by an *invisible hand* of enlightened self-interest to achieve the common good, even as we think we are being most selfish.

Adam Smith's theory of economic enterprise emerged in the natural law tradition of the eighteenth century. As was the fashion for that period, Smith presented his conclusions as a series of laws: the law of supply and demand, which links supply, demand, and price; the law that links efficiency with success; and, ultimately, the laws that link the absolute freedom of the market with the absolute growth of the wealth of the free-market country.

To these laws were added others, specifying the conditions under which business enterprise would be conducted in capitalist countries. The laws of *population* formulated by English clergyman and economist Thomas Malthus (1766–1834) concluded that population would always outstrip food production, ensuring that the bulk of humanity would always live at the subsistence level. Since Smith had already postulated that employers would purchase labor at the lowest possible price, it was a one-step derivation for English economist David Ricardo (1772–1823) to conclude that workers' *wages* would never exceed the subsistence level, no matter how prosperous industrial enterprise should become. From these capitalist theorists proceeded the nineteenth-century assumption that society would inevitably divide into two classes, a minority of fabulous wealth and a majority of subsistence-level workers.

These laws, like the laws of physics advanced at that time by Sir Isaac Newton (1642–1727) and the laws of psychology and government advanced at that time by John Locke (1632–1704), were held to be immutable facts of nature, true forever and not subject to change. No concept of progress, or of the historical fitness of a system to society at a point in time, was contemplated.

The Marxian Critique

Only within the last century and a half have we learned to think "historically." The notion of progress, the vision of a better future, and even the very idea that we might modify that future, in part by the discernment of historical trends, were unknown to the ancients and of no interest to medieval chroniclers. For Western political philosophy, history emerged as a factor in our understanding only with the work of the nineteenth-century German philosopher G. W. F. Hegel (1770–1831), who traced the history of the Western world as an ordered series of ideal forms, evolving one from another in logical sequence toward an ideal future. A young German student of Hegel's, Karl Marx (1818–1883), concluded from his study of philosophy and economics that Hegel had to be wrong: the phases of history were ruled not by ideas but by the *material conditions* of life, and their evolution one from another came about as the ruling class of each age generated its own revolutionary overthrow.

Marx's theory, especially as it applies to the evolution of capitalism, is enormously complex; for the purposes of this unit, it can be summarized simply. According to Marx, the *ruling class* in every age is the group that *owns the means of production* of the age's product. Throughout the seventeenth century, the product was almost exclusively agricultural, and the means of production was almost exclusively agricultural land: landowners were the aristocrats and rulers. With the coming of commerce and industry, the owners of the factories joined the ruling class and eventually dominated it. It was in the nature of such capital-intensive industry to concentrate within itself more capital: as Adam Smith had proved, its greater efficiency would drive all smaller labor-intensive industry out of business, and its enormous income would be put to work as more capital, expanding the domain of the factory and the machine indefinitely (at the expense of the cottage industry and the human being). Thus would the wealth of society concentrate in fewer and fewer hands, as the owners of the factories expanded their enterprises without limit into mighty industrial empires, dominated by machines and by the greed of their owners.

Meanwhile, all this wealth was being produced by a new class of workers, the unskilled factory workers. Taken from the ranks of the obsolete peasantry, artisans, and craftsmen, this new working class, the *proletariat,* expanded in numbers with the gigantic mills, whose "hands" they were. Work on the assembly line demanded no education or skills, so the workers could never make themselves valuable enough to command a living wage on the open market. They survived as a vast underclass, interchangeable with the unemployed workers (recently displaced by more machines) who gathered around the factory gates looking for jobs—*their* jobs. As capitalism and its factories expanded, the entire population, except the wealthy capitalist families, sank into this hopeless, pauperized class.

So Marx saw Western society under capitalism as one that ultimately would be divided into a small group of fabulously wealthy capitalists and a mass of paupers, mostly factory workers. The minority would keep the majority in strict control through its hired thugs (the state—the army and the police), control rendered easier by thought control (the schools and the churches). The purpose of the ideology taught by the schools and the churches—the value structure of capitalism—was to show both classes that the capitalists had a right to their wealth (through the sham of liberty, free enterprise, and the utilitarian benefits of the free market) and a perfect right to govern everyone else (through the sham of democracy and equal justice). Thus, the capitalists could enjoy their wealth in good conscience and the poor would understand their moral obligation to accept the oppression of the ruling class with good cheer.

Marx foresaw, and in his writings attempted to help bring about, the disillusionment of the workers: there would come a point when the workers would suddenly ask, *Why* should we accept oppression all our lives? Their search for answers to this question would show them the history of their situation, expose the falsehood of the ideology and the false consciousness of those who believe it, show them their own strength, and lead them directly to the solution that would usher in the new age of socialism—the revolutionary overthrow of the capitalist regime. Why, after all, should they not undertake such a revolution? People are restrained from violence against oppression only by the prospect of losing something valuable, and, as Marx concluded, the industrialized workers of the world had nothing to lose but their chains.

As feudalism had been swept away, then, by the "iron broom" of the French Revolution, so capitalism would be swept away by the revolt of the masses. After the first rebellions, Marx foresaw no lengthy problem of divided loyalties in the industrialized countries of the world. Once the scales had fallen from their eyes, the working-class hirelings of the army and police would quickly turn their guns on their masters and join their natural allies in the proletariat to create the new world.

After the revolution, Marx predicted, there would be a temporary "dictatorship of the proletariat," during which the last vestiges of capitalism would be eradicated and the authority to run the industrial establishment would be returned to the workers of each industry. Once the economy had been de-centralized, to turn each factory into an industrial commune run by its own workers and each landed estate into an agricultural commune run by its farm-ers, the state as such would simply wither away. Some central authority would certainly continue to exist, to coordinate and facilitate the exchange of goods within the country. But with no ruling class to serve and no oppression to carry out, there will be no need of the state to rule *people;* what is left will be confined to the administration of *things.*

Even as he wrote, just in time for the revolutions in Europe of 1848, Marx expected the end of capitalism as a system. Not that capitalism was evil in itself; Marx did not presume to make moral judgments on history. Indeed, capitalism was necessary as an economic system to concentrate the wealth of the country into the industries of the modern age. So, in Marx's judgment, capitalism had a respectable past and would still be necessary for awhile in the developing countries to launch their industries. But that task completed, it had no further role in history, and the longer it stayed around, the more the workers would suffer and the more violent the revolution would be when it came. The sooner the revolution, the better; the future belonged to communism.

As the collapse of the Communist governments in Eastern Europe demon-strates, the course of history has not proceeded quite as Marx predicted in 1848. In fairness, it might be pointed out that no other prophets of the time had any more luck with prognostication; the twentieth century took all of us by surprise. But there is much in Marx's analysis that is rock solid, possibly for reasons, especially ethical reasons, that he himself would have rejected. In any case, since Marx wrote, all participants in the debate on the nature and future of capitalism have had to respond to his judgments and predictions.

Law: Recovering for Damages Sustained

Life is full of misfortune. Ordinarily, if you suffer misfortune, you must put up with it and find the resources to deal with it. If your misfortune is my fault, however, the law may step in and make me pay for those damages.

Through *criminal law,* the public steps in and demands punishment for an offense that is serious enough to outrage public feeling and endanger public welfare. If I knock you on the head and take your wallet, the police will find me, restore your wallet to you, and imprison or otherwise punish me for the crime. Strictly speaking, you should recover from me not only your wallet, but you should also receive the money to sew up your head and damages for the fright and insult. But the average street criminal does not have the money to make full restitution to his victims; in fact, you will be lucky to get your wallet back.

Through *civil law,* if I do you damage through some action of mine, you may take me to civil court and ask a judge (and jury) to determine whether or not I have damaged you, if so by how much, and how I should pay you back for that damage. There are a number of forms of action under which you may make your claim; the most common for business purposes are *contract* and *torts*. If you and I agree to (or "contract for") some undertaking, and I back out of it after you have relied on our agreement to commit your resources to the undertaking, you have a right to recover what you have lost. In torts, if I simply injure you in some way, hurting you in health, life, or limb, or destroying your property, I have done you a wrong (*tort,* in French), and I must pay for the damage I have done. How much I will have to pay will depend (as the jury will determine) on (1) the amount of the damage that has been caused, (2) the extent to which I knew or should have known that my action or neglect to act would cause damage (my *culpability*), and (3) the extent to which *you* contributed to the damage, beyond whatever I did (*contributory negligence*).

Another kind of suit at law alleges *negligence,* which is a tort, on the part of a company, in that it made and put up for sale a product known to be defective and that the defect injured its users. To establish negligence, civil or criminal, four elements must be demonstrated: First, there must have been a *duty*—the party accused of negligence must have had a preexisting duty to the plaintiff. Second, there must have been a *breach of,* or failure to fulfill, that duty. Third, the plaintiff must have suffered an *injury.* And fourth, the breach of the duty must have been the *proximate cause* of the injury, or the thing that actually brought the injury about. Where negligence is alleged in a product liability case, it must be established that the manufacturer had a duty to make a product that could not do certain harm, that the duty was breached, that the harm was caused, that nothing else was to blame, and that the manufacturer therefore must compensate the victim for the damage done.

There are very similar allegations in other cases, even when no lawsuit is at issue. In all of these cases, one set of claims amounts to an accusation of deliberately damaging innocent consumers, placing them in harm's way for the sake of profit. The other set of claims counters that the company did not know, and could not have known, that the product was dangerous and/or that the freely chosen behavior of the consumers contributed in some way to the damage that was done. In all cases, *risk* and *responsibility* are the central issues. When a small car explodes and burns when hit by a much larger van, to what extent is the company responsible for the flimsiness of the car? To what extent did the consumer assume the risk of that happening when she bought a small economical car? (Furthermore, what ever happened to the responsibility of the driver of the van?)

Should companies ultimately be responsible for any harm that comes from the use of the products they profitably market and sell? Or should consumers be content to bear the responsibility for risks that they freely accept? When we are in a hurry, short of cash, or in need of a cigarette, then risky behavior looks to us to be our right, and we are resentful of the busybodies who would always have us play it safe. But when the risk materializes—when the accident or the disease happens—the perception of that risk (and the direction of that resentment) changes drastically. From the perspective of the hospital bed, it is crystal clear that the behavior was not worth the risk, that we never realized the behavior was risky, that we should have been warned, and that it was someone's duty to warn us. In that instantaneous change of perspective, three elements of negligence come into view: duty, breach, and injury. No wonder product liability suits are so common.

Yet the suit is a relatively recent phenomenon because of a peculiarity in the law. Until the twentieth century, a judge faced with a consumer who had been injured by a product (physically or financially) applied the principle of *caveat emptor*—"let the buyer beware"—and could ask the seller to pay damages only to the original buyer, and only if the exact defect in the product could be proven. For example, a defective kerosene lamp might explode and burn five people, but the exact defect (broken seam or shoddy wick) had to be brought into court or the case would be thrown out. In addition, the buyer could sue only the seller, not the manufacturer or designer, because the right to collect damages rested on the law of *contract*, not torts, and on the warrant of merchantability implied in the contractual relationship between buyer and seller. The cause of the action was understood to be a breach in that contract.

There matters stood until 1916, when an American judge allowed a buyer to sue the manufacturer of a product. A Mr. MacPherson had been injured when his car collapsed under him due to a defect in the wood used to build one of the wheels, and MacPherson went to court against the Buick Motor Company. The judge reasoned that the action was in torts, specifically "negligence," and not in contract, for a manufacturer is under a duty to make carefully any product that could be expected to endanger life, and this duty existed irrespective of any contract. So if MacPherson, or any future user of the product, was injured because the product was badly made, he could collect damages even if he had never dealt with the manufacturer in any way.

In the 1960s the automobile was still center stage in the arguments over the duties of manufacturers. Consumer advocate Ralph Nader's book *Unsafe at Any Speed* (1966) spearheaded the consumer rights movement with its scathing attack on General Motors and its exposé of the dangerous design of the Corvair. In response to the consumer activism resulting from that movement, Congress passed the Consumer Product Safety Act in 1972 and empowered the Consumer Product Safety Commission, an independent federal agency, to set safety standards, require warning labels, and order recalls of hazardous products. When three girls died in a Ford Pinto in 1978, the foundations of consumer rights against careless manufacturers were well established. What was new in the Ford Motor Company case was the allegation of *criminal* negligence—in effect, criminal homicide.

At present, product liability suits are major uncharted reefs in the navigational plans of American business. If a number of people die in a fire in a hotel, for instance, their families will often sue not only the hotel, for culpable negligence, but the manufacturers of the furniture that burned, alleging that it should have been fire-retardant; the manufacturers of the cushions on the furniture, alleging that they gave off toxic fumes in the fire; and the manufacturers of the chemicals that went into those cushions, alleging that there was no warning to the consumers on the toxicity of those chemicals in fire conditions. The settlements that can be obtained are used to finance the suit and the law firm that is managing it for the years that it will take to exhaust all the appeals. This phenomenon of unlimited litigation is relatively new on the American scene, and we are not quite sure how to respond to it.

The Corporation

The human being is a social animal. We exist in the herd and depend for our lives on the cooperation of those around us. Who are they? Anthropologists tell us that originally we traveled in extended families, then settled down into villages of intensely interlocked groups of families. With the advent of the modern era, we have found our identities in family, village, church, and nation. Yet, in the great transformation of the obligations of the Western world (see Henry Maine [1822–1888], *From Status to Contract*), we have abandoned the old family-oriented care systems and thrown ourselves upon the mercy of secondary organizations: club, corporation, and state. The French sociologist Emile Durkheim (1858–1917), in his classic work *Suicide,* suggested that following the collapse of the family and the church, the corporation would be the association in the future that would supply the social support that every individual needs to maintain a moral life.

Can the corporation do that? Or is the corporation merely the organization that implements Adam Smith's self-interested pursuit of the dollar, with no purpose but to maximize return on investment to the investors while protecting them from unlimited liability?

On the other hand, once formed, and having become a major community figure and employer, does the corporation have a right to exist that transcends at least the immediate pursuit of money? The issue of so-called hostile takeovers sends us back to the purpose and foundation of business enterprise in America. Let us review: When an entrepreneur gets a bright idea for how to make money, he or she secures the capital necessary to run the business from investors (venture capitalists); uses that capital to buy the land, buildings, and machinery needed to see the project through; hires the labor needed to do the work; and goes into production. As the income from the enterprise comes in, the entrepreneur pays the suppliers of raw materials; pays the workers; pays the taxes, rent, mortgages, and utility bills; keeps some of the money for him- or herself (salary); and then divides up the rest of the income (profit) among the investors (probably including him- or herself) in proportion to the capital they invested. Motives of all parties are presupposed: the entrepreneur wants money; the laborers and the landlords want money; and the investors, who are the shareholders in the company, want money. The investors thought that this enterprise would yield them a higher return on their capital than any other investment available to them at the time; that is why they invested. However, this is a free country, and people can move around. If the workers see better jobs, they will take them; if a landlord can rent for more, the lease will be terminated; and if the investors see a better place to put their capital, they will move it. The determiner of the flow of capital is the rate of return, no more and no less. Loyalty to the company, faithfulness to the corporation for the sake of the association itself, is not on anyone's agenda—not on the worker's, certainly not on the landlord's, and *most* certainly not on the shareholder's.

The shareholders are represented by a board of directors elected by them to see that the company is run efficiently; that is, that costs are kept down and income up to yield the highest possible return. The board of directors hires management—the cadre of corporate officers headed by the president and/or chief executive officer to do the actual running of the company. The corporate officers thus stand in a *fiduciary* relationship to the shareholders; that is, they are forbidden by the understandings on which the corporation is founded to do anything at all except that which will protect and enhance the interests of the shareholders. That goes for all the normal business decisions made by the management; even the decision not to break the law can be seen as a prudent estimate of the financial costs of lawbreaking.

Yet our dealings with the business world, as citizens and as consumers, have always turned on recognition and support of the huge reliable corporations in established industries; not just coal and steel, which had certain natural limitations built into their consumption of natural resources, but the automobile companies, the airlines, the consumer products companies, and even the banks. Companies had "reputations" and "integrity," and they cultivated (and bought and sold) "good will." Consumers cooperated with the companies that catered to them in developing "brand loyalty." And, most important, those working in business cooperated with their employers in developing "company loyalty," which became a part of their lives, just as loyalty to one's tribe or nation was part of the lives of their ancestors. Is the company that sought our loyalty—and got it—just a scrap of paper, to disappear as soon as return on investment falls below the nearest competition? What part do we want corporations to play in our associative lives? If we want them to be any more than profit maximizers for the investors, what sorts of protections would we have to offer them, and what sorts of limitations should we put on their extra-profit-making activities?

Current Issues

Business ethics ultimately rests on a base of political philosophy, economics, and philosophical ethics. As these underlying fields change, new topics and approaches will surface in business ethics. For example, hostile takeovers did not take place very often in the regulatory climate that existed prior to the Reagan administration. The change in political philosophy introduced by his administration resulted in new business practices, which resulted in new ethical problems. Also, the work of John Rawls, a professor of philosophy at Harvard University, profoundly influenced our understanding of distributive justice and, therefore, our understanding of acceptable economic distribution in the society. The work currently being done in postmodern philosophy will change the way we see human beings generally and, hence, the activity of business.

No single work can cover all the issues of ethical practice in business in all their range and particularity, especially since, as above, we are dealing with a moving target. Our task here is much more limited. The purpose of this book is to allow you to grapple with some of the ethical issues of current business practice in the safety of the classroom, before they come up on the job where human rights and careers are at stake and legal action looms outside the boardroom or factory door. We think that rational consideration of these issues now will help you prepare for a lifetime of the types of problems that naturally arise in a complex and pluralistic society. You will find here no dogmas, no settled solutions to memorize. These problems do not have preset answers but require that you use your mind to balance the values in conflict and to work out acceptable policies in each issue. To employ business ethics, you must learn to think critically, to look beyond short-term advantages and traditional ways of doing things, and to become an innovator. The exercise provided by these debates should help you in this learning.

There is no doubt that businesspeople think that ethics is important. Sometimes the reasons why they think ethics is important have to do only with the long-run profitability of a business enterprise. There is no doubt that greater employee honesty and diligence would improve the bottom line or that strict attention to environmental and employee health laws is necessary to protect the company from expensive lawsuits and fines. But ethics goes well beyond profitability, to the lives that we live and the persons we want to be. What the bottom line has taught us is that the working day is not apart from life. We must bring the same integrity and care to the contexts of the factory and the office that we are used to showing at home and among our friends. An imperative of business ethics is to make of your business life an opportunity to become, and remain, the person that you know you ought to be—and as far as it is within your capability, to extend that opportunity to others.

In this book, we attempt to present in good debatable form some of the issues that raise the big questions—of justice, of rights, of the common good —in order to build bridges between the workaday world of employment and the ageless world of morality. If you will enter into these dialogues with an open mind, a willingness to have it changed, and a determination to master the skills of critical thinking that will enable you to make responsible decisions in difficult situations, you may be able to help build the bridges for the new ethical issues that will emerge in the next century. At the least, that is our hope.

On the Internet . . .

Business Ethics Resources on WWW

Sponsored by the Centre for Applied Ethics, this page of business ethics resources links to corporate codes of ethics, business ethics institutions and
organizations, and online papers and publications, as well as other elements.

http://www.ethics.ubc.ca/resources/business/

Critical Thinking Across the Curriculum Project

This site, sponsored by Longview Community College in Lee's Summit, Missouri, links to resources in critical thinking. They are divided into the core
resources and discipline-specific resources.

http://www.kcmetro.cc.mo.us/longview/ctac/toc.htm

International Business Ethics Institute

The International Business Ethics Institute offers professional services to organizations interested in implementing, expanding, or modifying business ethics
and corporate responsibility programs. Its mission is to foster global business
practices that promote equitable economic development, resource sustainability, and democratic forms of government.

http://www.business-ethics.org

PART 1

Capitalism and the Corporation

*W*e know that businesspeople can do wrong sometimes during the practice of business. But can business as an enterprise be wrong in itself? Is business necessarily a matter of grasping profiteers who are organized for the systematic robbery of the larger society? Can business and corporations be morally good? The debates in this part raise the question of the moral worth of the business enterprise as a whole and the corporations of which it is constructed.

- The Classic Dialogue: Is Capitalism the Best Route to Human Happiness?

- Can Individual Virtue Survive Corporate Pressure?

- Can Restructuring a Corporation's Rules Make a Moral Difference?

- Should Corporations Adopt Policies of Corporate Social Responsibility?

ISSUE 1

The Classic Dialogue: Is Capitalism the Best Route to Human Happiness?

YES: Adam Smith, from *An Inquiry Into the Nature and Causes of the Wealth of Nations, vols. 1 and 2* (1869)

NO: Karl Marx and Friedrich Engels, from *The Communist Manifesto* (1848)

ISSUE SUMMARY

YES: Free-market economist Adam Smith (1723–1790) states that if self-interested people are left alone to seek their own economic advantage, the result, unintended by any one of them, will be greater advantage for all. He maintains that government interference is not necessary to protect the general welfare.

NO: German philosopher Karl Marx (1818–1883) and German sociologist Friedrich Engels (1820–1895) argue that if people are left to their own self-interested devices, those who own the means of production will rapidly reduce everyone else to virtual slaves. Although the few may be fabulously happy, all others would live in misery.

The rationale of capitalism is that an unintended coordination of self-interested actions will lead to the production of the greatest welfare of the whole. The logic is that as a natural result of free competition in a free market, quality will improve and prices decline without limit, thereby raising the real standard of living of every buyer; to protect themselves in competition, sellers will be forced to innovate, and discover new products and new markets, thereby raising the real wealth of the society as a whole. Products improve without limit, wealth increases without limit, and society prospers.

But how does the Common Man—the "least advantaged" member of society—fare under capitalism? According to communist theory, not very well. The most efficient factories are those that hire their workers at the lowest cost. And if all industry is accomplished by essentially unskilled labor, and every worker can be replaced by any other, there is no reason to pay any worker beyond the subsistence wage. Therefore only when free competition *fails*, because the economy is expanding so rapidly that it runs out of labor, can the working man's wages rise in a free market. According to capitalist theory, however, such a market imbalance—too few workers and therefore "artificially" high wages—will rapidly disappear because greater prosperity causes more of the working-class babies to survive to adulthood and enter into the workforce. Eighteenth-century economists Adam Smith, Thomas Malthus, and David Ricardo all agreed that as society as a whole approaches maximum efficiency, all except the capitalists (the owners) approach the subsistence level of survival. So most of the accumulated "wealth" of the nation actually ends up in the hands of the employers, who enjoy the low prices of bread themselves while saving the money they would need to spend to keep their workers alive if the bread were more expensive.

This is where Karl Marx comes in. He focused not on the making of the wealth but on how the wealth is distributed—who gets it and gets to enjoy it when it has been generated by the capitalist process. Marx found it unreasonable for the bulk of society's wealth to be languishing in the bank accounts of the super-rich. He argued that the welfare of the nation as a whole would be vastly increased if it could be shared systematically with the workers, which would allow them to join their employers as consumers of the manufactured goods of society. Lord John Maynard Keynes would later point out that such distribution would be an enormous spur to the economy; Marx, however, was more concerned that it would be a great gain in justice.

One empirical question that surrounds the issue of social justice in a free-market society is this: If the controllers of the wealth—the capitalists—are required to share it with the workers who produced it, will they not lose motivation to put their money at risk in productive enterprises? Other questions concern entitlement (aren't those who control the capital entitled to the entire return on it?) and the relative importance of liberty and equality as political values. As you read the following selections by Smith and Marx and Friedrich Engels, keep in mind that the debate is not bound by the historical controversies of Marx and his opponents; it goes to the core of contemporary notions of entitlement and justice.

Adam Smith

 **YES**

An Inquiry Into the Nature and Causes of the Wealth of Nations

Of the Division of Labour

The greatest improvement in the productive powers of labour, and the greater part of the skill, dexterity, and judgment with which it is anywhere directed or applied, seem to have been the effect of the division of labour.

The effects of the division of labour, in the general business of society, will be more easily understood by considering in what manner it operates in some particular manufactures. It is commonly supposed to be carried furthest in some very trifling ones; not perhaps that it really is carried further in them than in others of more importance: but in those trifling manufactures which are destined to supply the small wants of but a small number of people, the whole number of workmen must necessarily be small; and those employed in every different branch of the work can often be collected into the same workhouse, and placed at once under the view of the spectator. In those great manufactures, on the contrary, which are destined to supply the great wants of the great body of the people, every different branch of the work employs so great a number of workmen, that it is impossible to collect them all into the same workhouse. We can seldom see more, at one time, than those employed in one single branch. Though in such manufactures, therefore, the work may really be divided into a much greater number of parts than in those of a more trifling nature, the division is not near so obvious, and has accordingly been much less observed.

To take an example, therefore, from a very trifling manufacture, but one in which the division of labour has been very often taken notice of, the trade of the pin-maker; a workman not educated to this business (which the division of labour has rendered a distinct trade), nor acquainted with the use of the machinery employed in it (to the invention of which the same division of labour has probably given occasion), could scarce, perhaps, with his utmost industry, make one pin in a day, and certainly could not make twenty. But in the way

From Adam Smith, *An Inquiry Into the Nature and Causes of the Wealth of Nations*, vols. *1 and 2* (1869). Notes omitted.

in which this business is now carried on, not only the whole work is a peculiar trade, but it is divided into a number of branches, of which the greater part are likewise peculiar trades. One man draws out the wire, another straights it, a third cuts it, a fourth points it, a fifth grinds it at the top for receiving the head; to make the head requires two or three distinct operations; to put it on is a peculiar business, to whiten the pins is another; it is even a trade by itself to put them into the paper; and the important business of making a pin is, in this manner, divided into about eighteen distinct operations, which in some manufactories are all performed by distinct hands, though in others the same man will sometimes perform two or three of them. I have seen a small manufactory of this kind where ten men only were employed, and where some of them consequently performed two or three distinct operations. But though they were very poor, and therefore but indifferently accommodated with the necessary machinery, they could, when they exerted themselves, make among them about twelve pounds of pins in a day. There are in a pound upwards of four thousand pins of a middling size. Those ten persons, therefore, could make among them upwards of forty-eight thousand pins in a day. Each person, therefore, making a tenth part of forty-eight thousand pins, might be considered as making four thousand eight hundred pins in a day. But if they had all wrought separately and independently, and without any of them having been educated to this peculiar business, they certainly could not each of them have made twenty, perhaps not one pin in a day; that is, certainly, not the two hundred and fortieth, perhaps not the four thousand eight hundredth part of what they are at present capable of performing, in consequence of a proper division and combination of their different operations. . . .

This great increase of the quantity of work, which, in consequence of the division of labour, the same number of people are capable of performing, is owning to three different circumstances: first, to the increase of dexterity in every particular workman; secondly, to the saving of the time which is commonly lost in passing from one species of work to another; and lastly, to the invention of a great number of machines which facilitate and abridge labour, and enable one man to do the work of many. . . .

It is the great multiplication of the productions of all the different arts, in consequence of the division of labour, which occasions, in a well-governed society, that universal opulence which extends itself to the lowest ranks of the people. Every workman has a great quantity of his own work to dispose of beyond what he himself has occasion for: and every other workman being exactly in the same situation, he is enabled to exchange a great quantity of his own goods for a great quantity, or, what comes to the same thing, for the price of a great quantity of theirs. He supplies them abundantly with what they have occasion for, and they accommodate him as amply with what he has occasion for, and a general plenty diffuses itself through all the different ranks of the society.

Observe the accommodation of the most common artificer or day-labourer in a civilised and thriving country, and you will perceive that the number of people of whose industry a part, though but a small part, has been employed in procuring him this accommodation exceeds all computation. The woollen coat, for example, which covers the day-labourer, as coarse and rough as it may appear, is the produce of the joint labour of a great multitude of workmen. The shepherd, the sorter of the wool, the wool-comber or carder, the dyer, the scribbler, the spinner, the weaver, the fuller, the dresser, with many others, must all join their different arts in order to complete even this homely production. How many merchants and carriers, besides, must have been employed in transporting the materials from some of those workmen to others who often live in a very distant part of the country! How much commerce and navigation in particular, how many ship-builders, sailors, sail-makers, rope-makers, must have been employed in order to bring together the different drugs made use of by the dyer, which often come from the remotest corners of the world! What a variety of labour too is necessary in order to produce the tools of the meanest of those workmen! To say nothing of such complicated machines as the ship of the sailor, the mill of the fuller, or even the loom of the weaver, let us consider only what a variety of labour is requisite in order to form that very simple machine, the shears with which the shepherd clips the wool. The miner, the builder of the furnace for smelting the ore, the feller of the timber, the burner of the charcoal to be made use of in the smelting-house, the brickmaker, the bricklayer, the workmen who attend the furnace, the mill-wright, the forger, the smith, must all of them join their different arts in order to produce them. Were we to examine, in the same manner, all the different parts of his dress and household furniture, the coarse linen shirt which he wears next his skin, the shoes which cover his feet, the bed which he lies on, and all the different parts which compose it, the kitchen-grate at which he prepares his victuals, the coals which he makes use of for that purpose, dug from the bowels of the earth, and brought to him perhaps by a long sea and a long land carriage, all the other utensils of his kitchen, all the furniture of his table, the knives and forks, the earthen or pewter plates upon which he serves up and divides his victuals, the different hands employed in preparing his bread and his beer, the glass window which lets in the heat and the light and keeps out the wind and the rain, with all the knowledge and art requisite for preparing that beautiful and happy invention, without which these northern parts of the world could scarce have afforded a very comfortable habitation, together with the tools of all the different workmen employed in producing those different conveniences; if we examine, I say, all these things, and consider what a variety of labour is employed about each of them, we shall be sensible that without the assistance and co-operation of many thousands, the very meanest person in a civilised country could not be provided, even according to, what we very falsely imagine, the easy and simple manner in which he is commonly accommodated. Compared, indeed, with the more extravagant luxury of the great, his accommodation must no doubt appear extremely simple and easy; and yet it may be true, perhaps, that the accommodation of an European prince does not always so much exceed that of an industrious and frugal peasant, as the accommodation of the latter exceeds that of many an African king, the absolute master of the lives and liberties of ten thousand naked savages.

Of the Principle Which Gives Occasion to the Division of Labour

This division of labour, from which so many advantages are derived, is not originally the effect of any human wisdom, which foresees and intends that general opulence to which it gives occasion. It is the necessary, though very slow and gradual consequence of a certain propensity in human nature which has in view no such extensive utility; the propensity to truck, barter, and exchange one thing for another.

Whether this propensity be one of those original principles in human nature, of which no further account can be given; or whether, as seems more probable, it be the necessary consequence of the faculties of reason and speech, it belongs not to our present subject to inquire. It is common to all men, and to be found in no other race of animals, which seem to know neither this nor any other species of contracts.... But man has almost constant occasion for the help of his brethren, and it is in vain for him to expect it from their benevolence only. He will be more likely to prevail if he can interest their self-love in his favour, and show them that it is for their own advantage to do for him what he requires of them. Whoever offers to another a bargain of any kind, proposes to do this. Give me that which I want, and you shall have this which you want, is the meaning of every such offer; and it is in this manner that we obtain from one another the far greater part of those good offices which we stand in need of. It is not from the benevolence of the butcher, the brewer, or the baker, that we expect our dinner, but from their regard to their own interest. We address ourselves, not to their humanity but to their self-love, and never talk to them of our own necessities but of their advantages. Nobody but a beggar chooses to depend chiefly upon the benevolence of his fellow-citizens. Even a beggar does not depend upon it entirely. The charity of well-disposed people, indeed, supplies him with the whole fund of his subsistence. But though this principle ultimately provides him with all the necessaries of life which he has occasion for, it neither does nor can provide him with them as he has occasion for them. The greater part of his occasional wants are supplied in the same manner as those of other people, by treaty, by barter, and by purchase. With the money which one man gives him he purchases food. The old clothes which another bestows upon him he exchanges for other old clothes which suit him better, or for lodging, or for food, or for money, with which he can buy either food, clothes, or lodging, as he has occasion.

... Each animal is still obliged to support and defend itself, separately and independently, and derives no sort of advantage from that variety of talents with which nature has distinguished its fellows. Among men, on the contrary, the most dissimilar geniuses are of use to one another; the different produces of their respective talents, by the general disposition to truck, barter, and exchange, being brought, as it were, into a common stock, where every man may purchase whatever part of the produce of other men's talents he has occasion for....

Of Restraints Upon the Importation From Foreign Countries of Such Goods as Can Be Produced at Home

... The general industry of the society never can exceed what the capital of the society can employ. As the number of workmen that can be kept in employment by any particular person must bear a certain proportion to his capital, so the number of those that can be continually employed by all the members of a great society, must bear a certain proportion to the whole capital of that society, and never can exceed that proportion. No regulation of commerce can increase the quantity of industry in any society beyond what its capital can maintain. It can only divert a part of it into a direction into which it might not otherwise have gone; and it is by no means certain that this artificial direction is likely to be more advantageous to the society than that into which it would have gone of its own accord.

Every individual is continually exerting himself to find out the most advantageous employment for whatever capital he can demand. It is his own advantage, indeed, and not that of the society, which he has in view. But the study of his own advantage naturally, or rather necessarily, leads him to prefer that employment which is most advantageous to the society.

First, every individual endeavours to employ his capital as near home as he can, and consequently as much as he can in the support of domestic industry; provided always that he can thereby obtain the ordinary, or not a great deal less than the ordinary, profits of stock.

Thus, upon equal or nearly equal profits, every wholesale merchant naturally prefers the home trade to the foreign trade of consumption, and the foreign trade of consumption to the carrying trade. In the home trade his capital is never so long out of his sight as it frequently is in the foreign trade of consumption. He can know better the character and situation of the persons whom he trusts, and, if he should happen to be deceived, he knows better the laws of the country from which he must seek redress. In the carrying trade, the capital of the merchant is, as it were, divided between two foreign countries, and no part of it is ever necessarily brought home, or placed under his own immediate view and command. The capital which an Amsterdam merchant employs in carrying corn from Konigsberg to Lisbon, and fruit and wine from Lisbon to Konigsberg, must generally be the one half of it at Konigsberg and the other half at Lisbon. No part of it need ever come to Amsterdam. The natural residence of such a merchant should either be at Konigsberg or Lisbon, and it can only be some very particular circumstance which can make him prefer the residence of Amsterdam. The uneasiness, however, which he feels at being separated so far from his capital, generally determines him to bring part both of the Konigsberg goods which he destines for the market of Lisbon, and of the Lisbon goods which he destines for that of Konigsberg, to Amsterdam; and though this necessarily subjects him to a double charge of loading and unloading, as well as to the payment of some duties and customs, yet for the sake of having some part of his capital always under his own view and command, he willingly submits to this extraordinary charge; and it is in this manner that every country which has any considerable share of the carrying trade, becomes always the emporium, or general market, for the goods of all the different countries whose trade it carries on. The merchant, in order to save a second loading and unloading, endeavours always to sell in the home market as much of the goods of all those different countries as he can, and thus, so far as he can, to convert his carrying trade into a foreign trade of consumption. A merchant, in the same manner, who is engaged in the foreign trade of consumption, when he collects goods for foreign markets, will always be glad, upon equal or nearly equal profits, to sell as great a part of them at home as he can. He saves himself the risk and trouble of exportation, when, so far as he can, he thus converts his foreign trade of consumption into a home trade. Home is in this manner the centre, if I may say so, round which the capitals of the inhabitants of every country are continually circulating, and towards which they are always tending, though by particular causes they may sometimes be driven off and repelled from it towards more distant employments. But a capital employed in the home trade, it has already been shown, necessarily puts into motion a greater quantity of domestic industry, and gives revenue and employment to a greater number of the inhabitants of the country, than an equal capital employed in the foreign trade of consumption; and one employed in the foreign trade of consumption has the same advantage over an equal capital employed in the carrying trade. Upon equal, or only nearly equal profits, therefore, every individual naturally inclines to employ his capital in the manner in which it is likely to afford the greatest support to domestic industry, and to give revenue and employment to the greatest number of people of his own country.

Secondly, every individual who employs his capital in the support of domestic industry, necessarily endeavours so to direct that industry, that its produce may be of the greatest possible value.

The produce of industry is what it adds to the subject or materials upon which it is employed. In proportion as the value of this produce is great or small, so will likewise be the profits of the employer. But it is only for the sake of profit that any man employs a capital in the support of industry; and he will always, therefore, endeavour to employ it in the support of that industry of which the produce is likely to be of the greatest value, or to exchange for the greatest quantity either of money or of other goods.

But the annual revenue of every society is always precisely equal to the exchangeable value of the whole annual produce of its industry, or rather is precisely the same thing with that exchangeable value. As every individual, therefore, endeavours as much as he can both to employ his capital in the support of domestic industry, and so to direct that industry that its produce may be of the greatest value, every individual necessarily labours to render the annual revenue of the society as great as he can. He generally, indeed, neither intends to promote the public interest, nor knows how much he is promoting it. By preferring the support of domestic to that of foreign industry, he intends only his own security; and by directing that industry in such a manner as its produce may be of the greatest value, he intends only his own gain, and he is in this, as in many other cases, led by an invisible hand to promote an end which was no part of his intention. Nor is it always the worse for the society that it was no part of it. By pursuing his own interest he frequently promotes that of the society more effectually than when he really intends to promote it. I have never known much good done by those who affected to trade for the public good. It is an affectation, indeed, not very common among merchants, and very few words need be employed in dissuading them from it.

What is the species of domestic industry which his capital can employ, and of which the produce is likely to be of the greatest value, every individual, it is evident, can, in his local situation, judge much better than any statesman or lawgiver can do for him. The statesman, who should attempt to direct private people in what manner they ought to employ their capitals, would not only load himself with a most unnecessary attention, but assume an authority which could safely be trusted, not only to no single person, but to no council or senate whatever, and which would nowhere be so dangerous as in the hands of a man who had folly and presumption enough to fancy himself fit to exercise it.

To give the monopoly of the home market to the produce of domestic industry, in any particular art or manufacture, is in some measure to direct private people in what manner they ought to employ their capitals, and must, in almost all cases, be either a useless or a hurtful regulation. If the produce of domestic can be brought there as cheap as that of foreign industry, the regulation is evidently useless. If it cannot, it must generally be hurtful. It is the maxim of every prudent master of a family, never to attempt to make at home what it will cost him more to make than to buy. The tailor does not attempt to make his own shoes, but buys them of the shoemaker. The shoemaker does not attempt to make his own clothes, but employs a tailor. The farmer attempts to make neither the one nor the other, but employs those different artificers. All of them find it for their interest to employ their whole industry in a way in which they have some advantage over their neighbours, and to purchase with a part of its produce, or, what is the same thing, with the price of a part of it, whatever else they have occasion for.

What is prudence in the conduct of every private family, can scarce be folly in that of a great kingdom. If a foreign country can supply us with a commodity cheaper than we ourselves can make it, better buy it of them with some part of the produce of our own industry, employed in a way in which we have some advantage. The general industry of the country, being always in proportion to the capital which employs it, will not thereby be diminished, no more than that of the above-mentioned artificers, but only left to find out the way in which it can be employed with the greatest advantage. It is certainly not employed to the greatest advantage, when it is thus directed towards an object which it can buy cheaper than it can make. The value of its annual produce is certainly more or less diminished, when it is thus turned away from producing commodities evidently of more value than the commodity which it is directed to produce. According to the supposition, that commodity could be purchased from foreign countries cheaper than it can be made at home. It could, therefore, have been purchased with a part only of the commodities, or, what is the same thing, with a part only of the price of the commodities, which the industry employed by an equal capital would have produced at home, had it been left to follow its natural course. The industry of the country, therefore, is thus turned away from a more to a less advantageous employment, and the exchangeable value of its annual produce, instead of being increased, according to the intention of the lawgiver, must necessarily be diminished by every such regulation.

By means of such regulations, indeed, a particular manufacture may sometimes be acquired sooner than it could have been otherwise, and after a certain time may be made at home as cheap or cheaper than in the foreign country. But though the industry of the society may be thus carried with advantage into a particular channel sooner than it could have been otherwise, it will by no means follow that the sum total, either of its industry or of its revenue, can ever be augmented by any such regulation. The industry of the society can augment only in proportion as its capital augments, and its capital can augment only in proportion to what can be gradually saved out of its revenue. But the immediate effect of every such regulation is to diminish its revenue, and what diminishes its revenue is certainly not very likely to augment its capital faster than it would have augmented of its own accord, had both capital and industry been left to find out their natural employments.

Though for want of such regulations the society should never acquire the proposed manufacture, it would not, upon that account, necessarily be the poorer in any one period of its duration. In every period of its duration its whole capital and industry might still have been employed, though upon different objects, in the manner that was most advantageous at the time. In every period its revenue might have been the greatest which its capital could afford, and both capital and revenue might have been augmented with the greatest possible rapidity.

The natural advantages which one country has over another in producing particular commodities are sometimes so great, that it is acknowledged by all the world to be in vain to struggle with them. By means of glasses, hot-beds, and hot-walls, very good grapes can be raised in Scotland, and very good wine too can be made of them, at about thirty times the expense for which at least equally good can be brought from foreign countries. Would it be a reasonable law to prohibit the importation of all foreign wines, merely to encourage the making of claret and burgundy in Scotland? But if there would be a manifest absurdity in turning towards any employment thirty times more of the capital and industry of the country than would be necessary to purchase from foreign countries an equal quantity of the commodities wanted, there must be an absurdity, though not altogether so glaring, yet exactly of the same kind, in turning towards any such employment a thirtieth or even a three-hundredth part more of either. Whether the advantages which one country has over another be natural or acquired, is in this respect of no consequence. As long as the one country has those advantages and the other wants them, it will always be more advantageous for the latter rather to buy of the former than to make. It is an acquired advantage only which one artificer has over his neighbour who exercises another trade; and yet they both find it more advantageous to buy of one another than to make what does not belong to their particular trades.

Manifesto of the Communist Party

Aspectre is haunting Europe—the spectre of Communism. All the powers of old Europe have entered into a holy alliance to exorcise this spectre; Pope and Czar, Metternich and Guizot, French Radicals and German police-spies.

Where is the party in opposition that has not been decried as communistic by its opponents in power? Where the opposition that has not hurled back the branding reproach of Communism, against the more advanced opposition parties, as well as against its reactionary adversaries?

Two things result from this fact.

I. Communism is already acknowledged by all European Powers to be itself a Power.

II. It is high time that Communists should openly, in the face of the whole world, publish their views, their aims, their tendencies, and meet this nursery tale of the Spectre of Communism with a Manifesto of the party itself.

To this end, Communists of various nationalities have assembled in London, and sketched the following manifesto, to be published in the English, French, German, Italian, Flemish and Danish languages.

Bourgeois and Proletarians

The history of all hitherto existing society is the history of class struggles.

Freeman and slave, patrician and plebeian, lord and serf, guild-master and journeyman, in a word; oppressor and oppressed, stood in constant opposition to one another, carried on an uninterrupted, now hidden, now open fight, a fight that each time ended, either in a revolutionary re-constitution of society at large, or in the common ruin of the contending classes.

In the early epochs of history, we find almost everywhere a complicated arrangement of society into various orders, a manifold graduation of social rank. In ancient Rome we have patricians, knights, plebeians, slaves; in the Middle Ages, feudal lords, vassals, guild-masters, journeymen, apprentices, serfs; in almost all of these classes, again, subordinate gradations.

The modern bourgeois society that has sprouted from the ruins of feudal society, has not done away with class antagonisms. It has but established new

From Karl Marx and Friedrich Engels, *The Communist Manifesto* (1848).

classes, new conditions of oppression, new forms of struggle in place of the old ones.

Our epoch, the epoch of the bourgeoisie, possesses, however, this distinctive feature; it has simplified the class antagonisms. Society as a whole is more and more splitting up into two great hostile camps, into two great classes directly facing each other: Bourgeoisie and Proletariat.

From the serfs of the Middle Ages sprang the chartered burghers of the earliest towns. From these burgesses the first elements of the bourgeoisie were developed.

The discovery of America, the rounding of the Cape, opened up fresh ground for the rising bourgeoisie. The East-Indian and Chinese markets, the colonization of America, trade with the colonies, the increase in the means of exchange in commodities, generally, gave to commerce, to navigation, to industry, an impulse never before known, and thereby, to the revolutionary element in the tottering feudal society, a rapid development.

The feudal system of industry, under which industrial production was monopolized by closed guilds, now no longer sufficed for the growing wants of the new markets. The manufacturing system took its place. The guild-masters were pushed on one side by the manufacturing middle-class; division of labor between the different corporate guilds vanished in the face of division of labor in each single workshop.

Meantime the markets kept ever growing, the demand, ever rising. Even manufacturing no longer sufficed. Thereupon, steam and machinery revolutionized industrial production. The place of manufacture was taken by the giant, Modern Industry, the place of the industrial middle-class, by industrial millionaires, the leaders of whole industrial armies, the modern bourgeoisie.

Modern Industry has established the world-market, for which the discovery of America paved the way. This market has given an immense development to commerce, to navigation, to communication by land. This development has, in its turn, reacted on the extension of industry; and in proportion as industry, commerce, navigation, railways extended in the same proportion the bourgeoisie developed, increased its capital, and pushed into the background every class handed down from the Middle Ages.

We see, therefore, how the modern bourgeoisie is itself the product of a long course of development, of a series of revolutions in the modes of production and of exchange.

Each step in the development of the bourgeoisie was accompanied by a corresponding political advance of that class. An oppressed class under the sway of the feudal nobility, an armed and self-governing association in the medieval commune, here independent urban republic (as in Italy and Germany), there taxable "third estate" of the monarchy (as in France), afterwards, in the period of manufacturing proper, serving either the semi-feudal or the absolute monarchy as a counterpoise against the nobility, and in fact, cornerstone of the great monarchies in general, the bourgeoisie has at last, since the establishment of Modern Industry and of the world-market, conquered for itself, in a modern representative State, exclusive political sway. The executive of the modern State is but a committee for managing the common affairs of the whole bourgeoisie.

The bourgeoisie, historically, has played a most revolutionary part.

The bourgeoisie, wherever it has got the upper hand, has put an end to all feudal, patriarchal, idyllic relations. It has pitilessly torn asunder the motley feudal ties that bound man to his "natural superiors," and has left remaining no other nexus between man and man than naked self-interest, than callous "cash payment." It has drowned the most heavenly ecstasies of religious fervor, of chivalrous enthusiasm, of philistine sentimentalism, in the icy water of egotistical calculation. It has resolved personal worth into exchange value, and in place of the numberless indefeasible chartered freedoms, has set up that single, unconscionable freedom—Free Trade. In one word, for exploitation, veiled by religious and political illusions, it has substituted naked, shameless, direct, brutal exploitation.

The bourgeoisie has stripped of its halo every occupation hitherto honored and looked up to with reverent awe. It has converted the physician, the lawyer, the priest, the poet, the man of science, into its paid wage-laborers.

The bourgeoisie has torn away from the family its sentimental veil, and has reduced the family relation to a mere money relation.

The bourgeoisie has disclosed how it came to pass that the brutal display of vigor in the Middle Ages, which Reactionists so much admire, found its fitting complement in the most slothful indolence. It has been the first to show what man's activity can bring about. It has accomplished wonders far surpassing Egyptian pyramids, Roman aqueducts, and Gothic cathedrals; it has conducted expeditions that put in the shade all former Exoduses of nations and crusades.

The bourgeoisie cannot exist without constantly revolutionizing the instruments of production, and thereby the relations of production, and with them the whole relations of society. Conservation of the old modes of production in unaltered form, was, on the contrary, the first condition of existence for all earlier industrial classes. Constant revolutionizing of production, uninterrupted disturbance of all social conditions, everlasting uncertainty and agitation distinguish the bourgeois epoch from all earlier ones. All fixed, fast-frozen relations, with their train of ancient and venerable prejudices and opinions, are swept away, all newly-formed ones become antiquated before they can ossify. All that is solid melts into air, all that is holy is profaned, and man is at last compelled to face with sober senses, his real conditions of life, and his relations with his kind.

The need of a constantly expanding market for its products chases the bourgeoisie over the whole surface of the globe. It must nestle everywhere, settle everywhere, establish connections everywhere.

The bourgeoisie has through its exploitation of the world-market given a cosmopolitan character to production and consumption in every country. To the great chagrin of Reactionists, it has drawn from under the feet of industry the national ground on which it stood. All old-established national industries have been destroyed or are daily being destroyed. They are dislodged by new industries, whose introduction becomes a life and death question for all civilized nations, by industries that no longer work up indigenous raw material, but raw material drawn from the remotest zones; industries whose products are consumed, not only at home, but in every quarter of the globe. In place of the old wants, satisfied by the productions of the country, we find new wants, requiring for their satisfaction the products of distant lands and climes. In place of the old local and national seclusion and self-sufficiency, we have intercourse in every direction, universal inter-dependence of nations. And as in material, so also in intellectual production. The intellectual creations of individual nations become common property. National one-sidedness and narrow-mindedness become more and more impossible, and from the numerous national and local literatures there arises a world-literature.

The bourgeoisie, by the rapid improvement of all instruments of production, by the immensely facilitated means of communication, draws all, even the most barbarian, nations into civilization. The cheap prices of its commodities are the heavy artillery with which it batters down all Chinese walls, with which it forces the barbarians' intensely obstinate hatred of foreigners to capitulate. It compels all nations, on pain of extinction, to adopt the bourgeois mode of production; it compels them to introduce what it calls civilization into their midst, i.e., to become bourgeois themselves. In a word, it creates a world after its own image.

The bourgeoisie has subjected the country to the rule of the towns. It has created enormous cities, has greatly increased the urban population as compared with the rural, and has thus rescued a considerable part of the population from the idiocy of rural life. Just as it has made the country dependent on the towns, so it has made barbarian and semibarbarian countries dependent on the civilized ones, nations of peasants on nations of bourgeois, the East on the West.

The bourgeoisie keeps more and more doing away with the scattered state of the population, of the means of production, and of property. It has agglomerated population, centralized means of production, and has concentrated property in a few hands. The necessary consequence of this was political centralization. Independent, or but loosely connected provinces, with separate interests, laws, governments and systems of taxation, became lumped together in one nation, with one government, one code of laws, one national class-interest, one frontier and one customs-tariff.

The bourgeoisie, during its rule of scarce one hundred years, has created more massive and more colossal productive forces than have all preceding generations together. Subjection of Nature's forces to man, machinery, application of chemistry to industry and agriculture, steam-navigation, railways, electric telegraphs, clearing of whole continents for cultivation, canalization of rivers, whole populations conjured out of the ground—what earlier century had even a presentiment that such productive forces slumbered in the lap of social labor?

We see then: the means of production and of exchange on whose foundations the bourgeoisie built itself up, were generated in feudal society. At a certain stage in the development of these means of production and of exchange, the conditions under which feudal society produced and exchanged, the feudal organization of agriculture and manufacturing industry, in one word, the feudal relations of property became no longer compatible with the already developed productive forces; they became so many fetters. They had to be burst asunder; they were burst asunder.

Into their places stepped free competition, accompanied by a social and political constitution adapted to it, and by the economical and political sway of the bourgeois class.

A similar movement is going on before our own eyes. Modern bourgeois society with its relations of production, of exchange and of property, a society that has conjured up such gigantic means of production and of exchange, is like the sorcerer, who is no longer able to control the powers of the nether world whom he has called up by his spells. For many a decade past the history of industry and commerce is but the history of the revolt of modern productive forces against modern conditions of production, against the property relations that are the condition for the existence of the bourgeoisie and of its rule. It is enough to mention the commercial crises that by their periodical return put on trial, each time more threateningly, the existence of the entire bourgeois society. In these crises a great part not only of the existing products, but also of the previously created productive forces, are periodically destroyed. In these crises there breaks out an epidemic that, in all earlier epochs, would have seemed an absurdity—the epidemic of overproduction. Society suddenly finds itself put back into a state of momentary barbarism; it appears as if a famine, a universal war of devastation had cut off the supply of every means of subsistence; industry and commerce seem to be destroyed; and why? Because there is too much civilization, too much means of subsistence, too much industry, too much commerce. The productive forces at the disposal of society no longer tend to further the development of the conditions of bourgeois property; on the contrary, they have become too powerful for these conditions, by which they are fettered, and so soon as they overcome these fetters, they bring disorder into the whole of bourgeois society, endangering the existence of bourgeois property. The conditions of bourgeois society are too narrow to comprise the wealth created by them. And how does the bourgeoisie get over these crises? On the one hand by enforced destruction of a mass of productive forces; on the other, by the conquest of new markets, and by the more thorough exploitation of the old ones. That is to say, by paving the way for more extensive and more destructive crises, and by diminishing the means whereby crises are prevented.

The weapons with which the bourgeoisie felled feudalism to the ground are now turned against the bourgeoisie itself.

But not only has the bourgeoisie forged the weapons that bring death to itself; it has also called into existence the men who are to wield those weapons —the modern working-class—the proletarians.

In proportion as the bourgeoisie, i.e., capital, is developed, in the same proportion is the proletariat, the modern working-class, developed, a class of laborers, who live only so long as they find work, and who find work only so long as their labor increases capital. These laborers, who must sell themselves piecemeal, are a commodity, like every other article of commerce, and are consequently exposed to all the vicissitudes of competition, to all the fluctuations of the market.

Owing to the extensive use of machinery and to division of labor, the work of the proletarians has lost all individual character, and, consequently, all charm for the workman. He becomes an appendage of the machine, and it is only the most simple, most monotonous, and most easily acquired knack that is required of him. Hence, the cost of production of a workman is restricted, almost entirely, to the means of subsistence that he requires for his maintenance, and for the propagation of his race. But the price of a commodity, and also of labor, is equal to its cost of production. In proportion, therefore, as the repulsiveness of the work increases, the wage decreases. Nay more, in proportion as the use of machinery and division of labor increases, in the same proportion the burden of toil also increases, whether by prolongation of the working hours, by increase of the work enacted in a given time, or by increased speed of the machinery, etc.

Modern Industry has converted the little workshop of the patriarchal master into the great factory of the industrial capitalist. Masses of laborers, crowded into the factory, are organized like soldiers. As privates of the industrial army they are placed under the command of a perfect hierarchy of officers and sergeants. Not only are they the slaves of the bourgeois class, and of the bourgeois State, they are daily and hourly enslaved by the machine, by the over-looker, and, above all, by the individual bourgeois manufacturer himself. The more openly this despotism proclaims gain to be its end and aim, the more petty, the more hateful and the more embittering it is.

The less the skill and exertion or strength implied in manual labor, in other words, the more modern industry becomes developed, the more is the labor of men superseded by that of women. Differences of age and sex have no longer any distinctive social validity for the working class. All are instruments of labor, more or less expensive to use, according to their age and sex.

No sooner is the exploitation of the laborer by the manufacturer so far at an end, that he receives his wages in cash, than he is set upon by the other portions of the bourgeoisie, the landlord, the shopkeeper, the pawnbroker, etc.

The low strata of the middle class—the small trades-people, shopkeepers, and retired tradesmen generally, the handicraftsmen and peasants—all these sink gradually into the proletariat, partly because their diminutive capital does not suffice for the scale on which Modern Industry is carried on, and is swamped in the competition with the large capitalists, partly because their specialized skill is rendered worthless by new methods of production. Thus the proletariat is recruited from all classes of the population.

The proletariat goes through various stages of development. With its birth begins its struggle with the bourgeoisie. At first the contest is carried on by individual laborers, then by the workpeople of a factory, then by the operatives of one trade, in one locality, against the individual bourgeois who directly exploits them. They direct their attacks not against the bourgeois conditions of production, but against the instruments of production themselves; they destroy imported wares that compete with their labor, they smash to pieces machinery, they set factories ablaze, they seek to restore by force the vanished status of the workman of the Middle Ages.

At this stage the laborers still form an incoherent mass scattered over the whole country, and broken up by their mutual competition. If anywhere they unite to form more compact bodies, this is not yet the consequence of their own active union, but of the union of bourgeoisie, which class, in order to attain its own political ends, is compelled to set the whole proletariat in motion, and is moreover yet, for a time, able to do so. At this stage, therefore, the proletarians do not fight their enemies, but the enemies of their enemies, the remnants of absolute monarchy, the landowners, the non-industrial bourgeoisie, the petty bourgeoisie. Thus the whole historical movement is concentrated in the hands of the bourgeoisie; every victory so obtained is a victory for the bourgeoisie.

But with the development of industry the proletariat not only increases in number, it becomes concentrated in great masses, its strength grows, and it feels that strength more. The various interests and conditions of life within the ranks of the proletariat are more and more equalized, in proportion as machinery obliterates all distinction of labor, and nearly everywhere reduces wages to the same low level. The growing competition among the bourgeoisie, and the resulting commercial crises, make the wages of the worker ever more fluctuating. The unceasing improvement of machinery, ever more rapidly developing, makes their livelihood more and more precarious, the collisions between individual workmen and individual bourgeois take more and more the character of collision between two classes. Thereupon the workers begin to form combinations (Trades Unions) against the bourgeoisie; they club together in order to keep up the rate of wages; they found permanent associations in order to make provision beforehand for these occasional revolts. Here and there the contest breaks out into riots.

Now and then the workers are victorious, but only for a time. The real fruits of their battles lie, not in the immediate result, but in the ever expanding union of the workers. This union is helped on by the improved means of communication that are created by modern industry, and that place the workers of different localities in contact with one another. It was just this contact that was needed to centralize the numerous local struggles, all of the same character, into one national struggle between classes. But every class struggle is a political struggle. And that union, to attain which the burghers of the Middle Ages, with their miserable highways, required centuries, the modern proletarians, thanks to railways, achieve in a few years.

This organization of the proletarians into a class, and consequently into a political party, is continually being upset again by the competition between the workers themselves. But it ever rises up again, stronger, firmer, mightier. It compels legislative recognition of particular interests of the workers, by taking advantage of the divisions among the bourgeoisie itself. Thus the ten-hour bill in England was carried.

Altogether collisions between the classes of the old society further, in many ways, the course of development of the proletariat. The bourgeoisie finds itself involved in a constant battle. At first with the aristocracy; later on, with those portions of the bourgeoisie itself, whose interests have become antagonistic to the progress of industry; at all times, with the bourgeoisie of foreign countries. In all these battles it sees itself compelled to appeal to the proletariat, to ask for its help, and thus, to drag it into the political arena. The bourgeoisie itself, therefore, supplies the proletariat with its own elements of political and general education, in other words, it furnishes the proletariat with weapons for fighting the bourgeoisie.

Further, as we have already seen, entire sections of the ruling classes are, by the advance of industry, precipitated into the proletariat, or are at least threatened in their conditions of existence. These also supply the proletariat with fresh elements of enlightenment and progress.

Finally, in times when the class-struggle nears the decisive hour, the process of dissolution going on within the ruling class, in fact, within the whole range of old society, assumes such a violent, glaring character, that a small section of the ruling class cuts itself adrift, and joins the revolutionary class, the class that holds the future in its hands. Just as, therefore, at an earlier period, a section of the nobility went over to the bourgeoisie, so now a portion of the bourgeoisie goes over to the proletariat, and in particular, a portion of the bourgeois ideologists, who have raised themselves to the level of comprehending theoretically the historical movements as a whole.

Of all the classes that stand face to face with the bourgeoisie today, the proletariat alone is a really revolutionary class. The other classes decay and finally disappear in the face of Modern Industry; the proletariat is its special and essential product. . . .

In the conditions of the proletariat, those of old society at large are already virtually swamped. The proletarian is without property; his relation to his wife and children has no longer anything in common with the bourgeois family-relations; modern industrial labor, modern subjugation to capital, the same in England as in France, in America as in Germany, has stripped him of every trace of national character. Law, morality, religion, are to him so many bourgeois prejudices, behind which lurk in ambush just as many bourgeois interests.

All the preceding classes that got the upper hand, sought to fortify their already acquired status by subjecting society at large to their conditions of appropriation. The proletarians cannot become masters of the productive forces of society, except by abolishing their own previous mode of appropriation, and thereby also every other previous mode of appropriation. They have nothing of their own to secure and to fortify; their mission is to destroy all previous securities for, and insurances of, individual property.

All previous historical movements were movements of minorities, or in the interests of minorities. The proletarian movement is the self-conscious, independent movement of the immense majority, in the interest of the immense majority. The proletariat, the lowest stratum of our present society, cannot stir, cannot raise itself up, without the whole superincumbent strata of official society being sprung into the air.

Though not in substance, yet in form, the struggle of the proletariat with the bourgeoisie is at first a national struggle. The proletariat of each country must, of course, first of all settle matters with its own bourgeoisie.

In depicting the most general phases of the development of the proletariat, we traced the more or less veiled civil war, raging within existing society, up to the point where that war breaks out into open revolution, and where the violent overthrow of the bourgeoisie lays the foundation for the sway of the proletariat.

Hitherto, every form of society has been based, as we have already seen, on the antagonism of oppressing and oppressed classes. But in order to oppress a class, certain conditions must be assured to it under which it can, at least, continue its slavish existence. The serf, in the period of serfdom, raised himself to membership in the commune, just as the petty bourgeois, under the yoke of feudal absolutism, managed to develop into a bourgeois.

The modern laborer, on the contrary, instead of rising with the progress of industry, sinks deeper and deeper below the conditions of existence of his own class. He becomes a pauper, and pauperism develops more rapidly than population and wealth. And here it becomes evident that the bourgeoisie is unfit any longer to be the ruling class in society, and to impose its conditions of existence upon society as an over-riding law. It is unfit to rule, because it is incompetent to assure an existence to its slave within his slavery, because it cannot help letting him sink into such a state that it has to feed him, instead of being fed by him. Society can no longer live under this bourgeoisie, in other words, its existence is no longer compatible with society.

The essential condition for the existence, and for the sway of the bourgeois class, is the formation and augmentation of capital; the condition for capital is wage-labor. Wage-labor rests exclusively on competition between the laborers. The advance of industry, whose involuntary promoter is the bourgeoisie, replaces the isolation of the laborers, due to competition, by their revolutionary combination, due to association. The development of Modern Industry, therefore, cuts from under its feet the very foundation on which the bourgeoisie produces and appropriates products. What the bourgeoisie therefore produces, above all, are its own grave-diggers. Its fall and the victory of the proletariat are equally inevitable.

POSTSCRIPT

The Classic Dialogue: Is Capitalism the Best Route to Human Happiness?

As a society, Americans have always prized liberty over equality. The attitude within the United States seems to be that the wealth of the society as a whole is the only legitimate goal of economic enterprise and that distribution for the sake of equity or charity is a side issue best left to churches and private charities. Americans have resisted attempts to socialize such basic needs as medicine, communications (e.g., telephone companies), and economic security for the old, young, and infirm. In promoting capitalism, economists point to the failures of socialism in England and Sweden, and they cite the fall of communism in Eastern Europe and Russia.

The United States has built some safety nets: Social Security, Medicare and Medicaid, Aid to Dependent Children, and the like. But these and other elements of the welfare system have become a major political issue. People in the welfare system complain about its failure to provide adequately for those who need the most—babies and the infirm elderly, for example. Meanwhile, conservative members of Congress argue that welfare subsidies are costing the taxpayers too much. Can it be said that capitalism is "working" for people on welfare?

What about the "invisible hand" of Smith's free market; is it operating in the United States? Does America have true capitalism? The last two decades of economic reform have seen the richest persons in America absorbing more and more of the wealth and income, while the poorest people have been getting poorer. Should society strive to redistribute the productive assets of the country?

Suggested Readings

David Korten, "The Difference Between Money and Wealth: How Out-of-Control Speculation Is Destroying Real Wealth," *Business Ethics* (January/February 1999).

Richard John Neuhaus, "The Pope Affirms the 'New Capitalism,'" *The Wall Street Journal* (May 2, 1991).

David Schweickart, *Against Capitalism*, rev. ed. (Cambridge University Press, 1993).

John D. Bishop, "Adam Smith's Invisible Hand Argument," *Journal of Business Ethics* (March 1995).

Donald McCloskey, "A Bourgeois Virtue," *American Scholar* (vol. 63, 1994).

ISSUE 2

Can Individual Virtue Survive Corporate Pressure?

YES: Robert C. Solomon, from "Victims of Circumstances? A Defense of Virtue Ethics in Business," *Business Ethics Quarterly* (January 2003)

NO: Gilbert Harman, from "No Character or Personality," *Business Ethics Quarterly* (January 2003)

ISSUE SUMMARY

YES: Joining the long-standing debate on the possibility of free choice and moral agency in the business world, Quincy Lee Centennial Professor of Business and Philosophy at the University of Texas in Austin Robert C. Solomon argues that whatever the structures, the individual's choice is free, and therefore his character or virtue is of the utmost importance in creating a good moral tone in the life of a business.

NO: Stuart Professor of Philosophy at Princeton University Gilbert Harman employs determinist arguments to conclude that no individual can of his own free choice make a difference in a group enterprise.

We have long recognized that the world looks very different from internal and external perspectives.

From the inside, the choices people make are very clearly *their* choices. They wrestle with their fear, they encourage their generosity, they praise themselves for farsightedness and blame themselves for carelessness and haste—and at the end, they choose. "Character" is that foundation in right living that strengthens or enables people to make the right choices by prevailing against the external pressures to make the wrong choices. For example, an athlete is strengthened or enabled to win a contest because he has disciplined himself to exercise regularly.

From the outside, observers can easily explain one's choices by references to the external circumstances and incentives. One may protest that the observers know nothing of one's internal processes, but the standard response is, whatever you may have thought of the situation, given the circumstances, you had no choice but to do what you did.

Philosophically, one notes the difference in perspectives as "free will versus determinism," originally a dispute over whether actions are caused by free choice or by circumstances. Since the philosopher David Hume (1711–1776) explored the subject, we have learned to adopt a more sophisticated analysis of the dispute. One can conclude that, generally, all human actions are determined not just by external circumstances but also by the entire history and upbringing of the agent. One can also conclude that all human actions are free in that the agent, in choosing, builds creatively on that history and upbringing to adapt to the external circumstances.

Robert C. Solomon and Gilbert Harman address a more limited question: if agents (presumably employees in a corporation) are clearly people of good education, sound upbringing, and good character, can one expect that they will act rightly, no matter what external circumstances business life throws at them? Does virtue play a role in the conduct of business?

Certain experiments in social psychology, as mentioned in the selections, suggest that it does not. The Milgram experiments comprised a series of studies of human behavior conducted in several locations in New England, beginning in 1964. Dr. Stanley Milgram invited volunteers from the communities to participate in a "learning" experiment. The purpose, he explained to them, was to find out if negative reinforcement (punishment) speeded up learning of a simple task. Volunteers were directed to man a menacing board of "electrical shock administration" buttons, with one labeled "danger!" The volunteers drew lots to see who would be "student" and who "teacher." As the "teacher," they would administer shocks to the "student." Each time the "student" made a mistake, a higher level of shock would be administered, resulting in the "students" crying out in pain at the higher levels. If a "student" made enough mistakes, the instructions called for the "teacher" to press the "danger!" button; when that happened, there was only an ominous silence from the "student."

Of course the whole thing was a hoax. The lots the volunteers drew were all labeled "teacher." The "student" was an actor employed by Milgram, and the board was a phony. The question Milgram was really trying to answer concerned obedience to authority: would a normal adult, who knew that it was wrong to inflict pain on another human being and who was given no pressure but the instructions of someone in a white coat, obediently inflict what he had every reason to believe was serious and possibly lethal injury on an innocent stranger? The answer was—an alarming percent of the time—yes, he would.

What does one mean by "character"? Is character supposed to produce virtuous behavior automatically, even when the situation is completely staged and artificial? Is there still room for virtue among the fierce pressures of the business world?

Ask yourself, as you read these selections, just how prepared you are to meet demanding situations as an employee or as a citizen. Is your community of faith or ethics strong enough to enable you to do the right thing in a situation that frightens or constricts you? How would you teach new employees in a company to do the right thing in a difficult situation?

Robert C. Solomon

YES

Victims of Circumstances? A Defense of Virtue Ethics in Business

Abstract: Should the responsibilities of business managers be understood independently of the social circumstances and "market forces" that surround them, or (in accord with empiricism and the social sciences) are agents and their choices shaped by their circumstances, free only insofar as they act in accordance with antecedently established dispositions, their "character"? Virtue ethics, of which I consider myself a proponent, shares with empiricism this emphasis on character as well as an affinity with the social sciences. But recent criticisms of both empiricist and virtue ethical accounts of character deny even this apparent compromise between agency and environment. Here is an account of character that emphasizes dynamic interaction both in the formation and in the interplay between personal agency and responsibility on the one hand and social pressures and the environment on the other.

Business ethics is a child of ethics, and business ethics, like its parents, is vulnerable to the same threats and challenges visited on its elders. For many years, one such threat (or rather, a family of threats) has challenged moral philosophy, and it is time it was brought out in the open in business ethics as well. It is a threat that is sometimes identified by way of the philosophical term, "determinism," and though its status in the philosophy of science and theory of knowledge is by no means settled, it has nevertheless wreaked havoc on ethics. If there is determinism, so the argument goes, there can be no agency, properly speaking, and thus no moral responsibility. But determinism admits of at least two interpretations in ethics. The first is determination by "external" circumstances, including pressure or coercion by other people. The second is determination within the person, in particular, by his or her *character*. In the former case, but arguably not in the latter, there is thought to be a problem ascribing moral responsibility.[1]

The argument can be readily extended to business ethics. Versions of the argument have been put forward with regard to corporations, for instance, in the now perennial arguments whether corporations can be or cannot be held responsible.[2] One familiar line of argument holds that only individuals,

From Robert C. Solomon, "Victims of Circumstances? A Defense of Virtue Ethics in Business," *Business Ethics Quarterly,* vol. 13, no. 1 (January 2003). Copyright © 2003 by *Business Ethics Quarterly.* Reprinted by permission of The Philosophy Documentation Center, publisher of *Business Ethics Quarterly.*

not corporations, can be held responsible for their actions. But then corporate executives like to excuse their actions by reference to "market forces" that render them helpless, mere victims of economic circumstances, and everyone who works in the corporation similarly excuses their bad behavior by reference to those who set their agenda and policies. They are mere "victims of circumstances." They thus betray their utter lack of leadership. Moreover, it doesn't take a whole lot of research to show that people in corporations tend to behave in conformity with the people and expectations that surround them, even when what they are told to do violates their "personal morality." What (outside of the corporation) might count as "character" tends to be more of an obstacle than a boon to corporate success for many people. What seems to count as "character" in the corporation is a disposition to please others, obey superiors, follow others, and avoid personal responsibility.

In general philosophy, [Immanuel] Kant tried desperately to separate determinism and moral responsibility, defending determinism in the domain of science and "Nature" but preserving agency and responsibility in the domain of ethics. "I have found it necessary to limit knowledge to make room for faith," as he put in one of his most concise but rather misleading *bon mots*. Other philosophers were not so bold. They were willing to accept determinism (even if conjoined with skeptical doubts) and somehow fit agency and responsibility into its domain. David Hume and John Stuart Mill, the two most illustrious empiricist promoters of this strategy, suggested that an act is free (and an agent responsible) if it "flows from the person's character,"[3] where "character" stood for a reasonably stable set of established character traits that were both morally significant and served as the antecedent causal conditions demanded by determinism. Adam Smith, Hume's best friend and the father of not only modern economics but of business ethics too, agreed with this thesis. It was a good solution. It saved the notions of agency and responsibility, it was very much in line with our ordinary intuitions about people's behavior, and it did not try to challenge the scientific establishment. So, too, a major movement in business ethics, of which I consider myself a card-carrying member, is "virtue ethics," which takes the concept of character (and with it the related notions of virtue and integrity) to be central to the idea of being a good person in business. Among the many virtues of virtue ethics in business, one might think, is that, as in Hume and Mill, it would seem to keep at bay the threat of situational ("external") determinism.

Such a solution seems particularly appropriate for business ethics because the concept of character fills the void between institutional behaviorism ("organizational behavior") and an overblown emphasis on free will and personal autonomy that remains oblivious to context, the reality of office work, and the force of peer and corporate pressures. It provides a locus for responsibility without sacrificing the findings of "management science." But I have mixed feelings about the empiricist solution. On the one hand, it seems to me too weak. It does not account (or try to account) for actions "out of character," heroic or saintly or vicious and shockingly greedy behavior, which could not have been predicted of (or even by) the subject. And it does not (as Aristotle does) rigorously hold a person responsible for the formation of his or her character.

Aristotle makes it quite clear that a wicked person is responsible for his or her character not because he or she could *now* alter it but because he or she could have and should have acted differently early on and established very different habits and states of character. The corporate bully, the greedy entrepreneur, and the office snitch all would seem to be responsible for not only what they do but who they are, according to Aristotle's tough criterion.

On the other hand, however, the empiricist solution overstates the case for character. (This is what some psychologists, and Gilbert Harman, refer to as the "attribution error.") The empiricists make it sound as if character is something both settled and "robust" (the target of much of the recent psychological liter-ature). Character consists of such traits as honesty and trustworthiness that are more or less resistant to social or interpersonal pressures. But character is never fully formed and settled. It is always vulnerable to circumstances and trauma. People change, and they are malleable. They respond in interesting and some-times immediate ways to their environment, their peers and pressures from above. Put into an unusual, pressured, or troubled environment, many people will act "out of character," sometimes in heroic but more often in disappoint-ing and sometimes shocking ways. In the corporate setting, in particular, people joke about "leaving their integrity at the office door" and act with sometimes shocking obedience to orders and policies that they personally find unethical and even downright revolting.

These worries can be taken care of with an adequate retooling of the no-tion of character and its place in ethics, and this is what I will try to do here. But my real worry is that in the effort to correct the excesses of the empiricist em-phasis on character, the baby is being thrown out with the bath toys. In recent work by Gilbert Harman and John Doris, in particular, the very notion of char-acter is being thrown into question.[4] Indeed, Harman suggests that "there may be no such thing." Doris entitles his book, tellingly, *Lack of Character*. Both Harman and Doris argue at considerable length that a great deal of what we take as "character" is in fact (and demonstrably) due to specific social settings that reinforce virtuous conduct. To mention two often-used examples, clergy act like clergy not because of character but because they surround themselves with other clergy who expect them to act like clergy. So, too, criminals act like criminals not because of character but because they hang out with other crimi-nals who expect them to act like criminals. Harman argues vehemently against what he calls the illusion of "a robust sense of character." Doris argues, at book length, a very detailed and remarkably nuanced account of virtue and respon-sibility without character. The conclusion of both authors is that virtue ethics, construed in terms of character, is at best a mistake, and at worst a vicious political maneuver.

It is worth saying a word about this "vicious political maneuver" that is the political target of Harman's and Doris's arguments. I share in their concern, and I, too, would want to argue against those who, on the basis of an absurd notion of character, expect people to "pick themselves up by their own boot-straps," blaming the poor, for instance, for their own impoverishment and thus ignoring social and political (not to mention medical and racial) disadvantages that are certainly not their fault. I, too, reject such a notion of character, but I am not willing to dispense with the very notions of character and the virtues in order to do this.

So, too, in business ethics, there is a good reason to be suspicious of a notion of character that is supposed to stand up to overwhelming pressures without peer or institutional support. I would take Harman's and Doris's arguments as a good reason to insist on sound ethical policies and rigorous ethical enforcement in corporations and in the business community more generally, thus maximizing the likelihood that people will conform to the right kinds of corporate expectations. Nevertheless, something extremely important can get lost in the face of that otherwise quite reasonable and desirable demand. It is the idea that a person can, and should, resist those pressures, even at considerable cost to oneself, depending on the severity of the situation and circumstances. That is the very basis on which virtue ethics has proven to be so appealing to people in business. It is the hope that they can, and sometimes will, resist or even rise up against pressures and policies that they find to be unethical.

So whatever my worries, I find myself a staunch defender of character and the indispensability of talk about character in both ethics and business ethics.[5] To quote my friend and colleague Ed Hartman, "the difference between Peter Hempel [one of the most wonderful human beings we ever met] and Richard Nixon is not just a matter of environment." In both everyday life and in business, there are people we trust, and there are people we do not, often on the basis of a substantial history of disappointments and betrayal. And we trust or distrust those people in much the same circumstances and under much the same conditions. To be sure, character is vulnerable to environment but it is also a bulwark *against* environment. Character supplies that familiar and sometimes uncomfortable or even uncanny resistance to untoward pressures that violate our "principles" or morally disgust us or are damaging to our "integrity." It is character and not God or the Superego that produces that nagging inner voice called "conscience." (It has been suggested that conscience produces character rather than the other way around, but apart from religious predilections there seems to be little sound philosophical argument or empirical research to defend this.) One person refuses to obey a directive to short-change his customers while another refuses to cheat on her expense account despite the fact that everyone around her is doing so. It is character that makes the difference, though not, to be sure, *all* the difference.

Some of my concern with this issue is personal. Like most conscientious people, I worry about my integrity and character, what sorts of temptations and threats I could and would withstand. I feel ashamed (or worse) when I give into those temptations and humiliated when I succumb to (at least some of) those threats. I am occasionally even proud about those temptations and threats I have withstood. Philosophically ("existentially"), I worry about how we view ourselves when the balance of accounts is shifted over to causal and statistical explanations of behavior instead of a continuing emphasis on character, agency, and responsibility. Will that give almost everyone an excuse for almost everything?[6] . . .

The "New Empiricism" Virtue Ethics and Empirical Science

... Harman and Doris attack virtue ethics in general and the concept of character in particular on the grounds that they do not survive experimental findings in the past few decades. Exhibit number one for both of them is the infamous Stanley Milgram experiments in which people with supposedly good character performed the most despicable acts when encouraged to do so by an authority (the experimenter). But though empirical research in social psychology can on occasion shock us, surprise us, annoy us, and sometimes burst our illusions, it all gets weighed and accounted for, whether well or badly, in terms of our ordinary folk psychology observations and the ordinary concepts of belief, desire, emotion, character, and interpersonal influences, interactions, and institutions. There are no Copernican revolutions and no Michelson-Morley experiments. The Milgram and other experiments such as those by [J. M.] Darley and [C. D.] Batson that play a central role in Doris's and Harman's arguments get rationalized and explained in all sorts of ways, but none of them in violation of the basic forms of psychological explanation that Aristotle would have found perfectly familiar.[7] Of course, there remains a debate about the relative influence of "external" (environmental) and "inner" factors (character), but the debate, which ever way it goes, remains within the framework of folk psychology and our ordinary psychological concepts.

We might be disturbed, for example, that so many subjects followed the instructions of an authority figure to the point of (what they thought was) the torturing of another human being, but the various explanations in terms of "obedience to authority" or the unusual circumstances of the experiment (how often are most of us told to punish anyone?) do nothing to challenge our ordinary moral intuitions. It just reminds us of something we'd rather not remember, that ordinary people sometimes act very badly in group and institutional situations. This should come as no surprise to those of us who do corporate and organizational ethics....

I have long been an advocate of cooperation between moral philosophy and the social sciences in business ethics. I think that the more we know about how people actually behave in corporations, the richer and more informed our moral judgments and, more important, our decisions will be. In particular, it is very instructive to learn how people will behave in extraordinary circumstances, those in which our ordinary moral intuitions do *not* give us a clue. All of us have asked, say, with regard to the Nazi disease in Germany in the Thirties, how we would have behaved; or how we would behave, think, and feel if we worked for a tobacco company. But even in an ordinary corporation (which is not the same as a university in which there is at least the illusion of individual autonomy and "academic freedom"), the question of "obedience to authority" comes front and center.

Thus an experiment like the Milgram experiment is shocking precisely because it does not seem to presuppose any extraordinary context. Milgram's experiment, which would certainly be prohibited today, has to do with subjects inflicting potentially lethal shocks to victim-learners (in fact the experimenter's accomplices). Even when the victim-learners pleaded for them to stop, the majority of subjects continued to apply the shocks when ordered to do so by the authorities (the experimenters). One could easily imagine this "experiment" being confirmed in any corporation.[8] But I find the use of such research to undermine the notion of character not at all convincing.[9] Harman, for example, argues that

> Empirical studies designed to test whether people behave differently in ways that might reflect their having different character traits have failed to find relevant differences. It is true that studies of this sort are very difficult to carry out and there have been few such studies. Nevertheless, the existing studies have had negative results. Since it is possible to explain our ordinary belief in character traits as deriving from certain illusions, we must conclude that there is no empirical basis for the existence of character traits.[10]

But in addition to leaping from "very few studies" that are "difficult to carry out" to the conclusion that there is "no empirical basis for the existence of character traits," the whole weight of the argument comes to depend on the *possibility* of explaining our ordinary belief in character traits as "deriving from certain illusions." But what would such an explanation consist of? What illusions are we talking about? And what is our "ordinary belief in character"? I will argue that it does not require the "robust" notion attacked by Harman....

What Is a Virtue and Whence Character?

Harman does a nice job of delimiting the ordinary notions of virtue and character, namely those that are most relevant to business ethics. He distinguishes character from various psychological disorders (schizophrenia, mania, depression). More dubiously, he distinguishes character from "innate aspects of temperament such as shyness or being a happy or sad person.[11] Kant, oddly enough, quite correctly insists that being happy (though an "inclination") can be a virtue, as it makes us more inclined to do our duty. But Harman is not just attacking the virtues. He is after character traits in general. Shyness, for example, is a non-moral example of a character trait. Harman considers this a prime example of "false attribution." But I think Jean-Paul Sartre has his eye on something very important when he refers to the citing of such a character trait as "bad faith," namely, where we point to a causal syndrome where we should be talking about decisions and the cultivation (in a very strong sense) of character.[12] There is a certain element of such Sartrianism (an insistence on existential choices rather than robust character) in Harman's argument (with which I quite agree), but this is a very different set of reasons for questioning or qualifying the concepts of character and the virtues.[13] ...

In the ordinary conceptions of character traits and virtues, Harman and Doris tell us, people differ in their possession of such traits and virtues. People are different, and these differences explain their differences in behavior. Harman: "We ordinarily suppose that a person's character traits *help* to explain at least some of the things the person does" (italics mine). But, he says, "the fact that people regularly behave in different ways does not establish that they have different character traits. The difference *may* be due to their different situations rather than differences in their characters" (italics mine). But notice that there is no consistency whatever between insisting that a person's character traits *help* to explain their behavior and insisting that a difference in behavior *may* be due to the different situations in which two people find themselves. So, too, Doris's objection to globalism is that people (in experimental situations) fail to display the consistency and stability that explanations in terms of character require. But again, the short-term experiments that he cites do not undermine our more ordinary long-term judgments about personal propensities and dispositions. At best, they force us to face some hard truths about ourselves and consider other propensities and dispositions that may not be virtuous at all.

In our "ordinary conception" two people (one honest, one dishonest) in the same situation (discovering a lost wallet in the street, encountering a person in apparent desperate need, being ordered by an experimenter to "keep on punishing") will very probably act differently. But any philosopher worthy of his or her debating trophies will quickly point out that no two situations are sufficiently similar to make that case. It is only a very thin description of "the situation" (the experimental set-up) that makes it seem so. Subjects come from different backgrounds and different social classes. They are different genders. They may as a consequence have very different senses of the situation. I would not join Joel Feinberg in claiming that those students who do not stop for a stranger in need (in Darley and Batson's much-discussed "Good Samaritan" experiment) have a "character flaw," but neither would I conclude (with Doris) that their behavior is largely "situational."[14] The student's way of seeing and being in the situation may be very different, and this, of course, is just what Aristotle says about character. It is, first of all, a kind of perception, based on good up-bringing. Thus I think Harman is being a bit disingenuous when he argues that "they must be disposed to act differently in the same circumstances (as they perceive those circumstances)." The question of character begins with how they perceive those circumstances.

... Corporate managers and employees feel obliged and committed to act in conformity with corporate pressures and policies even when they are questionable or unethical, and they learn to rationalize accordingly. The question is, does any of this imply that we should give up or give in on character? Or should we say that character is both cultivated and maintained through the dynamic interaction of individuals and groups in their environment and they in turn develop those virtues (and vices) that in turn motivate them to remain in the situations in which their virtues are supported, reinforced, and not threatened?

In Milgram's famous "shocking people" experiment in the early 1960s (just as America was getting more deeply involved in the morass of Vietnam), the experimental data were indeed shocking, even to Milgram and his colleagues who expected no such result. In the social context of the times, questions about obedience to authority (left over from the Nuremberg trials not so many years before) had a special poignancy, especially in the face of the soon to be challenged American "innocence" of the time. It was very upsetting to find that good, solid, ordinary middle-class people could be ordered (but not coerced) to act so brutally (whether or not they had severe misgivings about their behavior at the time—a matter of no small importance here). The facts of the experiment are beyond dispute. But what the experiment means remains highly controversial, and it does not deserve the central place in the attack on character that it is now receiving. Doris claims that "Milgram's experiments show how apparently non-coercive situational factors may induce destructive behavior despite the apparent presence of contrary evaluative and dispositional structures." Accordingly, he "gives us reason to question the robustness of dispositions implicated in compassion-relevant moral behavior."[15]

Well, no. The disposition (virtue) that is most prominent and robust in this very contrived and unusual situation, the one that virtually all of the subjects had been brought up with and practiced everyday since childhood, was doing what they were told by those in authority. Compassion, by contrast, is a virtue more often praised than practiced, except on specially designated occasions (giving to the neediest at Christmas time) or stretching the term to include such common courtesies as restraining one's criticism of an unprepared student or letting the other car go first at a four-way intersection. (I would argue that such examples betray a lack of understanding of what compassion is.) Most often, people display compassion by "feeling sorry for" those much worse off than they, a very small expenditure of effort even when it is sincere. It seems to me that what the Milgram experiment shows—and what subsequent events in Vietnam made all too painfully obvious—was that despite our high moral opinions of ourselves and our conformist chorus singing about what independent individuals we all are, Americans, like Germans before them, are capable of beastly behavior in circumstances where their *practiced* virtues are forced to confront an unusual situation in which unpracticed efforts are required. In the Milgram experiment as in Vietnam, American subjects and soldiers were compelled by their own practiced dispositions to follow orders even in the face of consequences that were intolerable. Obedience may not always be a virtue....

In discussions of Vietnam, those who were not there (especially politicians) like to talk about the virtue of courage as the defining trait of the American forces. What they ignore, of course, is the very nature of the war. In several important memoirs by soldiers who served there, Bill Broyles and Tim O'Brien, it becomes clear that courage was just about the last thing on most of the soldiers minds.[16] They were terrified of losing legs and arms. They were moved by camaraderie and a sense of mutual obligation. (The virtue-name "loyalty" misses the mark.) The only discussion of courage in O'Brien's book has to do with a single heroic figure, a Captain Johansen whom he likens to Hector in Homer's *Iliad*. But this one character is exemplary in precisely the fact that he alone talked about and exemplified true courage. But the absence of courage (which is not to imply anything like cowardice on the part of the American troops) had a great deal to do with the nature of this particular war. It lacked any sense of purpose or progress. It lacked any sense of meaning for most of the men. And so, in that moral vacuum, all that was left for most soldiers was the worry about their own physical integrity and their keen sense of responsibility for each other. The atrocities at My Lai and Thanh Phong followed as a matter of course. There was no context in which either character or courage could be exercised.

Which brings us back to the misgivings and feelings of discomfort experienced by some (not all) of the subjects and the "grunts" in Vietnam. Feelings of compassion (and other moral sentiments) may not be definitive in motivating behavior, especially if one has not faced anything like the awful situation in which the subjects and soldiers found themselves. But it does not follow that there is nothing more for virtue ethics to say about such cases. Experiments such as Milgram's are no longer allowed on college campuses, and for good reason. The feelings provoked in the subjects were too painful, and often with lasting damage.[17] And this is nothing, of course, compared to the post-traumatic experiences of many of those who served in Vietnam. The robustness of compassion must be measured not simply in terms of whether the subjects refused to continue with the experiment or not (most did) or whether the soldiers continued to do as they were ordered but by how powerful and upsetting the feelings they experienced both during and after the experiment. It is worth noting that there were a few sadists who actually enjoyed cruelty. There were others that were brutalized by the experiment and many who were brutalized by the war. That, it seems to me, should not be discounted. Bosses today are once again being forced to lay off thousands of their managers and employees. ("Market forces is the inescapable explanation.) But there is all the difference in the world between those monsters like the infamous Al "Chainsaw" Dunlap who took such evident pride in cross the board cuts and virtual saints such as Aaron Feuerstein who felt so badly about having to lay off workers (after a fire gutted his factory) that he kept them on the payroll until the company got back on its feet.[18]

The Milgram Experiment Revisited: A Model of Corporate Life?

Is corporate life nothing but the vectors of peer pressures, leaving very little or even no room for the personal virtues? Does social psychology show that this is not the case only for corporate grinds but for all of us? Empirically-minded philosophers love to find a single experiment, or perhaps two, that make this case for them, that is, which provide the basis for speculative excursions that go far beyond the (usually rather timid) findings of the social psychologists themselves. Harman's appeal to the two famous experiments by Milgram and by Darley and Batson are illustrative. Doris takes in a much wider swath of the social science literature, but even he is forced to admit, throughout his admirable book, that there are profound reasons for not generalizing from particular experiments to a good deal of "real life."

Regarding the Milgram experiment, Harman (following Ross and Nisbett) rejects as implausible any explanation in terms of a "character defect" and suggests instead the "step-wise character of the shift from relatively unobjectionable behavior to complicity in a pointless, cruel, and dangerous ordeal." I think that this is indeed part of the explanation. Milgram's subjects needed to have their callousness cultivated even as they dutifully obeyed the authorities (like the proverbial frog in slowly boiling water). The subjects could not have been expected to simply shock strangers on command. But where Harman adds that we are tempted to make the "fundamental attribution error" of blaming the subject's destructive obedience on a personal defect, I would say instead that what the Milgram experiment shows is how foolish and tragic the otherwise important virtues of conformity and obedience can be. There is no "personal defect" on display here precisely because what the experiment shows is the consistency and stability of *that* virtue. And the fact that it is (like all virtues) not always a virtue is no argument against its status as part of the core of the explanation of the subjects' behavior. The rest of the explanation involves not just the incremental but also the disorienting nature of the situation. . . .

The other often-used case for "lack of character" is the case of the "good Samaritan," designed by Darley and Batson. Seminary students, on their way to give an assigned lecture (on "the good Samaritan") were forced to confront a person (an accomplice of the experimenter) on their way. Few of them stopped to help. It is no doubt true that the difference between subjects and their willingness to help the (supposed) victim can be partially explained on the basis of such transient variables as the fact that they were "in a hurry." And it is probably true as well (and not at all surprising to those of us who are not pushing "faith-based initiatives" these days) that people who were (or claimed to be) religious or who were about to talk on a religious topic of direct relevance to the experience did not act so differently as they would have supposed. But does it follow that character played no role? I would say that all sorts of character traits, from one's ability to think about time and priorities to one's feelings of anxiety and competence when faced with a (seemingly) suffering human being all come into play. Plus, of course, the sense of responsibility and obligation to arrive at an appointment on time, which once again slips into the background of the interpretation of the experiment and so blinds us to the obvious.

As in the Milgram experiment, how much is the most plausible explanation of the case precisely one that the experimenters simply assume but ignore, namely the character trait or virtue of promptness, the desire to arrive at the designated place on time? It is not lack of character. It is a *conflict* of character traits, one practiced and well-cultivated, the other more often spoken of than put in practice. Theology students have no special claims on compassion. They just tend to talk about it a lot. And as students they have had little opportunity to test and practice their compassion in ways that are not routine. . . .

What is not debatable, it seems to me, is that people present themselves differently, whether or not their presentations accurately represent their virtues and vices (which longer exposure is sure to reveal). I have long argued that the subject of explanation is not just the behavior of an agent but the behavior of an *agent-in-situation* (or some such odd locution). In business ethics, in particular, the behavior in question is the behavior of an *"individual-within-the-organization,"* which is not for a moment to deny that this context may not be the only one of relevance in moral evaluation. Context is essential but it isn't everything. Virtues and vices are important for our explanations of human behavior, but they make sense only in the context of particular situations and cultural surroundings. There is no such thing as courage or generosity in abstraction, but it does not follow that there is no such thing as courage or generosity.

Conclusion: In Defense of Business Virtue Ethics

Virtue ethics has a long pedigree, going back to Plato and Aristotle, Confucius in China, and many other cultures as well as encompassing much of Medieval and modern ethics—including, especially, the ethics of Hume, Adam Smith, and the other "Moral Sentiment Theorists." But we would do well to remind ourselves just why virtue and character have become such large concerns in the world today—in business ethics and in politics in particular. The impetus comes from such disparate sources as the Nuremberg trials and American atrocities in Vietnam, teenage drug use and peer pressure, and the frequently heard rationalization in business and politics that "everyone is doing it." The renewed emphasis on character is an attempt to build a personal bulwark (call it "integrity") against such pressures and rationalizations and (though half-heartedly) to cultivate virtues other than those virtues of unquestioning obedience that proved to be so dominant in the Milgram experiments and in Vietnam atrocities such as My Lai.

... If we are to combat intolerance, encourage mutual forgiveness, and facilitate human flourishing in contexts plagued by ethnic hatred, for instance, there is no denying the need for mediating institutions that will create the circumstances in which the virtues can be cultivated. Closer to home, the cultivation of the virtues in much-touted moral education also requires the serious redesign of our educational institutions. And much of the crime and commercial dishonesty in the United States and in the world today is due, no doubt, to the absence of such designs and character-building contexts. (The market, said the late great "Buddhist" economist E. F. Schumaker, "is the institutionalization of non-responsibility."[19]) We need less moralizing and more beneficent social engineering.

I could not agree more with these aims. But the existentialist twist to which Harman alludes (that we *choose* our circumstances) and the postmodern turn encouraged by Doris (that we acknowledge that for the most part our circumstances make us) convince me not that we should eliminate talk of the virtues and character but fully acknowledge both the role of the social sciences (*all* of the social sciences) and stop preaching the virtues without due emphasis upon *both* personal responsibility and the force of circumstances. Like Doris, we should appreciate more such "out of character" heroic and saintly behavior (he mentions Oscar Schindler in particular) and the exigencies of context and circumstances. But we should insist, first and foremost, that people—at any rate, people *like us*—are responsible for what they do, and what they make of themselves.

Notes

1. See, for example, Robert Young, "The Implications of Determinism," in Peter Singer, *A Companion to Ethics* (London: Blackwell, 1991). I am not considering

here the post-Freudian complications of determination by way of compulsion or personality disorder.

2. E.g., Kenneth Goodpaster and John B. Matthews, Jr., "Can a Corporation have a Conscience?" *Harvard Business Review*, Jan–Feb. 1982; John Ladd, "Morality and the Ideal of Rationality in Formal Organizations," *The Monist*, Oct. 1970; Peter A. French, *Collective and Corporate Responsibility* (New York: Columbia University Press, 1984). French, Peter A., "Responsibility and the Moral Role of Corporate Entities," in R. Edward Freeman, ed., *Business as a Humanity (Ruffin Lectures II)* (New York: Oxford, 1994); Peter A. French, "The Corporation as a Moral Person," *American Philosophical Quarterly* 16: 3 (1979). Manuel G. Velasquez, *Business Ethics* (Engelwood Cliffs, N.J.: Prentice-Hall, 1982 and further editions).

3. David Hume, *An Enquiry Concerning Human Understanding*, 2nd ed. L. A. Sleby; Biggee, ed. (Clarendon: Oxford University Press, 1902). John Stuart Mill, *A System of Logic* 8th ed. (New York: Harper & Row, 1874). Adam Smith, *Theory of the Moral Sentiments* (London: George Bell, 1880).

4. Gilbert Harman, "Moral Philosophy Meets Social Psychology: Virtue Ethics and the Fundamental Attribution Error," *Proceedings of the Aristotelian Society* 99(1998–99): 315–331. Revised version in Harman, G., *Explaining Value and Other Essays in Moral Philosophy* (Oxford: Clarendon Press, 2000), 165–178. See also, "The Nonexistence of Character Traits," *Proceedings of the Aristotelian Society* 100 (1999–2000): 223–226. John Doris, *Lack of Character: Personality and Moral Behavior* (New York: Cambridge University Press, 2002).

5. Two philosophical defenses of character are Joel Kupperman, "The Indispensability of Character," in *Philosophy*, April 2001, 76(2): 239–250, and Maria Merritt, "Virtue Ethics and Situationist Personality Psychology," in *Ethical Theory and Moral Practice* 3 (2000): 365–383.

6. The fight against the pervasiveness of excuses is something I learned early on from Jean-Paul Sartre and pursue in some detail in my series, *No Excuses: Existentialism and the Meaning of Life* (The Teaching Company, 2000).

7. I would plea for something of an exception in the case of the fascinating flow of neuropsychiatric research of the last thirty or so years, which does indeed go beyond folk psychology, not only in its particular findings but in the very vocabulary and structure of its explanations. Nevertheless, what is so dazzling in much of this research is precisely that way in which neurological anomalies violate our ordinary "folk psychology" explanations. I will limit my references to two. The first is a wonderful series of studies published by Oliver Sachs over the years, including *The Man Who Mistook His Wife for a Hat and Other Clinical Tales* (Touchstone, 1998). The second is the recent research of Antonio Damasio, esp. in *Descartes's Error* (Putnam, 1994).

8. Stanley Milgram, "Behavioral Study of Obedience," *Journal of Abnormal and Social Psychology*, vol. 67, 1963; *Obedience to Authority* (New York: Harpercollins, 1983).

9. I have argued with both Harman and Doris that they have made selective use of social science research. In particular, they have restricted their appeals and references almost entirely to social psychology and have been correspondingly neglectful of counter-arguments in personality theory. The difference in perspective—and consequently the tension—between these two branches of empirical psychology are extremely significant to the argument at hand. See, e.g., Todd F. Heatherton (ed.), Joel Lee Weinberger, (ed.), *Can Personality Change?* [edited book] (Washington, D.C.: American Psychological Association, 1994), xiv, 368. A. Caspi, and B. W. Roberts (1999), "Personality Continuity and Change Across the Life Course" in L. A. Pervin and O. P. John (eds.), *Handbook of Personality: Theory and Research*, 2nd ed., (New York: Guilford), 300–326. Thomas J. Bouchard, Jr., "The Genetics of Personality," [chapter], Kenneth Blum (ed.); Ernest P. Noble, (ed.) et al., *Handbook of Psychiatric Genetics* (Boca Raton, Fla.: CRC Press, Inc. 1997), 273–296.

10. Gilbert Harman, "Moral Philosophy Meets Social Psychology" (web version), 1.

11. But see a similar distinction defended by Ed Hartrnan, "The Role of Character in Business Ethics," in J. Dienhart, D. Moberg, and R. Duska, *The Next Phase of Business Ethics: Integrating Psychology and Ethics* (Amsterdam: JAI/Elsevier, 2001), 341–354.

12. Jean-Paul Sartre, *Being and Nothingness*, trans. H. Barnes (New York: Philosophical Library, 1956), see for instance 104f.

13. An essay that uses the Milgram experiment to talk about "excuses" is A. Strudler and D. Warren, "Authority, Heuristics, and the Structure of Excuses," in J. Dienhart, D. Moberg, and R. Duska, *The Next Phase of Business Ethics*, 355–375. My own view is that "everybody's doing it" is NO excuse, or at best a mitigating one. See my *No Excuses: Existentialism and the Meaning of Life*. See also the now classic essay by Ron Green, "Everybody's Doing It," in *Business Ethics Quarterly* 1(1): 75–94.

14. J. M. Darley and C. D. Batson, "From Jerusalem to Jericho: A Study of Situational and Disposition Variables in Helping Behavior," *Journal of Personality and Social Psychology 27*, 1973.

15. Doris, 69.

16. William Broyles, Jr. *Brothers in Arms* (New York: Knopf, 1986) and Tim O'Brien, *If I Die in a Combat Zone Box Me Up and Ship Me Home* (New York: Delacorte, 1973). Both books are discussed by Thomas Palaima in "Courage and Prowess Afoot in Homer and in Vietnam" in *Classical and Modern Literature*, 20/3/(2000).

17. See Milgram, *Obedience to Authority*.

18. See my discussion in *A Better Way to think about Business* (Oxford, 1999), 10.

19. E. F. Schumaker, *Small is Beautiful* (Harper and Row, 1973).

References

Blackburn, Simon. 1995. *Essays in Quasi-Realism* (New York: Oxford University Press.

Bouchard, Thomas J., Jr. 1997. "The Genetics of Personality" [chapter]. Kenneth Blum (ed.), Ernest P. Noble, (ed.) et al. *Handbook of Psychiatric Genetics*. Boca Raton, Fla.: CRC Press, Inc., 273–296.

Broyles, William, Jr. 1986. *Brothers in Arms*. New York: Knopf.

Carr, Alfred. Jan.–Feb. 1968. "Is Business Bluffing Ethical?" *Harvard Business Review*: 143–153.

Caspi, A., and B. W. Roberts. 1999. "Personality Continuity and Change Across the Life Course" in *Handbook of Personality: Theory and Research* 2nd ed. L. A. Pervin and O. P. John (eds.) New York: Guilford, 300–326.

Damasio, Antonio. 1994. *Descartes's Error*. New York: Putnam.

Darley, J. M., and C. D. Batson. 1973. "From Jerusalem to Jericho: A Study of Situational and Dispositional Variables in Helping Behavior." *Journal of Personality and Psychology 27*.

Doris, John. 2002. *Lack of Character: Personality and Moral Behavior*. New York: Cambridge University Press.

French, Peter A. 1984. Collective and Corporate Responsibility. New York: Columbia University Press.

_____. 1979. "The Corporation as a Moral Person." *American Philosophical Quarterly* 16 (3).

_____. "Responsibility and the Moral Role of Corporate Entities." 1994. In *Business as a Humanity (Ruffin Lectures II)*. R. Edward Freeman (ed.). New York: Oxford.

Funder, David C. 2001. "Personality." *Annual Review of Psychology*. 52: 197–221.

Goodpaster, Kenneth, and John B. Matthews, Jr. Jan.–Feb. 1982. "Can a Corporation Have a Conscience? *Harvard Business Review*.

Green, Ronald. "Everybody's Doing It." *Business Ethics Quarterly* 1(1): 75–94.

Griffiths, Paul. 1997. *What Emotions Really Are.* Chicago University of Chicago Press. 1998–99.

Harman, Gilbert. 1998–99. "Moral Philosophy Meets Social Psychology: Virtue Ethics and the Fundamental Attribution Error." *Proceedings of the Aristotelian Society* (99): 315–331.

———. 1999–2000. "The Nonexistence of Character Traits." *Proceedings of the Aristotelian Society* (100): 223–226.

———. 2000. *Explaining Value and Other Essays in Moral Philosophy.* Oxford: Claredon Press, 165–178.

Hartman, Edwin M., ed. 2001. "The Role of Character in Business Ethics." in *The Next Phase of Business Ethics: Integrating Psychology and Ethics.* J. Dienhart, D. Moberg, and R. Duska (eds.). Amsterdam: JAI/Elsevier, 341–354.

Heatherton, Todd F. and Joel Lee Weinberger (eds.). 1994. "Can Personality Change? [edited book]. Washington, D.C.: American Psychological Association, 368.

Hume, David. 1902. *An Enquiry Concerning Human Understanding,* 2nd ed. L. A. Sleby-Biggee (ed.). Clarendon: Oxford University Press.

Kenrick, D. T., and Funder, D. C. 1988. "Profiting from Controversy: Lessons from the Person-Situation Debate." *American Psychologist* (43): 23–34.

Kupperman, Joel. April 2001. "The Indispensability of Character." *Philosophy* 76(2): 239–250.

Ladd, John. Oct. 1970. "Morality and the Ideal of Rationality in Formal Organizations." *The Monist.*

MacIntyre, Alasdair. 1984. *After Virtue.* Notre Dame: Notre Dame University Press.

Merritt, Maria. 2000. "Virtue Ethics and Situationist Personality Psychology." *Ethical Theory and Moral Practice* (3): 365–383.

Milgram, Stanley. 1963. "Behavioral Study of Obedience." *Journal of Abnormal and Social Psychology* 67.

Milgram, Stanley. 1983. *Obedience to Authority.* New York: HarperCollins.

Mill, John Stuart. 1874. *A System of Logic.* 8th ed. New York: Harper & Row.

Nietzsche, Friedrich. 1954. *Thus Spoke Zarathustra.* Trans., Kaufmann. New York: Viking, 207.

Nisbett and Ross. 1980. *Human Inference: Strategies and Shortcomings of Social Judgement.* Englewood Cliffs, N.J.: Prentice-Hall.

O'Brien, Tim. 1973. *If I Die in a Combat Zone Box Me Up and Ship Me Home.* New York: Delacorte.

Palaima, Thomas. 2000. "Courage and Prowess Afoot in Homer and in Vietnam," in *Classical and Modern Literature* 20(3):1–22.

Sachs, Oliver. 1998. *The Man Who Mistook His Wife for a Hat and Other Clinical Tales.* New York: Touchstone.

Sartre, Jean-Paul. 1956. *Being and Nothingness.* Trans. H. Barnes. New York: Philosophical Library.

Schumaker, E. F. 1973. *Small is Beautiful.* New York: Harper and Row.

Smith, Adam. 1880. *Theory of the Moral Sentiments.* London: George Bell.

Solomon, Robert C. 1993. *Ethics and Excellence.* New York: Oxford University Press.

———. 1999. *A Better Way to Think about Business.* New York: Oxford University Press.

Strudler, A., and D. Warren. 2001. "Authority, Heuristics, and the Structure of Excuses" in *The Next Phase of Business Ethics.* J. Dienhart, D. Moberg, and R. Duska (eds.), 355–375.

Velasquez, Manuel G. 1982. *Business Ethics.* Engelwood Cliffs, N.J.: Prentice-Hall.

Young, Robert. 1991. "The Implications of Determinism" in *A Companion to Ethics.* Peter Singer (ed.). London Blackwell.

Gilbert Harman

← **NO**

No Character or Personality

Abstract: [Robert] Solomon argues that, although recent research in social psychology has important implications for business ethics, it does not undermine an approach that stresses virtue ethics. However, he underestimates the empirical threat to virtue ethics, and his a priori claim that empirical research cannot overturn our ordinary moral psychology is overstated. His appeal to seemingly obvious differences in character traits between people simply illustrates the fundamental attribution error. His suggestion that the Milgram and Darley and Batson experiments have to do with such character traits as obedience and punctuality cannot help to explain the relevant differences in the way people behave in different situations.

... I want to suggest that Solomon underestimates the force of the threat to his version of business virtue ethics and I want to say a bit more about how the evidence from social psychology implies such "fragmentation."

Psychology and Folk Psychology

It is uncontroversial that there is usually a difference between the study of ordinary conceptions of a given phenomenon and the study of the phenomenon itself. We distinguish between folk or common-sense physics, which is studied by certain psychologists, and physics, which is studied by physicists; these are both interesting subjects, but they are different. Similarly, there is a clear difference between the study of conceptions people at a certain time had about witches and witchcraft and the study of what was actually true about people who were taken to be witches and phenomena thought to be witchcraft. We distinguish between the study of how people conceive of God from the study of theology. We distinguish between the study of doctors' views about good medical treatment and an investigation into what sorts of treatment are actually effective. We distinguish interviewers' conceptions of the value of interviewing from whether interviews actually improve selection processes.[1] In the same way, there is a clear conceptual difference between what people generally think about character and personality and what is actually the case; the study of what people think about character and personality (as in "personality theory" or

From Gilbert Harman, "No Character or Personality," *Business Ethics Quarterly*, vol. 13, no. 1 (January 2003). Copyright © 2003 by *Business Ethics Quarterly*. Reprinted by permission of The Philosophy Documentation Center, publisher of *Business Ethics Quarterly*.

"personality psychology") is part of the study of folk psychology and is not the same as a study of character and personality.

Surprisingly, Solomon expresses doubts about this sort of difference with respect to the virtues. He says that "there is an easy but wholly misleading analogy with physics." He agrees that "many of our moral intuitions are erroneous or archaic," but insists that "our moral intuitions are not *like* our intuitions in physics. There is no 'matter of fact' independent of our intuitions and attitudes." Furthermore, he says, "*All* psychology, if it is psychology at all, is one or another version of 'folk psychology' ('the only game in town,' according to Jerry Fodor)."

In response, I have to say that, although it has often been argued (e.g., by Dennett, 1981; Fodor, 1987) that psychology has to be belief and desire psychology, I am not familiar with any similar argument that psychology must for that reason also include commitment to character and personality traits. In particular, I do not believe that Fodor has ever made such an argument. Fodor's (1975) "only game in town" is a supposed to be a certain sort of computational functionalism involving a "language of thought" with no reference whatsoever to character traits.

Furthermore, whether or not there is a matter of fact about what is right or wrong, it is obvious that many moral judgments presuppose matters of fact. To belabor the point, if I say you were wrong to hit Bob in the nose, I presuppose that in fact you hit Bob in the nose and, if you did not, I am mistaken. Similarly, if I say that you have a certain virtuous character, I presuppose that you have a character. Perhaps, as Solomon believes, it is not a matter of fact whether such a character is virtuous. But it is a matter of fact whether you have the character, and whether there are character traits at all.

In addition to offering these relatively a priori arguments for doubting that social psychology could undermine ordinary conceptions of character and personality traits, Solomon also notes the existence of the field of "personality theory." He has, he says, "long been an advocate of cooperation between moral philosophy and the social sciences in business ethics." But, he says,

> What about that voluminous literature *not* in social psychology but in the (artificially competing) field of personality theory?... If we want to play off moral philosophy and virtue ethics against the social sciences, let's make sure that all of the social sciences are represented and not just social psychology.

However, personality theory or personality psychology is in pretty bad institutional shape. Solomon refers to Funder (2001), a bravely upbeat review of the current (utterly dismal) state of personality psychology that nevertheless acknowledges that personality psychology has collapsed as an academic subject. So, Funder revealingly bemoans

> the permanent damage to the infrastructure of personality psychology wreaked by the person-situation debate of the 1970s and 1980s.... [O]ne reason for the trend... for so much personality research being done by investigators not affiliated with formal programs in personality may be that

there are so few formal programs to be affiliated with. The graduate programs in personality psychology that were shrunken beyond recognition or even abolished during the 1970s and 1980s have not been revived.(213)

Why does the critique of virtue ethics appeal to social psychology rather than to personality psychology? Because personality psychology has been concerned with characterizing ordinary folk conceptions of personality. Social psychology is concerned with the accuracy of these conceptions. To the extent that you are interested in the truth and accuracy of claims about character and personality, you need to consult social psychology, not "personality psychology."[2]

What Is the Fundamental Attribution Error?

The librarian carried the old woman's groceries across the street. The receptionist stepped in front of the old man in line. The plumber slipped an extra $50 into his wife's purse. Although you were not asked to make any inferences about any of these characters, chances are that you inferred that the librarian is helpful, the receptionist rude, and the plumber generous. Perhaps because we do not realize the extent to which behavior is shaped by situations, we tend to spontaneously infer such traits from behavior." (Kunda, 1999, 435)

Psychologists refer to this tendency as "correspondence bias" or "the fundamental attribution error." It is a bias toward explanations in terms of corresponding personality traits, the error of ignoring situational factors. The bias seems to be associated with a perceptual tendency to pay more attention to a figure than to its ground, and there appear to be significant cultural differences in the extent to which people are subject to this tendency and to the fundamental attribution error (Nisbett, 1998).

Having once attributed a trait to a given person, an observer has a strong tendency to continue to attribute that trait to the person even in the face of considerable disconfirming evidence, a tendency psychologists sometimes call "confirmation bias," a bias toward noting evidence that is in accord with one's hypothesis and toward disregarding evidence against it.[3]

Even in a world with no individual differences in character traits or personality traits, people would still strongly believe that there were such differences, as long as they were subject to the fundamental attribution error and to confirmation bias. This means that the apparent obviousness of the claim that people differ in such traits (as in Ed Hartman's comparison, endorsed by Solomon, between Hempel and Nixon) is less evidential than one may think. True, it is "obvious" that, some people have different character and personality traits than others. But our finding this fact so obvious is predicted by our tendency to the fundamental attribution error whether or not there are such differences.

...ceived situation some-
Doris (2002) discusses

plaza. As the caller
older full of papers
elp before the only
hungry throngs?...
perdropper was an
of callers, a dime
the slot was empty.
helped and 2 did
t.]... Finding a bit
k on in describing
not. (Doris, 2002,

meone who seems to
a hurry the student is
atson, 1973. Whether
er person who seems
d on whether there is
ned with the apparent

In the Milgram (1974) experiment, subjects were led by gradual steps to do something they would never have done straight away, namely to administer very severe electrical shocks to another person. The gradualness of the process with no obvious place to stop seems an important part of the explanation why they obeyed a command to shock the other person in that experiment although they would not have done so if directly ordered to give the severe shock at the very beginning.

Similarly, if you are trying not to give into temptation to drink alcohol, to smoke, or to eat caloric food, the best advice is not to try to develop "will-power" or "self-control." Instead, it is best to head the situationist slogan, "People! Places! Things!" Don't go to places where people drink! Do not carry cigarettes or a lighter and avoid people who smoke! Stay out of the kitchen!

Sometimes a person acts well or badly in a seemingly unusual way. Concerning any such case, there is an issue as to what makes the difference that leads to such seemingly unusual behavior. When you perceive or learn about someone you do not know doing such an unusual thing, you have a strong tendency to attribute the behavior to some good or bad trait of the person in question. When you learn that a certain seminary student walked right past someone who seemed to be having a heart attack, actually stepping right over the person, you tend to think of the student as incredibly callous.

The question is what makes the difference that leads to the unusual or surprising behavior. Is it that some theology students are more compassionate than others? Does the Milgram experiment show that almost everyone is basically evil?

Solomon says that certain character traits are relevant in these cases, namely, (1) obedience to (the experimenters') authority and (2) promptness. But relevant to what? Since Solomon thinks that all the experimental subjects had these traits, he does not suppose that these common traits are responsible for the *differences* in helping behavior that were observed. Nor do they account for the difference in obedience between a subject who is commanded to give an intense shock to someone at the very beginning and a subject who starts by giving a little shock and who increases the shock by very small steps.

No one supposes that these two experiments, taken by themselves, show that there are no character traits. What they show is that aspects of a particular situation can be important to how a person acts in ways that ordinary people do not normally appreciate, leading them to attribute certain distinctive actions to an agent's distinctive character rather than to subtle aspects of the situation. In particular, observers [of] some of the events that occur in these experiments are strongly inclined to blame those participants who did not stop to help or who provided intense shocks, thinking that the explanation of these agent's immoral actions lies in their terrible character. But the observers are wrong: that cannot be the explanation.

Near the end of his remarks, Solomon says, "Empirically-minded philosophers love to find a single experiment or perhaps two that... provide the basis for speculative excursions which go far beyond the (usually rather timid) findings of the social psychologists themselves." I need to emphasize that the Milgram experiment and others mentioned so far are only a very few large number of different experiments illustrating subtle effects of situations and the ways in which observers fail to understand those effects, leading observers to make the fundamental attribution error. Furthermore, as I have been insisting, the "speculative excursions" Solomon attributes to Doris and me do not go "far beyond the... findings of the social psychologists," but are in fact part of the settled core of the subject of social psychology.

Traits

We must distinguish individual acts of honesty or dishonesty, courage or cowardice, compassion or coldness from the corresponding character traits. The ordinary conception of a character or personality trait is of a relatively broad-based disposition to respond in the relevant way with acts of the corresponding sort. In an important discussion, Merritt (2000) shows that Aristotelian virtue ethics and most contemporary versions of virtue ethics (*but not Hume's theory*) appeal to character traits in this broad sense.

Now, the evidence indicates that people may differ in certain relatively narrow traits but do not have broad and stable dispositions corresponding to the sorts of character and personality traits we normally suppose that people have. Doris's (2002) defense of the fragmentation of character, derided by Solomon, is so widely accepted by social psychologists that a similar account can be found in any introductory textbook in social psychology. This is how Kunda (1999) puts the point:

> Our notion of traits as broad and stable dispositions that manifest themselves to the same extent in a variety of situations cannot hold water. However, this does not mean that there are no enduring and systematic differences among individuals. My intuitions that I am a very different person from my brother or that my children have predictably different patterns of behavior need not be wrong. Such intuitions may be based on meaningful and stable differences among individuals but not the kind of differences implied by the traditional understanding of traits.... [For example,] Carol is extremely extroverted in one-on-one situations, is only moderately extroverted when in small groups, and is not at all extroverted in large groups. She will appear very comfortable and outgoing if you meet with her alone, but will clam up and appear very shy and awkward if you encounter her in a large group setting. Linda has a very different profile. She is extremely extroverted in large groups but not at all extroverted in one-on-one situations. She may appear composed and comfortable when lecturing to a large audience but withdrawn and aloof if you approach her alone. (Kunda, 1999, 443-4)
>
> In conclusion, it appears that we are truly quite consistent in our behavior within each situation, and it is quite appropriate to expect such consistency in others. But we run into trouble when we expect this consistency to extend to other situations as well. Even slight variations in the features of a situation can lead to dramatic shifts in people's behavior. (Kunda, 1999, 499)

Free Will and Responsibility

Solomon worries that in the rejection of the sort of character and personality traits that are accepted in ordinary moral thinking and in his version of virtue ethics,

> something extremely important can get lost.... It is the idea that [one] can and should resist [certain] pressures, even at considerable cost to oneself, depending on the severity of the situation and circumstances. That is the very basis on which virtue ethics has proven to be so appealing to people in business.

This is clearly a different issue. Of course, people can and should resist such pressures and we should encourage them to do so. But the point has nothing to do with whether people have character traits. As Solomon would certainly agree, even a person without relevant character traits can and should resist.

Solomon worries about the philosophical consequences of denying the existence of character, because that would be to go "over to causal and statistical explanations of behavior instead of a continuing emphasis on character, agency, and responsibility." But people do not need character traits in order to have agency and responsibility. As Doris (2002, chaps. 7–8) persuasively argues, denying the existence of character traits in no way undermines the notions of agency and of responsibility.

Conclusion

Aristotelian style virtue ethics shares with folk psychology a commitment to broad-based character traits of a sort that people simply do not have. This does not threaten free will and moral responsibility, but it does mean that it is a mistake to base business ethics on that sort of virtue ethics. This leaves open the possibility of Merritt's (2000) Humean style virtue ethics in which virtuous behavior is socially supported and sustained.

Notes

1. For discussion of the well-known "interview illusion," see, e.g., Kunda (1999), 179–89, and references cited there. Interviews are simultaneously very unreliable indicators of later performance and also very vivid. Using interviews adds expensive vivid noise to a decision process. Solomon (who says the Princeton Philosophy Department's practice of not interviewing job candidates is "peculiar") suggests that the point of interviewing is to see how well the candidate will "fit in" with others on the job. The point about expensive vivid noise obviously applies here as well, as is noted in Miller and Cantor (1982), who nevertheless suggest that there is still a point to having a candidate for a teaching position give a talk to members of the hiring department, because these members will almost certainly all have the same impression of the talk, so their decision will tend to be unanimous. (When the Princeton Philosophy Department discussed whether to continue interviewing job candidates, it considered the Miller Cantor point but decided that it did not particularly care about unanimity.)

2. Doris (2002, 67–75) discusses the relation between social psychology and personality psychology in some detail.

3. Confirmation bias is discussed, e.g., in Gilovich (1993), chap. 3.

References

Darely, J.M. 1973. "From Jerusalem to Jericho: A Study of Situational and Dispositional Variables in Helping Behavior." *Journal of Personality and Social Psychology* 27: 100–8.

Dennett, D. C. 1981. *Brainstorms: Philosophical Essays on Mind and Psychology.* Cambridge, Mass.: MIT Press.

Doris, J. 2002. *Lack of Character: Personality and Moral Behavior.* New York: Cambridge University Press.

Fodor, J. A. 1975. *The Language of Thought.* New York: Thomas Crowell.

_____. 1987. *Psychosemantics: The Problem of Meaning in the Philosophy of Mind.* Cambridge, Mass.: MIT Press.

Funder, D. C. 2001. "Personality." *Annual Review of Psychology* 52: 197–221.

Gilovich, T. 1993. *How We Know What Isn't So: The Fallibility of Human Reason in Everyday Life.* New York: The Free Press.

Harman, G. 1998–99. "Moral Philosophy Meets Social Psychology: Virtue Ethics and the Fundamental Attribution Error." *Proceedings of the Aristotelian Society* 99: 315–31.

_____. 1999–2000. "The Nonexistence of Character Traits." *Proceedings of the Aristotelian Society* 100: 223–6.

Isen, A. M., and P.F. Levin. 1972. "Effect of Feeling Good on Helping: Cookies and Kindness." *Journal of Personality and Social Psychology* 21: 384–8.

Kunda, Z. 1999. *Social Cognition: Making Sense of People.* Cambridge, Mass.: MIT Press.

Latané, B., and J. M. Darley. 1970. *The Unresponsive Bystander: Why Doesn't He Help?* New York: Appleton-Century-Crofts.

Merritt, M. 2000. "Virtue Ethics and Situationist Personality Psychology." *Ethical Theory and Moral Practice* 3:365–83.

Milgram, S. 1974. *Obedience to Authority.* New York: Harper and Row.

Miller, G. A., and N. Cantor. 1982. Review of *Human Inference: Strategies and Shortcomings of Social Judgement.* In *Social Cognition* 1: 83–93.

Nisbett, R. 1998. "Essence and Accident." In *Attribution and Social Interaction: The Legacy of Edward E. Jones,* ed. J. M. Darley and J. Cooper. Washington, D.C.: American Psychological Association.

Solomon, R. 2003. "Victims of Circumstances? A Defense of Virtue Ethics in Business." *Business Ethics Quarterly* 13(1): 43–62.

POSTSCRIPT

Can Individual Virtue Survive Corporate Pressure?

This issue draws on the background of classic behavioral experiments, well known in the field of social psychology. One is often required to master portions of a scientific field in order to understand a question confronting the business world. For example, to understand the Pinto case (Issue 13) one may well have to know a bit of automotive engineering. To understand the dispute over the labeling of genetically modified organisms (Issue 14), one may have to learn how genes can be inserted into reproductive material of plants. Increasingly, business is about information and scientific knowledge, and the corporate officer is expected to be knowledgeable about the fields that interface his or her company's business.

Suggested Readings

Kenneth Goodpaster and John B. Matthews, Jr., "Can a Corporation Have a Conscience?" *Harvard Business Review* (January–February 1982).

John Ladd, "Morality and the Ideal of Rationality in Formal Organizations," *The Monist* (October 1970).

Peter A. French, *Collective and Corporate Responsibility* (Columbia University Press, 1984).

Gilbert Harman, "Moral Philosophy Meets Social Psychology: Virtue Ethics and the Fundamental Attribution Error," *Proceedings of the Aristotelian Society* (1998–1999).

J. Doris, *Lack of Character: Personality and Moral Behavior* (Cambridge University Press, 2002).

ISSUE 3

Can Restructuring a Corporation's Rules Make a Moral Difference?

YES: Josef Wieland, from "The Ethics of Governance," *Business Ethics Quarterly* (January 2001)

NO: Ian Maitland, from "Distributive Justice in Firms: Do the Rules of Corporate Governance Matter?" *Business Ethics Quarterly* (January 2001)

ISSUE SUMMARY

YES: Josef Wieland, director of the German Business Ethics Network's Centre for Business Ethics, argues that moral issues can be attributed to organizations (as well as to individual persons). After developing a concept of governance ethics for corporations, he asserts that the incorporation of moral conditions and requirements in the structures of the firm is the precondition for lasting beneficial effects of the virtues of the individuals within it. Wieland concludes that one can only be a moral person at work when the workplace, too, is moral.

NO: Ian Maitland, professor of business, government, and society at the University of Minnesota's Carlson School of Management, counters that changing the rules will only succeed in impairing the corporation's efficiency.

Josef Wieland notes that the question of whether or not an organization of some sort, as opposed to its human members, may assume the status of moral agent has been around for a very long time. (It actually goes back to Aristotle, who took up the question of the conditions under which a government is morally obligated to pay the debts incurred by its predecessor. It is more difficult with organizations than with humans to tell when one is dealing with the same entity that undertook the obligation.) New in Wieland's approach is the use of recent economic theory (referred to as the "New Economics of Organization"). Readers not exposed to the language of this theory may find it rough going at first, but the attempt to reach almost mathematical precision in the language of organizational ethics is a useful intellectual stretch.

Wieland asks, To what extent is my ability and inclination to act morally ("cooperate" with others) dependent on the institutional atmosphere, the communication from the highest levels that moral behavior is approved? Further, he states that what the moral agent in the corporation needs is a strong message that moral behavior will be rewarded even if it entails falling short on numerical goals set by management—even if it cuts into return on investment and the increase of shareholder wealth. That is the only message that matters, says Wieland.

Ian Maitland would disagree. He addresses himself to a different group of corporate reformers, those who hold that restructuring corporate rules to signal a new concern with morality can make the corporation more willing to take into account stakeholders other than the shareholders—the employees, for instance, or the natural environment. Rules are neutral, Maitland argues, at least as far as morality goes. But they can do a beautiful job of fouling up the corporate enterprise's efficiency, as people who should be worrying about how to get their job done faster and with less consumption of resources find themselves worrying instead about how to create a more moral world.

The fundamental conflict found in the following selections is just the conflict that defines business ethics. Should we expect moral behavior of the corporation? Should we hold corporations to moral standards? Should we engage in moral criticism of the corporation? Or, should we recognize, as many have argued, that the corporation is by right and by law no more than a legal device for turning money into more money? Should the corporation be held accountable only insofar as the law requires it to operate within the bounds of the public interest?

Ask yourself, as you read these selections, whether or not Wieland's conviction that the corporation can be a moral agent, and can make itself more moral if it chooses to, is helped by the theory he brings to bear. Also consider whether or not Maitland's skepticism about the usefulness of the enterprise is justified.

Josef Wieland

 **YES**

The Ethics of Governance

Introduction: Organization and Ethics

In this [selection] I want to pursue two questions. The first of these is as follows: what is the subject and scope of business ethics?[1] The second question is
this: in what way does it make sense to talk about the ethics of the firm-as-an-
organization?

The topic of this [selection]—the Ethics of Governance—already implies
a connection between corporate governance and business ethics; that is, between the management, governance, and control regimes of a firm and its ethics
as an organization. In practice these are interrelated: codes of ethics, ethics
management systems, and corporate ethics programs can be understood as governance structures by which firms control, protect, and develop the integrity of
their transactions. The theoretical investigation and integration of these ethical systems has hitherto been developed only to a limited extent and has been
confined to individual aspects, as far as I can see. There are reasons for this.

The theoretical explanation and integration of codes of ethics, ethics management systems, and other organizational measures for the implementation of
moral claims in organizational contexts requires a conceptual distinction between the moral values of an individual person (value ethics), the values of
an individual person in a given function or role (management ethics), and the
moral values of an organization (governance ethics). This distinction would
provide the basis for a better understanding of the trade-offs, conflicts, and
dilemmas contained in those distinct levels of business ethics.

In the following discussion I would like to focus my own investigation
on just one of the aspects mentioned—i.e., on the moral characteristics of an
organization as a distinct moral actor. There has been a lengthy, extensive, and
controversial debate on this issue. Its focus is the question of the attribution of
moral responsibility to collective actors.[2] Differing viewpoints revolve around
the issue as to whether firms as corporate actors are independent action systems or subjects, or whether their status as action systems or subjects is derived
from individual actors. Although this discussion has yielded important insights
for research on business ethics, the issue remains unresolved. I believe the reason for this deadlock is to be found in the individualistic notion of action that

From Josef Wieland, "The Ethics of Governance," *Business Ethics Quarterly*, vol. 11, no. 1 (January
2001). Copyright © 2001 by *Business Ethics Quarterly*. Reprinted by permission of The Philosophy
Documentation Center, publisher of *Business Ethics Quarterly*. References omitted.

grounds all the arguments. This emphasis is in full accordance with philosophical tradition. However, business ethics questions are questions about ethics in the context of a functional structure: they cannot be developed by analogy with the ethics of a person, but must be developed out of the characteristics and conditions of the structure itself. Is it then possible to develop a type of business ethics that does not resort to an action-theoretic notion of the person? In the following sections I will argue that this question can be answered affirmatively, and that its answer requires the substitution of the notion of person by that of governance, and of that of action by that of cooperation.…

Form and Process of the Organization

In this section, the notions of governance and governance ethics that so far have been introduced in a more intuitive way will be located in theoretical terms and further developed. In accordance with the discussion so far, only one particular form of governance will be the object of this endeavor: governance of the firm. Of course, rules and orders at the level of the state also are governance structures. However, for reasons of precision and simplicity they will not be dealt with systematically here.

Questions regarding the ethics of the firm are questions with regard to an organization. From the point of view of the institutionalist New Economics of Organization,[3] which this [selection] regards as normative, these are questions about the moral characteristics of a governance structure for the execution of economic transactions.

Governance structures are formal and informal arrangements for the "steering" of the different codes of a system or organization. They are a matrix within which distinct transactions are negotiated and executed, completely if possible.[4] For the purposes of this investigation it is useful to distinguish between global and local governance structures. Global governance structures refer to the constitutional parameters of an organization or a system; local governance structures to the micropolitical governance of transactions. State, market, and firms, frameworks, corporate charters, and ethical codes of conduct are global governance structures in this sense. In pursuing the question of business ethics I will interpret global governance structures as firm-specific assets (structures, resources, competences, skills) for the identification and processing of moral problems in the economy. Local governance structures are standard operating procedures, organizational structures, rites, and moral values within the firm that can constitute transaction-specific assets for the identification and processing of problem issues.

Governance structures differ with regard to their ability to support the efficient execution of a given transaction. Efficiency in the context of governance is defined as adaptive efficiency, that is, as comparison of at least two governance structures with regard to their capacity to cope with the uncertainties and contingencies that can occur during the process of transaction. Since such structures usually consist of formal and informal codes of practice, moral ambitions and values can without too much difficulty be interpreted as elements of the governance of economic transactions.

The above argument implies that business ethics is not about the moral standards and behavior of entrepreneurs, management teams, or employees. Those are personal virtues that can be attributed to acting persons, but not to the normativity of organizations. There seems to be general consensus in the literature that the moral constitution of an organization has to be different from the sum of the moral convictions of its members. However, it remains to a large extent unclear how the phenomenon of a structural ethics can be approached at all.[5] In the following I will develop my own views on this topic and locate them in the notion of governance ethics.

First of all it is important to introduce the convention that regarding their normativity organizations are contractually constituted systems of institution-alized behavioral constraints and thus also represent behavioral options.[6] In other words, business ethics cannot be developed based on the notion of action, but must be premised on the characteristics of a global governance structure for economic transactions that limits (and extends) behavioral options. The investigation into the theoretical problems this disposition entails must begin with a differentiated notion of the organization itself. We differentiate as follows: organization denotes the general *process* of organizing, and also the specific *form* within which this process takes place.

The introduction of this distinction between process and form has far-reaching consequences; these can be demonstrated by using the example of the distinction between market and hierarchy[7] common in economic theory. Market and hierarchy represent different global governance structures. As options for the execution of a transaction, e.g., a long-term employment relationship, they are equivalent. But as concrete "form" under whose regime this employment relationship takes place, they are not equivalent. It is precisely because markets and hierarchies have at their disposal different characteristics and capabilities for the governance of economic processes that the problem of cost-efficient assignments of transactions to the most efficient governance structure arises. In the case of a long-term employment relationship governance is optimally organized not via the market but via the hierarchical form of "firm."

The difference between process and form that is inherent in the notion of organization can be used for the theoretical construction of an institutional business ethics. Insofar as the process of organizing involves individual action, virtues and vices matter. But the organizational form within which this process is taking place—the firm—stands outside the realm of traditional value ethics. This decoupling of form and process is rooted in different temporal characteristics. The processual character of the organization called "firm" can in principle be set to infinite duration by the form character of the same organization to the extent that form is based on the exclusion of "human beings," "individuals," or "persons."[8] Because of this, business ethics—if we take the label seriously—has to refer constitutively to the form of a "firm" as a governance structure. It can be systematically developed as governance ethics only under conditions where individual virtues can and must have their effect.

Of course, the analysis and design of governance structures is part of institutional theory. However, it is important to realize that in the theoretical design developed here the notions of "governance" and "institution" are not synonyms. The notion of institution aims at directing behavior via formal or informal behavioral constraints and incentives (utility maximizing). In contrast, the notion of governance emphasizes the integration and interaction of formal and informal constraints with regard to any given problem and focuses on the problem of adaptivity, i.e., the reflexivity and recursiveness of structures. From a governance-theoretic perspective, whereas the notion of institution is more static (goal-oriented directing of behavior via narrowing of options), the notion of governance is dynamic (goal-oriented directing of behavior via adaptivity).

Two conclusions emerge from the foregoing discussion. First, business ethics needs to be developed as governance ethics. Second, the relationship between value ethics and governance ethics is as follows: whereas management virtues belong to the process of the firm, the proper locus of governance ethics is the form of the firm.

Governance Ethics: Contract and Organization

The foregoing argument leads to the consideration that the "shape" of business ethics has to be developed based on the characteristics of a particular form, i.e., that of the firm as organization. The New Economics of Organization, an institutionalist and simultaneously interdisciplinary research program, captures this form in descriptive and explanatory terms in two dimensions—contract and organization.

Contract

From an organization-economic perspective the firm constitutes itself as economic form by means of a constitutional contract, the corporate charter.[9] This establishes not only the goals and policies of the firm, but also the identity of its stakeholders.[10] The process of constitution can be reconstructed in contact-theoretical terms as a "nexus of contracts" between individual resource owners.[11] According to this theoretical architecture, the constituting process of the enterprise (or team) is taking place because the gains of each individual resource owner attainable by cooperation are above the level that could be reached by each alone. The motive for founding the firm is thus not profit making,[12] but the realisation of a cooperation rent. This rent from cooperation, although an organizational collective good, gives a strictly individualist and self-interested motive for the formation of a team.

Now the decisive question is: how can it be possible that actors who are exclusively self-oriented can bind themselves together permanently in an organization in order to produce this collective good? The answer is: by entering into chosen long-term and adaptively designed contractual arrangements in which all partners to the contract commit themselves to agreed contractual provisions. On the one hand they thereby agree to constraints on their present and future behavioral options: only in this way can teamwork among strictly self-interested actors become possible. On the other hand, however, the partners to a contract opt to combine their particular resources and capabilities and thus extend the range of their respective individual behavioral options in a way that is by definition not precisely spelled out by the terms of the contract, but is indicative of the adaptivity of the contractual arrangements. The initial sets of resources of all partners to the contract are not reciprocally known completely, since it is impossible to measure them precisely, nor can future learning processes and the appropriation of implicit knowledge be anticipated. This might be a disadvantage from the performance measurement and marginal productivity point of view. But in this disadvantage lies also the dynamic and adaptive potential of a team.

It is thus the systematic incompleteness of contracts, desired by the contracting parties because of its potential for innovation, that initially leads to a problem of adaptation to newly arising situations and contingencies in the market and organizational environment of a firm. For reasons of adaptivity discretionary behavior has to be acceptable. It would be easy to interpret discretionary behavior as shirking.[13] However, the potential for innovation and productivity, organizational learning, and implicit knowledge; the resources, competences, and skills of an organization and its members for the realization of competitive advantage—all of these can be practically activated and theoretically reconstructed only if incompleteness and uncertainty are allowed to exist in contractual relations. It is the problem of adaptivity that is the source of entrepreneurial dynamic and the origin of novelty. Thus, via incompleteness and uncertainty we reconstruct the firm in contract-theoretic terms as a bundle of resources, skills, and competencies[14] the activation of which is based on implicit contracts.[15]

It is precisely these trade-offs between constraint and extension, performance control and development, contract and resource that characterise the form "firm" as a contractually constituted organization. The constitution of a firm as a network of explicit and implicit contracts codifies behavioral constraints and justified expectations, and thus creates cooperative behavioral options and resource use possibilities. In other words, it is the agreed explicit and implicit contracts of individual resource owners that constitute the collective actor "firm" as a cooperation project, and demarcate the form "firm" from firm-as-process. This interpretation of the form "firm" as a set of constitutional (corporate charter, standards of conduct) and postconstitutional (employment contracts) explicit and implicit contracts between resource owners defines a first interface for questions of morality.

Those questions can be developed on the basis of the problem of cooperation; more precisely, the values "willingness to cooperate" and "capability to cooperate." "Willingness to cooperate" signifies an ability to cooperate successfully, given that cooperation benefits at least one of the partners. The notion thus captures both a resource dimension and a behavioral dimension. The capability to cooperate signifies those mental factors that activate the willingness to cooperate. Thus we can formulate more precisely: long-term contracts for the foundation of a cooperation project in and between firms are incomplete[16] regarding the willingness and capability to cooperate, and are therefore characterized by ambiguity and contingency. Their fulfillment thus always raises moral questions. The basis of those moral questions lies in the fact that self-interested actors have a strong incentive to exploit contractual incompleteness, ambiguity, and contingency in an opportunistic way whenever they can do so in a cost-efficient manner. Such behavior by its very nature represents a suspension of the willingness to cooperate and a destruction of the capability to cooperate. On the other hand, the rejection of such behavior on moral grounds and the productive use of incompleteness have the contrary effect. Both types are determinants of the realization of a cooperation rent by the actors, with inverted signs.[17] The governance-theoretic development of questions of morality thus makes it possible to approach business ethics via the values "willingness to cooperate" and "capability to cooperate" as the immanent problematic of the form of a cooperation project.

Organization

It follows from the foregoing that cooperation of self-interested economic actors can attain duration and stability only if conflict, dependence, and order in an organization and between organizations can be balanced and communicated in an appropriate way. In order to generate this balance economic incentive systems and organizational processes and controls are fundamental. However, during the last couple of years the discussion of corporate culture and an "economics of atmosphere"[18] has increasingly made clear that the management of "soft facts," atmosphere, and values is also of crucial importance. The integration of these economic and non-economic incentives and factors is the theoretical and practical core of the ethics of governance.

(i) Conflict in organizations initially and inevitably develop because of the self-interest and opportunism of team members, because of disagreements over the distribution of the cooperation rent, and because of differences in priorities given to the realization of tasks. Technical (procedure, control) and economic (incentives) methods of avoiding or overcoming such conflicts are aggravated by the bounded rationality of actors under conditions of informational, personal, and situational uncertainty and imperfect information. Shared moral values can make a contribution to the handling of conflict.

(ii) Dependency is a basic element in cooperative relationships. It arises from the fact that the success potential of actor A depends on the resources and behavior of actor B and vice versa. If resources were dependent but behavior-predictable, there would be no problem. If resources were independently controlled and behavior-unpredictable there would also be no problem. The problem consists in the exploitability of asymmetric dependencies between the actors by one of the actors via the collective cooperation rent that can be achieved only via this dependency. Shared moral values can make a contribution to containing opportunism.

(iii) Order is manifest in constitutions, standard operating procedures, management principles, guidelines, organizational charts, codes of ethics, ethics management systems, and implicit expectations of performance and behavior, all of which constitute the matrix of globally and locally effective governance structures. For this reason, cooperation projects can be described and analyzed as specific sets of rules and values. In doing so, we must distinguish between performance values (competence), interaction values (loyalty), and moral values (justice) that only together can enable economic cooperation of resource owners and that cannot be reduced to each other. Performance values, interaction values, and moral values form the basis of the two guiding values of firms as cooperation projects, i.e., the "willingness to cooperate" and the "capability to cooperate," and thus determine the number of the chances for cooperation a firm can attain.

(iv) Firms are communication systems. The significance of the role of formal and informal communication in production and cooperation has generated much organizational research in recent years.[19] For our topic it is important to note that firms are polylingual systems. Unlike the market, which has to code every event in prices in order to be able to communicate it, firms have to be able to simultaneously or selectively evaluate and process relevant events in many different "language games"—economy, technology, law, process, morality. The economic code—expenditure/return or cost/profit—has a lead function in the overall bundle of the polylingual resources of the firm when it comes to decisions; this reflects the fact that it is the market system that structures the environment of the firm. Firms are organizations of the economic system: everything relevant in firms has economic relevance or consequence. But not everything in the firm is economic.

We can draw three conclusions from the polylingual character of the firm. In the first place, firms have to build up a comprehensive incentive management that cannot be reduced to economic incentives.[20] In other words, moral values do matter. Secondly, an ethics that aims to achieve something in the firm can be incentive-sensitive and management-oriented without having to become economics. Thirdly, an ethics that seeks to protect itself against this and wants to be undertaken for its own sake is irrelevant in the real-life firms of the economy.

These conclusions follow from the polylingual character of economic cooperation projects, but they also have another basis. From an organizational point of view profits—as mentioned already—are not a maximization goal of firms as cooperation projects, but the inevitable limitation of the relevance of all language games in firms. In other words, profits are the most important, but not the only behavioral constraint of a firm. This methodological rearrangement of profit from a maximization function to a behavioral constraint is an immediate consequence of the rearrangement of the object of the discussion from "firms" to "governance structures for specific transactions." Whereas in the first case the focus of interest is the goal or purpose of the firm, in the second case the focus is on its capacity for adaptivity. A governance structure that would have "profit" as its only adaptive criterion would be inefficient with regard to its adaptive capability.

Moral Communication and Moral Incentives

We must now clarify the status of moral communication in firms. The "moral" does not structure the market environment of the firm, nor is it a behavioral constraint constituting the market. However, via the aspect of comprehensive incentive management and the polylingual character of organization, we have assigned it the status of a behavioral constraint and a resource for firms. Obviously it is relevant to take into account the management context and the way it functions when analyzing behavioral constraints and resources. But what is the role of moral communication in decisions of the firm as a cooperation project? In the economic literature this question often involves a focus on the social and informal character of moral rules and values.[21] These develop in an evolutionary way, exist in society, may well contain both threat and promise, and through these affect decisions of economic actors to a greater or lesser extent. We can accept this analysis, but we do not want to take on the implicit value-ethical interpretation of business ethics that comes with it. We prefer to focus on the ambiguity of evolutionary-derived and non-codified, that is, informal, social moral values. By doing so an interesting characteristic of moral values is exposed. Although in principle it is clear what is meant by moral values, in practice borders between the intended and the approved become fuzzy. Moral values are held in stock communicatively in society, but not in a form that is use-specific.[22] There is thus considerable demand for definition, control, and enforcement of those values that can be met on the level of persons, organizations, and social institutions. Personal societies such as ancient Europe found their moral base in the virtue of actors. Institutionalised societies such as modern Europe make use of specific governance structures for this purpose, e.g., the state or firms.

When firms design an explicit code of ethics,[23] they are attempting to transform moral ambiguity in their environment into organizational self-commitment by rules and values. Those codified rules and values then are firm-specific constitutional global governance structures, idiosyncratic moral resources, competences and capabilities of the organization.[24] From a transaction-cost economics perspective this represents an investment in "asset specificity,"[25] which I would designate "atmospheric specificity" for the execution of transactions. To the extent to which a firm invests in moral specificity and thus builds up a competency for the execution of transactions, it is committed to this investment. The factor-specific implications of moral communication in the firm are thus organizational identity as an economic and moral actor, transparency of claims to action and behavior, and the degree to which these are binding. Furthermore, the moral commitment involved is also an encouragement to a similar commitment on the part of organizational stakeholders (team members, customers, partners, suppliers). The ultimate intention is to attain stable behavioral expectations and control over the organizational and social environment of the firm by committing oneself and thus creating incentives for others to commit themselves as well. Self-commitment and commitment by others thus are the reasons for specific investments in the atmospheric parameters of a transaction.

At this point the significance of genuine moral incentives in polylingual organizations becomes obvious. Firms have economic incentives at their disposal, the relevance and effectiveness of which derive from the economic lead code of organizational systems. However, these have to be distinguished from moral incentives, which cannot be reduced to or transformed into economic incentives. But what do we know about moral incentives? In this investigation we implicitly distinguish between social, personal, and organizational moral incentives. Social moral incentives spring from enculturated moral convictions sanctioned by the majority of the members of society, which are thus intrinsically "intended." Virtues and notions of justice belong to this category. An example of personal moral incentives are lived virtues and credible role model behavior (moral character, charisma) by managers and leaders. Organizational moral incentives are, for instance, codes of ethics, ethics management systems, and ethics audit systems. Neither this characterization nor the examples cited are theoretically elaborated or complete. Their common characteristic, however, seems to be that their relevance depends on the fact that they are valued in themselves and because of their implications. It would be the task of a "theory of moral incentives"—which still needs to be written—to work out and account for these matters in detail.

We now proceed to investigate the specific efficiency of the governance mechanism of moral values. The investigation so far has led to the following conclusions: the economic lead code has a direct and long-acting effect on the cooperation rent achievable in firms via the expenditure/return and cost/profit conditions. The moral encoding works via organizational self-commitment (identity, transparency, binding nature) on the cooperation lead values "willingness to cooperate" and "capability to cooperate," and in this way on the cooperation chances of a firm. Moral self-commitment is activated selectively via reputation capital when transactions can affect this capital. This scheme explains firstly why governance ethics is not and should not be in demand by all firms; after all, manufacturers of screws have a different demand from social service providers. The scheme explains secondly why moral communication always carries a promise of performance that is contingent on self-commitment. We have already explained this in terms of the characteristics of firm- and transaction-specific investments in "atmosphere," but in this context we would like to point out that speech act theory in philosophy has arrived at similar results, in that it has shown that moral communication does have a performative character.[26] Those who talk about morality or codify moral values do not talk about facts but implicitly promise performance. Firms that have codes of ethics are not making statements about existent facts, but promising self-commitment to and self-organization of a performance promise. A firm thus commits itself through its moral communication and the communication's organization in a specific fashion, and thus creates behavioral expectations and behavioral standards for itself and others. If these expectations are disappointed this leads not only to the moral disregard of the collective actors, but also to costs due to loss of reputation or motivation or to political intervention. The reduction of cooperation chances has immediate effects on the level of the cooperation rent attainable. Economic and moral values and incentives thus, in their own distinctively specifiable ways, have an effect on the willingness to cooperate, the capability to cooperate, and the cooperation chances of a firm. Economic and moral values and incentives lose their respective identities only in the cooperation rent.

Definition of Governance Ethics

The differentiation of form- and process-determination of the firm and the ensuing differentiation of the form of the firm in the contract- and organizational relations of a cooperation project has enabled us to develop a view of business ethics on the basis of the governance characteristics of the firm itself. Business ethics, seen systemically, is neither external correction of negative external effects nor external enlightenment of economic stubbornness and blindness. It is rather a constitutive element of the firm itself, mediated by rules and values, governance ethics, and as such it is in every sense part of the economic problem of making possible the cooperation of self-interested actors in and via firms. "In every sense" implies that the economic and organizational relevance of the moral factor parallels its embeddedness in the economic and organizational context.

In conclusion we would like to draw consequences from the theoretical viewpoint outlined here which may be helpful in defining the role of an institutionalist business ethics as governance ethics.

1. The elements of governance ethics are the moral resources and behavioral constraints and extensions deriving from organizational rules and values as well as their communication in and via cooperation projects. Accordingly, it is not the notion of action, but of governance which is its point of reflexion. Governance structures are sets or matrices of communicated formal and informal rules and values that constitute the cooperative actor as constraints and furnish him or her with explicit and implicit rules of the game for contractual and organizational relations for the realisation of specific transactions.

2. Analytically, governance ethics investigates those global and local, formal and informal structures of a firm that constitute and transaction-specifically govern the moral behavior of the individual and collective actors in an organization (intrafirm-relations), between organizations (interfirm-relations), and between organizations and society (extrafirm-relations). The unit of analysis is thus a specific transaction in the context of and in its interaction with the governance structures surrounding it.

3. Methodologically, business ethics compares different structures for the governance of separate economic transactions; it asks which moral and immoral rules; values and incentives they reflect and which kind of economic behavior they reward. It explains the presence, relevance, and the change of moral preferences in the context of the economic and moral incentive structure of a given organization and its economic and social environment. Business ethics as governance ethics thus is a comparative research program.

4. In normative terms business ethics as governance ethics proposes the development and implementation of such ethical systems (e.g., ethics management systems, ethics audit systems[27]) in and by way of organizations. Those organizations—as governance structures for transactions

—foster the willingness to cooperate, the capability to cooperate, and the cooperation chances of economic actors. It does this by creating economic and moral certainty of expectations through providing self-commitment and indirect commitment of others. What is prioritised here is not profit maximization, but rents from the economizing of cooperation.

5. In conclusion: the governance ethics of the firm is the theory of the comparative analysis of a moral-sensitive design and communication of governance structures for specific economic transactions via cooperation.

Notes

1. For the translation of this essay I wish to thank Markus Becker. The original German term is *Unternehmensethik,* which carries the connotation of "corporate ethics."

2. Cf. Donaldson (1982), French (1984), Donaldson/Werhane (1988), Werhane (1985).

3. This research program was initiated by Williamson. For the interdisciplinary intentions connected to it cf. for example Williamson (1990, 1993). In this paper we will make use of contract-based, transaction-cost-based, and organizational (resource-based, economics of competencies; cf. Dosi/Teece 1998; Teece/Pisano/Shuen 1997) considerations in explaining the role of "soft factors" (culture, communication, morality) in firms. With this, we are continuing our efforts of building an economic theory which is integrating these "soft factors" without dissolving them in the process. Cf. Wieland 1996a.

4. Cf. Williamson 1985, and the 1996 volume edited by Williamson with the telling title *The Mechanisms of Governance.*

5. Contemporary philosophy/ethics has never heard of organization, or at best accepts it as a peripheral phenomenon amongst several other issues. This ignorance as to a central societal actor and addressee of ethical claims is one of the conceptual problems of applied ethics that is blocking its theoretical development in a major way.

6. Cf. Vanberg 1992 and Gifford 1991. For the distinction of the notions of system, institution, and organization cf. Wieland 1997, pp. 62ff. It was Schmoller who made the first institutionalist inspired proposition for a distinction between institution and organization. Whereas institution for him is "the firm container of the action of generations" (Schmoller 1901, p. 61), organization is "the personal side of the institution" (ibid). Organizations are combinations of commodities and persons for a specific purpose. In this distinction, all the problems of contemporary institutionalist theory are already present, i.e., a static notion of institutions and a neglect of the normativity of organizations.

7. Cf. Williamson 1975.

8. In our understanding this insight presents a substantial contribution of German institutionalism to the theory of the firm. Cf. only Sombart (1902–1927/1987, pp. 101ff.), where he states that "the elevation of an independent economic organism over the individual economic human beings is guaranteeing its continual existence over time." Barnard (1938/1968) has shown in systems theoretic terms why precisely it is the exclusion of actors that represents the essence of the firm.

9. This, by the way, is one of the weaknesses of resource based organization theory. It does not treat the process of the constitution of the firm. At this point, contract-based theories are indispensable.

10. For the connection between the management of morality and stakeholders cf. Donaldson/Preston 1995.

11. For an early contribution to that insight cf. Schmoller (1901, pp. 414, 428f, 453). For the relevance of a differentiation of various types of contracts for a theory of the firm cf. Williamson 1991.

12. Of course the resignation from the profit motive is not a new idea, but commences with the development of an independent theory of the firm, independent of the Walrasian equilibrium model and price theory. For this part of the history of ideas cf. the interesting investigation by Krafft/Ravix (1998).

13. Shirking respectively the trade off between performance and control are the central problem of that branch of the theory of the firm that is oriented towards property rights. The classical text is Alchian/Demsetz 1972. However, they already emphasize the potential importance of moral values for the containing of shirking.

14. Cf. Dosi/Teece 1998. They do not take into consideration such a reformulation. They distinguish between theories of firms as production function, as optimal contract, and as organization. As long as this tripartite distinction will remain, there indeed is not much hope for theoretical integration. But contract theories have more to offer than optimal contracts. The theories of incomplete and implicit contracts (cf. Wieland 1996a, pp. 120ff., 158ff.) open the possibility of treating organizational phenomena in organizational terms, and to their own advantage.

15. For an overview cf. Bull 1983.

16. In Wieland 1998 we have pointed out the central sociological and managerial importance of cooperation and a theoretical notion capturing this aspect. This importance forms the basis for the arguments developed here.

17. Hobbes (1651/1914, pp. 68ff.) has described this particularity of contractual cooperation as a game-theoretic dilemma, the only escape from which is represented by rational calculation of advantage plus the power of the state to enforce plus implicit contracts (the covenant in the contract).

18. For the economics of atmosphere cf. Wieland 1996b and the literature referenced there.

19. Cf. Casson 1997 as well as Wieland 1999.

20. This connection has been clear since Xenophon, who in his *Oikonomikos* is building his human resource management and development theory for the *oikos* on this foundation. Cf. Wieland 1989, pp. 196ff.

21. This, by the way, is true for Williamson as well (1985, pp. 44, 271). In this way he is losing the option of a theory-endogenous parameter against opportunism.

22. The ancient Europe has attempted to cope with this characteristic of social moral communication by casuistry with approved exceptions. In functionally differentiated and abstract societies, however, the experience that now exceptions are more or less the rule has led to the situation that moral values have to be kept in stock in an abstractly justified way.

23. For this phenomenon cf. Weaver 1993 as well as Wieland 2001.

24. Cf. the already mentioned paper by Dosi/Teece (1998) as well as Barney 1991.

25. Cf. Williamson 1985, pp. 84ff., which distinguished site specificity, physical assets, human assets, and dedicated assets specificity. We propose an extension of this distinction to the notion of atmospheric specificity. In this way soft factors

like culture, communication, and morals can be integrated into the theoretical framework of transaction cost theory.

26. Cf. in particular Searle 1969, chap. 8, and for the pertaining condition of sincerity Searle 1979, pp. 21ff.

27. Cf. the contributions of Center for Business Ethics (1992), Paine (1994), and Weaver/Trevino/Cochran (1999).

NO

Ian Maitland

Distributive Justice in Firms: Do the Rules of Corporate Governance Matter?

Can we achieve greater fairness by reforming the corporation? Some recent progressive critics of the corporation argue that it is possible to achieve greater social justice both inside and outside the corporation by simply rewriting or reinterpreting corporate rules to favor non-stockholders over stockholders. But the progressive program for reforming the corporation rests on a critical assumption, which I challenge in this [selection],[1] namely that the rules of the corporation matter, so that changing them can effect a lasting redistribution of wealth from stockholders to non-stockholders (for convenience I will refer to non-stockholders as "stakeholders"[2]). This [selection] uses a critique of the progressive reform program to make the case that the rules of the corporation are distributively neutral. The corporation as we know it isn't rigged against stakeholders, and changing its rules will not improve the bargaining power of stakeholders. However, the [selection] will show that while the rules may be epiphenomenal from the standpoint of distributive justice, they can have substantial impacts on the corporation's efficiency. As a result, the proposed reforms of the corporation may hurt its capacity to generate benefits for all the parties concerned.

The Progressive Program for Reforming the Corporation

This [selection] examines some recent "progressive" scholarship on the corporation and proposals for its reform.[3] In many respects, the progressive reformers advocate a model of the corporation strikingly similar to what business ethicists call the "stakeholder corporation." They favor rewriting the rules that govern the relations between stockholders and stakeholders to eliminate what they see as built-in biases in favor of stockholders. And they propose to use reform of the corporation as a vehicle for greater social justice in the work place and the marketplace. They view the rules of a corporation simultaneously as an embodiment of capitalist privilege and as a potential point of leverage for redistributing wealth and power.[4]

From Ian Maitland, "Distributive Justice in Firms: Do the Rules of Corporate Governance Matter?" *Business Ethics Quarterly*, vol. 11, no. 1 (January 2001). Copyright © 2001 by *Business Ethics Quarterly*. Reprinted by permission of The Philosophy Documentation Center, publisher of *Business Ethics Quarterly*.

It is a key premise of the progressive critique of the corporation that its rules are not neutral between the different constituencies of the corporation. Thus David Millon argues that the important rules that govern the relations between stockholders and stakeholders are systematically biased in favor of stockholders. The rules of the corporation do not simply mirror background inequalities in society but actually create and reinforce those inequalities. As Joseph Singer puts it, "[t]he current legal rules created that imbalance of power [between workers and corporations in the market], and they can be altered to equalize it."[5]

Some of these rules are rules of corporate law, and some are not. As examples of the former, Millon cites voting rights in the corporation, limited liability, and management's fiduciary duty to run the corporation in the exclusive interest of stockholders (the "stockholder primacy principle"). Employment-at-will, on the other hand, is a common law doctrine. All of these rules confer powers and immunities on stockholders while imposing disadvantages on stakeholders or exposing them to certain contingencies or costs.

However, this non-neutrality cuts both ways. If the rules of the corporation are rigged in favor of stockholders, then that bias can be eliminated by simply changing the rules. But why stop there? The reformers want to structure the rules of the corporation to advance the progressive agenda of redistributing power and wealth in the broader society. If the relative power of stockholders and stakeholders is a function (in part) of the current legal rules, then those rules can be rewritten to redress that imbalance or even to tip the scales in favor of stakeholders.

> To a large extent, it is contract and property law that will determine [the parties'] relative bargaining power. If we want to protect the most vulnerable party to the relationship in times of economic stress, we have no alternative but to make them less vulnerable. This means systematically interpreting and changing property and contract principles in ways that effectively re-distribute power and wealth to workers.[6]

In summary, the progressives claim that rules matter. Accordingly, the rules furnish a point of leverage for altering the outcomes of the corporation so that they favor stakeholder groups and thereby redistributing power and wealth in society.

Neutrality Thesis

In opposition to the progressive view, this [selection] argues that the rules don't matter. The null hypothesis, or neutrality thesis, proposed here, is that the corporation is distributively neutral. Appearances notwithstanding, the rules don't systematically favor stockholders, and they cannot be manipulated so as to favor stakeholder groups like employees. The corollary is that proposals to change the rules to favor stakeholders will not have any systematic effect on the distributive impacts of the corporation.

This does not mean that existing outcomes are in some way equitable or in conformity with distributive justice. It is simply to say that the rules are neutral, in the sense that they passively pass along or mirror pre-existing inequalities of resources (where resources are to be broadly conceived as wealth, energy, skill, cunning, etc.).

This [essay] does not present a fully rounded or comprehensive account of the progressive critique of the corporation but instead focuses on certain propositions concerning the impact of corporate rules on distributive justice inside the corporation.

The Rules of Corporate Governance

The case for the neutrality of the corporation is rooted in the observation that the rules of corporate governance are essentially voluntary. This claim may seem odd, given the fact that the rules are prescribed by law. But, although we refer to "corporate law," as if the rules were commanded by legislatures or by common law, the reality is that the rules of the corporation are more accurately viewed as being self-imposed. The law does not mandate the rules. Instead, it provides a framework or template of "default" rules, which the parties or groups making up the corporation (stockholders, employees, etc.) remain free to modify or waive by agreement.

Thus nothing in the law stops corporations from accepting unlimited liability for any debts they may incur or from agreeing to override the law's presumption of at-will employment. Nor does the law prevent representatives of employees from sitting on the board of the corporation or from bargaining for the right to have management owe them fiduciary duties. Many progressive scholars concede this point. Millon notes that, "It is true that... the affected parties can reverse the assignment of benefit and burden specified by the rule should they choose to do so. Thus, of course, a creditor can bargain for unlimited stockholder liability or for voting rights."[7] Another critic of the corporation, Margaret Blair, notes that, "[b]ecause U.S. corporation law, contract law, and securities law readily accommodate most experiments in new organizational forms, many new governance structures are emerging on their own. This is one of the strengths of the U.S. system."[8]

If the rules are voluntary, then what purpose is served by state law codes or common law rules of corporate governance? The standard answer is that such laws reduce the costs of contracting (or "transaction costs") for the parties by providing a standard contract for governing their relations. That way the parties do not need to re-invent the corporation by explicitly negotiating the whole set of rules from scratch. "[S]hareholders typically contract with management by entering into the standard-form agreement applied by the relevant state law code and corpus of common law. This 'off-the-rack' contract includes a collection of terms that stockholders would typically prefer, so including them greatly reduces transaction costs."[9] Many (though not all) can be modified by express contract if the stockholders so choose.

The fact that the corporate form of organization—with its familiar structure of entitlements and obligations—is the dominant one in our economy may leave the impression that it is somehow mandatory. But the law provides other organizational forms to choose from. These include sole proprietorships, partnerships, cooperatives, trusts, and non-firm relational contracts, such as franchises and long-term supply contracts. In addition, there is an almost infinite variety of arrangements that the parties might conceivably fashion by agreement. Of course, not only are the parties free to take or leave the rules provided by the law, but also nothing prevents them from choosing not to contract with a corporation at all, or from limiting their business to other types of business organization.[10] On this account, then, the corporation is essentially a voluntary association. It exists only because the parties that make it up choose it as a means of governing their relationships.

If the corporation is voluntary, why would some groups agree to terms that seem so clearly inequitable? Why would employees accept, say, rules providing for employment at will or exclusion from voting rights in the corporation? Answers to this question make up the heart of the financial or contractarian theory of the firm developed by Fama and Jensen and others.[11] I won't try to summarize that extensive literature here. But the gist of it is that rights in the firm (say, voting rights) go to the highest bidders. That leaves the question of why stockholders would consistently outbid other groups for management's fiduciary loyalty and for voting control. Contractarian theorists explain that stockholders have the greatest stake in the outcome of corporate decision making because they occupy a peculiarly vulnerable position in the corporation. As "residual claimants" they differ from other groups in that they are not entitled to a guaranteed return. Their share is what is left over (if anything) after every other groups' contractually specified claims have been met. That gives stockholders a special interest in the efficient management of the corporation. If efficiency is maximized, then, over the long run, the corporation is better able to provide benefits for all participants.

On this view of the firm, the distribution of rights in the corporation is the outcome of bargaining between the different groups or parties. Since nothing in the law bars it, employees might (and indeed frequently do) contract for protection from arbitrary dismissal. But they have to "buy" that protection with lower wages. Conversely, if stockholders value the right to lay off employees at will more than employees value their job security, they may buy that right with higher wages.

Interestingly, the progressive scholars largely accept the contractarian account of the corporation. Nevertheless they argue that the corporation is rigged against stakeholders. They charge that the corporation does not merely reproduce existing imbalances of social power and wealth but creates and reinforces them. This charge is difficult (if not impossible) to reconcile with the contractarian view of the firm as a voluntary association. It would mean that stakeholders are consistently duped or manipulated by stockholders into accepting bargains that are inferior to the ones they could have achieved.

The thesis of this [selection] is that the rules of the corporation are distributively neutral. If that is the case, then we should observe two things: (a) that existing rules don't discriminate against stakeholders, and (b) that proposed changes in the rules won't make non-stockholders better off. The next section examines specific rules and proposed changes to those rules in order to see if these two predictions hold.

Progressive Proposals for Changing the Rules of the Corporation

Extending Fiduciary Duties

One perennially popular rule change would extend management's fiduciary duties to other parties, like employees. Management would no longer operate the corporation in the exclusive interests of the stockholders but would be required by law to balance the interests of stockholders with those of employees and other stakeholders.[12]

What would be the distributive effects of such a rule change? There could be a once-for-all expropriation of current stockholders. That is, if the law was introduced, enacted, and signed overnight, stockholders would wake up the next day to find that they were no longer the sole beneficiaries of management's fiduciary obligations. They would (literally) be poorer because the anticipated lower returns and increased risk would be reflected in a lower stock market valuation of their shares.

But any benefit to employees would be short-lived as investors would hesitate to buy corporations' shares, would hold off investing, and/or would demand a premium to reflect the added risk and lower return. Investors cannot be compelled to supply capital to American corporations. They can instead buy real estate, gold, Treasury bonds or shares in Japanese corporations, or they can invest in orchards,[13] to mention a few examples. If the risk-adjusted return from owning shares in U.S. corporations falls below that from alternative investments, then we should expect a flight of capital to alternative investments.[14]

In such circumstances, in order to attract the capital necessary to finance their operations, corporations would be forced to take steps to increase the prospective return to stockholders. That would likely require cutting wages, raising prices, laying off workers, etc. In short, it would require changes that would defeat the purpose of changing the fiduciary rule in the first place. Of course, those actions might be complicated—if not barred altogether—by management's new fiduciary duties to stakeholders. In that case, corporations might simply be unable to raise new capital. In due course, this would mean that corporations would find it difficult to expand their operations, there would be a drastic reduction in business start-ups relying on equity capital, and employment would suffer. All the parties to the corporation would be losers from the resulting economic disruptions.[15]

Employment-at-Will

David Millon argues that the employment-at-will rule favors stockholders over employees. It "confers freedom of action on stockholders while imposing costs on employees that would not be present if the default rule were a presumption of employment security."[16] Millon admits that, like other corporate rules, the employment-at-will rule is an optional or default rule, but he claims that even "mere" default rules have distributive consequences. Thus, by replacing the employment-at-will rule by an employment-security rule, we can increase the bargaining leverage of employees and enable them to capture a greater share of the benefits of the corporation. If we reverse the existing biases, "starting points will differ, and outcomes therefore will too."[17]

According to Millon, "a rule like the employment-at-will doctrine makes stockholders wealthier than an employment-security doctrine would." Under employment-at-will, if employees want protection against arbitrary dismissal, they have to *pay* stockholders for it. By contrast, if the rule were reversed, "stockholders would either have to compensate employees following termination of employment or would have to bribe them into giving up a property right in their job. The bias... has the potential to affect significantly the respective wealth of stockholders and stakeholders."[18]

Employees are also disadvantaged by the employment-at-will rule in cases where transaction costs prevent the parties from agreeing on trading a wage reduction for job security. There may be substantial, and sometimes prohibitive, costs associated with negotiating and drafting a satisfactory agreement. These "transaction costs" may prevent employees from reaching an agreement even if both sides would gain from it. In such a case, the default rule, viz., employment-at-will, will hold, and employees will find themselves stuck with the *status quo,* namely no job protection.

But Millon's scenario can't withstand close scrutiny. For simplicity, suppose that there are two types of firms, ones that provide job security to their employees and ones that do not. Under an employment-at-will regime, it is reasonable to assume that, other things (like employee characteristics) equal, firms that provide job security pay lower wages than firms that do not. (Otherwise, firms providing job security would have higher labor costs and/or risks which would over time lead to their failure).

Now suppose that we adopt Millon's proposal to replace employment-at-will with employment security as our default rule. Under the new rule, firms that don't provide job security will be required to start doing so *or* to compensate their employees for giving up their right to job security. (Firms that already provide job security will be unaffected.) Recall, however, that firms without job security were *already* paying higher wages. As a result of the rule change, such firms will faced with a choice between (a) providing job security (*and* continuing to pay the higher wage) or (b) giving employees an additional wage increase (on top of the original premium they enjoy) in return for the right to dismiss at will. In either case, such firms will have unsustainably higher labor costs. Consequently, they will be forced to reduce wages to competitive levels or to go out of business. In either case, of course, there will be no lasting redistribution of wealth from stockholders to employees.

However, while the distributive effect of the initial default rules will be nonexistent or trivial, the real-world efficiency effects might be substantial. By "real-world," I mean that we reintroduce transaction costs into the example. Suppose employees value employment-security guarantees less than stockholders disvalue them, then a rule that provides for employment-security will—in the presence of significant transaction costs—make both stockholders and employees worse off. If the parties are unable to reach an agreement to override the employment-security guarantees in exchange for higher wages, then they will both be poorer than if the rule had been employment-at-will.

This example illustrates why (as economists urge) it is mutually beneficial if default rules are set to reflect the outcomes that the parties *would have* (but for transaction costs) agreed on. That way they can help the parties economize on transaction costs "by supplying standard contract terms the parties would otherwise have to adopt by [expensive] express agreement."[19] In other words, Millon's proposal, by trying to correct an imaginary bias in the rules, will likely make it more difficult for parties to reach a mutually advantageous bargain. As a result, the proposal to flip the rules so that they favor stakeholders may actually wind up hurting the very people it is intended to help.[20]

Limited Liability

Millon also charges that limited liability "benefit[s] stockholders while having a correspondingly negative effect on creditors, who ... lose a degree of financial security that a rule of unlimited liability would otherwise provide."[21] The rule "limit[s] stockholders' liability to corporate creditors to their capital contribution, leaving creditors to bear the risk of corporate insolvency."[22]

That account is accurate as far as it goes. But Millon is mistaken in thinking that limited liability has any distributive implications. That is because, as Posner has pointed out, creditors are paid to bear this risk. "The lender is fully compensated for the risk of default by the higher interest rate that the corporation must pay lenders by virtue of its limited liability."[23] Furthermore, creditors are "also free to insist as a condition of making the loan that the stockholders personally guarantee the corporation's debts, or insert in the loan agreement other provisions limiting the lender's risk. Any resulting reduction in the risk of default will of course reduce the interest rate."[24]

One risk facing creditors is the possibility of nonpayment because of limited liability. Another risk, according to Easterbrook and Fischel, is the "prospect, common to all debtor-creditor relations, that after the terms of the transaction are set the debtor will take increased risk, to the detriment of the lender."[25] However, as they go on to note,

> As long as these risks are known, the firm pays for the freedom to engage in risky activities. Any creditor can get the risk-free rate by investing in T-bills or some low-risk substitute. The firm must offer a better risk-return combination to attract investment. If it cannot make credible promises to refrain from taking on excessive risks, it must pay higher interest rates (or, when the creditors are employees and trade creditors, higher prices for the work or goods delivered on credit). Although managers may change the riskiness of the firm after borrowing, debt must be repaid; this drives the firm back to the credit market, where it must pay a rate of interest appropriate to the soundness and risk of its current projects.... Voluntary creditors receive compensation in advance for the chance that the firm will step up the risk of its projects and later be unable to meet its obligations.[26]

Of course, creditors, too, enjoy limited liability. What is more, in the event of bankruptcy their claims on the corporation's assets outrank the claims of stockholders. Finally, lenders are not compelled to extend credit to the corporation. If limited liability is such a bargain, they are free to use their funds to purchase stock in the corporation instead.

Legal Obligation Arising out of Interdependence

Another proposed reform would change the rules of the corporation to recognize a legally enforceable right to job security arising out of longstanding and/or dependent relationships. Marleen O'Connor advocates that the courts should recognize a right to job security in cases of long-run employment. Joseph Singer proposes that the courts should recognize employees' property rights in longstanding relationships on which they have come to depend. He says "It is morally wrong for the owner to allow a relationship of dependence to be established and then cut off the dependent party."[27]

What would be the distributional impacts of such a rule change? Stockholders would likely be able to defeat or circumvent such a rule or, failing that, shift its cost back to employees. In that event, employees would find themselves forced to purchase a right (job security or severance pay) which they value less than what they would give up (wages and employment opportunities) in exchange for it.[28]

The set of possible responses by stockholders is limited only by the imagination. One obvious move would be to write into all employment contracts a disclaimer by which employees expressly waived their right to such job protection. Of course, the courts might choose to ignore or override such disclaimers.[29] That would still leave stockholders with many options which they might use singly or in combination to get around the rule.

If courts chose to ignore waivers of job security, then stockholders' specific responses would depend on how the rule was framed or interpreted. If courts relied on employees' length of service to determine whether they were owed job security, then the rule would perversely encourage stockholders to dismiss employees shortly before their claims to job security vested. Alternatively, if the courts relied on some measure of dependency or intimacy, stockholders might avoid such relationships with their employees.

Alternatively corporations might develop a two-tier work force with a core of highly skilled workers (who would enjoy job security) and a peripheral floating population of casual or temporary or contract workers (without job security).[30] Only the first would qualify for the legal privileges that come with a long-term relationship with the corporation. In any case, corporations would be cautious about expanding employment because of the legal barriers in the way of lay-offs in the event of a downturn in business. Therefore they would likely respond to increased demand for their products by increasing overtime, speeding up the line or working employees more intensively.

Another possibility is that stockholders might try to offset the expected costs of job security by reducing wages or (if that was impractical) by granting smaller wage increases and/or cutting back on any discretionary benefits (subsidized lunches or parking, pension contributions, etc.). If payroll costs could not be stabilized in this way, stockholders would shift to more capital-intensive production methods, and would reduce employment or increase it more gradually.[31] If the real wages of workers were increased by the implicit cost of greater job security, the stockholders would find it unprofitable to hire "marginal" workers because the value of their marginal product would be less than the cost of employing them.

In the short run, it might be possible for stockholders to pay the higher real wages and pass their cost along to consumers in the form of higher product prices. However, such price increases would not be sustainable in the long run. Of course, any reduced demand as a result of the price increases would mean lower employment. If the stockholders found themselves unable to pass the increased real wages along to consumers or employees, the resulting lower rates of return would eventually cause firms to exit the industry and/or would reduce the flow of investment capital to the industry, thus limiting employment growth. If companies expect to face heavy costs if they have to close a plant, they are going to be more reluctant to open new plants, knowing that the penalty for misjudging the market will be more severe.

One of the ironies of such a rule is that it would impose an implicit "tax" on the very behaviors we would generally wish to encourage—long-term employment relationships, the hiring of marginal workers, and so on. In self-defense, stockholders would avoid relationships with employees that might lock them into an onerous commitment.

Employee Rights in Cases of Plant Closure

The same objections apply to Joseph Singer's proposal to rewrite the rules to give employees a right to purchase their plant for its "fair market value" in the event that the stockholders declare their intention to close it down.

Singer acknowledges that employees might not choose to exercise their right, under such a rule, to buy their plant and keep it in operation. But he says that the rule would be a useful bargaining chip for employees: "[I]f we ... give workers a right to assert an ownership interest in the plant when the company wants to close it or when the company fails to manage the plant well, then the company would have to offer the workers more than the workers would ask to give up this right. Because the workers would *own* this right, their wealth would be dramatically higher than if the company had the legal liberty to destroy the plant."[32]

As I have noted, employees would get the right to purchase the plant at its "fair market value." That is what Singer says, but it doesn't seem to be what he means. Nothing in the current rules stops employees from banding together and offering to buy the plant. If their bid is higher than the next best alternative bid, then stockholders will presumably accept their offer. That is, employees appear already to enjoy the right that Singer wants to confer on them. What's more, if the employees acquire the plant at its market value, there is no transfer of wealth.

A transfer of wealth from stockholders to employees would happen only if the rules permitted employees to buy the plant at *less* than its market value.

But a rule that permitted employees to buy the plant at less than what other bidders might pay for it would predictably lead stockholders to take certain actions in their self-defense.[33] Employees would presumably be paid less than they would absent the law. Stockholders would in effect withhold an implicit insurance "premium" from each worker's wage. They might attempt to mitigate the possible additional expense of closure by renting rather than buying plant and equipment. Macey's observations on compulsory plant closing notification apply *a fortiori* to Singer's rule. He says that "if a legislature unilaterally gives rank-and-file workers a right to prior notification of a layoff or a plant closing, the workers will benefit only if, to retain that right, they will not have to give up something worth more than the right itself. The price of the forced 'purchase' of a right to notification may take the form of lower wages, reduced pension benefits, or a reduction in the overall size of the work force."[34]

That is not all. The added difficulty or expense of closing down a money-losing plant would likely make corporations more wary of opening new plants in the first place—especially in marginal areas where alternative employment opportunities are few. As Richard McKenzie has said, restrictions on plant closings are restrictions on plant openings.[35]

In summary, Singer's rule would not have any obvious redistributive effects. But, once again, it might worsen the lot of *both* stockholders and stakeholders by putting obstacles in the way of their agreeing on the optimal contract terms.

Courts as Guardians of Employees' Interests

Some progressive critics of the corporation suggest that the courts should aggressively interpret the law in favor of stakeholders. Singer says that "means systematically interpreting and changing property and contract principles in ways that effectively redistribute power and wealth to workers."[36] O'Connor favors using an expansive interpretation of management's fiduciary duty to tip the scales in favor of the vulnerable. She says that the "courts can use the fiduciary duty to prevent opportunistic behavior even where the terms of the contract explicitly allow the stronger party to engage in this type of conduct."[37] She would have courts to set aside contracts or override contract terms on grounds of distributive justice or "common morality." Although O'Connor invokes supposed "implicit contracts" between stockholders and employees, it is clear that she intends the courts to disregard the actual intentions of the parties (whether express or implicit). The content of the corporations' duties to employees would no longer be defined by the parties' explicit or implicit agreements but by some external standard of social justice or the conscience of the court.

But it is doubtful whether such judicial activism could actually help stakeholders vis-à-vis stockholders. Once again, the crucial point is that investors are not compelled to invest their capital in corporations. If the courts deliberately tilted in favor of stakeholders, then to attract equity capital stakeholders would have to try to devise safeguards to reassure investors.

It is impossible to imagine exactly what forms such safeguards might take. If investors anticipate that the courts will systematically discriminate against them, and disregard the agreements they strike with stakeholders, then they have various (non-mutually exclusive) options. First, they might demand compensation from stakeholders for the additional risk they would have to bear. Second, they might insist on bypassing the courts and resolving their disputes by means of arbitration. (There would be an incentive for workers to band together in "firms" which would seek to acquire a reputation for *not* resorting to the courts in order to opportunistically renege on their agreements with stockholders. That reputation would permit them to lower the cost of capital to themselves.) Third, if it is too costly or impractical for investors to protect themselves by these means (or others), they might simply decide that it is pointless to invest in the stock of U.S. corporations. In that case, all the parties would forgo the benefits that the corporation might have created.

The point is that stockholders and stakeholders alike *need* the courts as a guarantor and/or impartial arbiter of their agreements with one another. Otherwise those (mutually advantageous) agreements may be too risky to enter into in the first place. Consequently, both sides are the losers when the courts define their mission as achieving their own conceptions of social justice in place of giving effect to the intent of the parties. As Easterbrook and Fischel have noted, "future contracting parties, viewing the court's selective enforcement of the present contract, will try to take steps to avoid the disappointment of having their contract selectively enforced. But these steps will cause the parties to incur additional contracting costs, additional over which they would be if the act simply enforced perfect contracts."[38]

Conclusion: How Liberty Upsets Patterns

This [selection] has shown that, on close examination, many corporate rules that appear to be biased in favor of stockholders prove to be neutral and non-discriminatory. That should not come as a surprise since the rules are essentially voluntary. What would have been surprising would have been the discovery that parties continued to do business with the corporation on terms that are manifestly disadvantageous.

Moreover, precisely because the corporation is a voluntary association, an externally mandated rule change that is intended to achieve greater distributive justice is bound to fail. The parties themselves, including the supposed beneficiaries of the rule, are likely to collude to defeat it, because they all have a stake in maintaining the corporation as a going concern. A rule change that redistributes benefits and costs among the parties without regard to their contributions jeopardizes the carefully constructed bargain on which the corporation is based. If the party that loses from the rule change is not compensated for its loss, then its contribution to the corporation will exceed its benefits, and it will look outside the corporation for returns commensurate with its contribution. Meanwhile, the beneficiary of the rule change will enjoy benefits that exceed its contribution, and it will have to compensate the loser(s) from the rule change in order to retain its cooperation.

Contractarian theorists call the firm a nexus of contracts. If the totality of contracts that make up the corporation (including mandated contract terms or rules) does not accurately value the contributions made respectively by employees, creditors, suppliers, etc. then it is likely to be unstable. In that case, the rules of the corporation cannot be rigged to favor stockholders—or to favor stakeholders either. Therefore the rules can't furnish the point of leverage the progressive reformers of the corporation want in order to implement their program of social reform.

Notes

1. I would like to thank Thomas L. Carson, Alexei Marcoux and Patricia H. Werhane for their comments on an earlier draft of this paper.
2. Strictly, of course, stockholders are stakeholders too, along with employees, customers, vendors, lenders, and, sometimes, local communities.
3. Some of this work is usefully collected in Lawrence E. Mitchell, ed., *Progressive Corporate Law* (Boulder, Col.: Westview Press, 1995). See also Amitai Etzioni, "A Communitarian Note on Stakeholder Theory," *Business Ethics Quarterly* 8 (1998): 679–691.
4. Stakeholder theories also invoke distributive justice. See Thomas Donaldson and L. E. Preston, "The Stakeholder Theory of the Corporation: Concepts, Evidence, and Implications," *Academy of Management Review* 20 (1995): 84.
5. Joseph William Singer, "The Reliance Interest in Property," *Stanford Law Review* 40 (1983): 729.
6. Singer, "Reliance Interest," p. 723.
7. David Millon, "Communitarianism in Corporate Law: Foundations and Law Reform Strategies," in Mitchell, *Progressive Corporate Law*, p. 24.
8. Margaret M. Blair, *Ownership and Control* (Washington, D.C.: Brookings, 1995), p. 277.
9. Millon, "Communitarianism," p. 3.
10. "[N]o one is forced to use the corporate form of organization.... Thus, we do not observe all economic activity being carried on through one type of economic activity. Instead, we observe millions of organizations of many types, sizes, and structures" (Henry N. Butler and Larry E. Ribstein, *The Corporation and the Constitution* [Washington, D.C.: AEI Press, 1995], p. 4).
11. Eugene F. Fama and Michael C. Jensen, "Separation of Ownership and Control," *Journal of Law and Economics* 26 (1983): 301–325; Michael C. Jensen and William H. Meckling, "Theory of the Firm: Managerial Behavior, Agency Costs and Ownership Structure," *Journal of Financial Economics* 3 (1976): 305–360. See also Frank H. Easterbrook and Daniel R. Fischel, *The Economic Structure of Corporate Law* (Cambridge, Mass.: Harvard University Press, 1991).
12. Kenneth E. Goodpaster terms this a "multi-fiduciary" theory of managerial responsibility in "Business Ethics and Stakeholder Analysis," *Business Ethics Quarterly* 1 (1991): 53–73. See also Etzioni: "The stakeholder argument... accepts the legitimacy of the claim that shareholders have ... rights and entitlements, but maintains that the same basic claim should be extended to all those who invest in the corporation. This often includes employees (especially those who worked for a corporation for many years and loyally); the community...; creditors...; and, under some conditions, clients" (Etzioni, "Stakeholder Theory," p. 682, emphasis omitted); and John Orlando, "The Fourth Wave: The Ethics of Corporate Downsizing," *Business Ethics Quarterly* 9 (1999): 295–313.

13. "When we adjust for the risks involved and for various other factors that influence the return to an activity, we see that the returns most firms earn are not excessive compared to what the same resources could have earned in such manifestly non-exploitative alternatives as tree growing" (Robert Frank, *Choosing the Right Pond* [New York: Oxford University Press, 1985], p. 39). See also Easterbrook and Fischel, *Corporate Law,* p. 213.

14. This would not take the form of a "capital strike," as suggested by Lindblom, but would be the result of uncoordinated actions of millions of investors each acting in rational self-defense (Charles E. Lindblom, *Politics and Markets* [New York: Basic, 1977]).

15. The cost of the rule change would be borne by its beneficiaries. "Any legal regime that 'protects' workers by making them the 'beneficiaries' of fiduciary duties will, by definition, make those same workers less valuable (in monetary terms) to their employers.... Since workers generally prefer to receive compensation in the form of cash wages rather than in other ways, even the workers themselves will prefer that fiduciary duties not be imposed on employers since such duties will, at the margin, result in lower cash compensation to workers" (Jonathan R. Macey, "An economic analysis of the various rationales for making shareholders the exclusive beneficiaries of corporate fiduciary duties," *Stetson Law Review* 21 (1991): 37–38).

16. Millon, "Communitarianism," p. 24.

17. Ibid., p. 31.

18. Ibid., p. 28.

19. Richard A. Posner, *Economic Analysis of Law* (Boston: Little, Brown and Co., 1977), p. 396.

20. Note that an employment-security rule might be more efficient than an employment-at-will rule. This essay is agnostic on that point. However, the rule change would be neutral from the standpoint of distributive justice.

21. Millon, "Communitarianism," p. 26.

22. Ibid., p. 23.

23. Posner, *Economic Analysis,* p. 395. Posner suggests various reasons why creditors (rather than stockholders) might be better placed to bear the risk of business failure. Assume the lender is a bank. The bank might be in a better position to appraise the risk than is the individual investor who may know little or nothing about the business he has invested in. Then, also, the stockholder is likely to be more risk-averse than the bank.

24. Ibid.

25. *Corporate Law,* p. 50.

26. Ibid., p. 51. "Equity investors and managers have incentives to make arrangements that reduce risk and thus reduce the [interest rate] premium they must pay to debt claimants" (p. 51). The parties may also purchase insurance. As Easterbrook and Fischel say, "The ability of potential victims to protect themselves against loss through insurance is a strong reason for disregarding distributional concerns in choosing among liability rules" (p. 52).

27. Singer, "Reliance Interest," p. 667. See also Marleen A. O'Connor, "Promoting Economic Justice in Plant Closings: Exploring the Fiduciary/Contract Law Distinction to Enforce Implicit Employment Agreements," in Mitchell, *Progressive Corporate Law,* pp. 224 *et seq.* According to Etzioni, "[a] fair number of court decisions recognize employees' rights to employment by the corporation for which they have been working, based on good faith implied by continuous satisfactory service" ("Stakeholder theory," p. 684).

28. Otherwise why would employees not already have purchased this right in return for lower wages? Or, what is probably the more usual case, why would they have chosen employment in a firm that insisted on its right to dismiss at will?

29. Millon, "Communitarianism," p. 10.

30. New jobs in Europe tend to be temporary or casual owing to the difficulty of firing regular staff. Moreover, in Europe "those out of work for more than a year account for one-third of the unemployed" (Gary Becker, "Unemployment in Europe and the United States," *Journal des Economistes et des Etudes Humaines,* 7 [1996]: 101. Cited by David Schmidtz in Schmidtz and Robert E. Goodin, *Social Welfare and Individual Responsibility* [New York: Cambridge University Press, 1996]).

31. "Laws in many European countries, including Germany, Italy, and France, make it all but impossible to fire people. So companies don't hire—they invest in equipment instead." Thomas K. Grose, "Labor, Social Costs, Taking Toll on Governments," *USA Today,* September 19, 1996, pp. B–1, 2. Cited in Schmidtz and Goodin, *Social Welfare.*

32. Singer, "Reliance Interest," pp. 722–723. See also Orlando, "The Fourth Wave."

33. It also assumes *employees* won't change their behavior. But, as Jonathan R. Macey has pointed out, if employees can acquire the plant at *less* than fair market value, then they will be tempted to sabotage its operations and drive it into bankruptcy. See "Symposium: Fundamental Corporate Changes: Causes, Effects, and Legal Responses: Externalities, Firm-specific Capital Investments, and the Legal Treatment of Fundamental Corporate Changes," *Duke Law Journal,* February 1989, p. 193.

34. Macey, "Symposium," p. 180.

35. Ian Maitland, "Rights in the Workplace: A Nozickian Argument," *Journal of Business Ethics,* 1989, p. 953; Richard B. McKenzie, "The Case for Plant Closures," *Policy Review* 15 (1981): 122.

36. Singer, "Reliance Interest," p. 723.

37. O'Connor, "Plant Closings," p. 233.

38. Easterbrook and Fischel, *Corporate Law,* p. 231.

POSTSCRIPT

Can Restructuring a Corporation's Rules Make a Moral Difference?

Can the corporation live a moral life? For that matter, can a human being live a moral life? This is not the kind of question one can answer in a day or a week after reading some contrary views on the subject. But it must be answered somehow, and the less we think about it, the more definitively will it be answered by our actions. Corporations have often developed corporate "codes of conduct" or "vision statements," affirming a fundamental recognition of the importance of ethical behavior in business, but just as often they have left us in doubt about the motivation for the code. Was the intention of the code to help people live more ethical lives for their own sake? Was the code a public relations ploy to impress neighbors and regulators and get more favorable treatment from the local zoning board and inspectors? Was it intended as a legal lever, to put corporate officers in a position to fire employees whose aggressive business practices became an embarrassment to the firm? Was it to get credit for an "ethics program" under the federal sentencing guidelines? Sometimes, corporate executives extol a moral life only to keep the lowest paid workers honest. Is this a legitimate practice?

Suggested Readings

Amar Bhide and Howard H. Stevenson, "Why Be Honest If Honesty Doesn't Pay?" *Harvard Business Review* (September–October 1990).

D. M. Messick and M. H. Bazerman, "Ethics for the 21st Century: A Decision Making Perspective," *Sloan Management Review* (1996).

R. Murray Lindsay, Linda M. Lindsay, and V. Bruce Irvine, "Instilling Ethical Behavior in Organizations: A Survey of Canadian Companies," *Journal of Business Ethics* (vol.15, no.4, 1996).

James C. Wimbusch, Jon M. Shepard, and Steven E. Markham, "An Empirical Examination of the Relationship Between Ethical Climate and Ethical Behavior From Multiple Levels of Analysis," *Journal of Business Ethics* (vol. 16, no. 16, 1997).

ISSUE 4

Should Corporations Adopt Policies of Corporate Social Responsibility?

YES: Robert D. Hay and Edmund R. Gray, from "Introduction to Social Responsibility," in David Keller, man. ed., *Ethics and Values: Basic Readings in Theory and Practice* (Pearson Custom Publishing, 2002)

NO: Milton Friedman, from "The Social Responsibility of Business Is to Increase Its Profits," in Thomas Donaldson and Patricia H. Werhane, eds., *Ethical Issues in Business: A Philosophical Approach,* 4th ed. (Prentice Hall, 1993)

ISSUE SUMMARY

YES: Robert D. Hay, professor of management at the University of Arkansas, and Edmund R. Gray, professor and chair of the Department of Management at Loyola Marymount University, argue that in the long run, businesses will only be successful if they are directed to the needs of the society. If they choose to ignore that advice, government regulation is likely to fill the gap between business operations and the welfare of the people the government is sworn to protect.

NO: In this classic defense of *laissez-faire*, Paul Snowden Russell Distinguished Service Professor Emeritus of Economics at the University of Chicago Milton Friedman states that businesses have neither the right, in law or morals, nor the ability to meddle with "social responsibility." Customers, employees, and the general public, he concludes, are best served when the company simply does its job with maximum efficiency.

Should a company think past the bottom line and try to do good (or at least avoid evil)? This question, probably the first one asked in the infant discipline of business ethics a quarter of a century ago, has received many answers along the spectrum between yes and no; this spectrum is one of the arcs along which the political pendulum swings. In the 1950s Milton Friedman's arguments were taken as gospel truth. Those who agreed with Robert D. Hay and Edmund R.

Gray were regarded as "do-gooders" who understood nothing of business. During the 1970s, in a very rapid switch brought on by the consumer movements of the 1960s, the pendulum moved to Hay and Gray's position. During the Reagan-Bush administrations, the pendulum swung back, to the point where at present Friedman is regarded as a prophet and Hay and Gray's orientation a "variant perspective." Many agree that in this debate, nothing is certain, save that the pendulum will eventually swing the other way.

Underneath the political pendulum is a fixed structure of partnership. Society retains the right to seek the maximum happiness—without leaving the poor behind. Nor would it be in accordance with justice to abandon the U.S. economy to businesses: after all, the public granted the rights that the corporations have exercised to make their profits, protected their operations at taxpayer expense, and created and maintained the infrastructures (e.g., roads, water, power, and sanitation) upon which corporations depend.

There are widely differing opinions on the costs and benefits of an economic regime oriented to liberty rather than protection, but the American consensus has always been that the free market is good, individual liberty to pursue self-interest in economic matters is good, and that if everyone pursues self-interest exclusively—if business increases profits, to the exclusion of all other goals—in the end we will all, even the poorest of us, be better off. Whenever possible, Americans adhere to the free-market ideology. Many insist that it must be balanced by a strong legal regime prohibiting the uses of force and fraud, banning toxins and other dangers invisible to the consumer, and actively intervening in the endemic tendency of businesses to create monopolies —designed to thwart the market for the greater profit of the combiners. When that regime fails, businesses turn into predators, citizens are robbed, poisoned, and impoverished; and citizens eventually become outraged. Then the government is re-empowered to defeat—through arrest, jail, fines, or banishment—the "malefactors of great wealth," and a period of protection and rehabilitation of the poor succeeds the period of liberty for the corporations. It has happened often, and many predict that it will happen again, with the only change being the sophistication of the technology.

Ask yourself, as you read these selections, what balance between the freedom of the entrepreneur and the protection of the rest of the citizenry would be appropriate for a free and affluent society. How much of the responsibility for the citizenry should be taken on by corporations?

Robert D. Hay and Edmund R. Gray  **YES**

Introduction to Social Responsibility

It was Jeremy Bentham, late eighteenth century English philosopher, who espoused the social, political, and economic goal of society to be "the greatest happiness for the greatest number." His cardinal principle was written into the Declaration of Independence as "the pursuit of happiness," which became a societal goal of the American colonists. Bentham's principle was also incorporated into the Constitution of the United States in the preamble where the goal was stated "to promote the general welfare."

The economic-political system through which we in America strive to achieve this societal goal emphasizes the economic and political freedom to pursue individual interests. Adam Smith, another English political economist of the late eighteenth century, stated that the best way to achieve social goals was as follows:

> Every individual is continually exerting himself to find out the most advantageous employment for whatever capital he can command. It is his own advantage, indeed, and not that of the society, which he has in view. But the study of his own advantage naturally, or rather necessarily, leads him to prefer that employment which is most advantageous to the society....
>
> As every individual, therefore, endeavors as much as he can both to employ his capital in the support of domestic industry, and so to direct that industry that its produce may be of the greatest value, every individual necessarily labours to render the annual revenue of the society as great as he can. He generally, indeed, neither intends to promote the public interest, nor knows how much he is promoting it By preferring the support of domestic to that of foreign industry, he intends only his own security; and by directing that industry in such a manner as its produce may be of the greatest value, he intends only his own gain, and he is in this, as in many other cases, led by an invisible hand to promote an end which was not part of his intention. Nor is it always the worse for the society that it was no part of it. By pursuing his own interest he frequently promotes that of the society more effectually than when he really intends to promote it. I have never known much good done by those who affected to trade for the public good. It is an affectation, indeed, not very common among merchants, and very few words need be employed in dissuading them from it.

From Robert D. Hay and Edmund R. Gray, "Introduction to Social Responsibility," in David Keller, man. ed., *Ethics and Values: Basic Readings in Theory and Practice* (Pearson Custom Publishing, 2002). Reprinted from Robert D. Hay and Edmund R. Gray, *Business and Society: Cases and Text*, 2d ed. (South-Western, 1980). Copyright © 1981 by South-Western, a division of Thomson Learning. Reprinted by permission of South-Western, a division of Thomson Learning. http://www.thomsonrights.com. Notes and references omitted.

Adam Smith's economic values have had an important influence on American business thinking. As a result, most business people for the first hundred and fifty years of our history embraced the theory that social goals could be achieved by pursuing individual interests.

By 1930 American values were beginning to change from that of the individual owner ethic to that of the group or social ethic. As part of this changing mood, it was felt that Smith's emphasis on owner's interests was too predominant at the expense of other contributors to a business organization. Consequently, a new philosophy of management took shape which stated that the social goals could be achieved by balancing the interests of several groups of people who had an interest in a business. It was stated by Charles H. Percy, then president of Bell and Howell, in the 1950s as follows:

> There are over 64 million gainfully employed people in the United States. One half of these work directly for American corporations, and the other half are vitally affected by business directly or indirectly. Our entire economy, therefore, is dependent upon the type of business management we have. Business management is therefore in many respects a public trust charged with the responsibility of keeping America economically sound. We at Bell & Howell can best do this by keeping our own company's program on a firm foundation and by having a growing group of management leaders to direct the activities of the company.
>
> Management's role in a free society is, among other things, to prove that the real principles of a free society can work within a business organization.
>
> Our basic objective is the development of individuals. In our own present program we are doing everything conceivable to encourage, guide, and assist, and provide an opportunity to everyone to improve their abilities and skills, thus becoming more valuable to the company and enabling the company to improve the rewards paid to the individual for such additional efforts.
>
> Our company has based its entire program for the future on the development of the individual and also upon the building of an outstanding management group. This is why we have emphasized so strongly the supervisory training program recently completed by all Bell & Howell supervisors, and why we are now offering this program to others in the organization training for future management responsibilities.
>
> But a company must also have a creed to which its management is dedicated. I hope that we can all agree to the following:
>
> We believe that our company must develop and produce outstanding products that will perform a great service or fill a need for our customers.
>
> We believe that our business must be run at an adequate profit and that the services and products that we offer must be better than those offered by competitors.
>
> We believe that management must serve employees, stockholders, and customers, but that we cannot serve the interests of any one group at the undue expense of the other two. A proper and fair balance must be preserved.
>
> We believe that our business must provide stability of employment and job security for all those who depend on our company for their livelihood.

We believe that we are failing in our responsibility if our wages are not sufficiently high to not only meet the necessities of life but provide some of the luxuries as well. Wherever possible, we also believe that bonus earning should be paid for performance and output "beyond the call of duty."

We believe that every individual in the company should have an opportunity for advancement and growth with the organization. There should be no dead-end streets any place in an organization.

We believe in the necessity for constantly increasing productivity and output. Higher wages and greater benefits can never be "given" by management. Management can only see that they are paid out when "earned."

We believe in labor-saving machinery. We do not think human beings should perform operations that can be done by mechanical or electronic means. We believe in this because we believe in the human dignity and creative ability of the individual. We are more interested in the intellect, goodwill, initiative, enthusiasm, and cooperativeness of the individual than we are in his muscular energy.

We believe that every person in the company has a right to be treated with the respect and courtesy that is due a human being. It is for this reason that we have individual merit ratings, individual pay increases, job evaluation, and incentive pay; and it is why we keep every individual fully informed—through The Finder, through our annual report, through Family Night, and through individual letters—about the present program of the company and also about our future objectives.

We believe that our business must be conducted with the utmost integrity. We may fight the principle of confiscatory taxation, but we will pay our full share. We will observe every governmental law and regulation, local, state, and national. We will deal fairly with our customers, we will advertise our product truthfully, and we will make every attempt to maintain a friendly relationship with our competitors while at the same time waging the battle of free competition.

Some business leaders, on the one hand, preach the virtues of the free enterprise, democratic system and, on the other hand, run their own business in accordance with autocratic principles—all authority stemming from the top with little delegation of responsibility to individuals within the organization. We believe in democracy—in government and in our business.

We hope that every principle we believe in is right and is actually being practiced throughout the company as it affects every individual.

Then in the late 1960s American business leaders began to take another look at the problems of society in light of the goal of "the greatest happiness for the greatest number." How could people be happy if they have to breathe foul air, drink polluted water, live in crowded cities, use very unsafe products, be misled by untruthful advertising, be deprived of a job because of race, and face many other problems? Thus, another philosophy of management emerged. It was voiced by several American business leaders:

Business must learn to look upon its social responsibilities as inseparable from its economic function. If it fails to do so, it leaves a void that will quickly be filled by others—usually by the government. (George Champion, Chase National Bank, 1966.)

I believe there is one basic principle that needs to be emphasized more than ever before. It is the recognition that business is successful in the long term only when it is directed toward the needs of the society. (Robert F. Hansberger, Boise Cascade, 1971.)

The actions of the great corporations have so profound an influence that the public has come to judge them not only by their profit-making record, but by the contribution of their work to society as a whole. Under a political democracy such as ours, if the corporation fails to perceive itself and govern its action in essentially the same manner as the public at large, it may find itself in serious trouble. (Louis B. Lundborg, Bank of America, 1971.)

With these remarks we can see that there has been a shift in managerial emphasis from owners' interests to group interests, and finally, to society's interests. Managers of some American businesses have come to recognize that they have a social responsibility.

Historical Perspective of Social Responsibility

The concept of the social responsibility of business managers has in recent years become a popular subject of discussion and debate within both business and academic circles. Although the term itself is of relatively recent origin, the underlying concept has existed as long as there have been business organizations. It rests on the logical assumption that because the firm is a creation of society, it has a responsibility to aid in the accomplishment of society's goals. In the United States concepts of social responsibility have moved from three distinct phases which may be labeled Phases I, II, and III.

Phase I—Profit Maximizing Management

The Phase I concept was based on the belief that business managers have but one single objective—maximize profits. The only constraint on this pursuit was the legal framework within which the firm operated. The origin of this view may be found in Adam Smith's *Wealth of Nations*. As previously noted, Smith believed that individual business people acting in their own selfish interest would be guided by an "invisible hand" to promote the public good. In other words, the individual's drive for maximum profits and the regulation of the competitive marketplace would interact to create the greatest aggregate wealth for a nation and therefore the maximum public good. In the United States this view was universally accepted throughout the nineteenth century and the early part of the twentieth century. Its acceptance rested not only on economic logic but also on the goals and values of society. America in the nineteenth and first half of the twentieth centuries was a society of economic scarcity; therefore, economic growth and the accumulation of aggregate wealth were primary goals. The business system with its emphasis on maximum profit was seen as a vehicle for eliminating economic scarcity. In the process employee abuses such as child labor, starvation wages, and unsafe working conditions could be tolerated. No questions were raised with regard to using up the natural resources and polluting streams and land. Nor was anyone really concerned about urban problems, unethical advertising, unsafe products, and poverty problems of minority groups.

The profit maximization view of social responsibility also complemented the Calvinistic philosophy which pervaded nineteenth and twentieth century American thinking. Calvinism stressed that the road to salvation was through hard work and the accumulation of wealth. It then logically followed that a business person could demonstrate diligence (and thus godliness) and accumulate a maximum amount of wealth by adhering to the discipline of profit maximization.

Phase II—Trusteeship Management

Phase II, which may be labeled the "trusteeship" concept, emerged in the 1920s and 30s. It resulted from structural changes in both business institutions and in society. According to this concept, corporate managers were responsible not simply for maximizing the stockholders' wealth but rather for maintaining an equitable balance among the competing claims of customers, employees, suppliers, creditors, and the community. In this view the manager was seen as "trustee" for the various contributor groups to the firm rather than simply an agent of the owners.

The two structural trends largely responsible for the emergence of this newer view of social responsibility were: (1) the increasing diffusion of ownership of the shares of American corporations, and (2) the development of a pluralistic society. The extent of the diffusion of stock ownership may be highlighted by the fact that by the early 1930s the largest stockholders in corporations such as American Telephone and Telegraph, United States Steel, and the Pennsylvania Railroad owned less than one percent of the total shares outstanding of these companies. Similar dispersion of stock ownership existed in most other large corporations. In such situations management typically was firmly in control of the corporation. Except in rare circumstances, the top executives were able to perpetuate themselves in office through the proxy mechanism. If an individual shareholder was not satisfied with the performance of the firm, there was little recourse other than to sell the stock. Hence, although the stockholder's legal position was that of an owner—and thus a principal-agent relationship existed between the stockholder and the managers—the stockholder's actual position was more akin to bondholders and other creditors of the firm. Given such a situation it was only natural to ask, "To whom is management responsible?" The "trusteeship" concept provided an answer. Management was responsible to all the contributors to the firm—that is, stockholders, workers, customers, suppliers, creditors, and the community.

The emergence of a largely pluralistic society reinforced the logic of the "trusteeship" concept. A pluralistic society has been defined as "one which has many semi-autonomous and autonomous groups through which power is diffused. No one group has overwhelming power over all others, and each has direct or indirect impact on all others. From the perspective of business firms this translated into the fact that exogenous groups had considerable impact upon and influence over them. In the 1930s the major groups exerting significant pressure on business were labor unions and the federal government. Today the list has grown to include numerous minority, environmental, and consumer groups among others. Clearly, one logical approach to such a situation is to consider that the firm has a responsibility to each interested group and that management's task is to reconcile and balance the claims of the various groups.

Phase III—Quality of Life Management

Phase III, which may be called the "quality of life" concept of social responsibility, has become popular in recent years. The primary reason for the emergence of this concept is the very significant metamorphosis in societal goals which this nation is experiencing. Up to the middle part of this century, society's principal goal was to raise the standard of living of the American people, which could be achieved by producing more goods and services. The fact that the U.S. had become the wealthiest nation in the world was testimony to the success of business in meeting this expectation.

In this process, however, the U.S. has become what John Kenneth Galbraith calls an "affluent society" in which the aggregate scarcity of basic goods and services is no longer the fundamental problem. Other social problems have developed as direct and indirect results of economic success. Thus, there are pockets of poverty in a nation of plenty, deteriorating cities, air and water pollution, defacement of the landscape, and a disregard for consumers to mention only a few of the prominent social problems. The mood of the country seems to be that things have gotten out of balance—the economic abundance in the midst of a declining social and physical environment does not make sense. As a result, a new set of national priorities which stress the "Quality of life" appear to be emerging.

Concomitant with the new priorities, societal consensus seems to be demanding that business, with its technological and managerial skills and its financial resources, assume broader responsibilities—responsibilities that extend beyond the traditional economic realm of the Phase I concept or the mere balancing of the competing demands of the sundry contributors and pressure groups of the Phase II concept. The socially responsible firm under Phase III reasoning is one that becomes deeply involved in the solution of society's major problems.

Personal Values of the Three Styles of Managers

Values are the beliefs and attitudes which form one's frame of reference and help to determine the behavior which an individual displays. All managers have a set of values which affect their decisions, but the values are not the same for each manager; however, once values are ingrained in a manager, they do not change except over a period of time. It is possible to group these values into a general pattern of behavior which characterizes three styles of managers—the profit-maximizing style, the trusteeship style, and the "quality of life" style of management.

Phase I Managers

Phase I, profit-maximizing managers have a personal set of values which reflects their economic thinking. They believe that raw self-interest should prevail in society, and their values dictate that "What's good for me is good for my country." Therefore, Phase I managers rationalize that making as much profit as is possible would be good for society. They make every effort to become as efficient as possible and to make as much money as they can. To them money and wealth are the most important goals of their lives.

In the pursuit of maximum profit the actions of Phase I managers toward customers are reflected in a *caveat emptor* philosophy. "Let the buyer beware" characterizes decisions and actions in dealing with customers. They are not necessarily concerned with product quality or safety, or with sufficient and/or truthful information about products and services. A profit-maximizing manager's view toward employees can be stated as, "Labor is a commodity to be bought and sold in the marketplace." Thus, chief accountability lies with the owners of the business, and usually the Phase I manager is the owner or part owner of the organization.

To profit maximizers technology is very important. Machines and equipment rank high on their scale of values, therefore, materialism characterizes their philosophy.

Social values do not predominate the thinking of Phase I managers. In fact, they believe that employee problems should be left at home. Economics should be separate from societal or family concerns. A Phase I manager's leadership style is one of the rugged individualist— "I'm my own boss, and I'll manage my business as I please." Values about minority groups dictate that such groups are inferior, so they must be treated accordingly.

Political values are based on the doctrine of laissez faire. "That government is best which governs the least" characterizes the thinking of Phase I managers. As a result anything dealing with politicians and governments is foreign and distasteful to them.

Their beliefs about the environment can be stated, "The natural environment controls one's destiny; therefore, use it to protect your interests before it destroys you. Don't worry about the physical environment because there are plenty of natural resources which you can use."

Aesthetic values to the profit maximizer are minimal. In fact, Phase I managers would say, "Aesthetic values? What are they?" They have very little concern for the arts and cultural aspects of life. They hold musicians, artists, entertainers, and social scientists in low regard.

The values that a profit-maximizing manager holds were commonly accepted in the economic textbooks of the 1800s and early 1900s although they obviously did not apply to all managers of those times. It is easy to see how they conflict with the values of the other two styles of management.

Phase II Managers

Phase II, trusteeship managers have a somewhat different set of values. They recognize that self-interest plays a large role in their actions, but they also recognize the interests of those people who contribute to the organization—the customers, employees, suppliers, owners, creditors, government, and community. In other words, they operate with self-interest plus the interests of other groups. They believe that "What is good for my company is good for the country." They balance profits of the owners and the organization with wages for employees, taxes for the government, interest for the creditors, and so forth. Money is important to them but so are people, because their values tells them that satisfying people's needs is a better goal than just making money.

In balancing the needs of the various contributors to the organization, Phase II managers deal with customers as the chief providers of revenue to the firm. Their values tell them not to cheat the customers because cheating is not good for the firm.

They are concerned with providing sufficient quantities of goods as well as sufficient quality for customer satisfaction. They view employees as having certain rights which must be recognized and that employees are more than mere commodities to be traded in the marketplace. Their accountability as managers is to owners as well as to customers, employees, suppliers, creditors, government, and the community.

To the trusteeship-style manager, technology is important, but so are people. Innovation of technology is to be commended because new machines, equipment, and products are useful to people to create a high standard of living. Materialism is important, but so is humanism.

The social values held by trusteeship managers are more liberal than those held by profit maximizers. They recognize that employees have several needs beyond their economic needs. Employees have a desire for security and a sense of belonging as well as recognition. Phase II managers see themselves as individualists, but they also appreciate the value of group participation in managing the business. They view minority groups as having their place in society. But, a trusteeship manager would add: "Their place is usually inferior to mine; they are usually not qualified to hold their jobs but that's not my fault."

The political values of Phase II managers are reflected in recognizing that government and politics are important, but they view government and politics as necessary evils. They distrust both, recognizing that government serves as a threat to their existence if their firms do not live up to the laws passed since the 1930s.

The environmental beliefs of trusteeship managers are stated as follows: "People can control and manipulate their environment. Therefore, let them do it for their own benefit and incidentally for society's benefit."

Aesthetic values are all right to the trusteeship manager, but "they are not for our firm although someone has to support the arts and cultural values."

Phase III Managers

In contrast to profit maximizers and trustee managers, "quality of life" managers believe in enlightened self-interest. They agree that selfishness and group interests are important, but that society's interests are also important in making decisions. "What's good for society is good for our company" is their opinion. They agree that profit is essential for the firm, but that profit in and of itself is not the end objective of the firm. As far as money and wealth are concerned, their set of values tells them that money is important but people are more important than money.

In sharp contrast to *caveat emptor* in dealings with customers, the philosophy of Phase II managers is *caveat venditor*, that is, let the seller beware. The company should bear the responsibility for producing and distributing products and services in sufficient quantities at the right time and place with the necessary quality, information, and services necessary to satisfy customers' needs. Their views about employees are to recognize the dignity of each, not treating them as a commodity to be bought and sold. Their accountability as managers is to the owners, to the other contributors of the business, and to society in general.

Technological values are important but people are held in higher esteem than machines, equipment, computers, and esoteric products. A "quality of life" manager is a humanist rather than a materialist.

The social values of "quality of life" managers dictate that a person cannot be separated into an economic being or family being. Their philosophy is, "We hire the whole person including any problems that person might have." Phase III managers recognize that group participation rather than rugged individualism is a determining factor in an organization's success. Their values about minority groups are different from the other managers. Their view is that "A member of a minority group needs support and guidance like any other person."

The political values of "quality of life" managers dictate that government and politicians are necessary contributors to a quality of life. Rather than resisting government, they believe that business and government must cooperate to solve society's problems.

Their environmental beliefs are stated as, "A person must preserve the environment, not for the environment's sake alone, but for the benefit of people who want to lead a quality life."

As far as aesthetic values are concerned, Phase III managers recognize that the arts and cultural values reflect the lives of people whom they hold in high regard. Their actions support aesthetic values by committing resources to their preservation and presentation.

NO ↩

Milton Friedman

The Social Responsibility of Business Is to Increase Its Profits

When I hear businessmen speak eloquently about the "social responsibilities of business in a free-enterprise system," I am reminded of the wonderful line about the Frenchman who discovered at the age of 70 that he had been speaking prose all his life. The businessmen believe that they are defending free enterprise when they declaim that business is not concerned "merely" with profit but also with promoting desirable "social" ends; that business has a "social conscience" and takes seriously its responsibilities for providing employment, eliminating discrimination, avoiding pollution and whatever else may be the catchwords of the contemporary crop of reformers. In fact they are— or would be if they or anyone else took them seriously—preaching pure and unadulterated socialism. Businessmen who talk this way are unwitting puppets of the intellectual forces that have been undermining the basis of a free society these past decades.

The discussions of the "social responsibilities of business" are notable for their analytical looseness and lack of rigor. What does it mean to say that "business" has responsibilities? Only people can have responsibilities. A corporation is an artificial person and in this sense may have artificial responsibilities, but "business" as a whole cannot be said to have responsibilities, even in this vague sense. The first step toward clarity in examining the doctrine of the social responsibility of business is to ask precisely what it implies for whom.

Presumably, the individuals who are to be responsible are businessmen, which means individual proprietors or corporate executives. Most of the discussion of social responsibility is directed at corporations, so in what follows I shall mostly neglect the individual proprietors and speak of corporate executives.

In a free-enterprise, private-property system, a corporate executive is an employee of the owners of the business. He has direct responsibility to his employers. That responsibility is to conduct the business in accordance with their desires, which generally will be to make as much money as possible while conforming to the basic rules of the society, both those embodied in law and those embodied in ethical custom. Of course, in some cases his employers may have a different objective. A group of persons might establish a corporation for an eleemosynary purpose—for example, a hospital or a school. The manager of

From Milton Friedman, "The Social Responsibility of Business Is to Increase Its Profits," in Thomas Donaldson and Patricia H. Werhane, eds., *Ethical Issues in Business: A Philosophical Approach,* 4th ed. (Prentice Hall, 1993). Reprinted from *The New York Times Magazine* (September 13, 1970). Copyright © 1970 by Milton Friedman. Reprinted by permission of The New York Times Syndication Sales Corp.

such a corporation will not have money profit as his objective but the rendering of certain services.

In either case, the key point is that, in his capacity as a corporate executive, the manager is the agent of the individuals who own the corporation or establish the eleemosynary institution, and his primary responsibility is to them.

Needless to say, this does not mean that it is easy to judge how well he is performing his task. But at least the criterion of performance is straightforward, and the persons among whom a voluntary contractual arrangement exists are clearly defined.

Of course, the corporate executive is also a person in his own right. As a person, he may have many other responsibilities that he recognizes or assumes voluntarily—to his family, his conscience, his feelings of charity, his church, his clubs, his city, his country. He may feel impelled by these responsibilities to devote part of his income to causes he regards as worthy, to refuse to work for particular corporations, even to leave his job, for example, to join his country's armed forces. If we wish, we may refer to some of these responsibilities as "social responsibilities." But in these respects he is acting as a principal, not an agent; he is spending his own money or time or energy, not the money of his employers or the time or energy he has contracted to devote to their purposes. If these are "social responsibilities," they are the social responsibilities of individuals, not of business.

What does it mean to say that the corporate executive has a "social responsibility" in his capacity as businessman? If this statement is not pure rhetoric, it must mean that he is to act in some way that is not in the interest of his employers. For example, that he is to refrain from increasing the price of the product in order to contribute to the social objective of preventing inflation, even though a price increase would be in the best interests of the corporation. Or that he is to make expenditures on reducing pollution beyond the amount that is in the best interests of the corporation or that is required by law in order to contribute to the social objective of improving the environment. Or that, at the expense of corporate profits, he is to hire "hardcore" unemployed instead of better qualified available workmen to contribute to the social objective of reducing poverty.

In each of these cases, the corporate executive would be spending someone else's money for a general social interest. Insofar as his actions in accord with his "social responsibility" reduce returns to stockholders, he is spending their money. Insofar as his actions raise the price to customers, he is spending the customers' money. Insofar as his actions lower the wages of some employees, he is spending their money.

The stockholders or the customers or the employees could separately spend their own money on the particular action if they wished to do so. The executive is exercising a distinct "social responsibility," rather than serving as an agent of the stockholders or the customers or the employees, only if he spends the money in a different way than they would have spent it.

But if he does this, he is in effect imposing taxes, on the one hand, and deciding how the tax proceeds shall be spent, on the other.

This process raises political questions on two levels: principle and consequences. On the level of political principle, the imposition of taxes and the expenditure of tax proceeds are governmental functions. We have established elaborate constitutional, parliamentary and judicial provisions to control these functions, to assure that taxes are imposed so far as possible in accordance with the preferences and desires of the public—after all, "taxation without representation" was one of the battle cries of the American Revolution. We have a system of checks and balances to separate the legislative function of imposing taxes and enacting expenditures from the executive function of collecting taxes and administering expenditure programs and from the judicial function of mediating disputes and interpreting the law.

Here the businessman—self-selected or appointed directly or indirectly by stockholders—is to be simultaneously legislator, executive and jurist. He is to decide whom to tax by how much and for what purpose, and he is to spend the proceeds—all this guided only by general exhortations from on high to restrain inflation, improve the environment, fight poverty and so on and on.

The whole justification for permitting the corporate executive to be selected by the stockholders is that the executive is an agent serving the interests of his principal. This justification disappears when the corporate executive imposes taxes and spends the proceeds for "social" purposes. He becomes in effect a public employee, a civil servant, even though he remains in name an employee of a private enterprise. On grounds of political principle, it is intolerable that such civil servants—insofar as their actions in the name of social responsibility are real and not just window dressing—should be selected as they are now. If they are to be civil servants, then they must be elected through a political process. If they are to impose taxes and make expenditures to foster "social" objectives, then political machinery must be set up to make the assessment of taxes and to determine through a political process the objectives to be served.

This is the basic reason why the doctrine of "social responsibility" involves the acceptance of the socialist view that political mechanisms, not market mechanisms, are the appropriate way to determine the allocation of scarce resources to alternative uses.

On the grounds of consequences, can the corporate executive in fact discharge his alleged "social responsibilities"? On the other hand, suppose he could get away with spending the stockholders' or customers' or employees' money. How is he to know how to spend it? He is told that he must contribute to fighting inflation. How is he to know what action of his will contribute to that end? He is presumably an expert in running his company—in producing a product or selling it or financing it. But nothing about his selection makes him an expert on inflation. Will his holding down the price of his product reduce inflationary pressure? Or, by leaving more spending power in the hands of his customers, simply divert it elsewhere? Or, by forcing him to produce less because of the lower price, will it simply contribute to shortages? Even if he could answer these questions, how much cost is he justified in imposing on his stockholders, customers and employees for this social purpose? What is his appropriate share and what is the appropriate share of others?

And, whether he wants to or not, can he get away with spending his stock-holders', customers' or employees' money? Will not the stockholders fire him? (Either the present ones or those who take over when his actions in the name of social responsibility have reduced the corporation's profits and the price of its stock.) His customers and his employees can desert him for other producers and employers less scrupulous in exercising their social responsibilities.

This facet of "social responsibility" doctrine is brought into sharp relief when the doctrine is used to justify wage restraint by trade unions. The conflict of interest is naked and clear when union officials are asked to subordinate the interest of their members to some more general purpose. If the union officials try to enforce wage restraint, the consequence is likely to be wildcat strikes, rank-and-file revolts and the emergence of strong competitors for their jobs. We thus have the ironic phenomenon that union leaders—at least in the U.S.—have objected to Government interference with the market far more consistently and courageously than have business leaders.

The difficulty of exercising "social responsibility" illustrates, of course, the great virtue of private competitive enterprise—it forces people to be respon-sible for their own actions and makes it difficult for them to "exploit" other people for either selfish or unselfish purposes. They can do good—but only at their own expense.

Many a reader who has followed the argument this far may be tempted to remonstrate that it is all well and good to speak of Government's having the responsibility to impose taxes and determine expenditures for such "social" purposes as controlling pollution or training the hard-core unemployed, but that the problems are too urgent to wait on the slow course of political pro-cesses, that the exercise of social responsibility by businessmen is a quicker and surer way to solve pressing current problems.

Aside from the question of fact—I share Adam Smith's skepticism about the benefits that can be expected from "those who affect to trade for the pub-lic good"—this argument must be rejected on grounds of principle. What it amounts to is an assertion that those who favor the taxes and expenditures in question have failed to persuade a majority of their fellow citizens to be of like mind and that they are seeking to attain by undemocratic procedures what they cannot attain by democratic procedures. In a free society, it is hard for "evil" people to do "evil," especially since one man's good is another's evil.

I have, for simplicity, concentrated on the special case of the corporate ex-ecutive, except only for the brief digression on trade unions. But precisely the same argument applies to the newer phenomenon of calling upon stockholders to require corporations to exercise social responsibility (the recent G.M. cru-sade for example). In most of these cases, what is in effect involved is some stockholders trying to get other stockholders (or customers or employees) to contribute against their will to "social" causes favored by the activists. Insofar as they succeed, they are again imposing taxes and spending the proceeds.

The situation of the individual proprietor is somewhat different. If he acts to reduce the returns of his enterprise in order to exercise his "social respon-sibility," he is spending his own money, not someone else's. If he wishes to spend his money on such purposes, that is his right, and I cannot see that there is any objection to his doing so. In the process, he, too, may impose costs on employees and customers. However, because he is far less likely than a large corporation or union to have monopolistic power, any such side effects will tend to be minor.

Of course, in practice the doctrine of social responsibility is frequently a cloak for actions that are justified on other grounds rather than a reason for those actions.

To illustrate, it may well be in the long-run interest of a corporation that is a major employer in a small community to devote resources to providing amenities to that community or to improving its government. That may make it easier to attract desirable employees, it may reduce the wage bill or lessen losses from pilferage and sabotage or have other worthwhile effects. Or it may be that, given the laws about the deductibility of corporate charitable contributions, the stockholders can contribute more to charities they favor by having the corporation make the gift than by doing it themselves, since they can in that way contribute an amount that would otherwise have been paid as corporate taxes.

In each of these—and many similar—cases, there is a strong temptation to rationalize these actions as an exercise of "social responsibility." In the present climate of opinion, with its widespread aversion to "capitalism," "profits," the "soulless corporation" and so on, this is one way for a corporation to generate goodwill as a by-product of expenditures that are entirely justified in its own self-interest.

It would be inconsistent of me to call on corporate executives to refrain from this hypocritical window-dressing because it harms the foundations of a free society. That would be to call on them to exercise a "social responsibility"! If our institutions, and the attitudes of the public make it in their self-interest to cloak their actions in this way, I cannot summon much indignation to denounce them. At the same time, I can express admiration for those individual proprietors or owners of closely held corporations or stockholders of more broadly held corporations who disdain such tactics as approaching fraud.

Whether blameworthy or not, the use of the cloak of social responsibility, and the nonsense spoken in its name by influential and prestigious businessmen, does clearly harm the foundations of a free society. I have been impressed time and again by the schizophrenic character of many businessmen. They are capable of being extremely far-sighted and clearheaded in matters that are internal to their businesses. They are incredibly short-sighted and muddle-headed in matters that are outside their businesses but affect the possible survival of business in general. This short-sightedness is strikingly exemplified in the calls from many businessmen for wage and price guidelines or controls or income policies. There is nothing that could do more in a brief period to destroy a market system and replace it by a centrally controlled system than effective governmental control of prices and wages.

The short-sightedness is also exemplified in speeches by businessmen on social responsibility. This may gain them kudos in the short run. But it helps to strengthen the already too prevalent view that the pursuit of profits is wicked and immoral and must be curbed and controlled by external forces. Once this view is adopted, the external forces that curb the market will not be the so-cial consciences, however highly developed, of the pontificating executives; it will be the iron fist of Government bureaucrats. Here, as with price and wage controls, businessmen seem to me to reveal a suicidal impulse.

The political principle that underlies the market mechanism is unanimity. In an ideal free market resting on private property, no individual can coerce any other, all cooperation is voluntary, all parties to such cooperation benefit or they need not participate. There are no values, no "social" responsibilities in any sense other than the shared values and responsibilities of individuals. Society is a collection of individuals and of the various groups they voluntarily form.

The political principle that underlies the political mechanism is confor-mity. The individual must serve a more general social interest—whether that be determined by a church or a dictator or a majority. The individual may have a vote and say in what is to be done, but if he is overruled, he must conform. It is appropriate for some to require others to contribute to a general social purpose whether they wish to or not.

Unfortunately, unanimity is not always feasible. There are some respects in which conformity appears unavoidable, so I do not see how one can avoid the use of the political mechanism altogether.

But the doctrine of "social responsibility" taken seriously would extend the scope of the political mechanism to every human activity. It does not differ in philosophy from the most explicitly collectivist doctrine. It differs only by professing to believe that collectivist ends can be attained without collectivist means. That is why, in my book *Capitalism and Freedom*, I have called it a "fun-damentally subversive doctrine" in a free society, and have said that in such a society, "there is one and only one social responsibility of business—to use its resources and engage in activities designed to increase its profits so long as it stays within the rules of the game, which is to say, engages in open and free competition without deception or fraud."

POSTSCRIPT

Should Corporations Adopt Policies of Corporate Social Responsibility?

Why should a business be moral? This question is different from the original question of ethics, which is, why should any human being be moral? Many argue that we should be moral as individuals because we are social animals, and we cannot fulfill our nature unless we recognize, honor, and work to protect the community that enfolds us. The corporation is different. It is an artificial entity, chartered by the state, for the sole purpose of enriching its owners. Corporations, then, have no interest but self-interest; in that respect, they are solitary animals, and they violate their nature if they try to live for others. As the selections by Hay and Gray and Friedman demonstrate, the essential difference between the social-responsibility theorist and the increase-profit theorist is one of long-range or short-range planning. The intelligent corporate officer knows that in the long run, government, customers, and the press will make life intolerable for the company unless he or she takes care of the community's needs as conscientiously as he or she does the corporation's.

Suggested Readings

John K. Galbraith, *The Affluent Society* (Random House, 1971).

George A. Steiner, *Business and Society* (Random House, 1971).

Manuel G. Velasquez, *Business Ethics* (Prentice-Hall, 1982).

Peter A. French, *Collective and Corporate Responsibility* (Columbia University Press, 1984).

R. Edward Freeman, "Fixing the Ethics Crisis in Corporate America," *Miller Center Report* (Fall 2002).

Bennett Daviss, *The Futurist* (March 1999).

Adam Smith, *The Wealth of Nations* (Clarendon Press, 1976).

Thomas Donaldson and L. E. Preston, "The Stakeholder Theory of the Corporation: Concepts, Evidence, and Implications," *Academy of Management Review* (vol. 20).

STAT-USA/Internet

This site, a service of the U.S. Department of Commerce, provides one-stop Internet browsing for business, trade, and economic information. It contains daily economic news, frequently requested statistical releases, information on export and international trade, domestic economic news and statistical series, and databases.

http://www.stat-usa.gov/stat-usa.html

PhRMA: America's Pharmaceutical Companies

PhRMA membership represents approximately 100 U.S. pharmaceutical companies that have a primary commitment to pharmaceutical research. Information on the effects of pharmaceutical price controls on research spending is one of the many topics covered at this site.

http://www.phrma.org

NumaWeb

This Numa Financial Systems site calls itself "the Internet's home page for financial derivatives." This site includes a reference index, a discussion forum, and links to many related sites.

http://www.numa.com/index.htm

PART 2

Current Issues in Business

*C*urrently, *the health care area of business—medicine, nursing homes, and pharmaceuticals—presents some very interesting profit areas; casinos, illegal until recently, are spreading across the country; and the geniuses of Wall Street are constructing ever more interesting products for the investing public. Do we need to consider the regulation of vital industries for the public good? Conflict arises immediately when any area is identified as "out of bounds" to the market and when buying and selling is limited for good, moral reasons. This is what these four debates are about.*

- Are Pharmaceutical Firms Obliged to Cut Their Prices for Poor AIDS Victims?

- Should Casino Gambling Be Prohibited?

- Should Prudent Managers Avoid Purchasing Derivative Instruments?

- Does the Enron Collapse Show That We Need More Regulation of the Energy Industry?

ISSUE 5

Are Pharmaceutical Firms Obliged to Cut Their Prices for Poor AIDS Victims?

YES: Debra Watson, from "U.S. Pharmaceutical Companies Reap Huge Profits From AIDS Drugs," World Socialist Web Site, http://www.wsws.org/articles/1999/jun1999/aids-j05_prn.shtml (June 5, 1999)

NO: Robert Goldberg, from "Wrong Prescription: Don't Rush to Embrace the Bush AIDS Plan," *National Review Online,* http://www.nationalreview.com/comment/comment-rgoldberg020703.asp (February 7, 2003)

ISSUE SUMMARY

YES: Writer Debra Watson argues that the greed of AIDS profiteers is killing impoverished people with AIDS all over the world—including in the United States. She concludes that only drastic price reductions will make necessary drugs available to the victims.

NO: Senior fellow at the Manhattan Institute Robert Goldberg doubts that reducing pharmaceutical prices will make much of a difference to AIDS sufferers, since the education and health infrastructures remain inadequate to reach and teach the victims.

Business—in its American capitalist incarnation—is squarely based on two normative propositions. The first is that free enterprise is always good. The social welfare of the entire nation will be increased without limit if we permit entrepreneurs and products to compete without limit. Government regulations are discouraged in favor of letting the market decide.

The second normative proposition is that private property is sacred. What a person owns they may dispose of or keep just as they like with no regard to "serving the public good." One's property, including intellectual property, is one's own, and it is protected by the law.

The problem with AIDS drugs, many say, is that they were developed by American companies not just to help treat AIDS but primarily to make money for their shareholders. The value of these drugs to the shareholder is the "patent," that is, the drugs' developers are granted exclusive legal rights to make and sell these drugs for a period of years, during which time they may charge whatever price they like and make whatever profit they desire. This profit is morally justified because (1) the law says they have a right to it, that this is intellectual property, and property is sacred; (2) it takes years of research to develop a good drug, and the high profit on a successful one helps to pay for the research; and (3) most research is unsuccessful, so high profit margins are needed to give companies the incentive to keep working on products that might not pan out. Attacking those patents, those exclusive rights, risks losing the whole enterprise in the future.

But what if some astute scientists figure out how to make that drug, and on their own initiative, develop a generic version of it that sells at a much lower price? One might propose putting both branded and generic drugs on the market and letting them compete because competition is good, and all will profit if the more efficient producer prevails, regardless of the investment the proprietary drug company put into developing the drug. Many argue that profits for drug companies are not a consideration, given that the vast number of sufferers from AIDS are terribly poor. Many live in India or sub-Saharan Africa, nations that have no money to spend on AIDS victims. In countries like Kenya, for instance, where the average health care expenditure per person is about $3 per year, one cannot expect public support for AIDS victims. The drugs for these victims, if paid at the company's normal asking price, would cost about $10,000 per year per victim. Cipla, the Indian company that develops many of the generics, can supply drugs for one AIDS victim for about $600 per year, and the company promises to get that price down further in the future.

But is this fair, or right? Bear in mind, as you read the following selections, that AIDS is a very politicized epidemic. What percentage of the annual health care allotment should AIDS sufferers receive?

Debra Watson ➡ **YES**

U.S. Pharmaceutical Companies Reap Huge Profits From AIDS Drugs

The international financial crisis and growing world inequality dominated much of the roundtable discussion at the 1999 Annual World Health Assembly (WHA 1999). The World Health Organization (WHO) held its fifty-second annual meeting in May in Geneva, Switzerland. The AIDS roundtable included discussion by health ministers concerning the exorbitant cost of drug cocktails for AIDS patients in poor countries. "WHO should lobby for medicines. If technology is available, no one should be denied it," said J. Kalweo, Minister of Health from Kenya.

Outbreaks of tuberculosis, malaria, sleeping sickness and meningitis, as well as the deepening AIDS crisis, have raised serious alarms from WHO. The AIDS crisis has put increasing health inequalities in the forefront of the major international health conferences.

The severe effects of the world economic crisis on AIDS treatment in one country were clear in the recent WHO report entitled "Funding Priorities for the HIV/AIDS Crisis in Thailand." The report compiled data first presented by the Thai Ministry of Public Health last year. According to the report, the 1998 national AIDS program budget was cut 33 percent in real terms and staggering reductions in prevention and care of AIDS patients were imposed. The budget for vertical transmission (from mother to newborn) was reduced by 76.4 percent. Out of 18,000 AIDS pregnancies expected, only 2,500 of the women could be treated in an attempt to keep their babies from being born with the disease. The budget for universal AIDS precautions was reduced by 72 percent.

The Thai doctors reported that in 1997 of 60,000 AIDS patients, one-third had opportunistic infections (infections taking advantage of the body's debilitated immune system). Treatment for these infections would require 920 million baht, but only 166 million was available. They also reported that the cost of four common drugs for opportunistic infections used at Ramathibodi Teaching Hospital in Bangkok increased an average of 10 percent from 1997 to 1998.

Inequality in medical care in the U.S. as well as between the developed and underdeveloped countries was the focus of a speech by Eric Sawyer of ACT

From Debra Watson, "U.S. Pharmaceutical Companies Reap Huge Profits From AIDS Drugs," World Socialist Web Site, http://www.wsws.org/articles/1999/jun1999/aids-j05_prn.shtml (June 5, 1999). Copyright © 1999 by World Socialist Web Site. Reprinted by permission of the author.

UP/NY at the 1996 XI International Conference on AIDS. "The headlines that PWAS [People With Aids] want you to write from this conference would read: 'Human Rights Violations and Genocide Continue to Kill Millions of Impoverished People With AIDS.' ... Drug companies are killing people by charging excessive prices. This limits access to treatments. The greed of AIDS profiteers is killing impoverished people with AIDS."

Many who attended the 1998 World AIDS Conference echoed these sentiments. The XIII AIDS Conference, scheduled for South Africa in 2000, will be even more explosive, as it is taking place in the area of the world where there are staggering numbers of people infected with HIV.

WHA 1999 pledged [that] special efforts would be made to allow countries to monitor world drug price levels, to provide resources related to drug quality, and to disseminate knowledge developed by member countries for promoting efficient use of drugs. The World Health Organization (WHO) has urged countries to use the Internet to advance health cost efficiency, especially in the area of essential drug policy.

WHA 1999 also passed a resolution concerning the World Trade Organization (WTO) law on drug costs. The debate on the resolution has raged for more than a year. In a statement to WHA 1999, Consumers International pointed out that "enforcement of the WTO regulations will remove a source of innovative quality drugs on which the poorer countries depend. Patent protection for 20 years will increase the access gap between the North and the South." Another organization providing testimony related to new trade laws and intellectual property was Health Action International (HAI).

In late March an international conference of 120 delegates from 30 countries met in Geneva under the auspices of HAI, Médecins Sans Frontières and U.S. consumer advocate Ralph Nader's Consumer Project on Technology to discuss the campaign surrounding Trade-Related Aspects of Intellectual Property (TRIPS.) Thai conference participants said that Thailand was forced to drop its plan to manufacture DdI, to be used as part of a double therapy AZT/DdI, after the U.S. threatened trade sanctions on some of Thailand's key exports. DdI is exclusively marketed by Bristol-Myers Squibb.

Trade sanctions have also been threatened against South Africa if a proposed South African Medicine Act passes. The act would take advantage of parallel importing and compulsory licensing, which are legal under World Trade Organization regulations. Nader contends that such processes can lower drug prices 75 percent or more.

Compulsory licensing enables countries to instruct a patent holder to license the right to use its patent to another party. The drug is manufactured by the country granted the license, at a substantially lower price. The monopoly on sales by the patent holder is thus broken, although royalties are usually mandated in the process. Parallel importing or "gray market" importing takes advantage of substantial price differences from country to country by importing a product to one country and reselling it to another without authorization by the original seller.

The Clinton administration is meeting all threats to the pharmaceutical companies' monopolies and profits with severe action. Nader has charged

Vice President Al Gore, the chair of the United States/South Africa Binational Commission, with using "bullying tactics" to prevent South Africa from implementing legal policies designed to expand access to HIV/AIDS drugs.

Nader referred to a State Department report to Congress [that] said Gore was leading an "assiduous, concerted campaign" by U.S. government agencies —including the Department of State, the Department of Commerce, the U.S. Patent Trademark Office, the Office of United States Trade Representative and National Security Council—to undercut South Africa's policies. Nader called the State Department and administration attack on the South African law an "affront to the sovereignty of Third World Nations."

The March conference took note of the fact that 26 million of the 33 million people infected worldwide with HIV live in sub-Saharan Africa, yet Africa accounts for only 1.3 percent of the global drug market. Currently 3.2 million or 16 percent of South Africans are HIV positive. While the average annual income is $2,600, the cost of retrovirals, drugs [that] can significantly lengthen a patient's life, run $1,000 per month in South Africa. Other infectious disease epidemics have resulted in record disease rates, which are causing the de-population of some parts of the African continent. Treatments for these diseases are severely curtailed by prohibitively high pharmaceutical prices. Most of the 100,000 people suffering from multi-drug-resistant strains of TB, for example, are unable to afford the new standard combination treatment at $15,000 per course.

The three organizations sponsoring the conference have supported the final draft of the WHA 1999 Revised Drug Strategy Resolution, saying the resolution "will soften the negative effect of new global trade rules." However, some countries that supported the resolution nevertheless voiced serious reservations. The Philippines delegation pointed out that the TRIPS agreement is not sufficient for the requirements of some WHO member states, particularly those who are developing or least developed. They maintained that provisions in the resolution urging member states to ensure that public health interests are paramount in pharmaceutical and health policies must mean "that in the formulation and implementation of pharmaceutical policies, public health concerns take precedence over commercial, trade and other economic interests."

In April, 16 people were arrested in the U.S. outside a Washington, DC pharmaceutical industry trade office. They were protesting a bill that would further undermine efforts to use special WTO provisions to encourage production of cheaper drugs. The Africa Growth and Opportunity Act, sponsored by Congressman Charles Rangel (Dem.-N.Y) and Philip Crane (Rep.-Ill.), would set up a Free Trade Zone in 48 sub-Saharan African countries. The bill is on a fast track in the U.S. Congress, and is backed by the Pharmaceutical Research and Manufacturers Association (PhRMA), the American pharmaceutical industry group.

Protesters said the bill contains language that gives additional protection to U.S. drug patents and would prop up the price of disease-fighting drugs on a continent where 70 percent of the world's new AIDS cases are reported. "We're not going to allow our president and vice president to bully and harass and kill people in Africa," Julie Davids of ACT UP/Philadelphia told the rally.

There are other health-related issues affected by the use of patents to support high profits. The burgeoning biotechnology industry is trying to protect investments that anticipated huge profits by taking advantage of patent law. Attempts are being made to patent whole genetic sequences. In one example, the Meningitis Research Foundation warned that Human Genome Sciences, which has applied for the patent on the sequence for bacterial meningitis, could use their patent to demand royalties for any vaccine developed by the foundation.

Recent history shows many examples of the use of patent law to protect drug companies' profits. In 1993 Bristol-Myers Squibb was criticized when they announced a wholesale price of $4.87 per milligram of Taxol, an important cancer drug. Bristol-Myers Squibb acquired the drug in bulk from a contractor at $.25 per milligram. DdI, the AIDS drug, was also priced far above Bristol-Myers Squibb costs. The life-saving drug was invented by the U.S. government but was exclusively licensed to Bristol-Myers Squibb.

Mergers between pharmaceutical companies have also created giant monopolies on health-related products that the merged partners once competed to produce.

U.S. domestic drug pricing has also received a boost from the Clinton administration. In April 1995 the administration sided with the pharmaceutical companies by repealing the 1989 law requiring products developed in part due to research at National Institute of Health (NIH) laboratories to be reasonably priced. It is estimated that the federal government funds fully 38 percent of U.S. healthcare research while 10 percent is funded by other government agencies and nonprofits. The private sector funds about 52 percent of total healthcare research, but reaps most of the profits.

At an AIDS trade show last year, AIDS activists demonstrated against Glaxo-Wellcome for "putting greed before people's lives." Glaxo said it would limit access to the new HIV drug Abacavir (1592) to 2,500 people worldwide. AIDS drugs currently on the market are failing more than 10,000 people with AIDS. Although 1592 was invented in 1989, the protesters say unnecessary deaths are due to Glaxo-Wellcome's plan to maximize profits on the marketing of AZT until the patent runs out.

They also accused the giant pharmaceutical company of dragging its feet on developing the protease inhibitor 141 W94 that it purchased from Vertex. Glaxo raised the price of AZT and 3TC 3 percent in 1998. AZT has reaped $2.6 billion in sales. ACT UP demanded lowered standards for viral load and CD4 cell counts to determine that older drugs have failed, and to determine who will get the new treatment. They were incensed when the company proposed lotteries to determine who gets the new drug.

Recently ACT UP/NY studied several companies' annual reports and cited figures for profits based on net income/sales. They were four to five times higher for the drug companies than for non-drug industries. While AT&T reported a 2 percent profit, Texaco 3 percent and Chrysler 3 percent; Merck reported 22 percent, Abbott 16 percent and Roche 18 percent. Glaxo-Wellcome, the maker of AZT, reported a 23 percent profit. A 1998 congressional minority report on pharmaceutical profits put them even higher, at nearly 29 percent for the U.S. drug manufacturers.

Robert Goldberg

 **NO**

Wrong Prescription: Don't Rush to Embrace the Bush AIDS Plan

If President Bush wants to stop the AIDS epidemic from laying waste to generations of people in the developing world, he should scrap his proposed $15 billion plan to seed the African continent and the Caribbean with AIDS drugs and spend the money elsewhere. It bolsters the tragic notion, held by activists and the liberal media, that drug prices are the barrier to treating HIV in developing countries, while virtually ignoring the bleak conditions and corruption that are at the heart of efforts to confront the epidemic.

Administration officials maintain that the proposal is based on Uganda's success in reducing HIV rates from the highest of any African nation—14 percent in 1993—to the lowest (5 percent in 2001). But most of the progress was made before generic drugs were hailed as the silver bullet by activists and before efforts were made to increase access by attacking prices and patents. Rather, Uganda's gains are the result of action taken by its president and religious leaders to promote abstinence and sexual fidelity among the young and to insure that its public-health activities were free of corruption. (That Uganda has been spared war is critical too.)

Instead, the Bush plan simply takes a page from the HIV-activist handbook: Focus attention on high drug prices and use generic medicines as a battering ram against patent protection; at the same time, ignore Africa's own failure to focus time, attention, and money on the horrific public-health situation, which can only be addressed through economic growth and free trade.

Indeed, the Bush plan resembles more a Nigerian program that attempts to solve the HIV problem with cheap drugs. The Nigerian program has failed miserably and has essentially incapacitated the country at a time when its HIV-infection rate is rising faster than ever.

Nigeria—on the advice of activists—spurned the help of pharmaceutical companies and decided it would purchase generic anti-AIDS drugs purchased from Cipla for 15,000 patients. Cipla, an Indian company that has illegally manufactured generic versions of AIDS drugs developed by American companies, offered to reduce the price of the HIV-drug cocktail from $600 per person (the going government rate) to $350, a below-cost price that Cipla extended to a Doctors Without Borders clinical trial of 150 patients. To deal with drug

From Robert Goldberg, "Wrong Prescription: Don't Rush to Embrace the Bush AIDS Plan," *National Review Online,* http://www.nationalreview.com/comment/comment-rgoldberg020703.asp (February 7, 2003). Copyright © 2003 by *National Review.* Reprinted by permission of United Feature Syndicate, Inc.

delivery and health infrastructure, the World Bank, the U.S. Agency for International Development, and the Gates Foundation, among others, donated over $150 million.

Two years later, only about 800 people have been treated, and the tons of drugs in the government stockpile will expire in less than six months. Much of the drug supply was stolen and the funds for infrastructure were largely frittered away by incompetence and corruption. Two years later, while everyone was congratulating each other for their victory over the drug companies, the Nigerian Directorate of the National Programme to Fight AIDS concluded that Nigeria's woeful health infrastructure was the real reason for the failure. Cipla could have given three times the tonnage for free, but it would have been for naught.

The White House, however, didn't even bother to check and see if Cipla offered the best drugs at the lowest prices. They don't. Many of Cipla's HIV products have not met World Health Organization quality standards. And in some important cases the brand-name drugs are one-third the price of an Indian generic. Merck sells products it patented cheaper than the cheapest Indian generic. But somehow neither the White House nor the plan's author, National Institutes of Health HIV expert Anthony Fauci, shopped around.

The administration's attack on drug prices could also take a toll on the biotech and pharmaceutical industry's ability to invest in new drugs for global diseases. The administration has stood firm on protecting pharmaceutical patents in World Trade Organization meetings on global health, but now appears to have bought the activist claim that only generic companies can solve the HIV problem. By declaring it will buy its drugs from Cipla, the administration is directly undermining its own efforts to protect pharmaceutical patents from similar piracy.

But prices and patents were never the reason the developing world has failed to contain HIV. The vast majority of HIV drugs have no patents in Africa. In all that time, generic companies never made a move to sell their copies there. And if generic companies were the salvation, India—which has thousands of them—would be HIV free. As it is, their infection rate is climbing faster than that of many other countries, and only one percent of all people infected with the virus are receiving treatment.

Tons of drugs sitting unused in supply depots (before they are stolen and resold). Infrastructure concerns left ignored. New drug investment stagnating because of a desire to look compassionate on a global scale. But at least the White House will have stood up to the evil drug companies. The press clippings will look great. But who will stop the dying?

POSTSCRIPT

Are Pharmaceutical Firms Obliged to Cut Their Prices for Poor AIDS Victims?

$\mathbf{A}$IDS is not a problem that is going to go away. Unlike smallpox, influenza, or even the bubonic plague, AIDS resists all efforts to contain it. First, it is contagious for years, an indefinitely large number of years, before it shows any symptoms, so the sufferer does not know that he or she has it. Second, protecting against AIDS means strictly regulating, monitoring, and restricting: (1) the illegal use of intravenous drugs, which has proved to be unresponsive to regulation for 75 years and more; and (2) sex, which has proved to be impervious to regulation for 75,000 years and more. Not long ago, AIDS was a short-term death sentence; the loss of an AIDS victim was a human tragedy. Now that AIDS is a long-term, life-with-drugs sentence, the loss of a victim is a resounding injustice. But dare we dismantle our protective patent system? If we do, then where will future drugs come from?

Suggested Readings

Laurie Garrett, *The Coming Plague: Newly Emerging Diseases in a World out of Balance* (Penguin Group, 1994).

Deutsche Presse-Agentur, "Pharmaceutical Companies Back UN on AIDS Drugs," *Global Policy Forum* (April 5, 2001).

Julia M. Hernandez, "The High Cost of AIDS Drugs in Africa," *Health Law and Policy Institute* (July 23, 2001), http://www.law.uh.edu/healthlawperspectives/.

Thomas Etehel, "AIDS and Pharmaceutical Firms," (September 1, 2003), http://www.amisuk.f9.co.uk/writings.html.

Anup Shah, "Pharmaceutical Companies and AIDS," http://www.globalissues.org/TradeRelated/Corporations/AIDS.asp.

ISSUE 6

Should Casino Gambling Be Prohibited?

YES: William A. Galston and David Wasserman, from "Gambling Away Our Moral Capital," *The Public Interest* (Spring 1996)

NO: William R. Eadington, from "The Proliferation of Commercial Gaming in America," *The Sovereign Citizen* (Fall 1994)

ISSUE SUMMARY

YES: Political theorist William A. Galston and research scholar David Wasserman argue that there are significant moral objections to widespread casino gambling: gambling is deleterious to family and social life, and gambling losses fall on the most vulnerable members of society. Worse, legalizing gambling masks the need for adequate taxing to meet social responsibilities.

NO: Professor of economics William R. Eadington counters that gambling is a normal extension of commercial activity and it can safely promote the welfare of the host areas. He is less concerned about the reported downside of the gaming enterprise.

Is gambling wrong? If so, why? Many argue that there is no overt coercion: gamblers happily spend their money. There is no injustice: the poor are not deprived as a result. There is no exploitation of the person (the effective objection against prostitution) unless the person is the gambler himself or herself, willingly exploited. So why not use casino gambling to support America's cities?

Formed over the course of the last century, growing to wealth and splendor with the expansion of heavy manufacturing and the American domination of the world markets following World War II, American cities attracted hundreds of thousands of immigrants in search of jobs, education, and a better life for themselves and their families. While the good times lasted, waves of immigrants educated their children and watched them move up into the mobile middle class and the suburban lifestyle. When the bad times came, the last of those waves of immigrants, notably the African Americans and Hispanics from the South and the Caribbean, were stranded in cities without jobs, without ways up or out, and without hope.

Can casino gambling help this situation? What other hope is there? The present initiatives to introduce casino gambling to U.S. cities and the issue here result from two stubborn facts.

First, no traditional economic remedy will help American cities. The services we demand that cities provide are too expensive to support with any available enterprise that might choose a city location. Manufacturing is gone, lost to technology and foreign competition, and the new "information" industries will not employ the city's discontented crowds, feed its hungry, or care for its sick.

Second, gambling has shown itself to be a cow of almost infinite cash. No coercive collection mechanisms are needed to transfer money from private pockets to the public good; people choose freely—and happily—to gamble, lavishly spending their own money at the gaming tables, in a way that they will never choose to pay their taxes. Costs are low and revenues are spectacular. For instance, the Foxwoods casino, run by the Mashantucket Pequot Indians in Connecticut, and the Mohegan Sun casino, also in Connecticut, now support and educate every member of those once destitute tribes with their income. The tribes also contribute handsomely to Native American cultural foundations, employs hundreds of non–Native American residents of the state, and on top of those contributions, transferred in 2000 to the state of Connecticut $319 million as quid pro quo for its monopoly on slot machines. The two casinos are located in neighboring towns, yet both made a considerable amount of money. Many see no downside: the sources of all this cash, the gamblers, are happy to give it up.

Why not lead the cow to the people who really need the milk? American inner cities are dying for lack of jobs and money; casinos supply both, without adding to the tax burden of the marginal industries and dwindling middle class that remains within the city boundaries. The argument certainly seems compelling.

Not everyone agrees. Columnist William Safire cites singer/songwriter Kenny Rogers's "The Gambler": "You have to know when to hold 'em, know when to fold 'em..." "On the issue of casino gambling—its promotion of a false something-for-nothing philosophy, its corruption of both parties' politics with millions in Big Gambling cash—I am folding my hand" (*The New York Times* [March 29, 1999]). Tracking the association of casino gambling with the growth in addictive gambling, divorce, jail, bankruptcy, and increased tax costs to pay for all of this unhappiness, Safire concludes, "Good ends do not justify bad means," and he recommends that government put an end to casino gambling—or at least get out of the business of promoting it. Other critics worry about the growth of crime, especially about the participation in the industry of organized crime; they cite the evils of compulsive gambling and the possible additional drain that impoverished gamblers may put on social services. Who is right? Remember, as you read the following selections, that no one can really know for certain how far the market for gaming can continue to expand and what the ripple effects of casinos will be on America's aging urban centers. Appropriately, the introduction of large-scale casino gambling to cities carries a risk; it makes gamblers of us all, whatever we decide.

William A. Galston and
David Wasserman

Gambling Away Our Moral Capital

Duri ng the past generation, there has been a dramatic expansion of legalized gambling. Beginning with New Hampshire in 1964, 37 states and the District of Columbia have instituted lotteries. As recently as 1988, only two states allowed casino gambling. Today, 24 states do so, as do a number of Native American reservations. And gambling has become very big business. Total wagers reached nearly half a trillion dollars in 1994. Gross revenues from gambling have surged —to $40 billion annually, from only $10 billion a decade ago. Casino gambling has quadrupled; lottery revenues have registered a sixfold increase; and gambling on Indian reservations, nonexistent until the late 1980s, now brings in more than $3 billion each year. State governments drain off about one-third of total lottery wagers to finance public-sector activities....

It may seem churlish and retrograde to raise moral objections against gambling, especially given its deep roots in American history. Indeed, as historian Jackson Lears has suggested, it's possible to construct a moral case in its favor. Gambling may be justified as a source of intense experience, against the grain of our otherwise routinized urban lives; as a temporary release from the bonds of reality and responsibility into a realm of fantasy and imagination; as the expression of an anti-utilitarian spirit (gambling is not really about accumulating money). Gambling can even be seen as a much-needed counterweight to a smug Protestant ethic. According to this argument, gambling helps us to focus on chance as a way of experiencing the world and instructs us in the lack of a direct link between effort, merit, and success. Besides, it may be asked, what's the difference between gambling and the kind of economic risk-taking that has always been celebrated as part of America's "go-getter" culture of striving?

Some arguments against gambling do seem puritanical or overly fastidious. Few of us regard ourselves as having so stringent a duty to preserve our assets that we refrain from squandering even small amounts of money on trivial pursuits. But we can take a more relaxed view of our stewardship obligations and still regard gambling as a vice. While we may have no objection to small wagers guided by informed judgment or skilled play, we must also recognize the danger of recklessness and compulsion in almost any form of gambling. The same qualities that make gambling so attractive—its intensity and fantasy— make it potentially destructive.

From William A. Galston and David Wasserman, "Gambling Away Our Moral Capital," *The Public Interest*, no. 123 (Spring 1996). Copyright © 1996 by National Affairs, Inc. Reprinted by permission of *The Public Interest*.

Moreover, the rejection of a smug Protestant ethic may mask an elitist contempt for bourgeois striving. While gambling allows people of all social classes to display what Lears terms a "fine, careless disregard for utilitarian standards," it is a display that is unbecoming in a society with egalitarian ambitions and very costly for the poorer members of that society. Anti-utilitarianism is particularly destructive for individuals with limited resources.

We hardly need gambling to display a healthy respect for the vicissitudes of fortune or the limitations of individual effort. We can acknowledge the uncertainty of life by mitigating its effects, through individual or social insurance schemes: by steeling ourselves against it, through a stoic regulation of our desires, hopes, and fears; or by living more fully in its shadow, giving over more of our lives to the enjoyment of the present moment. It is hardly necessary, and arguably perverse, to recognize the role of chance in our lives by increasing its sway.

But if gambling is a vice, why isn't capitalism? There are several reasons: While gambling is at best zero-sum, entrepreneurship creates advantages for others and for society as a whole. While stock markets do represent opposing gambles on price movements, they also provide essential liquidity for market systems. Even futures—apparently a pure gamble—allow risk-averse individuals to hedge against market fluctuations. There are also important differences of individual motivation and behavior between gambling and business risk-taking: The entrepreneur is focused on the future; the gambler, on the present. The entrepreneur innovates; the gambler at best calculates. The entrepreneur is compelled to think about ways of satisfying the needs of others; the gambler is not. The attempt to equate the two invites us to abandon, as sanctimonious or hypocritical, those very aspects of entrepreneurship that make it morally defensible. We should reject the invitation. The riverboat gambler is a dangerous icon just because he appeals to the darker side of capitalism.

Gambling and Civil Society

Gambling is even more problematic when it is viewed in a social context: when we look at who gambles, in what social settings, with what impact on other social institutions. First, expenditures on the most widespread form of gambling, state lotteries, are clearly regressive. In *Selling Hope,* a comprehensive review of contemporary state lotteries, Charles Clotfelter and Philip Cook found that "the relatively poor spend a much larger fraction of their income on lottery tickets than the relatively affluent." For example, a 1984 study of the Maryland lottery found that players with incomes over $50,000 spent an average of $2.57 a week on lottery tickets, while those with incomes under $10,000 spent $7.30.

While regressivity appears to be less acute for casino play—one study of Las Vegas found that expenditures increased disproportionately with income, and one study of Atlantic City found only slight regressivity—this difference may vanish as casinos become more accessible. Researchers have consistently found that members of minority groups and people with less education gamble more. In Maryland in 1984, 41 percent of blacks with incomes under $10,000 spent at least $10 a week on lottery tickets, compared to only 8 percent of whites in the same income class. These findings suggest that gambling losses fall disproportionately on some of the more vulnerable members of society.

Second, gambling is increasingly asocial. As gambling expert A. Alvarez observes:

> Back in the 1980s, the center of the casinos was the "table games"—blackjack, roulette, baccarat, craps, poker—games that involve some social exchange with other people—players, dealers, croupiers—and varying degrees of skill.... Gradually, however, casinos have cut back on the space allotted to table games and filled it with slot machines.... But compared to traditional forms of gambling, playing the slots is an autistic activity—mindless, solitary, and addictive—and its popularity is growing at a terrible speed.

We are now gambling alone as well as bowling alone, and the peculiar social function of gambling—as Alvarez describes it, "the only place where people from the straight world could rub shoulders with gangsters and not get in trouble"—is becoming an anachronism.

Third, the growing appeal and accessibility of gambling to middle class and poor families appears to have done less to domesticate gambling than to coarsen family life. While Alvarez is struck by the increasingly Disney-like face of Las Vegas—a proliferation of "pirate battles, jousting knights, and exploding volcanoes"—other observers are struck by the inappropriateness of the moral suggestions children receive and act out. Iowa State University professors Corly Peterson and Allison Engel observed unsupervised children carrying plastic cups filled with quarters, parked in front of interactive video games, looking like their cuptoting parents sitting in front of video slot machines... kids betting dollar bills on mechanical horse race games... kids rushing from video screen to video screen until their money was gone.

Even in the rare supervised child-care centers, they found, "the atmosphere... mimics the visual stimulation of a casino."

Fourth, the rise in the popularity of gambling not only reflects but also reinforces a loss of confidence in hard work as a source of social advancement. The flight of blue-collar jobs, the trend toward downsizing, and the vagaries of the service sector have all contributed to a sharp decline in the proportion of Americans who believe that hard work pays off, from 60 percent in 1960 to 33 percent by the 1980s. As Alvarez observes, "When work is no longer a reliable route to prosperity, a big kill in the lotteries or the slots becomes the one hope of escape from the economic trap." It is certainly possible to exaggerate the impact of gambling on the work ethic and the impact of cynicism about the work ethic on the current popularity of gambling. But the emphasis on luck as a route to prosperity should be especially troublesome to governments involved in the promotion of gambling.

Marketing Vice

This litany of concerns does not make the case for outlawing all forms of gambling. The costs of criminalizing it are likely to be very high, and the moral posture of the state in issuing such a wholesale condemnation is questionable.

But these concerns do suggest that states should not encourage gambling or make their own functions dependent on its proliferation. Indeed, many of these concerns are exacerbated by state sponsorship.

The practical impact of state sponsorship is troubling if uncertain. Although several studies have found large increases in compulsive and problem gambling following the introduction of state lotteries or casinos, the reliability of these findings is limited by inconsistency and vagueness in the definition of "compulsive" and "problem" gambling and by the possibility that much of the apparent increase is due to increased awareness and increased reporting. Similarly, we do not know for sure how much the state's endorsement of spendthrift ways in lottery promotion adds to the powerful social forces that subvert the inculcation of thrift and industry in the most beleaguered communities in the United States—forces such as the loss of working-class jobs and the perverse incentives of the present welfare system.

But claims about adverse consequences by no means exhaust the moral objections to state sponsorship of gambling. The more important objections, we think, concern the propriety of the state's role as gambling promoter. Even if it were appropriate for individuals to express, through gambling, their recognition of the role of chance in their lives, it would be unseemly for the state to do so. The state's promotion of gambling belies its commitment to reducing the influence of morally arbitrary factors on the lives of its citizens and to supporting the virtues of thrift, hard work, and responsibility. Consider the messages conveyed by state-sponsored ads promoting lottery sales:(1)

> Playing the lottery is exciting; you'll be bored if you don't: "It's the Pick/It's a Kick/Come on in and try your luck. You can't buy more excitement for a buck."

> Playing the lottery is smart; you can't win if you don't play: "Imagine this.... The numbers are picked. Your numbers. And suddenly, your life has changed. Suddenly you're rich. Could it happen? Absolutely! But, you have to do more than just imagine. You have to play."

> Playing will give you quick, even instant, results; no more need to defer gratification: "Just One Ticket... and It Could Happen to You."

> Playing the lottery is the way to get set for life: "The Rich. Join Them."

Those who believe that statecraft is "soulcraft" have good grounds for objecting to government promulgation of such messages. But even those who believe that families and religious communities are responsible for inculcating the virtues of thrift and industry should be appalled at the denigration of those virtues in state lottery advertising.

Some critics regard it as wrong for anyone to offer a vanishingly small chance of a huge windfall to people mired in poverty. It is particularly objectionable for that offer to come from the state. Even if we disagree about the extent of the state's obligation to reduce privation and ignorance, we should agree that it has an obligation not to exploit them.

Public and Private Vice

Equally disturbing is the deliberate exploitation of poverty to finance public projects that should be paid for by taxes if undertaken at all. As Fairfield University philosophy professor Lisa Newton has said:

> There is an ironic justice in the fact that our eagerness to legalize casino gambling for the sake of the revenues follows directly from our unwillingness to assess ourselves a fair and adequate amount in taxes. The problems with our public character dovetail with the problems in our private character.

Defenders of state-sponsored gambling deny that the use of lotteries to raise public funds is a sign of public vice. They insist that this is a time-honored practice, frequently employed in early American communities and fully consistent with republican civic virtue. But this defense overlooks the huge differences between today's lotteries and their predecessors.

Unlike current state lotteries, early American lotteries were public-spirited and progressive. A typical colonial lottery was instituted to finance specific public works projects, such as bridges or roads, and participation was seen more as a charitable contribution than a form of gambling. For example, lotteries supported the reconstruction of Boston's Faneuil Hall and new buildings for Harvard, Princeton, and Yale. For decades after the Declaration of Independence, nearly all states sponsored lotteries; in 1793, President George Washington helped promote one to finance improvements in the District of Columbia.

In contrast, present-day lotteries have become a permanent revenue source for the states and a permanent pastime for their citizens; their operations are contracted out to professional gambling firms, their economic burden is regressive rather than progressive, and their customers are largely indifferent to their objectives. Although the political approval of state lotteries has often been secured by promising to earmark their revenues for government functions such as public education and care for the elderly, the actual use of lottery revenues has rarely, if ever, been so constrained. When lottery revenues are indeed earmarked for specific projects, they are often ones that the legislature would balk at funding by direct taxation. And those who purchase lottery tickets are less likely to be rich citizens with a strong moral or economic interest in the uses to which the revenues are put than poor citizens with little say or interest in their uses.

The resurgence of legal gambling also raises classic issues of public morality. The willingness of the state to legalize and sponsor gambling has introduced large amounts of new special interest money into our politics. With contributions totaling $2 million at the national level during the 1993–1994 election cycle, gambling-financed political-action committees are now in the same league as the National Rifle Association. At the state level, proponents of casino gambling have been able to outspend opponents by as much as 50 to 1; this has led recently to major corruption scandals in Louisiana, Missouri, Arizona, Kentucky, South Carolina, and West Virginia. In Florida, backers of a pro-gambling referendum spent almost as much as the state's two gubernatorial candidates combined. It is time to ask ourselves how much civic corruption we are willing to tolerate.

William R. Eadington

NO

The Proliferation of Commercial Gaming in America

Commercial gaming has arrived in America in the 1990s. To understand this, it is worthwhile to begin by examining the phenomenal success of the Foxwood's Casino and High Stakes Bingo in Ledyard, Connecticut. This is an Indian casino, owned by the 260 tribal members of the Mashantuckett Pequot Indian tribe, which opened in February, 1992. The amount of revenue generated by the casino in gaming winnings—customer expenditures on table games—in its first year of operation exceeded $200 million. In their second year of operation, after they negotiated with the Governor of Connecticut for the right to have slot machines and an exclusive franchise on casinos in Connecticut in exchange for a minimum $100 million payment to the State, their gaming winnings will approach $500 million. In their third year of operation—1994— when they have doubled their size, their gross gaming revenues could approach $700 million. At that point, they will be generating almost as much revenue as all the casinos in Reno, Nevada.

For another comparison, if you were to take all the movie theaters in America, the Foxwood's Casino is already generating about 10% as much in revenue as is generated in all ticket sales to all movie theaters in this country. Furthermore, because of its monopoly status in New England, the casino's profit margins are likely to be approximately 50%. That is for a tribe that ten years ago only had three people living on the reservation.

The gaming industry in America is going through an unprecedented proliferation and expansion that carries with it some amazing stories, of which the Ledyard situation is one. It also poses some fascinating and quite complex challenges to public policy, with regard to the impact that gambling is likely to have on society.

We are in the midst of a near total reversal of legal commercial gaming opportunities for American citizens in terms of their presence and accessibility. We are actually in the midst of a phenomenon that is occurring world wide.

From William R. Eadington, "The Proliferation of Commercial Gaming in America," *The Sovereign Citizen*, no. 1 (Fall 1994). Copyright © 1994 by Nichols College Institute for American Values. Reprinted by permission.

I would like to address a number of questions that relate to this phenomenon. Generally the questions are:

- Why is this occurring at this particular point in time?
- What are the dimensions of the gaming industries that are emerging?
- Where are these changes likely to carry us?
- What challenges will society have to confront as gambling becomes more and more present, and more and more pervasive in modern society?

As with many other facets of society, the following axiom is a useful starting point. To understand where we are today, we must first have an understanding of where we have been and how we have evolved to the current situation. Then we must try to see the directions implied by the current momentum to project what the situation will be like over the next couple of decades.

If one looks back as recently as 1910, we could note that gambling in America was virtually illegal almost everywhere. 1910 is interesting because that was the year that Nevada made casinos illegal. It was the year that New York made pari-mutuel wagering and race track wagering illegal. The only legal gambling one could find that year was on race tracks in Kentucky and in parts of Maryland. Everywhere else in America, gambling was illegal.

A half century later, in the year 1960, gambling was still largely prohibited in America. There were, as of yet, no lotteries. Casinos could be found only in Nevada, but Nevada, clearly, in the eyes of the rest of the country, was an outlaw state, which had created an environment to allow outlaws to legitimize themselves in the casino business. Wagering on racing had proliferated to about twenty states. However, people in the racing industry had a tendency to claim they were not in the gambling business; rather, they were in the business of improving the bloodlines and breed stock of thoroughbred horses, and if wagering on horses could be used as a way to subsidize the improvement of the quality of horses in this country, all the better.

That was the extent of legal gaming. There was a lot of illegal gambling, to be sure, but it was often viewed with a very critical eye. It was often cited as being the major source of income for organized crime, and a common view of gambling at the time could be summed up by an article written by Robert Kennedy, soon to become Attorney General of the United States. The article was entitled, "A Two Dollar Bet Means Murder". That seemed to summarize the public attitude towards gambling as late as the 1960s.

Churches, governments and good citizens agreed that gambling was evil, or at least that gambling was not something that should be accepted and brought into society. What were the substantive reasons? It was felt that gambling corrupted officials and law enforcement; it undermined the Protestant ethic of linkages between hard work and reward. And gambling could destroy lives through compulsive gambling, which would also lead to thefts, embezzlement, suicides, or worse. In total, gambling was considered a thoroughly unwholesome activity. That did not mean it was not fun for customers, however.

The contrast with the status of commercial gaming in the 1990s, however, is striking. Lotteries, which did not exist at all in America in 1960, can now be found in thirty-seven states and the District of Columbia. More than eighty percent of Americans can walk down to their local convenience store and purchase a lottery ticket. In 1992 lottery sales in America were over $21 billion, and after payment of prizes to winners, lotteries generated gross revenues of about $10 billion to the various states that had them. Casinos, as late as 1989 still could only be found in two places in the United States, in Nevada and in Atlantic City. Yet only four years later, one could gamble legally casino style in Nevada and Atlantic City, New Jersey; in mining town small stakes casinos in South Dakota and Colorado; on riverboats in Iowa, Illinois and Mississippi, and soon Louisiana, Missouri and Indiana. Or one could go [to] Indian casinos in Connecticut, Michigan, Minnesota, Wisconsin, South Dakota, Washington, Arizona, California, Colorado, New York, and soon in Mississippi, Louisiana, Texas and Rhode Island. All of this has transpired in a period of four years.

There has also been an expansion of non-casino casino style gambling, in the form of slot machines, video poker machines, or—in the euphemistically more acceptable name—video lottery terminals. The spread of gaming devices has been quite rapid, with their introduction into bars and taverns or other age restricted locations in the states of Montana, South Carolina, South Dakota, Oregon, Louisiana, West Virginia and Rhode Island. It has also recently been considered by the legislature of the state of Massachusetts, among others.

What does the casino industry do? How big an industry is casino gaming? And how does it affect peoples lives?

In 1992, the gross winnings for the various gaming industries in the United States, including lotteries, casinos, race tracks, charitable gambling and Indian gaming, were nearly $30 billion. That is the total expenditure of all customers on various gambling products. This also reflects total player losses after payment of winnings, as well as gross revenues on gaming to the various operators and purveyors of gambling services. This is approximately 0.6% of disposable income in the United States; roughly one-dollar out of every $150 spent in America is spent on gambling. This represents about five times as much money as Americans spend on going out to the movies; it represents about the same amount of income that is earned by all stock brokerages and securities firms in America; it represents approximately one-fourth of the gross revenues of all attorneys in America. Gambling is not a small business, it is substantial in its revenues and in its presence in society, and it is in the midst of a phenomenal expansion.

What has happened to social attitudes concerning gambling, and why are we seeing this phenomenon occurring now, at this very point in time?

There have historically been three main arguments in opposition to gambling. All of these arguments have been undermined by trends in the past three decades. The arguments are as follows:

1. Gambling leads to political corruption and brings organized crime into the mainstream of society.

However, as has been discovered time and again, political corruption and the infiltration of organized crime into gambling occurs more often when gambling is illegal, or where it is set up legally with considerable discretion given to public officials who can essentially sell the economic rents from gambling to the highest bidders. Gambling, especially when it is presented with a high degree of competent and professional regulation, can be run without scandal, and it can be run by individuals and organizations who themselves have a high degree of honesty and integrity with regard to their business dealings. It can be run without the kind of corruption that had dominated the quasi-legal or illegal gambling that used to be the major form of gambling in this country.

Lotteries, which have been run predominantly by governments, have had virtually no scandal in the 25 years that they have existed. Indeed, lotteries have also taught Americans how to gamble more than any other single activity, certainly more than such personalities as Jimmy the Greek, and more than casinos. Lotteries have played a very important role in this phenomenon, both by teaching people that gambling can be fun—even though lotteries themselves are far less interesting and entertaining than casino style gambling—but they have also demonstrated that gambling can be run with a high degree of honesty.

In New Jersey, the integrity of the regulatory process and the competence and integrity of the gaming operations has been there almost from the start, with relatively few lapses. Nevada has had a long learning process where its casino industry has gone from one of questionable integrity to one of fairly decent integrity with competent and professional operations and regulation.

2. Gambling is immoral.

Gambling has been considered as sinful by many religions. In earlier times, the church and the state would argue a person should not gamble because it is not good for people; it runs against family values; it undermines a husband's work values and long term objectives of achieving prosperity through hard work and meeting family responsibilities.

Why has this changed? In the last thirty years the church and the state have become major purveyors of gambling services. They have co-opted themselves out of the ability to take a strong moral position with regard to gambling. For many churches and charities, gambling—in the form of bingo and pull-tab tickets—have become a major revenue source.

Governments have turned to lotteries as a major revenue generator, arguing, in a world of increasing demand on public services, they cannot increase taxes not without risking their political futures. They also claim gambling is really a free tax. It is a tax that is voluntary because people choose to gamble. Therefore, governments have gone through the process of taking an illegal activity—gambling—legalizing it through lottery, and attempting to hold an exclusive franchise on their gambling monopoly so that they could maximize revenue for the state out of lottery profit. One has to be only slightly cynical to suggest that this may not be the appropriate role of government in preying on the propensities of its citizens to participate in an activity many still consider immoral.

Another factor relating to the moral arguments against gambling is that if one examines the challenges of the modern world, which is characterized by such terrible moral dilemmas and controversies over policy aimed at such things as abortion, AIDS, genocide, homosexuality, homelessness, and drug abuse, the moral questions posed by these broader issues make the morality of gambling seem quaint in comparison, or perhaps even anachronistic.

3. Gambling creates compulsive gamblers.

The third argument against gambling, compulsive gambling, is a real issue. Society is gaining greater understanding over time of this phenomenon. Among those factors that have improved our understanding of compulsive gambling in recent years is that it is an affliction that affects only a small percentage of the population, estimated at between one and five percent of the adult population. It is unclear whether compulsive gambling is a psychological or a physiological phenomenon. It is also unclear whether it is truly an addiction or merely an irresponsibility, an immaturity, on the part of those who are so cursed. But society has chosen more and more to take the attitude that if most people want to gamble, and if most people can do so responsibly, than gambling should not be prohibited for the majority, just to protect a small minority who might be at fault anyway, and for whom prohibition of gambling might not stop them from destroying themselves through gambling or some other vice anyway.

In summary, society has changed its attitude from "gambling is wrong, gambling is a sin", to one of saying "It's ok to gamble". The policy questions have shifted from "Should we gamble or not?" to "Who gets to benefit by being the purveyors of gambling services?" With regard to this point, we have seen the various claimants come forward. The claimants on gambling are the following groups, all of whom are well deserving. Governments have said that they should be the purveyors of gambling services because clearly they must deal with the fiscal crisis that is pervasive throughout this country, and clearly the demands for public services cannot be met through continuing tax increases on the middle class and the poor. So if government gets to run gambling, they can generate important tax revenues, and turn around and spend it in a fashion that is beneficial for society.

A second group of claimants—charities—respond to this argument with the claim that, if we allow government to take the revenues from gambling, it is like throwing it into a black hole. Nothing good seems to come out of government. They can absorb as much income as they can without resolving their crises. Rather, society should let charities be the purveyors of gambling services. Charities throughout Canada, and charities in certain states in the United States such as North Dakota or Minnesota, have become major purveyors of gambling services. In Minnesota, for example—a state of about four million people—charitable organizations and not-for-profit organizations in 1990 grossed about $250 million from their legal charitable gambling, after payment of prizes. They certainly are in the gambling business, and their argument is, "Let us have the revenues from gambling because we will spend them directly on things of definite and distinct value for the community; as charities, we know how to do good things."

Another set of groups who are purporting to be the legitimate claimants to the right to offer gambling are cities, or regions, in partnership with private sector gambling corporations. We have seen a bit of this in Connecticut, with attempts to legalize casinos in Hartford and Bridgeport, and we have seen legalization of a number of casinos in the Midwest, on the basis that their communities need jobs; their communities need investments; their communities need to stimulate economic development and tourism. The way they do this is to try to capture the same kinds of economic benefits that have accrued to Nevada and—to a lesser extent—New Jersey. The argument is, if the state would authorize a casino or casinos, private sector firms in partnership with political jurisdictions will create jobs; they will create investments; they will bring in tourists to the area; and everybody will benefit.

The fourth group of claimants are the Indian tribes in America. There is little doubt that, among all the minorities who have been treated in various ways by government programs over time, Indians have probably been the least effectively treated. The worst of the welfare cases in America have been Indian stories. After a combination of the emergence of Indian sovereignty as a well-defined right and a quirky law—the Indian Gaming Regulatory Act of 1988— along with some quite opportunistic situations that evolved for certain tribes, Indian gaming has become the most powerful economic development tool ever to develop for Indian tribes in America. Some tribes—such as the Mashantuckett Pequot of Connecticut—are becoming wealthy beyond their wildest expectations because of being at the right place at the right time with a set of circumstances that could be fully exploited.

Of the various claimants, one should probably concentrate on private sector casino development in league with cities, which is probably going to be the most important one over time. What are the jurisdictions who are legalizing casinos trying to do, and how effective are they likely to be? The motivation for places such as New Orleans, Kansas City, St. Louis, Davenport, Biloxi/Gulfport, Chicago, Bridgeport, Hartford and in Canada, Windsor and Montreal and Winnipeg have been to attempt to capture the economic benefits from casinos in the same manner as Nevada has done. These cities have looked at Las Vegas, which is a very interesting city for a number of reasons. They argue that they should be able to achieve the same successes.

Las Vegas is a city that most people would have claimed in 1960 was "all mobbed up". The common perception outside of Nevada was that Las Vegas was a city run for mobsters, by mobsters, in a very corrupt political system. However, Las Vegas is a city that for each of the last three decades has been among the five fastest growing metropolitan areas in the United States. It is a city that now has the ten largest hotels in the world. In terms of number of rooms, Las Vegas has more hotel rooms than both New York and London. Las Vegas is probably the best large convention city in the world today. They have the ability to accommodate over 100,000 visitors at one time. Las Vegas is also evolving in the same general direction as Orlando, Florida, with the construction of major amusement parks at a number of destination resort casino properties. In fact, the term "Las Orlando", has been used more and more commonly in recent years, and the term is actually getting to the point where one wonders whether the term Las Orlando, is an attempt to describe Las Vegas as a variant of Orlando, or an attempt to describe Orlando as a variant of Las Vegas.

The process of a rush to legalization of gambling has pointed out some very interesting patterns, and indeed, weaknesses in the American system. The first such weakness is that the American political system can be very myopic. It tends to concentrate on a single issue and run with that issue as long as it can. With regard to gambling, the dominant policy consideration used to be organized crime. That was the only point of debate: the concern that gambling inevitably led to involvement by organized crime and consequent political corruption.

If one examines the way that New Jersey wrote its Casino Control Act in 1977, and tries to see what their concerns were as embodied in the Act, it becomes very clear. The concerns of the Casino Control Act were to keep organized crime out of the casino gaming business, because that is its natural tendency. And that was the dominant way of thinking about commercial gaming until the late 1980s, especially with regard to casinos. And then—all of a sudden—concerns about organized crime diminished; they seemed to pass into posterity, into nostalgia. What replaced it was the primacy of economic benefits to be derived from gaming. Gambling's greatest social value is in creating economic benefits; thus, state after state has moved toward the legalization of gambling to capture those economic benefits.

There is a second weakness inherent in the American political system. This is the belief that if legislation works well in one place, it can work just as well in another jurisdiction, even though the safeguards may be slightly more relaxed and the circumstances somewhat different. There has been a very interesting and clear evolution in the legalization of casino style gambling in America. If we examine the third jurisdiction to legalize casinos, after Nevada and Atlantic City, we find it in a little place called Deadwood, South Dakota. Deadwood is about thirty miles from Mount Rushmore, and its population is about 1600 people. It is a small, remote, rural area. Deadwood peaked economically in the 1890s as a mining town, and it has not had much economic stimulus ever since. It is most famous for being the town where Wild Bill Hickock was shot in the back while playing poker, holding a hand of aces and eights, now known as the "dead man's" hand. The tourist attraction of Deadwood was the tomb of Wild Bill in Boot Hill, buried next to Calamity Jane.

In the 1980s, the town of Deadwood was literally falling apart. The city fathers argued the only way Deadwood could be saved would be to create a revenue source that will allow them to put some money aside for historic preservation of Deadwood. They were able to convince the voters of South Dakota in the 1988 election to authorize small stakes limited casino gambling in Deadwood. Five dollar maximum wagers were allowed, and no license could have more than thirty slot machines or table games. In November, 1989, Deadwood opened its first casinos and became the third jurisdiction in America to have casinos. Within a year every business in Deadwood had become a casino, and every other business was pushed out. In one sense, it was phenomenally successful; in another sense it was a disaster. People would travel six or eight hours to get to the slot machines of Deadwood.

Shortly thereafter, Iowa set up constrained riverboat gaming legislation that would allow no more than five dollar maximum wagers, and a person could lose no more than $200 per excursion. There was a belief among the good people of Iowa that the evils of gambling would show up if large wagers were allowed and if people were allowed to lose too much money in any given visit. Therefore, they legislated against it. They also allocated three percent of the gross winnings from their casinos for compulsive treatment programs, so that any social damage created by the casinos would be taken care of. They also mandated that—at least when the river was not frozen—gambling would have to take place on the riverboats while they were floating on the water. The belief—or symbolism—was that if all the sinning from gambling was taking place on the Mississippi River, then those sins, as they work their way back to shore, would be washed pure by the time they reached shore so as to not infect the good people of Iowa.

So Iowa and South Dakota set the tone for responsible, remote, small stakes gambling. But what happened next? Illinois is right across the river from Iowa and so they decided they did not want Iowa to get all the gaming revenues from their citizens, so they passed a riverboat gaming bill as well. However, they failed to put in the maximum wager limitation, or the maximum loss limitation, and they even allowed casino credit about which Iowa would shudder at the thought. Within nine months after Iowa passed its legislation, Illinois had copied it.

Further down the Mississippi River, in the state of Mississippi, the legislature argued that they also should have riverboat gambling; but they carried it one step further. They legislated that their riverboats did not have to go out and sail on the river. Indeed, after the law was passed, the Attorney General of Mississippi offered an opinion that Mississippi gaming boats do not even need to have motors on the boats. Indeed, they did not even have to be boats. A license holder in Mississippi can build a casino as long as it sits over the water. So, in an analogy to Darwinian evolution, we have seen casinos crawl out of the rivers and position themselves on the banks of rivers to become land-based casinos.

By the time riverboats worked their way into Louisiana, not only were the riverboats getting closer to the shore; they were getting closer to the cities. Louisiana, over a period of a little over a year, passed legislation that authorized riverboats within New Orleans, a major metropolitan area. They also passed non-casino gaming legislation that allowed video lottery terminals in bars, taverns, truck stops and off-track betting parlors throughout the state. Then in 1992, they passed legislation for a land-based monopoly casino in the center of New Orleans, right in the heart of its tourism area.

Thus, there has been a very rapid evolution from harmless, distant, remote gambling, to wide-open urban style gambling, bringing for the first time casinos to where many people live. This has been part of a process that has moved very quickly. It is also being copied in a lot of other jurisdictions. Every new jurisdiction, in order to be competitive, takes the position that they have to be more aggressive than the previous competing jurisdiction which legalized. So as legislation has moved one step further each time, casinos and their presence have become less constrained, less remote, less socially responsible.

The Indian gaming issue—which has been more influenced through the courts—accelerates the process of legalization. If Indians have casinos in particular jurisdictions, the entire public policy debate changes, because once Indians have casinos, the debate in the state, as has already occurred in Connecticut, is no longer, "Should we have casinos?" Rather, the important questions shift to "Who should have the casinos?", "Who should benefit from them?", and "Where should they be located?"

So, at this point in time, America confronts a situation where the momentum for the spread of gambling is, in my opinion, still just beginning. The United States casino and gaming market could be characterized as being terribly under-supplied. That under-supply is being addressed in a variety of ways, and at a very rapid pace.

How much growth remains in the gaming industry in America? In the United States, as mentioned earlier, commercial gaming is nearly a $30 billion a year industry. That represents an expenditure of about $110 per capita.

How much can such expenditures grow? To gain some insight into that question, we can examine the experience of New South Wales, Australia, the largest Australian state, home of Sydney, the country's largest city. In many respects, Australia is similar to America. With regard to gambling, there is generally widely available and accessible gambling in New South Wales. Per capita expenditures in New South Wales are about $570, about four times that of America when corrected for exchange rate differences.

How large can the American gaming industry get? It is not unreasonable to project an industry with gross revenues of $100 billion to $125 billion at maturity with current population and current real income. It can expand by a factor of about four or five just by addressing the question of under-supply of gaming facilities in America. If this process continues unconstrained, we could go from about 300,000 slot machines in America, to about three million, within a decade or so.

One of the issues with this type of projection is, could this really occur? The one thing that is working to bring it about is, if one examines the reasons why politicians are legalizing gaming, especially casino style gaming, one sees the rationale shrouded in economic justifications. Legislatures legalize casinos because of jobs. As Mayor Richard Daly of Chicago said, "Why do we want casinos in Chicago? Jobs, jobs, jobs."

POSTSCRIPT

Should Casino Gambling Be Prohibited?

T wo major cities in Connecticut, Hartford and Bridgeport, have both considered the introduction of casino gambling. Thirty-seven states and the District of Columbia have lotteries; in 2000, lotteries brought in upwards of $10 billion in revenue. Many regions have instituted, or are considering instituting, riverboat casinos or other restricted gaming establishments. Nonprofit institutions have long supported themselves with gambling; can the private sector be far behind? Underlying the entire debate is the tension of passing time: the market for gambling cannot be infinite, and each casino that opens draws revenue that the next cannot tap. And video lotteries (casinos on the Internet), which bring income to no location whatsoever, threaten all gambling establishments.

Life is a gamble, and risk is a part of our daily lives. The questions before us are not, in that sense, new. But they are certainly more complex, and they will demand our full attention in the next decade. America's cities need more help than anyone knows how to give them. Are the gambler's solutions the best solutions?

Suggested Readings

"Canada: 'A Gamble'," *The Economist* (June 18, 1994).

"Gambling May Yield Revenue Windfall," *Aviation Week and Space Technology* (August 15, 1994).

Francis X. Clines, "Gambling, Pariah No More, Is Booming Across America," *The New York Times* (December 5, 1993).

Susan B. Garland, "Clinton vs. The Sin Lobby: All Bark," Government Lobbyists, *Business Week* (July 18, 1994).

Robert Goodman, "Legalized Gambling as a Strategy for Economic Development," *United States Gambling Study* (March 1994).

Dan Parker, "Night Moves—When an Industry Runs Around the Clock (Weekends and Holidays) It Leaves Workers and Families Run-down and Stressed Out," *The Atlantic City Press* (June 14, 1993).

Timothy P. Ryan, Patricia J. Connor, Janet F. Speyerer, *The Impact of Casino Gambling in New Orleans* (Division of Business and Economic Research, University of New Orleans, LA, May 1990).

Gerald Slusher, *The Casino Industry and Its Impact on Southern New Jersey* (Division of Economic Development, Atlantic City, NJ, January 1991).

Frank Wolfe, "Inherited Talents," *Forbes 400* (October 17, 1994).

ISSUE 7

Should Prudent Managers Avoid Purchasing Derivative Instruments?

YES: Frank Partnoy, from *F.I.A.S.C.O.: The Inside Story of a Wall Street Trader* (Penguin Books, 1999)

NO: Merton H. Miller, from *Merton H. Miller on Derivatives* (John Wiley & Sons, 1997)

ISSUE SUMMARY

YES: Frank Partnoy, former trader and salesman at Morgan Stanley, makes a case that the financial instruments known as "derivatives" are wildly risky and generally good only for making large commissions for the salesmen who push them on unwary insurance companies and pension funds.

NO: Merton H. Miller, a Nobel Prize–winning economist, contends that derivatives allow financial players to hedge their bets more efficiently, and in doing so they make the world a safer place.

$\mathbf{D}$erivatives are financial instruments whose returns are linked to the performance of an underlying asset, such as mortgages, bonds, currencies, or commodities. Although the commodities market has been around a long time and has had its share of criticism over the years, it operates on agreed contracts, contracts for the purchase of a commodity (eggs, coffee, pork bellies) at least grounded in reality and recognizable in ordinary life. If you buy futures in eggs, for instance, speculating that the price will go up at some future date, but you forget to sell as the market moves, when your date arrives, so will your eggs. This might become a big problem if you are not in need of a truckload of eggs. This possibility tends to regulate the futures commodities markets. The possibility of the commodity being delivered takes buying futures out of the realm of "gambling": the intent of the contract at purchase time (to make a profit by an advantageous trade) is, according to the law, limited by the words of the contract and the existence of a real commodity.

But derivatives operate without such an agreed contract; they are risk bets to hedge against changes in the marketplace. While derivatives are linked to performance of underlying assets, such as mortgages or bonds, that linkage has nothing to do with the way they operate. Take the case of Orange County, California, which went into default because its speculators bought derivative securities linked to movements in a multiple of the difference between Swiss and U.S. interest rates. As the Swiss and U.S. interest rates changed, so did the amount of difference between them; as the direction of the U.S. interest rates changed versus the Swiss, Orange County won or lost its bets on (a multiple of) the amount of the change. If the interest rates had moved in the right direction, the yield on the investment would have been very high. As it happened, U.S. interest rates were raised by the Federal Reserve to clamp down on inflation for most of 1994 and the first months of 1995. That was the wrong direction for Orange County; the rate hikes sent the value of Orange County's portfolio on a downward spiral (keep in mind if the yield is high, so are the risks).

What should be done to prevent this type of disaster? Some suggest telling the states and counties exactly what they can and cannot buy. Instead, Arthur Levitt, the chairman of the Securities and Exchange Commission, has asked state and local governments to monitor those who manage and invest the taxpayers' money. It is not now known if that request will be sufficient to protect local governments from uninformed or unscrupulous investment advisors.

As you read the following selections, keep in mind the reasons for the stock and commodities markets in the first place—to help business and farmers raise cash—but always to help investors to make a profit. Contrast these with the objectives in the management of public funds (security and liquidity). The history of these markets, especially of the events that led to their present regulation, suggests that the stock market, especially in the complex areas of options, futures, and derivatives in general, is a financial and ethical minefield. This may help you understand the ethical complexities of the exchanges, their investment houses, banks, and financial advisors. The investment houses are all in the business of giving professional advice (with the client's interest at heart) and selling products to the public with their own profit foremost. How can these two goals be compatible? The public in many cases has little or no understanding of the products and the risks involved and depends on these professionals to give them good advice.

What weight should be given the values of freedom and justice in investment activities? Should government curb, with careful regulation, the activities of those investment experts who manage the public money—more than those who speculate for their own profit or for the profit of private clients? Why, or why not? When looking at government regulation of the financial markets, think about what it could do to the choices for investors and the ability to raise money by those who wish to expand or gain from these markets. Can government do a better job of protecting the public till than a well-trained professional who knows the local territory? Can, or should, government save one from oneself or save the community from the consequences of its own bad judgment? If so, how can this be done most effectively?

F.I.A.S.C.O.

Keeping tabs on the derivatives obituaries column is nearly a full-time job these days, especially with the recent surge in activity. By the time you read this, the market is likely to be more than $100 trillion (it was estimated at $65–80 trillion as of mid-1998), headed for the astronomical $1 quadrillion mark. I can't resist the urge to abuse the late Senator Everett Dirksen's famous quote: a quadrillion here and a quadrillion there and pretty soon you're talking about some serious money.

⚖

... Derivatives, once again, are a horror show. The structured notes and leveraged swaps that rocked the financial markets with billion-dollar losses in 1994–95 are back. The same specters that haunted, and then broke Barings, and Orange County, and took a slice out of Procter & Gamble have returned from the dead. And in my opinion, the sequel is even more scary.

Derivatives remain unseen, yet ubiquitous. Time bombs are ticking away, concealed in the underbelly of our investment portfolios. Whether you realize it or not, most of you investors continue to have exposure to derivatives, typically through investments in mutual funds (yes, even Fidelity) and pension funds (yes, even TIAA/CREF). I was not happy to discover that my new hometown, sleepy San Diego, has a $3.3 billion public-employee pension fund chock full of derivatives. I own derivatives, indirectly, through a mutual fund I bought, and I'll bet you own them, too. If you still don't believe me, just call your mutual fund manager or read your prospectus. And get ready to weep.

Of course, Wall Street isn't weeping one tear. Derivatives continue to be hugely profitable for bankers, in part because fund managers who buy derivatives will pay a premium to take on risks they can hide from shareholders, and in part because other buyers don't fully understand what they are buying. Derivatives have helped Wall Street to its best year ever—bonuses were up more than 30 percent last year. Sellers of derivatives are ecstatic. Many buyers are happy, for now; ignorance is bliss. Yet 70 percent of derivatives professionals say they expect big losses in the coming year.

From Frank Partnoy, *F.I.A.S.C.O.: The Inside Story of a Wall Street Trader* (Penguin Books, 1999). Copyright © 1997, 1999 by Frank Partnoy. Reprinted by permission of W. W. Norton & Company, Inc.

Opinion about derivatives remains sharply divided. George Soros, billionaire trader, warns that derivatives traders cause instability that will "destroy society." ... [I believe that] derivatives carry hidden seeds of destruction, and that no one truly understands their risks. ...

Asian Fallout

Much of the [recent] derivatives action... has been in Asia, where the derivatives market is estimated to be in the tens of trillions of dollars, though no one really knows how big it is. Market participants are worried, and Hong Kong pension fund regulators even proposed forbidding derivatives use. Japan and the Asian "tigers"—Korea, Indonesia, Malaysia, the Philippines, Singapore, Taiwan, Thailand—were doing just fine until the summer of 1997. On July 2, 1997, Thailand, which had pegged its currency, the baht, to a basket of foreign currencies, based on Thailand's trade with other countries, finally had to eliminate the peg. The baht plunged more than 17 percent against the U.S. dollar that day, just as the Mexican Peso had collapsed on December 20, 1994. The effects were cataclysmic.

[For instance, there was a] mouth-watering Thai baht structured note. ... That note, and similar foreign exchange-linked notes, were issued by highly-rated corporations and government sponsored enterprises, such as General Electric Credit Corporation and the Federal Home Loan Banks. The notes looked safe, and paid a deliciously high coupon. But if you were an unlucky holder of a Thai baht structured note on July 2, 1997, you were suffering from more than mild digestive problems. A mountain of pink bismuth powder couldn't block the financial dysentery as the note ripped through the innards of your balance sheet, faster than a plate of bad paed ped.

The other Asian tigers followed Thailand into the dumpster. Asian banks had been feasting, like the fat Mexican banks of the early 1990s, making leveraged bets on their own markets and currencies using equity swaps, total return swaps, options, futures, forwards, and more complex derivatives. Now, they faced annihilation. Within months, the foreign currency value of investments in East Asia dropped by 50 percent or more.

Structured notes and swaps did far more than cause localized commercial collywobbles in Asia. They ensured that the ripple effects of the baht devaluation would reach well beyond the domestic markets. If a butterfly flapping its wings in Thailand can affect weather in the U.S., imagine what a currency devaluation can do. Individual investors, money managers, even hedge fund operators throughout the world were hurting.

Most of the derivatives causing the pain were "over-the-counter" rather than traded on any exchange. That means, for example, that Asian banks engaging in swaps had a counterparty, typically a U.S. or European bank, who expected repayment on the swap, just as I would expect repayment if you and I had bet $10 on whether the Asian markets would falter. In other words, the Asian banks and companies hadn't lost money to any centralized exchange; they had lost money to other companies, primarily Western banks. The bottom line was that if the Asian banks went bust, their counterparties might lose the entire amounts the Asian banks owed.

The over-the-counter nature of these derivatives trades created enormous potential for loss. For example, banking regulators warned that U.S. banks had more than $20 billion of exposure to Korea. One Korean investment firm, SK Securities Company, had bet with J. P. Morgan that the Thai baht would rise relative to the Japanese yen, and when the baht collapsed, SK owed J. P. Morgan about $300 million. Other banks—including Citicorp, Chase Manhattan, and Bankers Trust—each disclosed more than a billion dollars of exposure to Asia. This exposure to a counterparty's inability or unwillingness to repay is called "credit risk." Credit risk is a banal non-issue irrelevant to a counterparty until a so-called credit event actually occurs; then, credit risk is a central issue mattering all too much. Credit risk from derivatives was a major reason the U.S. was so concerned about rescuing Asia (and its banking counterparties) from financial meltdown.

One man who was suffering more than most during this period of financial indigestion in Asia was Victor Niederhoffer, the celebrated, and often barefooted, squash/derivatives maestro and hedge fund manager extraordinaire. Niederhoffer's imbroglio illustrates the interconnectedness of modern capital markets, and the amazing velocity of investments in derivatives.

In June 1997, Niederhoffer was on top of the world. His excellent autobiography, *The Education of a Speculator*, was selling well, and he was managing more than $100 million of investments, including much of his own considerable wealth. He was both popular and respected, and had an incredible track record: returns of 30 percent per year for fifteen years, with a 1996 return of 35 percent.

Unfortunately, Niederhoffer also had made a big bet on the baht. And when the Thai butterfly flapped its wings, he lost about $50 million, almost half of his fund.

Derivatives traders who lose $50 million, or more, seem to follow a pattern. I used to fall into that pattern playing blackjack in Las Vegas. Perhaps you've had a similar experience. You play a hand of blackjack for $100, thinking it wouldn't kill you to lose that much money. You lose the hand. Then, you play another hand, thinking it wouldn't be a big deal to lose $200. Besides, maybe you'll win the hand and get back to even. You lose that hand, too. Then, you lose another hand, and another hand, and another. Pretty soon, you're down $500, an amount of money you really would prefer *not* to lose. What do you do? Do you quit? Or course not. You do the opposite. You increase your wagers, and start betting to get even. That's the pattern. You look up to the eye-in-the-sky, and a little voice in your head trembles, "If only I could win that money back, *then* I would stop gambling. Forever."

Imagine adding five zeros to that $500. What does that voice sound like, now? It might sound awfully depressing if the $50 million was your money. But what if the money was, in the words of Justice Louis Brandeis, "other people's money"? Suddenly betting to get even doesn't seem foolish at all. Wouldn't you double-down, at least once, for $50 million of *someone else's* money? Why not? If you win, you're even and no one will ever care about your temporary loss. And if you lose, do you really think it matters much if you lose another $50 million of someone else's money. After the first $50 million, you've pretty much guaranteed that special someone won't be inviting you to Thanksgiving dinner.

So Niederhoffer, like others before him—Nick Leeson of Barings, Joseph Jett of Kidder, Peabody, Yasuo Hamanaka of Sumitomo, Toshihide Iguchi of Daiwa—began betting to get even, taking on additional risk in the hope that he could make back enough money to overcome his losses on the baht. Academics would refer to Niederhoffer, at this point in his life, as a rogue trader.

He had recovered a bit of the Thai loss by September, but was still down about 35 percent for the year. Going into October, Niederhoffer began doubling down by selling put options on the Standard & Poor's 500 index futures contract. This was a truly gutsy move. The S & P 500 index futures contract allows speculators to make leveraged bets on the performance of the S & P 500 index, an index that tracks 500 large stocks. You can sell put options on this contract in the same way you can sell put options on any other instrument.

. . . A put option is the right to sell some underlying financial instrument or index at a specified time and price. In the trader's parlance, or Corvette lingo, if you bought a put option, you might pay $1,000 today for the right to sell a Corvette for $40,000 some time during the next month. You would make money if the price of Corvettes dropped. If the price of a Corvette dropped to $30,000, you would make $10,000—the $40,000 you could sell a Corvette for, using the put option, minus the $30,000 you could buy a Corvette for in the market (less the $1,000 premium you had paid).

Whereas the buyer of a put option wants the price to go down, the seller of a put option wants the price to stay the same or go up—but definitely, *please,* not to go down. The more the price goes down, the more the seller of the put option must pay the buyer. In our example, if the price of Corvettes dropped to $30,000, and we had sold put options on 100 Corvettes, we would lose $900,000 ($1 million less the $100,000 premium we had received). The strategy of selling put options does not carry the one benefit Morgan Stanley touted for some of the riskier products it sold: "downside limited to size of initial investment." In this case, you could lose *more* than everything. A put seller's downside is limited only by the size of his or her imagination (and the fact that prices don't usually drop below zero).

Niederhoffer was looking OK through the weekend of October 25–26. October had not been an especially eventful month, the publication of my book notwithstanding. Niederhoffer was waiting, hoping the options would expire worthless so he could keep the premium and get back closer to even. Remember, he wanted the market to stay the same or go up—but definitely, *please,* not to go down.

On Monday, October 27, 1997, the U.S. stock market plummeted 554 points, or about 7 percent. The S & P index fell 64.67 points to 876.97. It had been almost exactly 10 years since the stock market crash of 1987, dubbed "Black Monday," October 19, 1987. A 7 percent drop didn't meet the definition of market crash, and it certainly couldn't match Black Monday. But for Niederhoffer, that Monday delivered a death blow. By noon, he was broke.

By Wednesday, his funds had been liquidated. The $100 million-plus of his investors' money was gone.

Take a guess at who Niederhoffer's investors were? That's right, believe it or not, my hometown favorite, the $3.3 billion San Diego public-employee pension fund was right there in the thick of it with Niederhoffer's other put option sellers. Well done, San Diego!

NO ↵

Merton H. Miller

Merton H. Miller on Derivatives

$\mathbf{F}$inancial derivatives, for those who may have been too preoccupied with their own concerns to notice, come these days in basically three different flavors, like the quarks in nuclear physics.

Historically, the first derivatives to burst on the scene in their modern form were exchange-traded futures and options in the early 1970s, in Chicago, naturally (though their ancestry traces back to Holland in the seventeenth century and, surprisingly, to Japan at about the same time). Next in time came so-called swaps. Swaps are contracts in which, as the name suggests, two counterparties exchange payment streams, typically a floating interest-rate stream for a fixed-interest rate stream or a stream in dollars for a stream in marks or yen. Finally, and most recently, has come an explosive revival in so-called "structured notes" that might, to take one wild example, let a Brazilian firm, say, borrow at 5% in U.S. dollars plus the amount by which the returns on the Brazilian stock market exceed that on the Mexican market. These customized structured deals, admittedly, may sometimes strike outsiders as a bit bizarre, but the fact remains that the use of derivatives of all three flavors has grown rapidly over the last twenty years. And why is that?

Their use has grown, I insist, because they have satisfied an important business need. They have allowed firms and banks, at long last, to manage effectively and at low cost, business and financial risks that have plagued them for decades, if not for centuries.

But despite what I and most other economists, at least of the Chicago variety, see as the social benefits of these financial derivatives, they have, let us face it, also been getting a very bad press recently. Everyone by now surely has read about Procter and Gamble, that sweet little old Ivory soap company that dropped $150 million or so on derivatives, and about the big German conglomerate, Metallgesellschaft, that supposedly dropped ten times that amount on oil futures. Derivatives horror stories have created the impression that derivatives have brought us close to a financial Chernobyl that threatens to bring the whole economy down around our ears unless derivatives are brought under strict government control and supervision.

From Merton H. Miller, *Merton H. Miller on Derivatives* (John Wiley, 1997). Copyright © 1997 by Merton H. Miller. Reprinted by permission of John Wiley & Sons, Inc. Notes omitted.

The Real Threat: Derivatives or Central Banks?

So, before going any further, let me emphasize that no serious danger of a derivatives-induced financial collapse really exists. Note, however, how I have carefully phrased that: no *derivatives-induced* financial collapse. Firms will continue to lose money on bad judgment and bad derivatives deals, just as they always have in deals on ordinary assets like stocks and real estate. And a major crack in one of the world's financial markets is always possible. But crashes in financial markets are not exogenous calamities like earthquakes. They are *policy* disasters, tracing not to transactions between *private-sector* parties, but to the deliberately deflationary actions of a central bank somewhere, usually overreacting to its previous policy errors in the other direction.

A classic example, of course, has been the turmoil in the U.S. bond market since the spring of 1994 after our Federal Reserve System suddenly nudged up short-term interest rates. And why did the Fed feel it had to nudge them up? Because the Fed had previously driven short rates far too low, hoping that lower short rates would lead to lower long rates which in turn, the Fed hoped, would pull the U.S. economy more rapidly out of recession. That announced policy of driving interest rates down gave the banks, the hedge funds, and the big institutional investors generally what seemed a surefire, money-coining strategy: borrow short and lend long. The low short rates kept their cost of borrowing small and the Fed's fears of throttling the then still-weak economic expansion would keep them low. Prices of long-term bonds, then, could go only one way: up. For more than a year, those leveraged bets on falling long-term interest rates paid off handsomely.

But the Fed eventually discovered, or should I say rediscovered, that the short-term rate could be held below its warranted level only by rapidly expanding the money supply and risking a resurgence of price inflation. The Fed thereupon suddenly stepped on the monetary brakes by raising short-term interest rates, hoping that its anti-inflation rhetoric would keep the more inflation-sensitive long-term rates from rising. But the Fed guessed wrong. Long-term rates rose right along with short-term rates and blood began to flow on Wall Street (and in Orange County). So far, the fallout on the U.S. real economy from the Fed's monetary tightening has been small. But more tightening may be on the way and we must not become complacent. We need only look to the mismanagement by the Federal Reserve System in the early 1930s to see how much permanent damage a central bank can inflict on an economy.

The Current State of Derivatives Regulation

For what further comfort it may offer to those worried about the dangers from unregulated derivatives, let me also assure them that derivatives already are very extensively regulated. The futures exchanges, for example, are regulated (and very heavy-handedly) by the Commodities Futures Trading Commission, or CFTC, one of the largest producers of bureaucratic red tape this side of Japan. The securities broker/dealer firms like Goldman Sachs or Salomon Brothers are regulated by the Securities and Exchange Commission, or SEC, an agency with a world-recognized reputation as a tough cop.

On that score, however, some critics, including our U.S. General Accounting Office, have complained recently that while the SEC may regulate the dealer firms and their capital requirements, the agency has no special or specific requirements for their derivatives operations. But if you know how the derivatives business is structured in Wall Street these days, that line of argument by our GAO makes no real sense. The name of the game in the derivatives business is *credit quality*. Nobody will deal swaps with you if you can't convince them that you have adequate capital, or unless you post substantial collateral if you don't. For further reassurance to the particularly credit-sensitive sector of the market, moreover, some of the big brokerage firms have even split parts of their derivatives business off into separate subsidiaries, with dedicated capital of their own. These "subs" have received triple-A credit ratings from the private credit-rating agencies like Moody's and Standard & Poors, agencies who do a more stringent capital and credit analysis, incidentally, than the SEC ever has or ever could. And far from suggesting any looming capital inadequacy, the ratings of the subs, in fact, are actually higher than that of the banks that do most of the derivatives business.

Those banks, moreover, which currently account for about 70% of the derivatives business, are themselves heavily regulated, to say the least. The derivatives activities of every bank dealer are regulated by at least one, and sometimes by as many as three, separate regulators. The bank officers often find themselves saying good-bye to one group of examiners going out the back door just as another group is being ushered in at the front door.

The S&L Crisis and the Supposed Dangers of Inadequate Regulation

But if derivatives, as I insist, are already adequately (or more than adequately) regulated, how do I answer people who say we've heard that same talk about overregulation back in the early 1980s when the savings and loan industry was insisting that *its* regulation was adequate. And look what happened.

But are the two cases really parallel? Very definitely not. The so-called deregulation of S&Ls in the early 1980s was less a matter of allowing free market magic to do its work than an attempt by Congress to prolong the life of an industry that a truly free market would have ended years before. The industry was not allowed to die a natural death because residential housing and everything connected with it had become a sacred cow of U.S. politics. Congress in the 1930s and even more so in the years after World War II was encouraging U.S. citizens to buy homes and finance them with thirty-year fixed-rate mortgages from local savings and loan associations funded by insured deposits. By the mid 1960s however, as inflation and hence interest rates began to rise in the United States, the S&Ls found themselves having to pay 6% or more to keep from losing their deposits, while the thirty-year fixed-rate mortgages on their books had been made years before at 4 to 5%. By the late 1970s, in fact, as inflation accelerated, more of the industry had become technically insolvent on a mark-to-market basis.

At that point, rather than face up to closing down the politically potent local S&L industry and bailing out their federally insured depositors with tax money, Congress gave the S&Ls one last chance to stay alive, by allowing them to invest in more than just the mortgages on single-family homes, their traditional market niche. They could now invest in commercial real estate, luxury condos, and resort properties, a form of diversification which, by itself, might not have been so troublesome. But the S&Ls were allowed to support commercial property developments of that kind, without having to face the normal market tests for funding such risky ventures. Congress, in the dark of night (that is to say without holding hearings or any public debate), had raised the limit on government guaranteed deposit accounts of S&Ls from $10,000 to $100,000 per *account*. Not per individual or per family, but per account. In today's prices that would be equivalent to close to $200,000 per account, a non-trivial sum. S&Ls could thus raise virtually unlimited funds for speculative property development merely by offering to pay fifty or seventy-five basis points above the going deposit rate. Deposit brokers would then funnel them money from all over the country. The depositors didn't ask any questions about how the S&Ls hoped to earn those extra fifty or seventy-five basis points. Why should they care? The U.S. government was guaranteeing their deposits.

To cite the S&L bailouts as grounds for regulating derivatives is thus not only to miss the point of that government-spawned disaster, but is doubly ironic. Financial derivatives, if they had only been more readily available in the early 1980s, could have kept the S&L industry viable as a residential housing lender without massive life support from subsidized deposits. If maturity mismatch between floating-rate deposits and fixed-rate mortgages is your problem, then interest-rate swaps and futures and options can be your solution. Indeed, that is precisely the direction in which what's left of the S&L industry is going at the moment. The industry has also been helped, of course, by the development of variable-rate mortgages and even more by its ability to securitize its locally raised mortgages by bundling them into mortgage pools. Those pools in turn, serve as inputs to still another class of derivatives securities, the so-called CMOs or collateralized mortgage obligations. CMOs support many new strategies for controlling interest-rate risks, though, alas, also some new ways for the unskilled or the unlucky to lose big chunks of money.

Derivatives and the Safety of the Banking System

Not only are the S&Ls much safer institutions today, thanks to derivatives, than they were in the past, but so too are the commercial banks. Despite all the hullabaloo in the press, and all the bad publicity surrounding derivatives, banks are safer today, not riskier. And for several reasons.

For one thing, the customers in a bank's derivatives book are now much better credit risks, on the whole, than those in their regular loan portfolio. Top-rated, blue-chip clients had been leaving the banks steadily for many years in favor of public-market funding, especially commercial paper. Swaps and options have brought them back. And even for some of the banks' so-so, intermediate credits, swaps strengthen a bank's hand on long-term fixed rate credits. They let a bank pull the plug on a firm when its condition is just beginning to deteriorate, without having to wait for an actual default.

The swaps and options book, moreover, is typically highly diversified whereas banks' commercial portfolios are often heavily concentrated by region, or by industry (like Continential Bank and its oil credits) or by foreign country (like Citibank and its Latin American credits). And, of course, as noted earlier for the S&Ls, a bank's swaps and derivatives book can be managed to control interest-rate risk. If more of a bank's customers want to take the floating-rate side than want the fixed-rate side of interest-rate swaps, the bank simply lays off the excess directly with other dealers who happen to have the reverse position. Or, I am happy to say, the bank can make an offsetting transaction using exchange-traded financial futures, like the Eurodollar futures of the Chicago Mercantile Exchange, or CME.

But if swaps and derivatives have really made the financial system safer, not riskier, as I have claimed, why are we hearing so many calls these days for more regulation? Part of the answer, I suspect, comes from misunderstanding by the public and the financial press about how serious the risks really are.... A telltale sign of how deep those misunderstandings go is the almost universal practice of citing the nominal size of swaps outstanding and treating that number as if it were the amount at risk. Last year the conventional number was $8 trillion, this year it's $12 trillion. But whether eight or twelve, it's a huge amount. If it really did measure the risk exposure, it would be hard to blame people for being worried.

Those multitrillion dollar numbers, however, are just bookkeeping entries, or better, score-keeping entries, not transaction amounts. And similarly for interest-rate swaps. What gets swapped is *not* the trillions of principal amount, but only the *interest* on the principal, which is an order of magnitude smaller. And even that is an overstatement, because only the *difference* between the fixed and the floating rates is exchanged, which cuts it in half again. So we're talking not about $12 trillion at risk, but something like 1 to 2% of that amount, which is certainly not trivial, but it's not terribly frightening either, given the elaborate risk-control programs installed by all the major banks and dealers.

POSTSCRIPT

Should Prudent Managers Avoid Purchasing Derivative Instruments?

W hat is happening in the financial markets? Are derivatives a safe hedge in large portfolios to reduce the risks of institutional investors? Is this true, and does it apply to the small investor in a mutual fund who buys derivatives as a hedge against loss? Experienced investment advisors characterize the risk-taking "day traders" as "the folks who missed the bus to Atlantic City (and its gambling casinos)." Would a comparison to poker or blackjack at the many casinos around the country be a better way of describing the stock and commodities markets and the many investment advisors, with their "unique" investment instruments, who operate in these markets? Can the Securities and Exchange Commission (SEC) and/or the government keep these markets from being "casinos" without eliminating the "free market" system upon which they operate?

The derivatives question may best be seen as part of a larger question: In a free market economy is self-regulation and consumer choice sufficient to protect the public, or must the government take responsibility for protecting the common good?

Suggested Readings

Tim W. Ferguson, "The Dynamite and the Derivatives," *The Wall Street Journal* (February 28, 1995).

Roger Lowenstein, "Will Orange County Squeeze California?" *The Wall Street Journal* (June 15, 1995).

Suzanne McGee, "Derivatives Could Hedge Career Growth," *The Wall Street Journal* (August 24, 1995).

Donald G. Simonson, "Vignettes From the Derivatives 'Crisis'," *United States Banker* (September 1994).

Jeffrey Taylor, "Securities Firms Agree to Set Controls on Derivatives," *The Wall Street Journal* (March 9, 1995).

R. S. Wurman, A. Siegel, and K. M. Morris, *The Wall Street Journal Guide to Understanding Money and Markets* (Prentice Hall, 1990).

ISSUE 8

Does the Enron Collapse Show That We Need More Regulation of the Energy Industry?

YES: Richard Rosen, from "Regulating Power: An Idea Whose Time Is Back," *The American Prospect* (March 25, 2002)

NO: Christopher L. Culp and Steve H. Hanke, from "Empire of the Sun: An Economic Interpretation of Enron's Energy Business," *Policy Analysis* (February 20, 2003)

ISSUE SUMMARY

YES: Writer Richard Rosen contends that the disastrous collapse of the Enron energy company—accompanied by soaring prices in California, disruptions of the market in the United States and abroad, and accusations of fraud all around—means that America needs more government oversight.

NO: Christopher L. Culp, adjunct professor of finance at the Graduate School of Business at the University of Chicago, and Steve H. Hanke, professor of applied economics at the Johns Hopkins University, maintain that it was unwise regulation that caused the Enron problem in the first place. They conclude that only deregulation will let the market clear up the problems with the industry.

Many people since free-market economist Adam Smith have acknowledged that no matter what the virtues of the free market—and they are many—there are areas where the public needs protection. For example, the state, in order to be called a state, must assert and maintain an absolute monopoly on the use of force, not just force that would deprive of life, health, or liberty, but any force at all. Force, therefore, or the threat of violence, cannot be part of any legal negotiation. For another instance, there are products so dangerous to human health and welfare that by law they cannot be sold on the open market under any circumstances, even though a high demand and lucrative trade could be predicted. These include hand grenades, crack cocaine, and canisters of poison gas. Other restrictions on open trade include drugs available only by prescription, bans on the sale of wild or endangered animals or their parts, and bans on pesticides that endure in the environment. The state creates such restrictions in the exercise of its inalienable "police power," the responsibility to protect the health, welfare, and morals of the people. The exercise of that responsibility in most developed nations includes the provision of a free educational system and free health care for all citizens; the United States, as a matter of policy, has exempted itself from the latter and, according to some, seems to be aiming at phasing out the former.

At least since the beginning of the twentieth century, state monopoly and regulation has been extended to a large variety of "utilities"—public goods that cannot fall into private hands without putting the public at serious risk of exploitation. These include transportation corridors (e.g., roads, railways, and all waterways), communications pathways (e.g., airwaves, telegraph lines, and telephone services), and all provision of water and energy (e.g., heat and light). For most of that period, at least a portion of most of those services has been in private hands, but all were subject to regulation of rates and choice of services to provide and areas to be served. They were also expected to serve the public interest. Evidence to the contrary could result in government intervention at any time.

Deregulation began as part of the antiregulatory climate during the Reagan administration, in the period when companies were led by mergers and acquisitions departments. At that time Kenneth Lay took over the Enron company's predecessor and rapidly picked up several more unexciting pipeline companies. He cultivated friends in high places and furthered his deregulation agenda all through the Clinton administration. (In 1993, for instance, Wendy Gramm, wife of Senator Phil Gramm (R-TX), ushered a ruling exempting futures contracts from government oversight through the Commodity Futures Trading Commission, which she chaired. Shortly thereafter, she left that post and accepted a position on Enron's board of directors.) Lay, and Enron generally, spent a large amount of money on contributions to political campaigns, including at least $6 million to federal candidates and parties as well as $1.8 million or more to candidates for state office. Very large contributions went to George W. Bush's presidential campaign. By the time Bush was elected, Lay was a close friend—and Enron was the most persistent and loudest voice for deregulation.

Was deregulation a good idea? In California, deregulation led to skyrocketing prices, draining the state's coffers. Enron profited as a result. Is this just free enterprise at work? There are two sides to this dispute, which were both silenced on October 18, 2002, when Enron officers pleaded guilty to conspiracy to manipulate energy prices in California. Maybe the damage to California was due to regulation, maybe it was due to deregulation, but many would agree that probably it was due to criminal conspiracies undertaken by criminals under cover of the deregulation agenda. We will have to await a more honest trial of deregulation to discover the public's real best interest.

Richard Rosen  **YES**

Regulating Power: An Idea
Whose Time Is Back

Ignored in the scandal about Enron's off-the-books deals is the fact that Enron's core businesses—trading and selling energy—made little economic sense. Starting in the early 1990s, Enron claimed it could make electricity generation more efficient through a system to trade more electric power than regulated utilities. To that end, the company urged the Federal Energy Regulatory Commission (FERC) to promote the deregulation of wholesale electric markets.

But whenever there was an opportunity to reduce consumers' electric rates by trading power at the wholesale level, the old regulated electric utilities had always done so. Indeed, most electric utilities had already grouped themselves into "power pools" or other voluntary energy-swapping systems set up to trade power at its cost of production—the cheapest approach for consumers. If we calculate the relative costs of producing and selling electricity, new wholesale traders like Enron could have reduced our national average electric rates by perhaps 1 percent, if that.

So most of the supposed efficiencies of deregulation were already being realized by regulated utilities. To the extent that Enron could reap large profits, it was only by amassing market power, monopolizing transmission lines, and taking advantage of temporary scarcity—thus raising prices and frustrating the whole supposed point of deregulation. Any efficiency gains were more than wiped out by the cost of administering a new, complex trading system pursuing its own quest for profit.

When it lobbied state legislatures and public-utility commissions to deregulate electric utilities, Enron promised to sell retail electricity to all types of customers. Instead, because it was too costly to compete with traditional utilities for small customers, Enron wound up selling retail electricity primarily to large industrial and commercial companies under long-term contracts. Because government takes ultimate responsibility for the power supply, even in states that have deregulated generation, utilities will remain providers of last resort for at least the next few years. Regulated retail rates, meanwhile, have always been a fallback option for large and small consumers. Enron and other similar companies could seldom beat the regulated price.

From Richard Rosen, "Regulating Power: An Idea Whose Time Is Back," *The American Prospect*, vol. 13, no. 6 (March 25, 2002). Copyright © 2002 by *The American Prospect*, 5 Broad Street, Boston, MA 02109. Reprinted by permission.

Ultimately, Enron never made a profit in its retail business. The costs of gaining market share were just too high—and they were probably hidden by some of Enron's now famous off-balance-sheet debt. In some cases, very large customers saved a few percentage points on their electricity bills, but often only until wholesale prices rose, forcing them to turn back to the regulated utilities for the best rates.

The small savings that deregulation might deliver to some customers must be weighed against the higher costs to others—and against the huge risks of overcharges like those seen during the California debacle, well before Enron's collapse. Analysts who deny that Enron was a failure of deregulation, or who paint Enron as just an isolated case of corporate mismanagement, forget that the firm never realized its original promises—even though deregulated electricity sales, at both the wholesale and retail levels, were its primary reason for being.

How, then, should we regulate electricity? Contrary to the current fashion, our old system—state regulation of vertically integrated electric utilities—makes sense. Regulators need to stress state-of-the-art, "least cost" planning for new investments in generation and transmission. Traditional regulation means that utilities charge consumers their costs plus a reasonably low regulated return on equity.

Utilities should be grouped into power pools—like those we've had in the Northeast—in order to make possible economically efficient sharing of their generating plants. Under a regulated system, concentrated market power is a strength, not a threat, because utilities are prohibited from gouging consumers.

It turns out that it is not economically efficient to divide electric-utility services and create an unregulated market for each. We probably don't even need a competitive wholesale power market. Ironically, by the early 1990s many state regulatory commissions were getting quite good at keeping electric rates in check, thanks in part to growing investments in energy conservation. It was the big industrial customers who thought that they could get better deals in a deregulated market for electricity. On the whole, they didn't. While co-generation and other energy-saving technology surely make sense, deregulation doesn't.

Christopher L. Culp and
Steve H. Hanke

 **NO**

Empire of the Sun: An Economic Interpretation of Enron's Energy Business

Executive Summary

The collapse of Enron Corporation has been portrayed as the result of accounting fraud and greed. Not everything that Enron did, however, was wrong or fraudulent. Fraud contributed to the timing of Enron's failure but was not the root cause of that failure. In analyzing Enron, it is critically important to distinguish what Enron did wrong from what it did right.

Enron's basic business strategy, known as "asset lite," was legitimate and quite beneficial for the marketplace and consumers. By combining a small investment in a capital-intensive industry such as energy with a derivatives-trading operation and a market-making overlay for that market, Enron was able to transform itself from a small, regional energy market operator into one of America's largest companies.

Enron contributed to the creation of the natural gas derivatives market, and, for a while, it was the sole market maker, entering into price risk management contracts with all other market participants. Its physical market presence, as a wholesale merchant of natural gas and electricity, placed the Houston-based company in an ideal position to discover and transmit to the market relevant knowledge of energy markets and to make those markets more efficient.

When Enron applied that same strategy in other markets in which it had no comparative informational advantage or deviated from the asset-lite strategy, it had to incur significant costs to create the physical market presence required to rectify its relative lack of market information. The absence of a financial market overlay in several of those markets further prevented Enron from recovering its costs. It was at that point that Enron abused accounting and disclosure policies to hide debt and cover up the fact that its business model did not work in those other areas.

For its innovations, Enron should be commended; for their alleged illegal activities, Enron's managers should be prosecuted to the full extent of the law. But under no circumstance should Enron's failure be used as an excuse to enact policies and regulations aimed at eliminating risk taking and economic failure,

From Christopher L. Culp and Steve H. Hanke, "Empire of the Sun: An Economic Interpretation of Enron's Energy Business," *Policy Analysis,* no. 470 (February 20, 2003). Adapted from Christopher L. Culp and William A. Niskanen, eds., *Corporate Aftershock: The Public Policy Lessons From the Collapse of Enron and Other Major Corporations* (John Wiley, 2003). Copyright © 2003 by Christopher L. Culp and William A. Niskanen. Reprinted by permission of John Wiley & Sons, Inc.

because unless a firm takes the risk of failure, it will never earn the premium of success. As was demonstrated in the case of Enron, markets—not politicians—are the best judges of success and failure.

Introduction

By the time the Enron Corporation filed for Chapter 11 bankruptcy protection on December 2, 2001, virtually everyone with a television set knew that things were not as they had once seemed in Houston. How could a company go from a market capitalization of more than $100 billion and being ranked fifth in the *Fortune 500* list to bust within two years? How could a stock that had seen highs of nearly $90 per share become a penny stock in record time? How could the six-time consecutive winner (1996–2001) of *Fortune's* "most innovative company in the United States" have engineered its own financial destruction? *And more important, what can be done to make sure this never happens again?*

One must be careful, however, when defining "this" in the phrase "make sure this never happens again." Not everything Enron ever did, after all, was illegal, unethical, or even questionable. In fact, what actually caused Enron to fail is still subject to contentious debate. It is clear, however, that Enron did not fail because it was engaged in commercial and merchant commodity businesses.[1] Nor did a "rogue trader" or Enron's use of creative and sometimes-complex financial contracts bring Enron to its knees. Nor, finally, did Enron's corrupt financial activities—concealing its true indebtedness, lining the pockets of select senior managers at the expense of shareholders, hiding major losses, and the like—cause Enron to fail.[2] Enron's financial deception undoubtedly allowed it to remain in business longer than an otherwise similar firm engaged in accurate financial disclosures might have, but that is a question of timing alone and not causality.

This [selection] argues that Enron's ultimate financial failure most likely occurred for the very same reason that WorldCom, Global Crossing, and many other firms periodically have gone bankrupt or run into trouble. In short, those firms all lacked the ability to identify their true comparative advantage. In some cases that meant Enron overinvested in new markets and technologies that never took off; in other cases it simply meant that the company overestimated the value that it could add. But is *that* something that new policies and regulations should strive to ensure "never happens again"? Or, as argued in this study, is this aspect of Enron's failure simply a testimonial to the fact that competitive markets are effective judges of success and failure?

This study begins with an overview of Enron to stress that it was first and foremost an energy business that employed an innovative "asset-lite" strategy that accounted for many of its genuinely successful years. A discussion of those businesses in which Enron failed follows because it is in those areas where Enron departed from the successful asset-lite strategy employed in the energy business. The next section formally frames Enron's asset-lite strategy in the context of competitive economic theory. Standard "neoclassical" economic models do not explain firms such as Enron, and consequently a more "disequilibrium-oriented," or "neo-Austrian," approach is required. The [selection] concludes by considering whether Enron's failure *as a business* either offers lessons for other firms or provides a proscriptive case for greater regulation.

Neoclassical vs. Neo-Austrian Economic Theory

In addition to providing an analysis of Enron's business strategy through the lens of economic theory, this study illustrates the limitations of the traditional neoclassical theory of the price system for explaining entrepreneurship and innovation—terms that, despite Enron's illegal and fraudulent activities in some areas, nevertheless do describe that company in other areas. The neoclassical perspective views markets as existing in a stationary state in which the relevant knowledge about demand and supply is known; market prices are static, or given; and data are available to be used by individuals and firms. In this world without change, there is no need to ask how that stationary state came about. That knowledge simply falls into the category of irrelevant bygones.

Neoclassical economics does, of course, also deal with change. It does so by employing comparative statics. For example, we can conceive of a quasi-stationary state in which changes in the relevant knowledge in a market are few and far between, and analysis of the full repercussions is dealt with by evaluating and comparing the stationary states before and after changes in relevant knowledge occur. In the neoclassical world, prices act as signposts, guiding consumers to substitute goods for one another and producers to learn which lines of production to abandon or toward which to turn. In this neoclassical conception, the price system acts as a network of communication in which relevant knowledge is transmitted at once throughout markets that jump from one stationary state to the next.

In the neo-Austrian, or disequilibrium-oriented, context, by contrast, the market is viewed as a process that is in a constant state of flux.[3] In consequence, there are no stationary or quasi-stationary states. Indeed, expectations about the current and future state of affairs are always changing because the state of relevant knowledge is always changing. And with changing expectations, market prices are also changing. In consequence, the price system functions as a network for communicating all relevant knowledge. It is also a discovery process that is in continuous motion, working toward creating unity and coherence in the economic system. The speed of adjustment and of the dissemination of knowledge in the price system depends on the scope and scale of the markets, however.

As it relates to the discussion here, the full force of market integration is realized when both spot and forward markets exist. Indeed, the function of forward, or derivatives, markets is to spread relevant knowledge now about what market participants think the future will be. Forward markets connect and integrate those expectations about the future with the present in a consistent manner.[4] Although the future will always remain uncertain, it is possible for individuals to acquire information about the expected future and to adjust their plans accordingly. In addition, they can—via forward markets—express their views about the future by either buying or selling forward. Forward markets, then, bring expectations about the future into consistency with each other

Figure 1

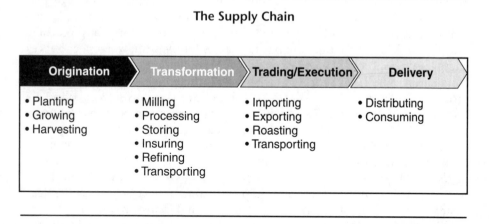

The Supply Chain

Origination	Transformation	Trading/Execution	Delivery
• Planting • Growing • Harvesting	• Milling • Processing • Storing • Insuring • Refining • Transporting	• Importing • Exporting • Roasting • Transporting	• Distributing • Consuming

and also bring forward prices into consistency with spot prices, with the difference being turned into "the basis."

In a neo-Austrian world, relevant knowledge and expectations are in a constant state of flux. And not surprisingly, spot and forward prices, as well as their difference (the basis), are constantly changing, too. Individuals' ever-changing expectations, therefore, keep the market process in motion. In consequence, disequilibrium is a hallmark of the neo-Austrian orientation. While the neo-Austrian market process is in a constant state of flux, it is working toward integrating and making consistent both spot and forward prices.[5]

As the analysis in this [selection] will demonstrate, the explicit incorporation of neo-Austrian variables such as time, knowledge, and market process into the traditional price-theoretic framework for microeconomic analysis is fundamental to understanding fully the financial and commercial market strategies of a company such as Enron.

Enron's Energy Business

Understanding Enron's business model for its core activities requires a brief explanation of how commodity markets function. The usefulness of many physical commodities to producers (e.g., wheat that can be milled into flour) and consumers (e.g., bread) depends on the "supply chain" through which the commodity is transformed from its raw, natural state into something of practical use. Figure 1 shows a typical supply chain for a variety of commodities.

When a commodity moves from one part of the supply chain to the next, transportation, distribution, and delivery services are almost always involved. Those services are the glue that keeps the supply chain linked. To put it simply, Enron was a firm that specialized in those transportation, distribution, and transformation services—often called "intermediate supply chain," or "midstream," services. Accordingly, Enron acted as a wholesale merchant. It acquired the latest information about alternative sources of supply and set prices for goods in a process that would maximize Enron's turnover. Enron was therefore an ideal vehicle for the discovery and transmission of relevant knowledge.

In its *2000 Annual Report,* Enron described itself as "a firm that manages efficient, flexible networks to reliably deliver physical products at predictable prices."[6] This involved four core business areas for the firm: wholesale services, energy services, broadband services, and transportation services.

Enron Wholesale Services was by far the largest—and generally the most profitable—operation of Enron Corp. The bulk of that business involved the transportation, transmission, and distribution of natural gas and electricity. On a volume basis, Enron accounted for more than twice the amount of gas and power delivery of its next-largest competitor in the United States.[7] In addition, Enron maintained an active (and, in several cases, growing) market presence in the supply chains for other commodities, including coal, crude oil, lique-fied natural gas, metals, steel, and pulp and paper. Enron Wholesale Services' customers were generally other large producers and industrial firms.

Enron Energy Services dealt mainly at the retail end of the energy mar-ket supply chains. Enron Wholesale Services' operation might deliver electrical power to a utility, for example, whereas Enron Energy Services might contract directly with a large grocery store chain to supply their power directly.

Enron Broadband was focused on the nonenergy business of broadband services, or the use of fiber optics to transmit audio and video. Capacity on fiber-optic cables is known as "bandwidth." Enron Broadband had three busi-ness goals. The first was to deploy the largest open global broadband network in the world, called the Enron Intelligent Network and consisting of 18,000 miles of fiber-optic cable. The second commercial objective in broadband was for En-ron to dominate the market for buying and selling bandwidth. Finally, Enron sought to become a dominant provider of premium content, mainly through streaming audio and video over the worldwide web.

Enron's fourth operating division was Enron Transportation Services, formerly the Gas Pipeline Group. Enron Transportation Services concentrated on operating interstate pipelines for the transportation of natural gas, long a core competency of Enron. Albeit highly specialized and narrowly focused, gas transportation was perhaps the core brick on which the Enron Corp. foundation was laid.

The Houston Natural Gas Production Company was founded in 1953 as a subsidiary of Houston Natural Gas [HNG] to explore, drill, and transport gas. From 1953 to 1985, the firm underwent a slow but steady expansion, respectably keeping pace with the gradual development of the gas market.

Natural gas was deregulated in the late 1980s and early 1990s. During that time, supplies increased substantially, and prices fell by more than 50 percent from 1985 to 1991 alone. As competition increased, the number of new entrants into various parts of the natural gas supply chain grew dramatically, and many existing firms restructured.

One such restructuring was the acquisition in 1985 of HNG by InterNorth, Inc. The takeover of HNG was largely the brainchild of Kenneth Lay, who had joined HNG as its CEO in 1984. Working closely with Michael Milken, Lay helped structure the InterNorth purchase of HNG as a leveraged buyout relying heavily on junk-bond finance.[8] Lay wrested the position of CEO of the merged firm from InterNorth CEO Samuel Segnar in 1985.

In 1986 InterNorth changed its name to Enron Corporation and incorporated Enron Oil & Gas Company, reflecting its expansion into oil markets to supplement its gas market presence. By then, most firms active in oil markets were also involved in gas—and conversely—given complementarities in exploration, drilling, pumping, distribution, and the like. With the exception of a brief hiatus toward the end, Kenneth Lay remained CEO of Enron Corp. until the firm failed.[9]

In 1985 the Federal Energy Regulatory Commission allowed "open access" to gas pipelines for the first time. In consequence, Enron was able to charge other firms for using Enron pipelines to transport gas, and, similarly, Enron was able to transport gas through other companies' pipelines.

Around that time, Jeffrey Skilling, then a consultant for McKinsey, began working at Enron. He was charged with developing a creative strategy to help Enron—recall, it had just been created through the InterNorth-HNG merger—leverage its presence in the emerging gas market. Skilling argued that the benefits of open access might well be more than offset by the decline in revenues associated with the general decline in prices and margins that greater competition would bring. Add to that Enron's mountain of debt, and Skilling maintained that Enron would not last very long unless a creative solution was identified.

Skilling argued, in particular, that natural gas would never be a serious source of revenues for the firm as long as natural gas was traded exclusively in a "spot" physical market for immediate delivery. Instead, he argued that a key success driver in the coming era of post-deregulation price volatility would be the development of a "derivatives market" in gas in which Enron would provide its customers with various price risk management solutions—forward contracts in which consumers could control their price risk by purchasing gas today at a fixed price for future delivery, and option contracts that allowed customers the right but not obligation to purchase or sell gas at a fixed price in the future.

Viewed from a neo-Austrian perspective, Skilling was functioning as a classic entrepreneur. Once FERC changed the rules of the game and natural gas became deregulated, Skilling spotted an entrepreneurial opportunity, literally, to develop new forward markets. Once forward markets were introduced, individuals could acquire information and knowledge about the future and express their own expectations by either buying or selling forward. Moreover, with both spot and futures prices revealed, "the basis"—the difference between spot and futures prices—could be revealed, and a more unified and coherently integrated natural gas "market" could be created. Although such a new setup would not eliminate risk and uncertainty, it promised to allow much more relevant knowledge to be discovered and disseminated, allowing firms to adjust their expectations and plans accordingly and to manage their risk more effectively.[10]

To create that market in natural gas derivatives, Skilling urged Enron set up a "gasbank." Much as traditional banks intermediate funds, Enron's GasBank intermediated gas purchases, sales, and deliveries by entering into long-term, fixed-price delivery and price risk management contracts with customers. Soon thereafter, other natural gas firms began to offer clients similar risk management solutions. And those producers, in turn, also came to Enron for their risk management needs—that is, to "swap" the exposure to falling prices they created by offering fixed-price forwards to customers back into the "natural" exposure to price increases those producers had before offering their customers fixed-price protection.

Enron acted as a classic market maker, standing ready to enter into natural gas derivatives on "both sides of the market"—that is, both buying and selling gas (or, equivalently, buying and selling at both fixed and floating prices or swapping one for the other). Enron thus became the primary supplier of liquidity to the market, earning the spread between bid and offer prices as a fee for providing the market with liquidity. And in a broader sense, Enron was functioning to spread knowledge about what market participants expected prices to be.

Did that mean Enron was exposed to *all* of the price risks that its trading counter parties were attempting to avoid? No. Many of the contracts into which Enron entered naturally offset one another. True, a consumer seeking to lock in its future energy purchase price with Enron would create a risk exposure for Enron. If prices rose above the fixed price at which Enron agreed to sell energy to a consumer, Enron could lose big money. But that might be offset by a risk exposure to *falling* prices that Enron would assume by agreeing to *buy* that same asset from a producer at a fixed price, thus allowing the producer to hedge its own price risk.[11] Enron was left only with the *residual* risk across all its customer positions in its GasBank, which, in turn, Enron could manage by using derivatives with other emerging market makers, generally known as "swap dealers," or on organized futures exchanges such as the New York Mercantile Exchange.[12]

For a long time, Enron was not merely a market maker for natural gas derivatives—it was *the* market maker. Having virtually created the market, Enron enjoyed wider spreads, higher margins, and more revenues as the sole real liquidity supplier to the market. But that also meant few counterparties existed with which Enron could hedge its own residual risks.

Here is where Enron's physical market presence comes back into the picture. In addition to allowing Enron to discover and reveal a great deal of "local" knowledge, Enron's presence in the physical market meant that it could control some of the residual price risks from its market-making operations. That could be accomplished because of *offsetting positions in its physical pipeline and gas operations*. Consider, for example, a firm that is buying natural gas in Tulsa, Oklahoma, from a pipeline with a supply source in San Angelo, Texas. If that firm seeks to lock in its future purchase price for gas to protect against unexpected price spikes, it might enter into a forward purchase agreement with Enron, thus leaving Enron to bear the risk of a price increase. But if Enron also *owns the pipeline* and charges a price for distribution proportional to the spot price of gas, then the net effect will be roughly offsetting.

Operating that kind of a gas bank also gave Enron very valuable information about the gas market itself. Knowing from its pipeline operations that congestion was likely to occur at Point A, for example, Enron could anticipate price spikes at delivery points beyond Point A arising from the squeeze in available pipeline capacity. And Enron could very successfully "trade around" such congestion points. Conversely, when prices in derivatives markets signaled surplus or deficit pipeline capacity in the financial market, Enron could stand ready to exploit that information in the physical market.

Gradually, thanks to Enron's role as marketmaker, the natural gas derivatives market became increasingly standardized and liquid. Accordingly, relevant knowledge was spread more rapidly and the natural gas market became more integrated and coherent. Enron still offered customized solutions to certain consumers and producers, but much of the volume of the market shifted to exchanges like the NYMEX that began to provide standardized gas futures. Nevertheless, Enron's role as dominant market maker left the GasBank well placed to profit from supplying liquidity to those standardized markets, as well as from retaining much of the custom over-the-counter derivatives-dealing business.

The Enron GasBank division eventually became Enron Gas Services, and later Enron Capital and Trade Resources. In 1990 Jeff Skilling left McKinsey to become a full-time Enron employee, and he later became CEO of both EGS and EC&TR. In early 2001 Skilling replaced Lay as CEO of the whole firm, marking the only time in the history of Enron that Lay was not at the helm.

Asset Lite as a More General Business Strategy

When Skilling formally joined Enron in 1990, he maintained that the future success of the firm would be in repeating the GasBank experience in other markets. To accomplish that, Skilling developed a business concept known as "asset lite" in which Enron would combine small investments in capital-intensive commodity markets with a derivatives-trading and market-making "overlay" for those markets. The idea was to begin with a small capital expenditure that was used to acquire portions of assets and establish a presence in the physical market. That allowed Enron to learn the operational features of the market and to collect information about factors that might affect market price dynamics. Then, Enron would create a new financial market overlaid on top of that underlying physical market presence—a market in which Enron would act as market maker and liquidity supplier to meet other firms' risk management needs. As Skilling described it: "[Enron] is a company that makes markets. We create the market, and once it's created, we make the market."[13] Needless to say, that encapsulates the essence of one of the central roles of an Austrian entrepreneur.

One reason for the appeal of asset lite was that it enabled Enron to exploit some presence in the physical market without incurring huge capital expenditures on bulk fixed investments. Enron quickly discovered that this was best accomplished by focusing on investing in *intermediate* assets in commodity supply chains. In natural gas, this meant that Enron could get the biggest bang for its buck in midstream activities such as transportation, pipeline compression, storage, and distribution. In fact, Enron's Transwestern Pipeline Company eventually became the first U.S. pipeline that was exclusively for transportation, neither pumping gas at the wellhead nor selling it to customers.[14]

Other markets in which Enron applied its asset-lite business expansion strategy with a large degree of success included coal, fossil fuels, and, to some extent, pulp and paper. But after its successful experience with gas, Enron remained much more interested in markets that were being deregulated. Electricity thus became a major focus of the firm in the mid-1990s and was a key success driver for Enron.[15]

Oil and Water Do Not Mix

Throughout its history, Enron's consistent financial and market successes occurred in the energy sector. On more than one occasion, however, Enron tried to expand its business outside the energy area, albeit rarely with any success.

Asset Heavy at Enron International

When it became clear that Kenneth Lay was preparing to turn over the reins in the latter half of the 1990s, an extremely contentious struggle for the leadership of Enron ensued.[16] That occurred in no small part because of the success of Enron GasBank and the power-marketing operations of EC&TR. When the dust settled, Lay named EC&TR CEO and asset-lite inventor Jeff Skilling as the new CEO of Enron Corp. in February 2001. That Skilling would rise to this level, however, was not at all a foregone conclusion. Right up to the announcement date, debates over whose shoulder Kenneth Lay would tap were popular coffee shop banter. Skilling's chief competitor was Rebecca Mark.

In 1993 Mark prevailed upon Lay to establish Enron International, of which she became the first president. Mark did not adhere to an asset-lite strategy. Instead, she pursued an "asset-heavy" strategy of attempting to acquire or develop large capital-intensive projects *for their own sake*. In other words, there was no financial-trading activity overlay component for most of her initiatives. She tried instead to identify projects whose revenues promised to be sizable based purely on the capital investment component with no need for a market maker component. Unlike asset lite, that did not prove to be an area in which Enron Corp. had much comparative advantage.

Water-Trading Rights

The EI operations delved into the asset-heavy water-supply industry. At least here there was some pretense of eventually developing a "water rights trading market," but that possibility was so far down the road that the firm's water investments have to be regarded as largely self-contained capital projects, the largest of which was Azurix and its Wessex Water initiative.

In 1998 Enron spun off the water company Azurix. Enron retained a major interest in the firm, which focused its efforts on water markets in a single purchase—the British firm Wessex Water, for which Enron paid about $1.9 billion. But in this case, deregulation did not help Enron. There was no market-making function and no trading overlay—there was only a British water company serving a market with plummeting prices. (That experience also underscores the fundamentally correct view that Skilling advanced when he was still at McKinsey—namely, that expanding in a deregulating market makes little sense if you are limited to selling a commodity whose price is falling sharply in the spot markets.)

At the same time that the falling prices caused by deregulation in Britain were eating away Wessex's margins, Azurix itself was hit with staggering losses on several of its other operations, mainly in Argentina. In light of that failure, as well as the spectacular failure of EI's Dhabhol, India, power plant project, which may have cost Enron as much as $4 billion, Mark resigned as CEO of Enron International in the summer of 2000. Enron eventually sold Wessex in 2002, about three years after financing its acquisition by Azurix, to a Malaysian firm for $777 million, or $1.1 billion less than it paid for the firm.[17]

The Broadband Black Hole

Like its forays into the water industry, Enron's broadband efforts were plagued with problems from the start. In gas and powermarkets, Enron acquired its physical market presence by investing in assets sold mainly by would-be competing energy companies. It then used those investments to help create and develop a financial market, the growth of which, in turn, helped *increase* the value of Enron's physical investments. But that increase did not come at the expense of Enron's competitors, which in turn were benefiting from the new price risk management market. In broadband technologies, by contrast, Enron's asset-lite effort required the firm to acquire assets not just from competitors but from the *inventors* of the technology. Even then, Enron was paying for a technology that was essentially untested with no guarantee that the "emerging" bandwidth market would bolster asset values. Enron therefore had to pay dearly to acquire a market presence from firms that viewed Enron's effort not as a constructive market-making move but as essentially an intrusive one.

Several other drags on Enron's broadband expansion efforts contributed to its ultimate failure. One was that demand for the technology failed to materialize as expected. Enron is also alleged to have been using the "bandwidth market" to mislead investors—and possibly certain senior managers and directors—about its losses on underlying broadband technologies. On the one hand, Enron was optimistic about the eventual success of the broadband strategy; it "pointed at" significant trading in the bandwidth market. On the other hand, few other market participants observed any appreciable trading activity, and Enron was openly disclosing millions of dollars of losses on its quarterly and annual reports on its broadband efforts. Much of that "market activity" now seems to have come from Enron's "wash," or "roundtrip," trades or transactions in which Enron was essentially trading with itself.[18] To take a simple example, a purchase and sale of the same contract within a one- or two-minute period of time in which prices have not changed will show up as "volume," but the transactions wash out and amount to no real bottom-line profits.

In addition to apparently using wash trades to exaggerate the state of the market's development, Enron was also alleged to have used some of its bandwidth derivatives for "manufacturing" exaggeratedly high valuations for its technological assets. Specifically, Enron and Qwest are under investigation for engaging in transactions with one another that are alleged to have been designed specifically to create artificial mark-to-market valuations. Enron and Qwest engaged in a $500 million bandwidth swap negotiated just prior to the end of the 2001 third-quarter financial reporting period. Many observers would argue that Enron and Qwest were swapping one worthless thing for another worthless thing, given the lack of a market for bandwidth and the lack of *interest* in bandwidth. Nevertheless, both firms apparently used the swaps to justify having acquired a much more valuable asset than the one of which they were getting rid. With essentially no "market," no market prices were available for evaluating the validity of those claims at the time.

The Economics of Asset Lite and "Basis Trading"

Through its investments in the underlying commodity supply chains, the trading-room "overlay" on the physical markets allowed Enron to generate substantial revenues as a market maker. But that was not the only source of profits associated with the asset-lite strategy of combining physical and financial market positions. Specifically, Enron engaged in significant "basis trading." Understanding what that is and when a company might be able to do it profitably is essential for recognizing the differences between businesses on which Enron "made money" and those on which it did not.

To understand the economics of basis trading (sometimes called spread trading), one must first recognize the important finance proposition that commodity derivatives—contracts for the purchase or sale of a commodity in the future—are economic substitutes for physical market operations.[19] Buying a forward oil purchase contract, for example, is economically equivalent to buying and storing oil.[20] In a competitive equilibrium of the physical and derivatives markets, the forward purchase price—denoted $F(t,T)$ and defined as the fixed price negotiated on date t for the purchase of a commodity to be delivered on later date T—can be expressed using the famed "cost of carry model" as[21]

$$F(t,T) = S(t)[1 + b(t,T)]$$

Where $b(t,T)$ $r(t,T) + w(t,T) - d(t,T)$

and $S(t)$ = time t spot price of the commodity to be delivered at T

$r(t,T)$ = the interest rate prevailing from t to T

$w(t,T)$ = the cost of physical storage of the commodity from t to T

$d(t,T)$ = the benefit of holding the commodity from t to T

such that w and d are expressed as a proportion of $S(t)$ and are denominated in time T dollars.

The term $b(t,T)$—the "basis"—is also often called the "net cost of carry," to convey the fact that its three components together makeup the cost of "carrying" the commodity across time and space to the delivery location on future date T. The term $d(t,T)$ that reflects the benefit of physical storage is called the "convenience yield," a concept developed by John Maynard Keynes, Nicholas

Kaldor, Holbrook Working, Michael J. Brennan, and Lester G. Telser.[22] The convenience yield is driven mainly by what Working calls the "precautionary demand for storage," or concerns by firms that unanticipated shocks to demand or supply could precipitate a costly inventory depletion.[23] Airlines store fuel at different airports, for example, to avoid the huge costs of grounding their local fleets in the case of a jet fuel outage. Gas pipeline owners store gas to help ensure that there is always an adequate supply of gas in the lines to maintain the flow and avoid a shutdown.

Keynes, Working, and others have observed how the "supply of storage" (i.e., the amount of a commodity in physical storage) is related to the convenience yield and, by extension, to the "term structure of futures prices."[24] That relation defines the economic linkage between derivatives, physical asset markets, and the allocation of physical supplies across time. Specifically, the supply of storage is directly related to the premium placed on selling inventory *in the future* relative to selling spot *today*. When inventories are high, the *relative* premium that a commodity commands in the future vis-à-vis the present is reasonably small; plenty of the commodity is on hand today to assure producers and intermediaries that a stock-out will not occur, leading to a very low convenience yield. As current inventories get smaller, however, the convenience yield rises (at an increasing rate) and the spot price rises relative to the futures price in order to induce producers to take physical product out of inventory and sell it in the current spot market. A high spot price *alone* would not do that. But a high spot price *relative* to the futures price signals the market that inventories are tight *today* relative to the future.

We can now see more meaningfully where cost-of-carry pricing comes from. Namely, it is the condition that must hold in equilibrium to make market participants indifferent toward physical storage or "synthetic storage" using forwards or other derivatives. Here's how it works. Suppose a firm borrows $S(t)$ in funds at time t and uses the proceeds to buy a commodity worth $S(t)$. At time T, the firm is holding an asset then worth $S(T)$ and repays the money loan. In the interim, the firm incurs physical storage costs w but earns the convenience yield d. Table 1 shows the net effect of this physical storage operation.

In turn, a short position in a forward contract involves no initial outlay and has a time T value of $F(t,T) - S(T)$. From the last line of Table 1, it should be clear that physical storage plus borrowing can be used to hedge the short forward contract (or vice versa). The net of the hedged position is then just $F(t,T) - S(t)[1+r(t,T) + w(t,T) - d(t,T)]$, all of which is known at time t and thus is riskless. If all market participants are price takers and face identical benefits and costs of storage, cost-of-carry futures pricing thus holds purely through the mechanism of arbitrage.

Because not every firm has the same convenience yield or storage costs, however, commodity forward prices are driven to the cost-of-carry expression instead by the dynamics of a competitive equilibrium.[25] To see how it works, suppose the forward purchase price is

$$F° = S(t)[1+b°(t,T)]$$

Table 1

Physical Commodity Storage

	t	T
Money loan		
Borrow dollars	$S(t)$	-
Repay dollars and interest	-	$-S(t)[1+r(t,T)]$
Buy and store the asset		
Buy commodity	$-S(t)$	-
Pay storage costs	-	$-S(t)w(t,T)$
Earn convenience yield	-	$S(t)d\,(t,T)$
Still own the commodity	-	$S(T)$
Net	0	$S(T) - S(t)[1+r(t,T) + w(t,T) - d(t,T)]$

---

where $b°(t,T)$ denotes any arbitrary net cost of carry. All firms for which $S(t)[1+b(t,T)] < F°$ can earn positive economic profits by going short the forward and simultaneously buying and storing the commodity. They will continue to do this until the forward price falls and $S(t)[1+b(t,T)] = F°$. As long as any firm can make positive profits from this operation, the selling will continue, until

$$S(t)[1+b(t,T)] = F^*$$

where $F^* = S(t)[1 + b^*(t,T)]$ and where $b^*(t,T)$ denotes the marginal net cost of carry from t to T for the marginal storer. This marginal entrant earns exactly zero economic profits since its own net cost of carry is equal to b^*.

Things work in the other direction for any firms for which $S(t)[1 + b(t,T)] > F°$. Those firms will go long the forward and then engage in a commodity repurchase agreement (i.e., lending the commodity at time t and repurchasing it at time T).[26] Again, entry occurs until $F°$ exactly equals F^* and reflects the marginal basis of the marginal storer.

In the short run, the basis b^* thus reflects the marginal cost of carrying an incremental unit of the commodity over time. In the long run, b^* will also correspond to the minimum point on a traditional U-shaped long-run average-cost curve.[27] Suppose all firms have b^* below this minimum long-run average cost. In this case, at least one firm will expand output until the marginal cost rises to the minimum average cost and equals the marginal price of the cost of carry and the new b^* will also be reflected in the forward price.

The process by which commodity derivatives and the underlying asset market simultaneously grope toward a competitive equilibrium helps illustrate an important point: namely, the relation between forward and spot prices—the "basis"—is really a "third market" implied by the prices of the two explicit ones.[28] In the example above, the two explicit markets are the spot and forward markets, and the relation between the two implicitly defines *the price of physical storage*. Such "third markets" are also called "basis" or "spread" relations. The implicit market for storage over time is called the "calendar basis or spread," the implicit market for transportation is called the "transportation basis or spread," and so on.

Firms can also use derivatives *based* on *different assets* in order to conduct spread trades to synthesize a third market. Going short crude oil and simultaneously long heating oil and gasoline, for example, is called trading the "crack spread" and is economically equivalent in equilibrium to synthetic refining. Short soybeans and long bean oil and meal are likewise "synthetic crushing." And trading the "spark spread" through a short position in natural gas and a long position in electricity is called "synthetic generation" because the derivatives positions replicate the economic exposure of a gas-fired electric turbine.

A Neo-Austrian Explanation for Basis Trading

Armed with an understanding of how commodity derivatives are priced in equilibrium, we want now to consider the economic rationale for why Enron and firms like it sometimes dedicate substantial resources to "basis trading." We want to recognize what can happen out of *equilibrium*—a state of affairs that typically prevails. Indeed, expectations and relevant knowledge (data) are in a constant state of flux. Accordingly, a neoclassical stationary state—one that treats the data as constant—is of limited use in explaining the market process.[29]

We have seen how equilibrium emerges from the interactions of numerous firms competing to drive prices to their marginal cost. Specifically, suppose b^* reflects the marginal net cost of carry reflected in the prevailing natural gas forward price. This is the price of transportation and delivery in equilibrium. The net cost of carry b^* may only conform to the actual physical and capital costs of carry less the convenience yield for one firm—the marginal entrant into the gas transportation market. Or b^* may be shared by all firms in the short run, but aggregate output may need to adjust in the long run if b^* does not also reflect the minimum average long-run cost of carry. The point is this: the cost of carry reflected in the forward price may or may not be the optimal cost of carry for any given firm at any given time. As is standard in neoclassical microeconomic theory, the price that "clears the market" in the long run will equal the short-run marginal cost for any given firm only by pure coincidence.

Suppose we begin in a situation where b^* is the cost of carry reflected in the forward price and is equal to the short-run marginal costs of all market participants at their production optima. Now consider a new entrant into the market and suppose that new entrant is Enron with its large amount of pipelines and strong economies of scale that lead to a cost of distributing and transporting natural gas at some point in time of $b^e < b^*$, where b^e is Enron's marginal cost of carry. In this case, Enron can physically move gas across time and space at a lower cost than gas can be moved "synthetically" using derivatives.

By going short or selling gas for future delivery using forwards, or futures, Enron is selling gas at an implied net cost of carry of b^*. But its own net cost of carry—a cost that is quite relevant to Enron's ability to move the gas across time and space in order to honor its own future sale obligation created by the forward contract—is less. Accordingly, in *disequilibrium*—or, more properly, on the way to equilibrium—Enron can make a profit equal to the difference between its own net cost of storage and the cost reflected in the market.

The reason that that profit is a short-run profit inconsistent with a long-run equilibrium is that Enron's sale of the forward contract drives the b^* reflected in forward prices closer to b^e. If Enron is the lowest-cost producer and other firms can replicate its production techniques (i.e., Enron owns no unique resources), ultimately b^* will become b^e, which will also eventually approach the long-run minimum average cost of carry. Enron's capacity to earn supranormal profits will vanish in this new equilibrium—in fact, zero economic profits earned by every producer is basically the very meaning of a long-run equilibrium.

Because markets are constantly adjusting to new information, new trading activity, and new entrants, however, it is quite hard to determine when a market actually is in some kind of "final equilibrium resting state," as opposed to when it is adjusting from one state to another. The inevitability of a long-run competitive equilibrium in which profits are not possible thus must be considered relative to the inability of market participants to identify slippery concepts such as "long-run" and "in equilibrium." Strictly speaking, a market is "in equilibrium" as long as supply equals demand. But the term is used here in a more subtle fashion, where "equilibrium" refers to the steady state in which firms earn zero supranormal economic profits in the long run. Accordingly, firms may engage in basis trading to try and exploit the differences in prices reflected in derivatives and their own ability to conduct physical market "pseudoarbitrage" operations that are economically equivalent to those derivatives transactions.[30]

Now consider a situation in which the market is *always* adjusting and never reaches a long-run competitive equilibrium.[31] In this situation, the tendency is still toward the archetypical neoclassical long-run competitive equilibrium, but we never quite get there. Why not? Certainly economic agents are responding in the manner here described, and their behavior should ultimately lead to a steady-state long-run equilibrium. The only reason it does not is, quite simply, that too much is happening at any given moment to make the leap from "short run" to "long run."

In that situation, all firms are always, by definition, inframarginal in some sense of the term. The kind of "pseudoarbitrage" between physical and synthetic storage described above thus can be expected to occur *quite regularly*. And at least some firms will earn supranormal profits quite regularly. Those profits are not riskless, but at least some firms are sure to be right at least some of the time.

Does that mean that physical and synthetic storage are not really equivalent? Technically, it does. But it was never said otherwise. It was only claimed that the two are equivalent in *equilibrium*. When a market is in disequilibrium, what you actually pay to store a commodity physically may well differ from what you actually pay to store it synthetically. But that is not important.

What is important is that, even if new information and other market activities drive a wedge between $b°$ and $b*$, maximizing decisions by firms *always* lead *toward* the convergence of the two prices of storage. Conversely, the price mechanism *never* sends a signal that will lead maximizing firms to engage in physical or derivatives transactions that drive $b°$ and $b*$ further apart. The very fact that maximizing firms are constantly seeking to exploit differences between $b°$ and $b*$ itself is what gives the theory meaning. That the two might never end up exactly equal is not very relevant because, as explained below, information changes before the long-run equilibrium is ever reached.

Asymmetric Information

Now suppose that the net cost of storage is a random variable about which some firms are better informed than others—for example, the impact of supply or demand shocks on particular locational prices, the impact of pipeline congestion on the transportation basis, and the like. Suppose further that we assume a competitive long-run equilibrium *does* hold. Because of the information asymmetry, a rational expectations equilibrium (REE) in which expected supranormal profits are zero in the long run will result. But *expected by whom?*

In that case, firms such as Enron may engage in basis, or spread, trading in an effort to exploit a perceived comparative informational advantage. If a firm owns physical pipelines, for example, it may have a superior capability for forecasting congestion or regional supply-and-demand shocks. That creates a situation quite similar to a market that is out of or on the way to equilibrium —that is, the net cost of carry that the *firm* observes may be *different* from the net cost of carry market participants expect, given the different information on which the two numbers are based. Just as in the disequilibrium case, firms may engage in basis trading to exploit those differences.

In a traditional REE that type of behavior is akin to inframarginal firms attempting to exploit their storage cost advantage relative to the marginal price of storage reflected in forward markets. And as noted, that cannot go on for very long, because the trading actions of the lower-cost firm eventually lead it to become the marginal entrant, thus driving $b*$ to $b°$ for that firm. The same is true in a REE, where trading *itself* is informative. Every time a well-informed trader attempts to exploit its superior information through a transaction, it reveals that superior information to the market. So, the paradox for the firm with better information is that the firm must either *not trade* based on that information in order to preserve its informational advantage, or it must *give away* its informational advantage while simultaneously trying to exploit it in the short run through trading.

In a study written with the late Nobel laureate economist Merton H. Miller, one of this paper's authors argues,[32] however, that that sort of classic equilibrium assumes that the trading activities of the better-informed firm are, indeed, informative. But what if other market participants cannot see all the firm's trades? And what if the trades are occurring in highly opaque, bilateral markets rather than on an exchange? In this case, better-informed firms can profit from their superior information without necessarily having all of their valuable information reflected in the new marginal price. Anecdotal evidence certainly seems to support this in the case of Enron, given how heavily the firm focused on less-liquid and less-transparent markets.

Why Not Speculate Outright?

Trading to exploit disequilibrium, market imperfections, or asymmetric information is hardly riskless. On the contrary, it can be quite risky. That helps explain why many firms engaged in such trading do so with *relative*, or *spread*, positions in third markets rather than take outright positions in one of the two explicit markets. Suppose, for example, that a firm perceives the "true" net cost of storage of gas to be b* (which is equal to the firm's own net cost of carry) but that the current net cost of carry reflected in listed gas futures prices is b' > b*. It is a good bet that b' will fall toward b*. In that case, an outright short position in forward contracts would make sense. But that is *extremely risky*.

A position that exploits the same information asymmetry without the high degree of risk is to go short futures and *simultaneously* buy and hold gas. In this manner, the firm is protected from wild short-term price swings and instead is expressing a view solely on the *relative* prices of storage as reflected in the futures market and storage by the firm itself.

In essence, asset lite is a basis-trading or "third-market" trading strategy in which physical assets are traded vis-à-vis derivatives positions. A physical market combined with the *residual risk* of a market-making function is essentially one big spread trade.

Putting Enron in Context

Reading the marketing and business materials of Enron's energy business lines is eerily similar to reading an example of a firm putting all the theories of basis trading just discussed into practice. And in that sense, Enron was hardly the first firm to leverage its physical market presence into financial- and basis-trading opportunities. Perhaps the best-known example of a firm engaged in the same practice is Cargill.[33] Cargill is the largest private company in the world, with $50 billion in annual sales and 97,000 employees deployed in 59 countries. For 137 years, Cargill has employed an asset-lite strategy that has allowed it to basis trade and manage risks for a wide variety of agricultural commodities, among other things. For the commodities it deals in, Cargill is involved in every link of the supply chains. As a result of its commodity trading, processing, freight shipping, and futures businesses, Cargill has been able to develop an effective intelligence network that generates valuable information. Indeed, via its people on the ground, Cargill knows where every ship and rail car hauling commodities is in real time and what that implies about prospective prices over time and space. By being able to ferret out valuable local information, Cargill has been able to obtain an edge, one that accounts for much of its success.[34]

Basis trading can make economic sense to a firm *ex ante* without making profits *ex post*. The key driver underlying most basis traders' behavior is the *perception* that they have some comparative informational advantage about some basis relation. But perception need not be reality. Markets are, after all, relatively efficient. Indeed, most of the inefficiencies that give rise to profitable trading opportunities can be linked to taxes, regulations, and other institutional frictions that essentially prevent markets from reflecting all available information at all times.

Enron did indeed attempt to focus its efforts on markets riddled with inefficiencies, often created by overregulation, poorly defined property rights, or a slow deregulation process. But that did not mean Enron had a comparative informational advantage in all of those markets.

Structural inefficiencies that prevent prices from fully reflecting all available information are only part of what it takes to run a successful basis-trading operation. The other requisite component is for a firm to perceive itself as (and, it is hoped, actually be) *better informed*. In oil and power, Enron achieved that informational superiority like many other firms do in their own industries—by dominating the financial market. That allowed Enron to develop informationally rich customer relationships that in turn could be extrapolated into superior knowledge of firm-specific supply-and-demand considerations, congestion points along the supply chain, and other important factors.

Now consider, by contrast, a market such as broadband in which Enron was *not* the primary inventor of the technology, *not* the primary buyer or seller of the supply chain infrastructure, and *not* a regular player in the consumer telecommunications arena. The mere existence of market frictions in broadband attracted Enron, but without the requisite information, Enron could not achieve the market dominance required to make asset lite in that market profitable.

Buying Time and the End of Enron

As Culp and Miller explain,[35] firms best suited to the asset-lite kind of strategy that Enron pursued typically require fairly significant amounts of capital —not invested capital assets necessarily but *equity capital* in a financial market sense. Equity capital is a necessary component of successful basis trading and the asset-lite strategy for several reasons. First, equity is required to absorb the occasional loss inevitably arising from the volatility that basis trading can bring to cash flows. Second, maintaining a strong market-making and financial-market presence requires at least the perception by other participants of financial integrity and credit worthiness. Especially in long-dated, credit-sensitive over-the-counter (OTC) derivatives, financial capital is essential to support the credit requirements that other OTC derivatives users and dealers demand.[36]

Unfortunately, Enron's cash management skills were no match for its apparent trading savvy. Despite being "asset lite," Enron's expenditures on intermediate supply chain assets were still not cheap. Add to this EI's asset-heavy investment programs and a corporate culture under Skilling and Lay that emphasized high and stable *earnings* often at the expense of high and stable *cash flows*,[37] and the net result was financial trouble for the firm.[38]

Enron's Deceptions

Much of the public controversy about Enron focuses on how Enron abused accounting and disclosure policies. In short, Enron's abuses in those areas included the following:

- Using inappropriate or aggressive accounting and disclosure policies to conceal assets owned and debt incurred by Enron through special purpose entities (SPEs);[39]
- Using inadequately capitalized subsidiaries and SPEs for "hedges" that reduced Enron's earnings volatility on paper, despite in many cases being dysfunctional or nonperforming in practice;[40] and
- Allegedly engaging in "wash trades" with undisclosed subsidiaries designed to increase trading revenues or mark-to-market valuations artificially.[41]

At first, Enron's abuses of those structures seem to have been driven more by a desire to manage earnings than by anything else. But as time passed, Enron used aggressive accounting and disclosure policies to "buy time" for itself. Especially as Enron moved into new markets in which its comparative advantage was more questionable (e.g., broadband) or in which Enron's success depended strongly on the rate of government deregulation (e.g., water), Enron's financial shenanigans amounted to "robbing Peter to pay Paul." In other words, as Enron's cash balances got lower and lower, concealing its true financial condition was the only way that Enron could sustain itself long enough to hope that its next big investment program would pay off. That might have worked had Enron stuck to markets in which its success with asset lite was more assured. Unfortunately, as has been argued, the firm's end became inevitable once it decided to start moving into areas that deviated from its core business strategy.

There is also the question of whom Enron was actually deceiving with its accounting and disclosure policies. Over the course of many years, one could argue that Enron seduced investors, monitors (e.g., rating agencies and accounting firms), creditors, and even its own employees into believing that the firm was stronger financially than it actually was through a mixture of aggressive marketing, cultural arrogance, and, in some cases, outright deception. But especially as the end of Enron neared, many institutions had begun to view the company with deepening suspicion.[42] By the time Enron failed, a surprisingly large number of firms dealing with Enron commercially had come to fear that the worst for Enron might lie ahead.[43] In the end, those who seem to have been the most deceived—and for the longest time—were Enron's own employees, who, unlike other firms dealing with Enron, had more cause to be inherently optimistic and were doubtless taken almost completely off-guard.

Conclusion

Enron's main business was asset lite—exploiting the synergies between a small physical market presence, a market-making function on derivatives, and a basis-trading operation to "arbitrage" the first two. Many observers have questioned the wisdom of Enron's asset-lite strategy. Most of the criticisms are hard to address without getting into deeper details of Enron's financial situation. In short, people argue that although asset lite did not require a lot of capital *expenditures* and investments in fixed capital, the strategy *did* require Enron to have a fairly large chunk of equity capital—enough to convince its numerous financial counterparties that it was creditworthy. If indeed Enron was camouflaging its capital structure to hide a massive amount of debt, then Enron probably *was* undercapitalized to exploit asset lite effectively. But that is not a criticism of asset lite —it is a criticism of Enron.

In fact, asset lite has become a very common practice for many firms engaged in energy market activities, especially at intermediate points along the various physical supply chains—transmission and distribution of power and midstream transportation and distribution of oil and gas, to name two. One firm that has been consistently successful at playing the asset-lite game, for example, is Kinder Morgan, founded by Enron's former president Richard Kinder when he left Enron in 1996. Kinder Morgan was started in part by Kinder's successful acquisition from Enron of Enron Gas Liquids, for which he outbid six other firms, including Mobil Oil.[44]

In nonenergy markets, firms such as Cargill have also long practiced their version of asset lite, often going the way of Enron in electricity and becoming asset heavy overtime. The key common denominators are two: the use of a physical market presence to acquire specific information about the underlying market and the use of a financial-trading operation to make markets and engage in basis trading to leverage off that underlying asset infrastructure.

Unfortunately, there is no exact answer to the question of when asset lite and basis trading might work for a firm versus when they might fail dismally. The comparative informational advantage that allows some firms to earn positive economic profits is exceedingly hard to analyze or identify except through trial and error. That process of trial and error is what Austrian economist Joseph Schumpeter meant by the "creative destruction" of capitalism, and great economists such as Frank H. Knight and Keynes went on to emphasize further that the success or failure of a given firm cannot ever really be predicted. "Animal spirits," as Keynes put it, ultimately dictate the success or failure of a business as much as any other variable.

Economists are uneasy with that notion. As noted earlier, the neoclassical model postulates that markets tend to be "in equilibrium," whereas the neo-Austrian perspective merely argues that markets "lean in that direction." To be in equilibrium implies some steady state of profits resting on an identifiable cost advantage or structural informational asymmetry. But concepts such as "information asymmetry" are completely nontestable. That makes theoretical economists nervous because it means that the success or failure of a firm cannot be related to a defined set of assumptions and parameters *ex ante*. And empirical economists get even more disgruntled because the success or failure of a firm cannot be explained *ex post*.

Nevertheless, that is the state of affairs. Economic theory merely says that firms will strive to exploit perceived comparative informational advantages in disequilibrium situations where prices do not reflect every market participant's information equally. Theory says nothing about firms being correct in their perceived advantages, nor does theory help us pinpoint precisely what those advantages are. Those things are what *the market* is for.

Can Enron's experience be generalized to suggest a "failure" of the theory underlying basis trading? In fact, Enron cannot be generalized at *all*. Looking purely at the firm's *legitimate* business activities, Enron perceived a comparative informational advantage, pursued it, and was wrong. That does not make the underlying economic model wrong, nor even Enron's managers and shareholders. If we could generalize the economic factors that explain why one firm succeeds and another fails, then competition in the open market would serve no purpose. Instead, competition and the market are both judge and jury to a company's perceived informational advantage. And unless a firm takes the risk of failure, it will never earn the premium of success.[45]

There can be little doubt that Enron did a lot wrong. Indeed, where it deviated from its asset-lite strategy, Enron tended to engage in businesses that were unprofitable. In addition, many of the firm's senior managers were basically unethical. But amid all those legitimate criticisms of Enron, we must be careful not to indict everything the firm did. In some instances, Enron got it right. And at a minimum, the firm moved entrepreneurially into new areas and put itself to the ultimate test of the market. Finally, Enron failed that test, but we must at least tip our hats to that part of Enron that was willing to try. Without that spirit of innovation, the process of capitalism would grind to a screeching halt.

Notes

1. See *Corporate Aftershock: The Public Policy Lessons from the Collapse of Enron and Other Major Corporations*, ed. Christopher L. Culp and William A. Niskanen (New York: John Wiley and Sons, forthcoming 2003), part I.

2. See ibid., part II.

3. The Austrian school of economics was developed in the 19th and 20th centuries by a group of principally Austrian economists in response to several noted shortcomings in the neoclassical theory of the price system. The approach adopted here, however, is more properly called *neo*-Austrian. Following Sir John Hicks's use of the term, a neo-Austrian approach recognizes some of the deficiencies of the neoclassical school and seeks to address those problems from a more Austrian perspective. We do not consider, as some do, the pure Austrian school to be a viable stand-alone theory of the price system. Rather than forcing a choice of theories in either/or fashion, the neo-Austrian approach recognizes instead that a little bit of Austrian insight can go a long way toward salvaging the neoclassical paradigm. For an example of this theoretical approach, see John R. Hicks, *Capital and Time: A Neo-Austrian Theory* (1973; reprint, Oxford: Oxford University Press, 2001).

4. That does not require that forward prices always be unbiased expectations of future spot prices, although they frequently are, especially for physical commodities. But even if forward prices are not unbiased predictors of future spot prices, as in some currency markets, there is still a strong and consistent relation between spot and forward prices—just not an unbiased one. For further discussion of this issue, see Christopher L. Culp, *Risk Transfer: Derivatives in Theory and Practice* (New York: John Wiley and Sons, forthcoming 2003).

5. For a full elaboration of these concepts, see Ludwig M. Lachmann, *Capital and Its Structure* (Kansas City, Mo.: Sheed Andrews and McMeel, 1978).

6. See Enron Corporation, *2000 Annual Report*, 2001, cover page.

7. Ibid., p. 9.

8. A typical use of junk bonds during this period was providing funds to companies with otherwise questionable access to capital, given their credit risk. Highly leveraged transactions like leveraged buyouts were thus a natural candidate for junk-bond financing.

9. EOG continued for two decades to spearhead all of Enron Corp.'s exploration and production activities in oil and gas. In 1999, EOG exchanged the shares in EOG held by Enron for its operations in India and China. In so doing, EOG became independent of Enron Corp. and, in fact, changed its name the same year to EOG Resources, Inc. This firm still exists today.

10. See Lachmann.

11. For more discussion of these different types of contracts, see Andrea M. P. Neves, "Wholesale Electricity Markets and Products after Enron," in *Corporate Aftershock*; and Barbara T. Kavanagh, "An Introduction to the Business of Structure Finance," in *Corporate Aftershock*.

12. In the huge interest rate swap market, dealers did essentially the same thing as the Enron GasBank—they used other swaps and futures contracts to manage the *residual* risks of running a dealing portfolio, called a "swap warehouse."

13. Quoted in Joel Kurtzman and Glenn Rifkin, *Radical E: From GE to Enron—Lessons on How to Rule the Web* (New York: John Wiley & Sons, 2001), p. 47.

14. See Ronnie J. Clayton, William Scroggins, and Christopher Westley, "Enron: Market Exploitation and Correction," *Financial Decisions* (Spring 2002): 1–16.

15. See Neves.

16. See Peter C. Fusaro and Ross M. Miller, *What Went Wrong at Enron?* (New York: John Wiley & Sons, 2002).

17. Ibid.

18. This can be accomplished in various ways. For examples, see Andrea S. Kramer, Paul J. Pantano, and Doron F. Ezickson, "Regulation of Electricity Trading after Enron," in *Corporate Aftershock*; and Paul Palmer, "The Market for Complex Credit Risk," in *Corporate Aftershock*.

19. Early discussions of the economic rationale for basis, or spread, trading can be found in L. Leland Johnson, "The Theory of Hedging and Speculation in Commodity Futures," *Review of Economic Studies* 27, no. 3 (1960): 139–51; Holbrook Working, "Theory of the Inverse Carrying Charge in Futures Markets," *Journal of Farm Economics* 30 (1948): 1–28; Holbrook Working, "The Theory of Price of Storage," *American Economic Review* 39 (1949): 1254–62; and Holbrook Working, "New Concepts Concerning Futures Markets and Prices," *American Economic Review* 52 (1962): 432–59.

20. See, for example, Jeffrey B. Williams, *The Economic Function of Futures Markets* (New York: Cambridge University Press, 1986); Culp, *Risk Transfer*; and Steve H. Hanke, "Backwardation Revisited," *Friedberg's Commodity and Currency Comments* 8, no. 11 (December 20, 1987).

21. Alternative versions of this rely on different types of discounting and compounding assumptions, as well as allowing certain variables in the equation to be stochastic (i.e., subject to random variation). But the spirit of all versions of the model is well captured by the representation here. See Culp, *Risk Transfer*, for more detail.

22. See John Maynard Keynes, *The Theory of Money*, vol. II, *The Applied Theory of Money* (London: Macmillan, 1930); Nicholas Kaldor, "Speculation and Economic Stability," *Review of Economic Studies* 7 (1939): 1–27; Working, "Theory of the Inverse Carrying Charge in Futures Markets"; Working, "The Theory of Price of Storage"; Michael J. Brennan, "The Supply of Storage," *American Economic Review* 48 (1958): 50–72; and Lester G. Telser, "Futures Trading and the Storage of Cotton and Wheat," *Journal of Political Economy* 66 (1958): 233–55.

23. See Working, "New Concepts Concerning Futures Markets and Storage."

24. See Keynes; Working, "The Theory of Price of Storage"; Culp, *Risk Transfer*; and Hanke.

25. Cost-of-carry pricing for forwards on financial assets, by contrast, is enforced by direct "cash-and-carry" arbitrage because financial assets pay *observable* and *explicit* dividends that are the same regardless who holds the asset. See Culp, *Risk Transfer*.

26. Commodity lending does occur, so this example is in no way unrealistic. See Williams.

27. The classical U-shape is consistent with a production technology that demonstrates increasing returns to scale up to b^* and diminishing returns thereafter.

28. See Williams.

29. For a more general discussion, see John H. Cochrane and Christopher L. Culp, "Equilibrium Asset Pricing: Implications for Risk Management," in *The Growth of Risk Management: A History* (London: Risk Books, 2002).

30. This is pseudoarbitrage because it has the flavor of an arbitrage transaction but is far from riskless.

31. This seems heretical in the neoclassical microeconomic paradigm, but is typical of the notion of "equilibrium" developed by economists in the "Austrian" and "neo-Austrian" tradition, such as Carl Menger, *Principles of Economics* (1871; reprint, Grove City, Pa.: Libertarian Press, 1974); F. A. Hayek, "Economics and Knowledge," *Economica* 4 (1937): 33–54; F. A. Hayek, "The Use of Knowledge in Society," *American Economic Review* 35, no. 4 (1945): 519–30; F. A. Hayek, "The Meaning of Competition," in *Individualism and Economic Order* (1948; reprint, London: Routledge and Kegan Paul, 1978), pp. 92–107; F. A. Hayek, "Competition as a Discovery Procedure," in *New Studies in Philosophy, Politics, Economics, and the History of Ideas* (Chicago: University of Chicago Press, 1978), pp. 179–91; F. A. Hayek, "The New Confusion about 'Planning,'" in *New Studies in Philosophy, Politics, Economics, and the History of Ideas*, pp. 232–49; Hicks; and Lachmann.

32. See Christopher L. Culp and Merton H. Miller, "Hedging in the Theory of Corporate Finance," *Journal of Applied Corporate Finance* 8, no.1 (Spring 1995): 121–27.

33. See, for example, Wayne G. Broehl Jr., *Cargill: Trading the World's Grains* (Hanover, N.H.: University Press of New England, 1992).

34. See, for example, Neil Weinberg and Brandon Copple, "Going against the Grain," *Forbes*, November 25, 2002, pp. 158–68.

35. See Culp and Miller, "Hedging in the Theory of Corporate Finance"; Christopher L. Culp and Merton H. Miller, "Metallgesellschaft and the Economics of Synthetic Storage," *Journal of Applied Corporate Finance* 7, no. 4 (Winter 1995): 62–76; and Christopher L. Culp and Merton H. Miller, "Introduction: Why a Firm Hedges Affects How a Firm Should Hedge," in *Corporate Hedging in Theory and Practice: Lessons from Metallgesellschaft*, ed. Christopher L. Culp and Merton H. Miller (London: Risk Books, 1999).

36. See David Mengle, "Do Swaps Need More Regulation?" in *Corporate Aftershock*; and Christopher L. Culp, "Credit Risk Management Lessons from Enron," in *Corporate Aftershock*.

37. See Richard Bassett and Mark Storrie, "Accounting at Energy Firms after Enron: Is the 'Cure' Worse than the Disease?" in *Corporate Aftershock*.

38. Cash flow mismanagement was not always the norm at Enron. Jeffrey Skilling's predecessor Richard Kinder was actually known for being a cash flow "tight-wad" and kept the firm's financial health relatively strong during his tenure at the operational helm of Enron.

39. See Bassett and Storrie; Kavanagh; and Keith A. Bockus, W. Dana Northcut, and Mark E. Zmijewski, "Accounting and Disclosure Issues in Structured Finance," in *Corporate Aftershock*.

40. See Bassett and Storrie; and Kavanagh.

41. See ibid.; Neves; Kramer, Pantano, and Ezickson; John Herron, "Online Trading and Clearing after Enron," in *Corporate Aftershock*; and Bockus, Northcut, and Zmijewski.

42. See Bassett and Storrie.

43. See Culp, *Risk Transfer*.

44. See Fusaro and Miller.

45. See Frank H. Knight, *Risk, Uncertainty, and Profit* (Boston: Houghton Mifflin, 1933).

POSTSCRIPT

Does the Enron Collapse Show That We Need More Regulation of the Energy Industry?

The Enron case is in many ways a poor example for any discussion of business activity, since it involves so many activities that were clearly criminal. Had the officers of the corporation been honest people, what might we have found out about the operations of deregulated markets in public utilities?

Suggested Readings

Michael K. Block, "Energy Deregulation: Moving Ahead Quickly (and Wisely)," The Progress and Freedom Foundation (June 1996).

Peter Behr and April Witt, "Visionary's Dream Led to Risky Business," *Washington Post* (July 28, 2002).

Allan Sloan, "Who Killed Enron?" *Newsweek* (January 21, 2002).

Brian Cruver, *Anatomy of Greed: The Unshredded Truth From an Enron Insider* (Caroll & Graff, 2002).

Kurt Eichenwald and Floyd Norris, "Early Verdict on Audit: Procedures Ignored," *The New York Times*, C5 (June 6, 2002).

Kurt Eichenwald, "Flinging Billions to Acquire Assets That No One Else Would Touch," *The New York Times* (October 18, 2002).

Rural Utilities Service, *Connecting Rural America*, RUS Press Releases and Official Statements (2002), http://www.usda.gov/rus/index2/press.htm.

Workplace Fairness

Workplace Fairness is a nonprofit organization that was founded to assist individuals, both employed and unemployed, in understanding, enforcing, and expanding their rights in the workplace.

http://www.nerinet.org

WorkNet@ILR

The School of Industrial and Labor Relations at Cornell University offers this site consisting of an index of Internet sites relevant to the field of industrial and labor relations; a list of centers, institutes, and affiliated groups; and an electronic archive that contains full-text documents on the glass ceiling, child labor, and more.

http://www.ilr.cornell.edu/workplace.html

WorkNet: Alcohol and Other Drugs in the Workplace

This site of the Canadian Centre on Substance Abuse provides news, databases, bibliographies, resources, and research on alcohol and other drugs in the workplace.

http://www.ccsa.ca/wise.htm

Employee Incentives and Career Development

This site is dedicated to the proposition that effective employee compensation and career development is a valuable tool in obtaining, maintaining, and retaining a productive workforce. It contains links to pay-for-knowledge, incentive systems, career development, wage and salary compensation, and more.

http://www.snc.edu/socsci/chair/336/group1.htm

Executive PayWatch

Executive PayWatch, sponsored by the American Federation of Labor–Congress of Industrial Organizations (AFL-CIO), is a working families' guide to monitoring and curtailing the excessive salaries, bonuses, and perks in CEO compensation packages.

http://www.aflcio.org/corporateamerica/paywatch/

PART 3

Human Resources: The Corporation and the Employee

*W*hat does the company owe the employee, and what does the employee owe the company? When the company acts in a morally reprehensible way, and the employee "blows the whistle" on it, whose fault is the resulting damage to the company's reputation? The company has a right to monitor job performance and protect itself against hazards—but at what price to the employee's right of privacy? What is a "just wage" for a worker, or a manager, or the CEO of a company? The debates in this section follow some of these issues.

- Does Blowing the Whistle Violate Company Loyalty?

- Is Controlling Drug Abuse More Important Than Protecting Privacy?

- Is CEO Compensation Justified by Performance?

ISSUE 9

Does Blowing the Whistle Violate Company Loyalty?

YES: Sissela Bok, from "Whistleblowing and Professional Responsibility," *New York University Education Quarterly* (Summer 1980)

NO: Robert A. Larmer, from "Whistleblowing and Employee Loyalty," *Journal of Business Ethics* (vol. 11, 1992)

ISSUE SUMMARY

YES: Philosopher Sissela Bok asserts that although blowing the whistle is often justified, it does involve dissent, accusation, and a breach of loyalty to the employer.

NO: Robert A. Larmer, an associate professor of philosophy, argues that attempting to stop illegal or unethical company activities may be the highest type of company loyalty an employee can display.

Whistle-blowing occurs when an employee discovers a wrong at his or her place of employment and exposes it, thereby saving lives or a great deal of money, but almost always at great expense to him- or herself. Since the readings that follow are theoretical, some specific cases might be useful. In "The Whistle Blowers' Morning After," *The New York Times* (November 9, 1986), N. R. Kleinfeld portrays five of the early whistle-blowers, some of whom have become famous as case studies in business schools across the country. Each one has an interesting story to tell; each claims that if he had it to do over again he would, for he likes living with a clear conscience. But each has also paid a price: great stress, sometimes ill health, career loss, financial ruin, and/or loss of friends and family.

Charles Atchinson blew the whistle on the Comanche Park nuclear plant in Glen Rose, Texas, a power station that was unsafe. It cost him his job, plunged him into debt, and left emotional scars on his family. Kermit Vandivier, who blew the whistle on the B. F. Goodrich Aircraft brakes scandal, also lost his job. He has since begun a new career as a journalist. James Pope claimed that the Federal Aviation Administration (FAA) found in 1975 an effective device, known as an airborne collision avoidance system, that would prevent mid-air crashes; but it chose instead to pursue an inferior device it had had a hand in developing. Mr. Pope was "retired" early by the FAA. The most famous whistle-blower of all may be A. Ernest Fitzgerald, the U.S. Air Force cost analyst who found huge cost overruns on Lockheed cargo planes that were being developed for the Air Force. After his revelations, he was discharged from the Air Force. He fought for 13 years to be reinstated, which he was, at full rank, in 1982. For some first-hand accounts by Fitzgerald, see *Pentagonists: An Insider's View of Waste, Mismanagement, and Fraud in Defense Spending* (Houghton Mifflin, 1989) and *The High Priests of Waste* (W. W. Norton, 1972). The common thread of these stories is that when someone detected a wrong and properly reported it, he was demoted, labeled a troublemaker, and disciplined or fired, even when the evidence was very much in his favor. All of them, incidentally, initially believed in their organizations, and not only were all of them sure that they were acting in an ethical manner, but they also believed that they would be thanked for their efforts and diligence.

Professors Myron Peretz Glazer and Penina Migdal Glazer, in *The Whistle Blowers: Exposing Corruption in Government and Industry* (Basic Books, 1989), tell the story of 55 whistle-blowers—why they did what they did, and what the consequences were for themselves and their families. The Glazers found that the dominant trait in these whistle-blowers was a strong belief in individual responsibility. As one of the spouses of a whistle-blower stated, "A corrupt system can happen only if the individuals who make up that system are corrupt. You are either going to be part of the corruption or part of the forces working against it. There isn't a third choice. Someone, someday, has to take a stand; if you don't, maybe no one will. And that is wrong."

The Glazers write that the strong belief in individual responsibility that drove these ethical resisters was often supported by professional ethics, religious values, or allegiance to a community. But the personal costs of public disclosure were high, and the results were less than satisfactory. In some cases the accused corporations made no changes. The whistle-blowers, however, had to recreate careers, relocate, and settle for less money in new jobs. For most resisters, the worst part was the devastating months or even years of dislocation, unemployment, and temporary jobs. In response to a question posed by the Glazers, 21 of the whistle-blowers advised other potential whistle-blowers to "forget it" or to "leak the information without your name attached." If blowing the whistle is unavoidable, however, then "be prepared to be ostracized, have your career come to a screeching halt, and perhaps even be driven into bankruptcy."

As you read the following selections by Sissela Bok and Robert A. Larmer, think about these cases and others you may have heard about. Consider the motivations involved in whistle-blowing and whether they reflect loyalty or disloyalty to the company. How would you view an instance of whistle-blowing if you or your company were the target? Who deserves the greatest consideration in potential whistle-blowing situations: the individual, the company, or the public?

Sissela Bok

 **YES**

Whistleblowing and Professional Responsibility

Whistleblowing" is a new label generated by our increased awareness of the ethical conflicts encountered at work. Whistleblowers sound an alarm from within the very organization in which they work, aiming to spotlight neglect or abuses that threaten the public interest.

The stakes in whistleblowing are high. Take the nurse who alleges that physicians enrich themselves in her hospital through unnecessary surgery; the engineer who discloses safety defects in the braking systems of a fleet of new rapid-transit vehicles; the Defense Department official who alerts Congress to military graft and overspending: all know that they pose a threat to those whom they denounce and that their own careers may be at risk.

Moral Conflicts

Moral conflicts on several levels confront anyone who is wondering whether to speak out about abuses or risks or serious neglect. In the first place, he must try to decide whether, other things being equal, speaking out is in fact in the public interest. This choice is often made more complicated by factual uncertainties: Who is responsible for the abuse or neglect? How great is the threat? And how likely is it that speaking out will precipitate changes for the better?

In the second place, a would-be whistleblower must weigh his responsibility to serve the public interest against the responsibility he owes to his colleagues and the institution in which he works. While the professional ethic requires collegial loyalty, the codes of ethics often stress responsibility to the public over and above duties to colleagues and clients. Thus the United States Code of Ethics for Government Servants asks them to "expose corruption wherever uncovered" and to "put loyalty to the highest moral principles and to country above loyalty to persons, party, or government."[1] Similarly, the largest professional engineering association requires members to speak out against abuses threatening the safety, health, and welfare of the public.[2]

From Sissela Bok, "Whistleblowing and Professional Responsibility," *New York University Education Quarterly,* vol. 11 (Summer 1980), pp. 2–7. Copyright © 1980 by Sissela Bok. Reprinted by permission.

A third conflict for would-be whistleblowers is personal in nature and cuts across the first two: even in cases where they have concluded that the facts warrant speaking out, and that their duty to do so overrides loyalties to colleagues and institutions, they often have reason to fear the results of carrying out such a duty. However strong this duty may seem in theory, they know that, in practice, retaliation is likely. As a result, their careers and their ability to support themselves and their families may be unjustly impaired.[3] A government handbook issued during the Nixon era recommends reassigning "undesirables" to places so remote that they would prefer to resign. Whistleblowers may also be downgraded or given work without responsibility or work for which they are not qualified; or else they may be given many more tasks than they can possibly perform. Another risk is that an outspoken civil servant may be ordered to undergo a psychiatric fitness-for-duty examination,[4] declared unfit for service, and "separated" as well as discredited from the point of view of any allegations he may be making. Outright firing, finally, is the most direct institutional response to whistleblowers.

Add to the conflicts confronting individual whistleblowers the claim to self-policing that many professions make, and professional responsibility is at issue in still another way. For an appeal to the public goes against everything that "self-policing" stands for. The question for the different professions, then, is how to resolve, insofar as it is possible, the conflict between professional loyalty and professional responsibility toward the outside world. The same conflicts arise to some extent in all groups, but professional groups often have special cohesion and claim special dignity and privileges.

The plight of whistleblowers has come to be documented by the press and described in a number of books. Evidence of the hardships imposed on those who chose to act in the public interest has combined with a heightened awareness of professional malfeasance and corruption to produce a shift toward greater public support of whistleblowers. Public service law firms and consumer groups have taken up their cause; institutional reforms and legislation have been proposed to combat illegitimate reprisals.[5]

Given the indispensable services performed by so many whistleblowers, strong public support is often merited. But the new climate of acceptance makes it easy to overlook the dangers of whistleblowing: of uses in error or in malice; of work and reputations unjustly lost for those falsely accused; of privacy invaded and trust undermined. There comes a level of internal prying and mutual suspicion at which no institution can function. And it is a fact that the disappointed, the incompetent, the malicious, and the paranoid all too often leap to accusations in public. Worst of all, ideological persecution throughout the world traditionally relies on insiders willing to inform on their colleagues or even on their family members, often through staged public denunciations or press campaigns.

No society can count itself immune from such dangers. But neither can it risk silencing those with a legitimate reason to blow the whistle. How then can we distinguish between different instances of whistleblowing? A society that fails to protect the right to speak out even on the part of those whose warnings turn out to be spurious obviously opens the door to political repression. But from the moral point of view there are important differences between the aims, messages, and methods of dissenters from within.

Nature of Whistleblowing

Three elements, each jarring, and triply jarring when conjoined, lend acts of whistleblowing special urgency and bitterness: dissent, breach of loyalty, and accusation.

Like all dissent, whistleblowing makes public a disagreement with an authority or a majority view. But whereas dissent can concern all forms of disagreement with, for instance, religious dogma or government policy or court decisions, whistleblowing has the narrower aim of shedding light on negligence or abuse, or alerting to a risk, and of assigning responsibility for this risk.

Would-be whistleblowers confront the conflict inherent in all dissent: between conforming and sticking their necks out. The more repressive the authority they challenge, the greater the personal risk they take in speaking out. At exceptional times, as in times of war, even ordinarily tolerant authorities may come to regard dissent as unacceptable and even disloyal.[6]

Furthermore, the whistleblower hopes to stop the game; but since he is neither referee nor coach, and since he blows the whistle on his own team, his act is seen as a violation of loyalty. In holding his position, he has assumed certain obligations to his colleagues and clients. He may even have subscribed to a loyalty oath or a promise of confidentiality. Loyalty to colleagues and to clients comes to be pitted against loyalty to the public interest, to those who may be injured unless the revelation is made.

Not only is loyalty violated in whistleblowing, hierarchy as well is often opposed, since the whistleblower is not only a colleague but a subordinate. Though aware of the risks inherent in such disobedience, he often hopes to keep his job.[7] At times, however, he plans his alarm to coincide with leaving the institution. If he is highly placed, or joined by others, resigning in protest may effectively direct public attention to the wrongdoing at issue.[8] Still another alternative, often chosen by those who wish to be safe from retaliation, is to leave the institution quietly, to secure another post, and then to blow the whistle. In this way, it is possible to speak with the authority and knowledge of an insider without having the vulnerability of that position.

It is the element of accusation, of calling a "foul," that arouses the strongest reactions on the part of the hierarchy. The accusation may be of neglect, of willfully concealed dangers, or of outright abuse on the part of colleagues or superiors. It singles out specific persons or groups as responsible for threats to the public interest. If no one could be held responsible—as in the case of an impending avalanche—the warning would not constitute whistleblowing.

The accusation of the whistleblower, moreover, concerns a present or an imminent threat. Past errors or misdeeds occasion such an alarm only if they still affect current practices. And risks far in the future lack the immediacy needed to make the alarm a compelling one, as well as the close connection to particular individuals that would justify actual accusations. Thus an alarm can be sounded about safety defects in a rapid-transit system that threaten or will shortly threaten passengers, but the revelation of safety defects in a system no longer in use, while of historical interest, would not constitute whistleblowing. Nor would the revelation of potential problems in a system not yet fully designed and far from implemented.[9]

Not only immediacy, but also specificity, is needed for there to be an alarm capable of pinpointing responsibility. A concrete risk must be at issue rather than a vague foreboding or a somber prediction. The act of whistleblowing differs in this respect from the lamentation or the dire prophecy. An immediate and specific threat would normally be acted upon by those at risk. The whistleblower assumes that his message will alert listeners to something they do not know, or whose significance they have not grasped because it has been kept secret.

The desire for openness inheres in the temptation to reveal any secret, sometimes joined to an urge for self-aggrandizement and publicity and the hope for revenge for past slights or injustices. There can be pleasure, too—righteous or malicious—in laying bare the secrets of co-workers and in setting the record straight at last. Colleagues of the whistleblower often suspect his motives: they may regard him as a crank, as publicity-hungry, wrong about the facts, eager for scandal and discord, and driven to indiscretion by his personal biases and shortcomings.

For whistleblowing to be effective, it must arouse its audience. Inarticulate whistleblowers are likely to fail from the outset. When they are greeted by apathy, their message dissipates. When they are greeted by disbelief, they elicit no response at all. And when the audience is not free to receive or to act on the information—when censorship or fear of retribution stifles response—then the message rebounds to injure the whistleblower. Whistleblowing also requires the possibility of concerted public response: the idea of whistleblowing in an anarchy is therefore merely quixotic.

Such characteristics of whistleblowing and strategic considerations for achieving an impact are common to the noblest warnings, the most vicious personal attacks, and the delusions of the paranoid. How can one distinguish the many acts of sounding an alarm that are genuinely in the public interest from all the petty, biased, or lurid revelations that pervade our querulous and gossip-ridden society? Can we draw distinctions between different whistleblowers, different messages, different methods?

We clearly can, in a number of cases. Whistleblowing may be starkly inappropriate when in malice or error, or when it lays bare legitimately private matters having to do, for instance, with political belief or sexual life. It can, just as clearly, be the only way to shed light on an ongoing unjust practice such as drugging political prisoners or subjecting them to electroshock treatment. It can be the last resort for alerting the public to an impending disaster. Taking such clear-cut cases as benchmarks, and reflecting on what it is about them that weighs so heavily for or against speaking out, we can work our way toward the admittedly more complex cases in which whistleblowing is not so clearly the right or wrong choice, or where different points of view exist regarding its legitimacy—cases where there are moral reasons both for concealment and for disclosure and where judgments conflict....

Individual Moral Choice

What questions might those who consider sounding an alarm in public ask themselves? How might they articulate the problem they see and weigh its injustice before deciding whether or not to reveal it? How can they best try to make sure their choice is the right one? In thinking about these questions it helps to keep in mind the three elements mentioned earlier: dissent, breach of loyalty, and accusation. They impose certain requirements—of accuracy and judgment in dissent; of exploring alternative ways to cope with improprieties that minimize the breach of loyalty; and of fairness in accusation. For each, careful articulation and testing of arguments are needed to limit error and bias.

Dissent by whistleblowers, first of all, is expressly claimed to be intended to benefit the public. It carries with it, as a result, an obligation to consider the nature of this benefit and to consider also the possible harm that may come from speaking out: harm to persons or institutions and, ultimately, to the public interest itself. Whistleblowers must, therefore, begin by making every effort to consider the effects of speaking out versus those of remaining silent. They must assure themselves of the accuracy of their reports, checking and rechecking the facts before speaking out; specify the degree to which there is genuine impropriety; consider how imminent is the threat they see, how serious, and how closely linked to those accused of neglect and abuse.

If the facts warrant whistleblowing, how can the second element—breach of loyalty—be minimized? The most important question here is whether the existing avenues for change within the organization have been explored. It is a waste of time for the public as well as harmful to the institution to sound the loudest alarm first. Whistleblowing has to remain a last alternative because of its destructive side effects: it must be chosen only when other alternatives have been considered and rejected. They may be rejected if they simply do not apply to the problem at hand, or when there is not time to go through routine channels or when the institution is so corrupt or coercive that steps will be taken to silence the whistleblower should he try the regular channels first.

What weight should an oath or a promise of silence have in the conflict of loyalties? One sworn to silence is doubtless under a stronger obligation because of the oath he has taken. He has bound himself, assumed specific obligations beyond those assumed in merely taking a new position. But even such promises can be overridden when the public interest at issue is strong enough. They can be overridden if they were obtained under duress or through deceit. They can be overridden, too, if they promise something that is in itself wrong or unlawful. The fact that one has promised silence is no excuse for complicity in covering up a crime or a violation of the public's trust.

The third element in whistleblowing—accusation—raises equally serious ethical concerns. They are concerns of fairness to the persons accused of impropriety. Is the message one to which the public is entitled in the first place? Or does it infringe on personal and private matters that one has no right to invade? Here, the very notion of what is in the public's best "interest" is at issue: "accusations" regarding an official's unusual sexual or religious experiences may well appeal to the public's interest without being information relevant to "the public interest."

Great conflicts arise here. We have witnessed excessive claims to executive privilege and to secrecy by government officials during the Watergate scandal in order to cover up for abuses the public had every right to discover. Conversely, those hoping to profit from prying into private matters have become adept at invoking "the public's right to know." Some even regard such private matters as threats to the public: they voice their own religious and political prejudices in the language of accusation. Such a danger is never stronger than when the accusation is delivered surreptitiously. The anonymous accusations made during the McCarthy period regarding political beliefs and associations often injured persons who did not even know their accusers or the exact nature of the accusations.

From the public's point of view, accusations that are openly made by identifiable individuals are more likely to be taken seriously. And in fairness to those criticized, openly accepted responsibility for blowing the whistle should be preferred to the denunciation or the leaked rumor. What is openly stated can more easily be checked, its source's motives challenged, and the underlying information examined. Those under attack may otherwise be hard put to defend themselves against nameless adversaries. Often they do not even know that they are threatened until it is too late to respond. The anonymous denunciation, moreover, common to so many regimes, places the burden of investigation on government agencies that may thereby gain the power of a secret police.

From the point of view of the whistleblower, on the other hand, the anonymous message is safer in situations where retaliation is likely. But it is also often less likely to be taken seriously. Unless the message is accompanied by indications of how the evidence can be checked, its anonymity, however safe for the source, speaks against it.

During the process of weighing the legitimacy of speaking out, the method used, and the degree of fairness needed, whistleblowers must try to compensate for the strong possibility of bias on their part. They should be scrupulously aware of any motive that might skew their message: a desire for self-defense in a difficult bureaucratic situation, perhaps, or the urge to seek revenge, or inflated expectations regarding the effect their message will have on the situation. (Needless to say, bias affects the silent as well as the outspoken. The motive for holding back important information about abuses and injustice ought to give similar cause for soul-searching.)

Likewise, the possibility of personal gain from sounding the alarm ought to give pause. Once again there is then greater risk of a biased message. Even if the whistleblower regards himself as incorruptible, his profiting from revelations of neglect or abuse will lead others to question his motives and to put less credence in his charges. If, for example, a government employee stands to make large profits from a book exposing the inequities in his agency, there is danger that he will, perhaps even unconsciously, slant his report in order to cause more of a sensation.

A special problem arises when there is a high risk that the civil servant who speaks out will have to go through costly litigation. Might he not justifiably try to make enough money on his public revelations—say, through books or public speaking—to offset his losses? In so doing he will not strictly speaking have *profited* from his revelations: he merely avoids being financially crushed by their sequels. He will nevertheless still be suspected at the time of revelation, and his message will therefore seem more questionable.

Reducing bias and error in moral choice often requires consultation, even open debate[10]: methods that force articulation of the moral arguments at stake and challenge privately held assumptions. But acts of whistleblowing present special problems when it comes to open consultation. On the one hand, once the whistleblower sounds his alarm publicly, his arguments will be subjected to open scrutiny; he will have to articulate his reasons for speaking out and substantiate his charges. On the other hand, it will then be too late to retract the alarm or to combat its harmful effects, should his choice to speak out have been ill-advised.

For this reason, the whistleblower owes it to all involved to make sure of two things: that he has sought as much and as objective advice regarding his choice as he can *before* going public; and that he is aware of the arguments for and against the practice of whistleblowing in general, so that he can see his own choice against as richly detailed and coherently structured a background as possible. Satisfying these two requirements once again has special problems because of the very nature of whistleblowing: the more corrupt the circumstances, the more dangerous it may be to seek consultation before speaking out. And yet, since the whistleblower himself may have a biased view of the state of affairs, he may choose not to consult others when in fact it would be not only safe but advantageous to do so; he may see corruption and conspiracy where none exists.

Notes

1. Code of Ethics for Government Service passed by the U.S. House of Representatives in the 85th Congress (1958) and applying to all government employees and office holders.

2. Code of Ethics of the Institute of Electrical and Electronics Engineers, Article IV.

3. For case histories and descriptions of what befalls whistleblowers, see Rosemary Chalk and Frank von Hippel, "Due Process for Dissenting Whistle-Blowers," *Technology Review* 81 (June–July 1979); 48–55; Alan S. Westin and Stephen Salisbury, eds., *Individual Rights in the Corporation* (New York: Pantheon, 1980); Helen Dudar, "The Price of Blowing the Whistle," *New York Times Magazine,* 30 October 1979, pp. 41–54; John Edsall, *Scientific Freedom and Responsibility* (Washington, D.C.: American Association for the Advancement of Science, 1975), p. 5; David Ewing, *Freedom Inside the Organization* (New York: Dutton, 1977); Ralph Nader, Peter Petkas, and Kate Blackwell, *Whistle Blowing* (New York: Grossman, 1972); Charles Peter and Taylor Branch, *Blowing the Whistle* (New York: Praeger, 1972).

4. Congressional hearings uncovered a growing resort to mandatory psychiatric examinations.

5. For an account of strategies and proposals to support government whistleblowers, see Government Accountability Project, *A Whistleblower's Guide to the Federal Bureaucracy* (Washington, D.C.: Institute for Policy Studies, 1977).

6. See, e.g., Samuel Eliot Morison, Frederick Merk, and Frank Friedel, *Dissent in Three American Wars* (Cambridge: Harvard University Press, 1970).

7. In the scheme worked out by Albert Hirschman in *Exit, Voice and Loyalty* (Cambridge: Harvard University Press, 1970), whistleblowing represents "voice" accompanied by a preference not to "exit," though forced "exit" is clearly a possibility and "voice" after or during "exit" may be chosen for strategic reasons.

8. Edward Weisband and Thomas N. Franck, *Resignation in Protest* (New York: Grossman, 1975).

9. Future developments can, however, be the cause for whistleblowing if they are seen as resulting from steps being taken or about to be taken that render them inevitable.

10. I discuss these questions of consultation and publicity with respect to moral choice in chapter 7 of Sissela Bok, *Lying* (New York: Pantheon, 1978); and in *Secrets* (New York: Pantheon Books, 1982), Ch. IX and XV.

Robert A. Larmer

← **NO**

Whistleblowing and Employee Loyalty

Whistleblowing by an employee is the act of complaining, either within the corporation or publicly, about a corporation's unethical practices. Such an act raises important questions concerning the loyalties and duties of employees. Traditionally, the employee has been viewed as an agent who acts on behalf of a principal, i.e., the employer, and as possessing duties of loyalty and confidentiality. Whistleblowing, at least at first blush, seems a violation of these duties and it is scarcely surprising that in many instances employers and fellow employees argue that it is an act of disloyalty and hence morally wrong.[1]

It is this issue of the relation between whistleblowing and employee loyalty that I want to address. What I will call the standard view is that employees possess *prima facie* duties of loyalty and confidentiality to their employers and that whistleblowing cannot be justified except on the basis of a higher duty to the public good. Against this standard view, Ronald Duska has recently argued that employees do not have even a *prima facie* duty of loyalty to their employers and that whistleblowing needs, therefore, no moral justification.[2] I am going to criticize both views. My suggestion is that both misunderstand the relation between loyalty and whistleblowing. In their place I will propose a third more adequate view.

Duska's view is more radical in that it suggests that there can be no issue of whistleblowing and employee loyalty, since the employee has no duty to be loyal to his employer. His reason for suggesting that the employee owes the employer, at least the corporate employer, no loyalty is that companies are not the kinds of things which are proper objects of loyalty. His argument in support of this rests upon two key claims. The first is that loyalty, properly understood, implies a reciprocal relationship and is only appropriate in the context of a mutual surrendering of self-interest. He writes,

> It is important to recognize that in any relationship which demands loyalty the relationship works both ways and involves mutual enrichment. Loyalty is incompatible with self-interest, because it is something that necessarily requires we go beyond self-interest. My loyalty to my friend, for example, requires I put aside my interests some of the time.... Loyalty depends on ties that demand self-sacrifice with no expectation of reward, e.g., the ties of loyalty that bind a family together.[3]

From Robert A. Larmer, "Whistleblowing and Employee Loyalty," *Journal of Business Ethics*, vol. 11 (1992), pp. 125–128. Copyright © 1992 by D. Reidel Publishing Co., Dordrecht, Holland, and Boston, U.S.A. Reprinted by permission of Kluwer Academic Publishers.

The second is that the relation between a company and an employee does not involve any surrender of self-interest on the part of the company, since its primary goal is to maximize profit. Indeed, although it is convenient, it is misleading to talk of a company having interests. As Duska comments,

> A company is not a person. A company is an instrument, and an instrument with a specific purpose, the making of profit. To treat an instrument as an end in itself, like a person, may not be as bad as treating an end as an instrument, but it does give the instrument a moral status it does not deserve...[4]

Since, then, the relation between a company and an employee does not fulfill the minimal requirement of being a relation between two individuals, much less two reciprocally self-sacrificing individuals, Duska feels it is a mistake to suggest the employee has any duties of loyalty to the company.

This view does not seem adequate, however. First, it is not true that loyalty must be quite so reciprocal as Duska demands. Ideally, of course, one expects that if one is loyal to another person that person will reciprocate in kind. There are, however, many cases where loyalty is not entirely reciprocated, but where we do not feel that it is misplaced. A parent, for example, may remain loyal to an erring teenager, even though the teenager demonstrates no loyalty to the parent. Indeed, part of being a proper parent is to demonstrate loyalty to your children whether or not that loyalty is reciprocated. This is not to suggest any kind of analogy between parents and employees, but rather that it is not nonsense to suppose that loyalty may be appropriate even though it is not reciprocated. Inasmuch as he ignores this possibility, Duska's account of loyalty is flawed.

Second, even if Duska is correct in holding that loyalty is only appropriate between moral agents and that a company is not genuinely a moral agent, the question may still be raised whether an employee owes loyalty to fellow employees or the shareholders of the company. Granted that reference to a company as an individual involves reification and should not be taken too literally, it may nevertheless constitute a legitimate shorthand way of describing relations between genuine moral agents.

Third, it seems wrong to suggest that simply because the primary motive of the employer is economic, considerations of loyalty are irrelevant. An employee's primary motive in working for an employer is generally economic, but no one on that account would argue that it is impossible for her to demonstrate loyalty to the employer, even if it turns out to be misplaced. All that is required is that her primary economic motive be in some degree qualified by considerations of the employer's welfare. Similarly, the fact that an employer's primary motive is economic does not imply that it is not qualified by considerations of the employee's welfare. Given the possibility of mutual qualification of admittedly primary economic motives, it is fallacious to argue that employee loyalty is never appropriate.

In contrast to Duska, the standard view is that loyalty to one's employer is appropriate. According to it, one has an obligation to be loyal to one's employer and, consequently, a *prima facie* duty to protect the employer's interests. Whistleblowing constitutes, therefore, a violation of duty to one's employer and needs strong justification if it is to be appropriate. Sissela Bok summarizes this view very well when she writes

> the whistleblower hopes to stop the game; but since he is neither referee nor coach, and since he blows the whistle on his own team, his act is seen as a violation of loyalty. In holding his position, he has assumed certain obligations to his colleagues and clients. He may even have subscribed to a loyalty oath or a promise of confidentiality. Loyalty to colleagues and to clients comes to be pitted against loyalty to the public interest, to those who may be injured unless the revelation is made.[5]

The strength of this view is that it recognizes that loyalty is due one's employer. Its weakness is that it tends to conceive of whistleblowing as involving a tragic moral choice, since blowing the whistle is seen not so much as a positive action, but rather the lesser of two evils. Bok again puts the essence of this view very clearly when she writes that "a would-be whistleblower must weigh his responsibility to serve the public interest *against* the responsibility he owes to his colleagues and the institution in which he works" and "that [when] their duty [to whistleblow] ... *so overrides loyalties to colleagues and institutions,* they [whistleblowers] often have reason to fear the results of carrying out such a duty."[6] The employee, according to this understanding of whistleblowing, must choose between two acts of betrayal, either her employer or the public interest, each in itself reprehensible.

Behind this view lies the assumption that to be loyal to someone is to act in a way that accords with what that person believes to be in her best interests. To be loyal to an employer, therefore, is to act in a way which the employer deems to be in his or her best interests. Since employers very rarely approve of whistleblowing and generally feel that it is not in their best interests, it follows that whistleblowing is an act of betrayal on the part of the employee, albeit a betrayal made in the interests of the public good.

Plausible though it initially seems, I think this view of whistleblowing is mistaken and that it embodies a mistaken conception of what constitutes employee loyalty. It ignores the fact that

> the great majority of corporate whistleblowers ... [consider] themselves to be very loyal employees who ... [try] to use 'direct voice' (internal whistle-blowing), ... [are] rebuffed and punished for this, and then ... [use] 'indi-rect voice' (external whistleblowing). They ... [believe] initially that they ... [are] behaving in a loyal manner, helping their employers by calling top management's attention to practices that could eventually get the firm in trouble.[7]

By ignoring the possibility that blowing the whistle may demonstrate greater loyalty than not blowing the whistle, it fails to do justice to the many instances where loyalty to someone constrains us to act in defiance of what that person believes to be in her best interests. I am not, for example, being disloyal to a friend if I refuse to loan her money for an investment I am sure will bring her financial ruin; even if she bitterly reproaches me for denying her what is so obviously a golden opportunity to make a fortune.

A more adequate definition of being loyal to someone is that loyalty involves acting in accordance with what one has good reason to believe to be in that person's best interests. A key question, of course, is what constitutes a good reason to think that something is in a person's best interests. Very often, but by no means invariably, we accept that a person thinking that something is in her best interests is a sufficiently good reason to think that it actually is. Other times, especially when we feel that she is being rash, foolish, or misinformed we are prepared, precisely by virtue of being loyal, to act contrary to the person's wishes. It is beyond the scope of this paper to investigate such cases in detail, but three general points can be made.

First, to the degree that an action is genuinely immoral, it is impossible that it is in the agent's best interests. We would not, for example, say that someone who sells child pornography was acting in his own best interests, even if he vigorously protested that there was nothing wrong with such activity. Loyalty does not imply that we have a duty to refrain from reporting the immoral actions of those to whom we are loyal. An employer who is acting immorally is not acting in her own best interests and an employee is not acting disloyally in blowing the whistle.[8] Indeed, the argument can be made that the employee who blows the whistle may be demonstrating greater loyalty than the employee who simply ignores the immoral conduct, inasmuch as she is attempting to prevent her employer from engaging in self-destructive behaviour.

Second, loyalty requires that, whenever possible, in trying to resolve a problem we deal directly with the person to whom we are loyal. If, for example, I am loyal to a friend I do not immediately involve a third party when I try to dissuade my friend from involvement in immoral actions. Rather, I approach my friend directly, listen to his perspective on the events in question, and provide an opportunity for him to address the problem in a morally satisfactory way. This implies that, whenever possible, a loyal employee blows the whistle internally. This provides the employer with the opportunity to either demonstrate to the employee that, contrary to first appearances, no genuine wrongdoing had occurred, or, if there is a genuine moral problem, the opportunity to resolve it.

This principle of dealing directly with the person to whom loyalty is due needs to be qualified, however. Loyalty to a person requires that one acts in that person's best interests. Generally, this cannot be done without directly involving the person to whom one is loyal in the decision-making process, but there may arise cases where acting in a person's best interests requires that one act independently and perhaps even against the wishes of the person to whom one is loyal. Such cases will be especially apt to arise when the person to whom one is loyal is either immoral or ignoring the moral consequences of his actions. Thus, for example, loyalty to a friend who deals in hard narcotics would not imply that I speak first to my friend about my decision to inform the police of his activities, if the only effect of my doing so would be to make him more careful in his criminal dealings. Similarly, a loyal employee is under no obligation to speak first to an employer about the employer's immoral actions, if the only response of the employer will be to take care to cover up wrongdoing.

Neither is a loyal employee under obligation to speak first to an employer if it is clear that by doing so she placed herself in jeopardy from an employer who will retaliate if given the opportunity. Loyalty amounts to acting in another's best interests and that may mean qualifying what seems to be in one's own interests, but it cannot imply that one take no steps to protect oneself from the immorality of those to whom one is loyal. The reason it cannot is that, as has already been argued, acting immorally can never really be in a person's best interests. It follows, therefore, that one is not acting in a person's best interests if one allows oneself to be treated immorally by that person. Thus, for example, a father might be loyal to a child even though the child is guilty of stealing from him, but this would not mean that the father should let the child continue to steal. Similarly, an employee may be loyal to an employer even though she takes steps to protect herself against unfair retaliation by the employer, e.g., by blowing the whistle externally.

Third, loyalty requires that one is concerned with more than considerations of justice. I have been arguing that loyalty cannot require one to ignore immoral or unjust behaviour on the part of those to whom one is loyal, since loyalty amounts to acting in a person's best interests and it can never be in a person's best interests to be allowed to act immorally. Loyalty, however, goes beyond considerations of justice in that, while it is possible to be disinterested and just, it is not possible to be disinterested and loyal. Loyalty implies a desire that the person to whom one is loyal take no moral stumbles, but that if moral stumbles have occurred that the person be restored and not simply punished. A loyal friend is not only someone who sticks by you in times of trouble, but someone who tries to help you avoid trouble. This suggests that a loyal employee will have a desire to point out problems and potential problems long before the drastic measures associated with whistleblowing become necessary, but that if whistleblowing does become necessary there remains a desire to help the employer.

In conclusion, although much more could be said on the subject of loyalty, our brief discussion has enabled us to clarify considerably the relation between whistleblowing and employee loyalty. It permits us to steer a course between the Scylla of Duska's view that, since the primary link between employer and employee is economic, the ideal of employee loyalty is an oxymoron, and the Charybdis of the standard view that, since it forces an employee to weigh conflicting duties, whistleblowing inevitably involves some degree of moral tragedy. The solution lies in realizing that to whistleblow for reasons of morality is to act in one's employer's best interests and involves, therefore, no disloyalty.

Notes

1. The definition I have proposed applies most directly to the relation between privately owned companies aiming to realize a profit and their employees. Obviously, issues of whistleblowing arise in other contexts, e.g., governmental organizations or charitable agencies, and deserve careful thought. I do not propose, in this paper, to discuss whistleblowing in these other contexts, but I think my development of the concept of whistleblowing as positive demonstration of loyalty can easily be applied and will prove useful.

2. Duska, R.: 1985, 'Whistleblowing and Employee Loyalty', in J. R. Desjardins and J. J. McCall, eds., *Contemporary Issues in Business Ethics* (Wadsworth, Belmont, California), pp. 295–300.

3. Duska, p. 297.

4. Duska, p. 298.

5. Bok, S.: 1983, 'Whistleblowing and Professional Responsibility', in T. L. Beauchamp and N. E. Bowie, eds., *Ethical Theory and Business,* 2nd ed. (Prentice-Hall Inc., Englewood Cliffs, New Jersey), pp. 261–269, p. 263.

6. Bok, pp. 261–2, emphasis added.

7. Near, J. P. and P. Miceli: 1985, 'Organizational Dissidence: The Case of Whistle-Blowing', *Journal of Business Ethics* **4**, pp. 1–16, p. 10.

8. As Near and Miceli note 'The whistle-blower may provide valuable information helpful in improving organizational effectiveness . . . the prevalence of illegal activity in organizations is associated with declining organizational performance' (p. 1).
    The general point is that the structure of the world is such that it is not in a company's long-term interests to act immorally. Sooner or later a company which flouts morality and legality will suffer.

POSTSCRIPT

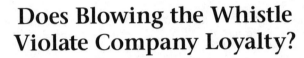

Does Blowing the Whistle Violate Company Loyalty?

W histle-blowing is a difficult choice. What would you do when faced with such a choice? The corporation is not the only setting for whistle-blowers. Would you report a friend for drug abuse, cheating on exams, or stealing? How do you weigh the possibility of damage being done to the community against the security of your own career (some damage done to many people versus much damage done to a few people)? If you see only painful consequences if you blow the whistle, does that settle the problem—or does simple justice and fidelity to law have a claim of its own?

Should we, as a society, protect the whistle-blower with legislation designed to discourage corporate retaliation? Richard T. DeGeorge and Alan F. Westin, two of the earliest business ethics writers to take whistle-blowing seriously, agree that companies should adopt policies that preclude the need for employees to blow the whistle. "The need for moral heroes," DeGeorge concludes in *Business Ethics,* 2d ed. (Macmillan, 1986), "shows a defective society and defective corporations. It is more important to change the legal and corporate structures that make whistle blowing necessary than to convince people to be moral heroes." In *Whistle Blowing: Loyalty and Dissent in the Corporation* (McGraw-Hill, 1981), Westin writes, "The single most important element in creating a meaningful internal system to deal with whistle blowing is to have top leadership accept this as a management priority. This means that the chief operating officer and his senior colleagues have to believe that a policy which encourages discussion and dissent, and deals fairly with whistle-blowing claims, is a good and important thing for their company to adopt.... They have to see it, in their own terms, as a moral duty of good private enterprise."

Suggested Readings

Tim Barnett, Ken Bass, and Gene Brown, "Religiosity, Ethical Ideology, and Intentions to Report a Peer's Wrongdoing," *Journal of Business Ethics* (November 1996), pp. 1161–1174.

Terry Morehead Dworkin and Janet P. Near, "A Better Statutory Approach to Whistle-Blowing," *Journal of the Society for Business Ethics* (January 1997), pp. 1–16.

Kenneth Kernaghan, "Whistle-Blowing in Canadian Governments: Ethical, Political, and Managerial Considerations," *Optimum* (1991–1992).

Is Controlling Drug Abuse More Important Than Protecting Privacy?

YES: Michael A. Verespej, from "Drug Users—Not Testing—Anger Workers," *Industry Week* (February 17, 1992)

NO: Jennifer Moore, from "Drug Testing and Corporate Responsibility: The 'Ought Implies Can' Argument," *Journal of Business Ethics* (vol. 8, 1989)

ISSUE SUMMARY

YES: Michael A. Verespej, a writer for *Industry Week,* argues that workers are the hardest hit when their coworkers use drugs, and he suggests that, for this reason, a majority of employees are tolerant of drug testing.

NO: Jennifer Moore, a researcher of business ethics and business law, asserts that a right is a right and that any utilitarian concerns that employers can cite to justify drug testing should not override the right of the employee to dignity and privacy on the job.

In 1928 U.S. Supreme Court justice Louis Brandeis defined the right of privacy as "the right to be let alone, the most comprehensive of rights and the right most valued by civilized men." The constitutional origins of that right are hazy, found variously in the Fourth Amendment (prohibiting illegal searches and seizures), the Fifth Amendment (prohibiting compulsory testimony), and parts of the Ninth Amendment. But the U.S. Constitution only limits *government* action, and worried Americans increasingly find that their employers can be a more dangerous threat to their privacy.

What right does an employee have to be "let alone" by his or her employer? Historically, none at all. Dictatorial employers had no qualms about making and enforcing rules governing not only job performance but dress and personal behavior on the job as well. Many also had rules for off-the-job behavior. School boards, for example, routinely enforced rules that required teachers to abstain from smoking and drinking, to attend church regularly, and to limit courting to one day a week. But with the advent of organized labor, the freedom of the employer to dictate the employee's lifestyle off the job almost disappeared. On-the-job requirements also ceased to be absolute. Although certain obvious safety rules could be enforced (such as prohibiting alcohol on the job and requiring that safety equipment be worn), the presumption was that rules should not be extended beyond necessity. Until very recently, we had seemed to be approaching an understanding that the employee's choices of amusements and associations off the job were sacrosanct and that his or her personal style of dress and grooming on the job could be regulated only to the extent that such appearances were reasonably job-related.

Then came drugs. Unlike alcohol, drugs can be easily concealed in one's clothing and cannot be detected on a person's breath after they are consumed. Seasoned foremen who would have no trouble spotting the slurred speech and wobbly walk caused by alcohol may not be able to detect drug use in their employees. The effect of drug use on judgment and behavior, especially for such people as pilots, bus drivers, and military personnel, can and does cause deaths.

While many may agree that this fact alone justifies testing for on-the-job drug use, there are many factors that complicate the issue. First, the only tests currently available to determine drug use are seriously invasive (unlike the Breathalyzer test for alcohol, for instance). In practice, the tester must take a blood sample from the worker or require the worker to give up a urine sample. The blood test requires a needle stick that some find painful and terrifying, and the urination must be observed to ensure that the test is valid—at an imaginable cost in embarrassment to the worker and to the observer. Second, the tests cannot distinguish between drug-use behavior on the job and off the job. Marijuana smoked on a Friday night may show up in urine that is expelled on the following Tuesday. So the worker subjected to testing at random may find his off-the-job activities severely restricted by the tests. To be sure, no one is interested in condoning off-the-job drug use, but the move from on-the-job regulation to 24-hour regulation is an unintended consequence that raises further legal and ethical issues.

Third, the tests are not always accurate. Most employers have a policy that if an employee fails one drug test, he or she can take another in order to ensure accuracy. If the employee fails twice, he or she is out. But the tests are only 90 to 95 percent accurate, at best. That means that 1 out of 10, or at best 1 out of 20, will yield a false positive (the employee will appear to have drugs in his or her system). One out of 100, or at best 1 out of 400, will yield a false positive upon retest of a false positive. But some firms have thousands of workers. Is it fair to impose a testing routine that commits gross injustice once in 100 cases —or even only once in 400 cases?

As you read the following selections by Michael A. Verespej and Jennifer Moore, ask yourself how society ought to balance the conflicting demands of privacy for the worker and safety for society. Given the doubts surrounding the practice, is routine randomized drug testing justified? On the other hand, given the terrible dangers that attend drug use on the job, can society afford to do without it?

Michael A. Verespej  **YES**

Drug Users—Not Testing—
Anger Workers

D rug testing by companies still elicits an emotional response from employees. But it's a far different one from four years ago.

Back then, readers responding to an IW [*Industry Week*] survey angrily protested workplace drug testing as an invasion of privacy and argued that drug testing should be reserved for occasions in which there was suspicion of drug use or in an accident investigation.

Today's prevailing view, based on a recent IW survey covering essentially the same questions, stands as a stark contrast. Not only do fewer employees see drug testing as an invasion of privacy, but a significantly higher percentage think that companies should extend the scope of drug testing to improve safety and productivity in the workplace.

Why aren't employees as leery of workplace drug testing as they were four years ago?

First, both the numbers and the comments suggest that employees and managers are less worried that inaccurate drug tests will brand them as drug users. Just 19.3% of those surveyed say that they consider drug testing an invasion of privacy, compared with 30% in the earlier survey.

Second, the tight job market appears to have made non-drug-users resent the presence of drug users in the workplace. Third, in contrast to four years ago, employees and managers are more concerned about the potential safety problems that drug users cause them than whatever invasion of privacy might result from a drug test. The net result: Unlike four years ago, employee thinking is now in sync with the viewpoints held for some time by top corporate management. "Job safety and performance are more important than the slight invasion of privacy caused by drug testing," asserts Lee Taylor, plant manager at U.S. Gypsum Co.'s Siguard, Utah, facility. "Freedom and privacy end when others are likely to be injured," adds the president of a high-tech business in Fort Collins, Colo.

G. A. Holland, chief estimator for a Bloomfield, Conn., construction firm, agrees: "Drug testing may be an invasion of privacy, but, because drug use puts

From Michael A. Verespej, "Drug Users—Not Testing—Anger Workers," *Industry Week* (February 17, 1992). Copyright © 1992 by Penton Publishing, Inc., Cleveland, OH. Reprinted by permission.

others in danger, [drug testing] is an acceptable practice. The safety of employees overrides the right to privacy of another." Adds D. S. McRoberts, manager of a Green Giant food-processing plant in Buhl, Idaho: "The risks employees put themselves and their peers under when they use drugs justify testing."

Perhaps the most blunt response comes from Louis Krivanek, a consulting engineer with Omega Induction Services, Warren, Mich.: "I certainly wouldn't ride with a drinking alcoholic. Why should I work with a drug addict not under control?"

And the anti-drug-user attitude is not just a safety issue, either. "Drug users are also a financial risk to the employer," declares John Larkin, president of Overland Computer, Omaha, Nebr. "It's time to begin thinking about the health and welfare of the company," says William Pence, vice president and general manager of Kantronics Inc., Lawrence, Kans. "Drug testing is simply a preventive measure to ensure the future stability of a company."

The competitive factor also appears to be influencing workers' viewpoints. "A drug-free environment must exist if the quality of product and process is to be continuously improved," writes one employee.

"Productivity and company survival are too important to trust to an employee with a drug problem," says Jack VerMeulen, director of quality assurance at C-Line Products, Des Plaines, Ill. "Employees are a company's most valuable assets, and those assets must perform at the peak of their ability. Test them." One could argue that workers—and managers—have simply become conditioned to drug testing in the workplace because it is no longer the exception, but the rule. After all, 56% of the managers responding to the survey—twice as many as four years ago—say their companies have drug-testing programs in place.

But the real reason for the change in opinion appears to be that four years of day-in, day-out experience with workplace drug problems have made managers and employees less tolerant of users. The attitude appears to be: Drug users are criminals and shouldn't be protected by the absence of a drug-testing program.

"Users are, by definition, criminals," declares Nick Benson, senior automation engineer at Babcock & Wilcox, Lynchburg, Va. "Drug users are breaking the law," states Naomi Walter, a data-processing specialist at Gemini Marketing Associates, Carthage, Mo. "So why let them get an advantage?"

Layoffs and plant and store closings are also behind the new lack of tolerance for the drug user. "I believe that if a company is paying a person to work for them," says one IW reader, "that person should be drug-free. A job is a privilege, not a right."

⋯⊙⋯

That lack of tolerance is reflected in significantly changed ideas of who in the workplace should be tested for drug use. A significantly higher percentage of respondents think that more workers should be tested at random or that *all* employees should be tested.

More than 45% of IW readers—compared with 29.6% four years ago—say that drug tests should be conducted at random. And 70.5% think all employees should be required to take drug tests. Only 60% felt that way in the last IW drug-testing survey. Not surprisingly, then, the percentage of readers who would take a drug test and who think that employers should be able to test employees for drug use is now 93%; it was 88% four years ago.

But several attitudes haven't changed. Workers and managers still think that when companies use drug testing, they should be required to offer rehabilitation through employee-assistance programs, that management should be tested as well as employees, and that alcohol problems are equally troublesome. "Employers should be prepared to help—not just fire someone if the drug or alcohol abuse is exposed," says H. A. Dellicker, programming manager at Siemens Nixdorf, Burlington, Mass. "You need a properly monitored rehabilitation program."

Readers are just as adamant that if the majority of employees is to be tested, then everyone should be included—all the way up to the CEO. "Drug testing should be conducted on all employees, from top management down to the lowest position," asserts Sharon Hyitt, a drafting technician at Varco Pruden Buildings, Van Wert, Ohio. And IW readers contend that any drug-testing program should test for alcohol abuse as well. "Drug testing stops short," argues a reader in Muncie, Ind. "Alcoholism is more widespread in our workplace and just as destructive."

A plant superintendent in Ohio agrees and laments, "Alcohol is the most abused drug in our workplace, but it is not covered under our testing program. While the 'heavy' drugs get the spotlight because of the violence associated with their distribution, alcohol does the most damage in the workplace."

A product-testing engineer agrees, "Alcohol should be included in the tests and then perhaps lunch-time drinking would decrease. Why is it O.K. for those who have three-martini lunches to come back to work and try to function?"

NO ⤶

Drug Testing and Corporate Responsibility: The "Ought Implies Can" Argument

In the past few years, testing for drug use in the workplace has become an important and controversial trend. Approximately 30% of Fortune 500 companies now engage in some sort of drug testing or screening, as do many smaller firms. The Reagan administration has called for mandatory testing of all federal employees. Several states have already passed drug testing laws; others will probably consider them in the future. While the Supreme Court has announced its intention to rule on the testing of federal employees within the next few months, its decision will not settle the permissibility of testing private employees. Discussion of the issue is likely to remain lively and heated for some time.

Most of the debate about drug testing in the workplace has focused on the issue of privacy rights. Three key questions have been: Do employees have privacy rights? If so, how far do these extend? What kinds of considerations outweigh these rights? I believe there are good reasons for supposing that employees do have moral privacy rights,[1] and that drug testing usually (though not always) violates these, but privacy is not my main concern in this paper. I wish to examine a different kind of argument, the claim that because corporations are responsible for harms committed by employees while under the influence of drugs, they are entitled to test for drug use.

This argument is rarely stated formally in the literature, but it can be found informally quite often.[2] One of its chief advantages is that it seems, at least at first glance, to bypass the issue of privacy rights altogether. There seems to be no need to determine the extent or weight of employees' privacy rights to make the argument work. It turns on a different set of principles altogether, that is, on the meaning and conditions of responsibility. This is an important asset, since arguments about rights are notoriously difficult to settle. Rights claims frequently function in ethical discourse as conversation-stoppers or non-negotiable demands.[3] Although it is widely recognized that rights are not absolute, there is little consensus on how far they extend, what kinds of considerations should be allowed to override them, or even how to go about

From Jennifer Moore, "Drug Testing and Corporate Responsibility: The 'Ought Implies Can' Argument," *Journal of Business Ethics,* vol. 8 (1989), pp. 279–287. Copyright © 1989 by D. Reidel Publishing Co., Dordrecht, Holland, and Boston, U.S.A. Reprinted by permission of Kluwer Academic Publishers.

settling these questions. But it is precisely these thorny problems that proponents of drug testing must tackle if they wish to address the issue on privacy grounds. Faced with the claim that drug testing violates the moral right to privacy of employees, proponents of testing must either (1) argue that drug testing does not really violate the privacy rights of employees;[4] (2) acknowledge that drug testing violates privacy rights, but argue that there are considerations that override those rights, such as public safety; or (3) argue that employees have no moral right to privacy at all.[5] It is not surprising that an argument that seems to move the debate out of the arena of privacy rights entirely appears attractive.

In spite of its initial appeal, however, I will maintain that the argument does not succeed in circumventing the claims of privacy rights. Even responsibility for the actions of others, I will argue, does not entitle us to do absolutely anything to control their behavior. We must look to rights, among other things, to determine what sorts of controls are morally permissible. Once this is acknowledged, the argument loses much of its force. In addition, it requires unjustified assumptions about the connection between drug testing and the prevention of drug-related harm.

An "Ought Implies Can" Argument

Before we can assess the argument, it must be set out more fully. It seems to turn on the deep-rooted philosophical connection between responsibility and control. Generally, we believe that agents are not responsible[6] for acts or events that they could not have prevented. People are responsible for their actions only if, it is often said, they "could have done otherwise". Responsibility implies some measure of control, freedom, or autonomy. It is for this reason that we do not hold the insane responsible for their actions. Showing that a person lacked the capacity to do otherwise blocks the normal moves of praise or blame and absolves the agent of responsibility for a given act.

For similar reasons, we believe that persons cannot be obligated to do things that they are incapable of doing, and that if they fail to do such things, no blame attaches to them. Obligation is empty, even senseless, without capability. If a person is obligated to perform an action, it must be within his or her power. This principle is sometimes summed up by the phrase "ought implies can". Kant used it as part of a metaphysical argument for free will, claiming that if persons are to have obligations at all, they must be autonomous, capable of acting freely.[7] The argument we examine here is narrower in scope, but similar in principle. If corporations are responsible for harms caused by employees under the influence of drugs, they must have the ability to prevent these harms. They must, therefore, have the freedom to test for drug use.

But the argument is still quite vague. What exactly does it mean to say that corporations are "responsible" for harms caused by employees? There are several possible meanings of "responsible". Not all of these are attributable to corporations, and not all of them exemplify the principle that "ought implies can". The question of how or whether corporations are "responsible" is highly complex, and we cannot begin to answer it in this paper.[8] There are, however, four distinct senses of "responsible" that appear with some regularity in the argument. They can be characterized, roughly, as follows: (a) legally liable; (b) culpable or guilty; (c) answerable or accountable; (d) bound by an obligation. The first is purely legal; the last three have a moral dimension.

Legal Liability

We do hold corporations legally liable for the negligent acts of employees under the doctrine of *respondeat superior* ("let the master respond"). If an employee harms a third party in the course of performing his or her duties for the firm, it is the corporation which must compensate the third party. *Respondeat superior* is an example of what is frequently called "vicarious liability". Since the employee was acting on behalf of the firm, and the firm was acting through the employee when the harmful act was committed, liability is said to "transfer" from the employee to the firm. But it is not clear that such liability on the part of the employer implies a capacity to have prevented the harm. Corporations are held liable for accidents caused by an employee's negligent driving, for example, even if they could not have foreseen or prevented the injury. While some employee accidents can be traced to corporate negligence,[9] there need be no fault on the part of the corporation for the doctrine of *respondeat superior* to apply. The doctrine of *respondeat superior* is grounded not in fault, but in concerns of public policy and utility. It is one of several applications of the notion of liability without fault in legal use today.

Because it does not imply fault, and its attendant ability to have done otherwise, legal liability or responsibility **a** cannot be used successfully as part of an "ought implies can" argument. Holding corporations legally liable for harms committed by intoxicated employees while at the same time forbidding drug-testing is not inconsistent. It could simply be viewed as yet another instance of liability without fault. Of course, one could argue that the notion of liability without fault is itself morally unacceptable, and that liability ought not to be detached from moral notions of punishment and blame. This is surely an extremely important claim, but it is beyond the scope of this paper. The main point to be made here is that we must be able to attribute more than legal liability to corporations if we are to invoke the principle of "ought implies can". Corporations must be responsible in sense **b, c,** or **d**—that is, *morally* responsible —if the argument is to work.

Moral Responsibility

Are corporations morally responsible for harms committed by intoxicated employees? Perhaps the most frequently used notion of moral responsibility is sense **b**, what I have called "guilt" or "culpability".[10] I have in mind here the strongest notion of moral responsibility, the sense that is prevalent in criminal law. An agent is responsible for an act in this sense if the act can be imputed to him or her. An essential condition of imputability is the presence in the agent of an intention to commit the act, or *mens rea*.[11] But does an employer whose workers use drugs satisfy the *mens rea* requirement? The requirement probably would be satisfied if it could be shown that the firm intended the resulting harms, ordered its employees to work under the influence of drugs, or even, perhaps (though this is less clear) turned a blind eye to blatant drug abuse in the workplace.[12] But these are all quite farfetched possibilities. It is reasonable to assume that most corporations do not intend the harms caused by their employees, and that they do not order employees to use drugs on the job. Drug use is quite likely to be prohibited by company policy. If corporations are morally responsible for drug-related harms committed [by] employees, then, it is not in sense **b**.

Corporations might, however, be morally responsible for harms committed by employees in another sense. An organization acts through its employees. It empowers its employees to act in ways in which they otherwise would not act by providing them with money, power, equipment, and authority. Through a series of agreements, the corporation delegates its employees to act on its behalf. For these reasons, one could argue that corporations are responsible, in the sense of "answerable" or "accountable" (responsibility **c**), for the harmful acts of their employees. Indeed, it could be argued that if corporations are not morally responsible for these acts, they are not morally responsible for any acts at all, since corporations can only act through their employees.[13] To say that corporations are responsible for the harms of their employees in sense **c** is to say more than just that a corporation must "pay up" if an employee causes harm. It is to assign fault to the corporation by virtue of the ways in which organizational policies and structures facilitate and direct employees' actions.[14]

Moreover, corporations presumably have the same obligations as other agents to avoid harm in the conduct of their business. Since they conduct their business through their employees, it could plausibly be argued that corporations have an obligation to anticipate and prevent harms that employees might cause in the course of their employment. If this reasoning is correct, corporations are morally responsible for the drug-related harms of employees in sense **d**—that is, they are under an obligation to prevent those harms. The "ought implies can" argument, then, may be formulated as follows:

1. If corporations have obligations, they must be capable of carrying them out, on the principle of "ought implies can".
2. Corporations have an obligation to prevent harm from occurring in the course of conducting their business.
3. Drug use by employees is likely to lead to harm.
4. Corporations must be able to take steps to eliminate (or at least reduce) drug use by employees.
5. Drug testing is an effective way to eliminate/reduce employee drug use.
6. Therefore corporations must be permitted to test for drugs.[15]

The Limits of Corporate Autonomy

This is surely an important argument, one that deserves to be taken seriously. The premise that corporations have an obligation to prevent harm from occurring in the conduct of their business seems unexceptionable and consistent with the actual moral beliefs of society. There is not much question that drug use by employees, especially regular drug use or drug use on the job, leads to harms of various kinds. Some of these are less serious than others, but some are very serious indeed: physical injury to consumers, the public, and fellow employees —and sometimes even death.[16]

Moreover, our convictions about the connections between responsibility or obligation and capability seem unassailable. Like other agents, if corporations are to have obligations, they must have the ability to carry them out. The argument seems to tell us that corporations are only able to carry out their obligations to prevent harm if they can free themselves of drugs. To prevent corporations from drug testing, it implies, is to prevent them from discharging their obligations. It is to cripple corporate autonomy just as we would cripple the autonomy of an individual worker if we refused to allow him to "kick the habit" that prevented him from giving satisfactory job performance.

But this analogy between corporate and individual autonomy reveals the initial defect in the argument. Unlike human beings, corporations are never fully autonomous selves. On the contrary, their actions are always dependent upon individual selves who are autonomous. Human autonomy means self-determination, self-governance, self-control. Corporate autonomy, at least as it is understood here, means control over others. Corporate autonomy is essentially derivative. But this means that corporate acts are not the simple sorts of acts generated by individual persons. They are complex. Most importantly, the members of a corporation are frequently not the agents, but the objects, of "corporate" action. A good deal of corporate action, that is, necessitates doing something not only *through* corporate employees, but *to* those employees.[17] The act of eliminating drugs from the workplace is an act of this sort. A corporation's ridding itself of drugs is not like an individual person's "kicking the habit". Rather, it is one group of persons making another group of persons give up drug use.

This fact has important implications for the "ought implies can" argument. The argument is persuasive in situations in which carrying out one's obligations requires only *self*-control, and does not involve controlling the behavior of others. Presumably there are no restrictions on what one may do to oneself in order to carry out an obligation.[18] But a corporation is not a genuine "self", and there *are* moral limits on what one person may do to another. Because this is so, we cannot automatically assume that the obligation to prevent harm justifies employee drug testing. Of course this does not necessarily mean that drug testing is *unjustified*. But it does mean that before we can determine whether it is justified, we must ask what is permissible for one person or group of persons to do to another to prevent a harm for which they are responsible.

Are there any analogies available that might help to resolve this question? It is becoming increasingly common to hold a hostess responsible (both legally and morally) for harm caused by a drunken guest on the way home from her party. In part, this is because she contributes to the harm by serving her guest alcohol. It is also because she knows that drunk driving is risky, and has a general obligation to prevent harm. What must she be allowed to do to prevent harms of this kind? Persuade the guest to spend the night on the couch? Surely. Take her car keys away from her? Perhaps. Knock her out and lock her in the bathroom until morning? Surely not.

Universities are occasionally held legally and morally responsible for harms committed by members of fraternities—destruction of property, gang rapes, and injuries or death caused by hazing. What may they do to prevent such harms? They may certainly withdraw institutional recognition and support from the fraternity, refusing to let it operate on the campus. But may they expel students who live together off-campus in fraternity-like arrangements? Have university security guards police these houses, covertly or by force? These questions are more difficult to answer.

We sometimes hold landlords morally (though not legally) responsible for tenants who are slovenly, play loud music, or otherwise make nuisances of themselves. Landlords are surely permitted to cancel the leases of such tenants, and they are justified in asking for references from previous landlords to prevent future problems of this kind. But it is not clear that a landlord may delve into a tenant's private life, search his room, or tap his telephone in order to anticipate trouble before it begins.

Each of these situations is one in which one person or group of persons is responsible, to a greater or a lesser degree, for the prevention of harm by others, and needs some measure of control in order to carry out this responsibility.[19] In each case, there is a fairly wide range of actions which we would be willing to allow the first party, but there are some actions which we would rule out. Having an obligation to prevent the harms of others seems to permit us some forms of control, but not all. At least one important consideration in deciding what kinds of actions are permissible is the *rights* of the controlled parties.[20] If these claims are correct, we must examine the rights of employees in order to determine whether drug testing is justified. The relevant right in the case of drug testing is the right to privacy. The "ought implies can" argument, then, does not circumvent the claims of privacy rights as it originally seemed to do.

The Agency Argument

A proponent of drug testing might argue, however, that the relation between employers and employees is significantly different from the relation between hosts and guests, universities and members of fraternities, or landlords and tenants. Employees have a special relation with the firm that employs them. They are *agents,* hired and empowered to act on behalf of the employer. While they act on the business of the firm, it might be argued, they "are" the corporation. The restrictions that apply to what one independent agent may do to another thus do not apply here.

But surely this argument is incorrect, for a number of reasons. First, if it were correct, it would justify anything a corporation might do to control the behavior of an employee—not merely drug testing, but polygraph testing, tapping of telephones, deception, psychological manipulation, whips and chains, etc.[21] There are undoubtedly some people who would argue that some of these procedures are permissible, but few would argue that all of them are. The fact that even some of them appear not to be suggests that we believe there are limits to what corporations may do to control employees, and that one consideration in determining these limits is the employees' rights.

Secondly, the argument implies that employees give up their own autonomy completely when they sign on as agents, and become an organ or piece of the corporation. But this cannot be true. Agency is a moral and contractual relationship of the kind that can only obtain between two independent, autonomous parties. This relationship could not be sustained if the employee ceased to be autonomous upon signing the contract. Employees are not slaves, but autonomous agents capable of upholding a contract. Moreover, we expect a certain amount of discretion in employees in the course of their agency. Employees are not expected to follow illegal or immoral commands of their employers, and we find them morally and legally blameworthy when they do so. That we expect such independent judgment of them suggests that they do not lose their autonomy entirely.[22]

Finally, if the employment contract were one in which employees gave up all right to be treated as autonomous human beings, then it would not be a legitimate or morally valid contract. Some rights are considered "inalienable" —people are forbidden from negotiating them away even if it seems advantageous to them to do so. The law grants recognition to this fact through anti-discrimination statutes, minimum wage legislation, workplace health and safety standards, etc. Even if I would like to, I may not trade away, for example, my right not to be sexually harassed or my right to know about workplace hazards.

Again, these arguments do not show that drug testing is unjustified. They do show, however, that *if* drug testing is justified, it is not because the "ought implies can" argument bypasses the issue of employee rights, but because drug testing does not impermissibly violate those rights.[23] To think that obligation, or responsibility for the acts of others, can circumvent rights claims is to misunderstand the import of the "ought implies can" principle. The principle tells us that there is a close connection between obligation or responsibility and capability. But it does not license us to disregard the rights of others any more than it guarantees us the physical conditions that make carrying out our obligations possible. It may well prove that employees' right to privacy, assuming they have such a right, is secondary to some more weighty consideration. I take up this question briefly below. What has been shown here is that the issue of the permissibility of drug testing will not and cannot be settled *without* a close scrutiny of privacy rights. If we are to decide the issue, we must eventually determine whether employees have privacy rights, how far they extend, and what considerations outweigh them—precisely the difficult questions the "ought implies can" argument sought to avoid.

Is Drug Testing Necessary?

The "ought implies can" argument also has another serious flaw. The argument turns on the claim that forbidding drug testing prevents corporations from carrying out their obligation to prevent harm. But this is only true if drug testing is *necessary* for preventing drug-related harm. If it is merely one option among many, then forbidding drug testing still leaves a corporation free to prevent harm in other ways. For the argument to be sound, in other words, premise 5 would have to be altered to read, "drug testing is a necessary element in any plan to rid the workplace of drugs."

But it is not at all clear that drug testing *is* necessary to reduce drug use in the workplace. Its necessity has been challenged repeatedly. In a recent article in the *Harvard Business Review,* for example, James Wrich draws on his experience in dealing with alcoholism in the workplace and suggests the use of broadbrush educational and rehabilitative programs as alternatives to testing. Corporations using such programs to combat alcohol problems, Wrich reports, have achieved tremendous reductions in absenteeism, sick leave, and on-the-job accidents.[24] Others have argued that impaired performance likely to result in harm could be easily detected by various sorts of performance-oriented tests— mental and physical dexterity tests, alertness tests, flight simulation tests, and so on. These sorts of procedures have the advantage of not being controversial from a rights perspective.[25]

Indeed, many thinkers have argued that drug testing is not only unnecessary, but is not even an effective way to attack drug use in the workplace. The commonly used and affordable urinalysis tests are notoriously unreliable. They have a very high rate both of false negatives and of false positives. At best the tests reveal, not impaired performance or even the presence of a particular drug, but the presence of metabolites of various drugs that can remain in the system long after any effects of the drug have worn off.[26] Because they do not measure impairment, such tests do not seem well-tailored to the purpose of preventing harm—which, after all, is the ultimate goal. As Lewis Maltby, vice president of a small instrumentation company and an opponent of drug testing, puts it,

> ... [T]he fundamental flaw with drug testing is that it tests for the wrong thing. A realistic program to detect workers whose condition put the company or other people at risk would test for the condition that actually creates the danger.[27]

If these claims are true, there is no real connection between the obligation to prevent harm and the practice of drug testing, and the "ought implies can" argument provides no justification for drug testing at all.[28]

Conclusion

I have made no attempt here to determine whether drug testing does indeed violate employees' privacy rights. The analysis ... above suggests that we have reason to believe that employees have some rights. Once we accept the notion of employee rights in general, it seems likely that a right to privacy would be among them, since it is an important civil right and central for the protection of individual autonomy. There are also reasons, I believe, to think that most drug testing violates the right to privacy. These claims need much more defense than they can be given here, and even if they are true, this does not necessarily mean that drug testing is unjustified. It does, however, create a *prima facie* case against drug testing. If drug testing violates the privacy rights of employees, it will be justified only under very strict conditions, if it is justified at all. It is worth taking a moment to see why this is so.

It is generally accepted in both the ethical and legal spheres that rights are not absolute. But we allow basic rights to be overridden only in special cases in which some urgent and fundamental good is at stake. In legal discourse, such goods are called "compelling interests".[29] While there is room for some debate about what counts as a "compelling interest", it is almost always understood to be more than a merely private interest, however weighty. Public safety might well fall into this category, but private monetary loss probably would not. While more needs to be done to determine what kinds of interests justify drug testing, it seems clear that if testing does violate the basic rights of employees, it is only justified in extreme cases—far less often than it is presently used. Moreover, we believe that overriding a right is to be avoided wherever possible, and is only justified when doing so is *necessary* to serve the "compelling interest" in question. If it violates rights, then drug testing is only permissible if it is necessary for the protection of an interest such as public safety and if there is no other, morally preferable, way of accomplishing the same goal. As we have seen above, however, it is by no means clear that drug testing meets these conditions. There may be better, less controversial ways to prevent the harm caused by drug use; if so, these must be used in preference to drug testing, and testing is unjustified. And if the attacks on the effectiveness of drug testing are correct, testing is not only unnecessary for the protection of public safety, but does not serve any "compelling interest" at all.

What do these conclusions tell us about the responsibility of employers for preventing harms caused by employees? If it is decided that drug testing is morally impermissible, then there can be no duty to use it to anticipate and prevent harms. Corporations who fail to use it cannot be blamed for doing so. They cannot have a moral obligation to do something morally impermissible. Moreover, if it turns out that there is no other effective way to prevent the harms caused by drug use, then it seems to me we may not hold employers morally responsible for those harms. This seems to me unlikely to be the case— there probably are other effective measures to control drug abuse in the work-place. But corporations can be held responsible only to the extent that they are permitted to act. It would not be inconsistent, however, to hold corporations legally liable for the harms caused by intoxicated employees under the doctrine of *respondeat superior*, even if drug testing is forbidden, for this kind of liability does not imply an ability to have done otherwise.

Notes

1. Employees do not, of course, have legal privacy rights, although the courts seem to be moving slowly in this direction. Opponents of testing usually claim that employees have *moral* rights to privacy, even if these have not been given legal recognition. See, for example, Joseph Des Jardins and Ronald Duska, "Drug Testing in Employment", in *Business Ethics: Readings and Cases in Corporate Morality*, 2nd edition, ed. W. M. Hoffman and J. M. Moore (McGraw-Hill, forthcoming).

2. See, for example, "Work-Place Privacy Issues and Employer Screening Policies," Richard Lehr and David Middlebrooks, *Employee Relations Law Journal* 11, 407. Lehr and Middlebrooks cite the argument as one of the chief justifications for

drug testing used by employers. I have also encountered the argument frequently in discussion with students, colleagues, and managers.

3. Ronald Dworkin has referred to rights as moral "trumps". This kind of language tends to suggest that rights overwhelm all other considerations, so that when they are flourished, all that opponents can do is subside in silence. Rights are frequently asserted this way in everyday discourse, and in this sense rights claims tend to close, rather than open, the door to fruitful ethical dialogue.

4. In his article "Privacy, Polygraphs, and Work," *Business and Professional Ethics Journal* 1, Fall, 1981, 19, George Brenkert has developed the idea that my privacy is violated when some one acquires information about me that they are not entitled, by virtue of their relationship to me, to have. My mortgage company, for example, is entitled to know my credit history; a prospective sexual partner is entitled to know if I have any sexually transmitted diseases. Thus their knowledge of this information does not violate my privacy. One could argue that employers are similarly entitled to the information obtained by drug tests, and that drug testing does not violate privacy for this reason. A somewhat different move would be to argue that testing does not violate privacy because employees give their "consent" to . . . drug testing as part of the employment contract. For a sustained attack on these and other Type 1 arguments, see Joseph Des Jardins and Ronald Duska, "Drug Testing in Employment".

5. One might defend this position on the ground that the employer "owns" the job and is therefore entitled to place any conditions he wishes on obtaining or keeping it. The problem with this argument is that it seems to rule out *all* employee rights, including such basic ones as the right to organize and bargain collectively, or the right not to be discriminated against, which have solid legal as well as ethical grounding. It also implies that ownership overrides all other considerations, and it is not at all clear that this is true. One might take the position that by accepting a job, an employee has agreed to give up all his rights save those actually specified in the employment contract. But this makes the employment contract look like an agreement in which employees sell themselves and accept the status of things without rights. And it overlooks the fact that we believe there are some things ("inalienable" rights) that persons ought not to be permitted to bargain away. Alex Michalos has discussed some of the limitations of the employment contract in "The Loyal Agent's Argument", in *Ethical Theory and Business,* 2nd edition, ed. Tom L. Beauchamp and Norman E. Bowie (Englewood Cliffs, NJ: Prentice-Hall, 1983), p. 247.

6. The term "responsibility" is deliberately left ambiguous here. Several different meanings of it are examined below.

7. See Immanuel Kant, *Critique of Practical Reason,* trans. Lewis White Beck (Indianapolis: Bobbs-Merril, 1956), p. 30.

8. In this paper I have tried to avoid getting embroiled in the question of whether or not corporations are themselves "moral agents", which has been the question to dominate the corporate responsibility debate. The argument I offer here does, I believe, have important implications for the problem of corporate agency, but does not require me to take a stand on it here. I am content to have those who reject the notion of corporations as moral agents read my references to corporate responsibility as shorthand for some complex form of individual or group responsibility.

9. One example would be negligent hiring, which is an increasingly frequent cause of action against an employer. Employers can also be held negligent if they give orders that lead to harms that they ought to have foreseen. Domino's Pizza is now under suit because it encouraged its drivers to deliver pizzas as fast as possible, a policy that accident victims claim should have been expected to cause accidents.

10. This understanding of moral responsibility often seems to overshadow other notions. In an article on corporate responsibility, for example, Manuel Velasquez concludes that because corporations are not responsible in this sense, they are "not responsible for anything they do". "Why Corporations Are Not Responsible For Anything They Do", *Business and Professional Ethics Journal* 2, Spring, 1983, 1.

11. There is also an *actus reus* requirement for this type of responsibility—that is, the act must be traceable to the voluntary bodily movements of the agent. Obviously, corporations do not have bodies, but the people who work for them do. The question, then, has become when may we call an act by one member of the corporation a "corporate act". If it is possible to do so at all, the decisive feature is probably the presence of some sort of corporate "intention." This is why I focus on intention here, and why intention has been central to the discussion of corporate responsibility.

12. There are some, like Velasquez, who hold that a corporation can never satisfy the *mens rea* requirement because this would require a collective mind. If this were true, the argument would collapse at the outset. Others believe that a *mens rea* can be attributed to corporations metaphorically, if it can be shown that company policy includes an "intention" to harm, and it is this model I follow here.

13. There are, of course, those who take precisely this position. See Velasquez, "Why Corporations Are Not Responsible For Anything They Do".

14. See, for example, Peter French, *Collective and Corporate Responsibility* (New York: Columbia University Press, 1984).

15. It is tempting to conclude from this argument that drug testing is not only permissible, but obligatory, but this is not the case. The reason why it is not provides a clue to one of the major weaknesses of the argument. Drug testing would be obligatory only if it were *necessary* for the prevention of harm due to drug use, but it is not clear that this is so. But [it] also means that it is not clear that corporations are deflected from their duty to prevent harm by a prohibition against drug testing. See below for a fuller discussion of this problem.

16. For example, it has been claimed that employees who use drugs cause four times as many work-related accidents as do other employees. The highly publicized Conrail crash in 1987 was determined to be drug-related. Of course there are harms to the company itself as well, in the form of higher absenteeism, lowered productivity, higher insurance costs, etc. But since these types of harm raise the question of what a company may do to preserve its self-interest, rather than what it may do to prevent harms to others for which they are responsible, I focus here on harm to employees, consumers, and the public.

17. In our eagerness to assign "corporate responsibility", this fact has frequently been overlooked. This in turn has led, I believe, to an oversimplified view of corporate action. I discuss this problem more fully in a paper in progress entitled "The Paradox of Corporate Autonomy".

18. It is an interesting question whether there are limitations on what individuals can do to themselves to control their own behavior. What about individuals who undergo hypnosis, or who have their jaws wired shut in order to lose weight? Are they violating their own rights? Undermining their own autonomy? It could be argued plausibly that these kinds of things are not permissible, on the Kantian ground that we have a duty not to treat ourselves as merely as means to an end. Of course, if there are such restrictions, it makes the "ought implies can" argument as applied to corporations even weaker.

19. None of these analogies is perfect. In the case of the hostess and guest, for example, the guest is clearly intoxicated. This is rarely true of employees who are tested for drugs; if the employee were visibly intoxicated, there would be no need to test. Moreover, in the hostess/guest case the hostess contributes directly to the

intoxication. There are important parallels, however. In each case one party is held morally (and in two of the cases, legally) responsible for harms caused by others. Moreover, the first parties are responsible in close to the same way that employers are responsible for the acts of their employees: they in some sense "facilitate" the harmful acts, they have some capacity to prevent those acts, and they are thus viewed as having an obligation to prevent them. One main difference, of course, is that employees are "agents" of their employers....

20. There are other, utility-related considerations, as well—for example, harm to employees who are unjustly dismissed, a demoralized workforce, the costs of testing, etc. I concentrate here on rights because they have been the primary focal point in the drug testing debate.

21. The assumption here is that persons are entitled to do whatever they wish to themselves. See Note 18.

22. See Michalos, "The Loyal Agent's Argument".

23. Some violations of right, of course, are permissible....

24. James T. Wrich, "Beyond Testing: Coping with Drugs at Work", *Harvard Business Review* Jan.–Feb. 1988, 120.

25. See Des Jardins and Duska, "Drug Testing in Employment", and Lewis Maltby, "Why Drug Testing is a Bad Idea", *Inc.* June 1987. While other sorts of tests also have the potential to be abused, they are at least a direct measurement of something that an employer is entitled to know—performance capability. Des Jardins and Duska offer an extended defense of this sort of test.

26. See Edward J. Imwinkelried, "False Positive", *The Sciences,* Sept.–Oct. 1987, 22. Also David Bearman, "The Medical Case Against Drug Testing", *Harvard Business Review* Jan.–Feb. 1988, 123.

27. Maltby, "Why Drug Testing is a Bad Idea", pp. 152–153.

28. It could still be argued that drug testing *deters* drug use, and thus has a connection with preventing harm, even though it doesn't directly provide any information that enables companies to prevent harm. This is an important point, but it is still subject to the restrictions discussed in the previous section. Not everything that has a deterrent value is permissible. It is possible that a penalty of capital punishment would provide a deterrent for rapists, or having one's hand removed deter shoplifting, but there are very few advocates for these penalties. Effectiveness is not the only issue here; rights and justice are also relevant.

29. The principle that fundamental rights may not be overridden by the state unless doing so is necessary to serve a "compelling state interest" is a principle of constitutional law, but it also reflects our moral intuitions about when it is appropriate to override rights. The legal principle would not apply to all cases of drug testing in the workplace because many of these involve private, rather than state, employees. But the principle does provide us with useful guidelines in the ethical sphere. Interestingly, Federal District Judge George Revercomb recently issued an injunction blocking the random drug testing of Justice Department employees on the ground that it did not serve a compelling state interest. Since there was no evidence of a drug problem among the Department's employees, the Judge concluded, there is no threat that would give rise to a compelling interest. See "Judge Blocks Drug Testing of Justice Department Employees", *New York Times* July 30, 1988, 7.

POSTSCRIPT

Is Controlling Drug Abuse More Important Than Protecting Privacy?

In the controversy over drug testing, the two sides seem to be reasoning from different moral principles and to different consequences. The proponents of randomized drug testing cite the principle of Least Harm: left to themselves to take drugs, the workforce is likely to turn out terribly harmful results—damaged products, derailed trains, and the pervasive negligence that makes products unsafe and the workplace dangerous.

The opponents of drug testing, however, find more harm than good resulting from drug testing. Given the potential for error, good employees will not only be fired but also be stigmatized; the morale of the workforce will suffer as the invasions of privacy threaten the dignity and self-esteem of the worker; and the atmosphere of suspicion built up by the testing policy will result in worker resentment.

It is difficult to predict the future of drug testing in the workplace. If it is to be allowed—and, according to the surveys reported by Verespej, it should be—more reliable tests are needed on the front line. There is now a very expensive test for which 99.9 percent accuracy is claimed, which is often used as a backup if an employee fails a drug test once. But generally, it is not used to screen candidates for employment, so there is still the risk of excluding good employees because of false positives or ruining credibility with too many false negatives. Primarily, drugs are not a company problem or an affliction of American business or capitalism. They are proliferating in the society at large, and until drugs are removed from the street, there is little hope of getting them out of the workplace. Under these circumstances, it seems that the certainty of invasion outweighs the possibility of preventing drug use. On the other hand, the corporations may be the perfect place to begin to confront drug abuse.

Suggested Readings

Rob Brookler, "Industry Standards in Workplace Drug Testing," *Personnel Journal* (April 1992).

Michael Janofsky, "Drug Use and Workers' Rights," *The New York Times* (December 28, 1993).

Laura Lally, "Privacy Versus Accessibility: The Impact of Situationally Conditioned Belief," *Journal of Business Ethics* (November 1996).

Rita C. Manning, "Liberal and Communitarian Defenses of Workplace Privacy," *Journal of Business Ethics* (June 1997).

ISSUE 11

Is CEO Compensation Justified by Performance?

YES: Kevin J. Murphy, from "Top Executives Are Worth Every Nickel They Get," *Harvard Business Review* (March/April 1986)

NO: Lisa H. Newton, from "The Care and Feeding of the Truly Greedy: CEO Salaries in World Perspective," An Original Essay Written for This Volume (2000)

ISSUE SUMMARY

YES: Professor of finance and business economics Kevin J. Murphy argues that chief executive officers (CEOs) are simply paid to do what they were hired to do—bring up the price of the stock to increase shareholder wealth. He concludes that for large increases in shareholder wealth, CEOs deserve large compensation.

NO: Professor of philosophy Lisa H. Newton finds the ultimate effect of large compensation packages on U.S. business to be negative. She asserts that the disparity between CEOs' wealth and the pay of their workers—let alone the poverty-stricken developing world—is unjust and a case of bad stewardship of resources.

CEOs are paid a lot to face facts, however unpleasant," writes Geoffrey Colvin in *Fortune* (1992), "so it's time they faced this one: The issue of their pay has finally landed on the national agenda and won't be leaving soon." He ticks off the sources of national discontent with the enormous sums (and stocks, etc.) paid to the corporate chiefs: layoffs continue; the lowest paid workers advance only slowly; Japanese CEOs are paid much less for much more productivity; but mostly, paying one person more money than he can ever spend on anything worthwhile for himself or his family, while the world's millions struggle, just seems to be wrong.

According to John Cassidy's *New Yorker* article, "Gimme" (November, 1997), since Colvin wrote, CEO compensation has gone much higher—by a factor of 4 for the average compensation up to factors of 15 and 20 for fortunate individuals. Colvin expresses disapproval of compensation from $1.5 million to $3 million per year, and in his article, Cassidy writes of compensation from

$18 million to $20 million per year. By 2000 compensation was observed as high as $90 million per year. The reason for the increase is clear enough to Cassidy: stock prices have gone up; shareholder wealth has increased enormously; and for reasons detailed in the following selections, shareholders wish to compensate managers of their companies according to the increase in the price of the stock. Is this right? The shareholders' interests legitimately dictate some aspects of corporate policy, and the salaries have been agreed upon by the legally appropriate parties, but if the result is substantially unjust, should not the people as a whole step in and rectify the situation?

Recent news on the CEO compensation front shows that as of early April 2001, stocks have undergone a correction and many have decreased significantly. Shareholder wealth has also decreased substantially. However, has CEO compensation decreased proportionally? Not in the least. As David Leonhardt states in "Executive Pay: A Special Report; For the Boss, Happy Days Are Still Here," *The New York Times* (April 1, 2001), "While typical investors lost 12 percent of their portfolios last year, based on the Wilshire 5000 total market index, and profits for the Standard & Poor's 500 companies rose at less than half their pace in the 1990's, chief executives received an average 22 percent raise in salary and bonus." Among the highest paid executives were Steven Jobs at $775.0 million for the year, Sanford Weill of Citigroup at $315.1 million, Lawrence Ellison of Oracle at $216.4 million, Dennis Kozlowski of Tyco at $205.2 million, and John Welch of General Electric at $144.5 million. You will see how these new figures dwarf those quoted in the selections that follow.

Should the American people step in and claim the right to set limits in the name of justice to the outsized amounts lavished on the fortunate sons of capitalism? That possibility is precisely what troubles Colvin. If CEOs will not regulate their own compensation, Congress and the Securities and Exchange Commission (SEC) will surely step in and do a bit of regulating on their own. The prospect is not enticing to the business community. On the other hand, is this not exactly why we have government—so that when private motives get out of hand, the people can step in and defend their long-term interests?

As you read the following selections, bear in mind that the corporation was set up as a private enterprise; it is a voluntary contract among investors to increase their wealth by legal means. But it is chartered and protected by the state, in the service of the state's long-term interest in a thriving economy. Economist Adam Smith would be pleased; he argued that leaving investors to make money as best they could for their own selfish interests would best increase the welfare of the whole body of the people. The question is, At what point do we conclude that the legal means set up for private parties to serve our interests by serving their own have failed of their purported effect and should be modified or revised? Or, do we have any right to make such a judgment?

 **YES**

Top Executives Are Worth Every Nickel They Get

Each spring, critics, journalists, and special-interest groups devour hundreds of corporate proxy statements in a race to determine which executive gets the most for allegedly doing the least. They're running the wrong race.

The "excessive" compensation paid these greedy types, we are told, gouges the nation's 30 million shareholders. Their salaries are arbitrarily set at outrageous levels without regard to either profitability or performance. Moreover, the six- and seven-digit base salaries are just the tip of the compensation iceberg—executives fatten their already sizable paychecks severalfold through bonuses, stock options, and other short- and long-term incentive plans. As a result, the public view prevails that executives are paid too much for what they do and that compensation policies are irrational and ignore the needs of shareholders.

Simply put, the public view is wrong and based on fundamental misconceptions about the managerial labor market. One reason for these misconceptions is that executive compensation is an emotional issue. And because critics become wound up in their emotions, they rely on a blend of opinion, intuition, and carefully selected anecdotes to prove their points.[1] Of course, such anecdotal evidence is not useless and may even be valuable in identifying abuses in the compensation system when carefully interpreted. Critics cannot use such evidence, however, to show compensation trends or to support across-the-board condemnations of compensation policies.

I have devised a better way to test the validity of the complaints about executive pay by subjecting each proposition to a series of logical and statistical tests. My data are drawn, in part, from an examination of the compensation policies of almost 1,200 large U.S. corporations over ten years and are supplemented by the findings of a 1984 University of Rochester symposium, "Managerial Compensation and the Managerial Labor Market."[2] My results paint a very different picture of executive compensation by showing that:

- The pay and performance of top executives are strongly and positively related. Even without a direct link between pay and performance, executives' incomes are tied to their companies' performance through

From Kevin J. Murphy, "Top Executives Are Worth Every Nickel They Get," *Harvard Business Review* (March/April 1986). Copyright © 1986 by The President and Fellows of Harvard College. Reprinted by permission of *Harvard Business Review*.

stock options, long-term performance plans, and, most important, stock ownership.

- Compensation proposals like short- and long-term incentive plans and golden parachutes actually benefit rather than harm shareholders.
- Changes in SEC reporting requirements and a shift toward compensation based on long-term performance explain most of the apparent compensation "explosion." This shift links compensation closely to shareholder wealth and motivates managers to look beyond next quarter's results.

Of course, some executives are overpaid or underpaid or paid in a way unrelated to performance. But, on average, I have found that compensation policies encourage executives to act on behalf of their shareholders and to put in the best managerial performance they can.

Pay & Performance

Because shareholders are the owners of the corporation, it makes sense to analyze the executive compensation controversy from their perspective. One way to motivate managers is to structure compensation policies that reward them for taking actions that benefit their shareholders and punish them for taking actions that harm their shareholders. Shareholders measure corporations in terms of stock price and dividend performance. Thus a sensible compensation policy would push an executive's pay up with good price performance and down with poor performance.

A common criticism of compensation policies is that they encourage executives to focus on short-term profits rather than on long-term performance. Assuming efficient capital markets, current stock price reflects all available information about a company, thus making its stock market performance the appropriate measure of its long-term potential. My analysis... indicates that compensation gives executives the incentive to focus on the long term since it is implicitly or explicitly linked to their companies' stock market performance.

The statistics in *Table 1* compare the rate of return on common stock (including price appreciation and dividends) with percentage changes in top executives' salaries and bonuses over ten years. I have grouped the data, which represent sample averages, by the companies' stock price performance, but experiments with alternative measures like sales growth and return on equity yield similar qualitative results.

Throughout the ten-year period, executives received inflation-adjusted average annual increases in salary and bonus of 7.8%; more important is the positive relationship shown between the rate of return on common stock and average percentage changes in salary and bonus. When returns were less than −20%, executives received pay increases of only .4%; when performance exceeded 40%, pay increases averaged 13.8%.

As *Table 1* shows, the relationship between pay and performance has remained positive over time and has actually become stronger in recent years.

Table 1

Relationship Between Rate of Return on Common Stock and Percentage Changes in Executive Salary and Bonus 1975–1984

Annual rate of return on common stock	1975-1984		1975-1979		1980-1984	
	Number of executive-years in sample	Average annual change in salary and bonus	Number of executive-years in sample	Average annual change in salary and bonus	Number of executive-years in sample	Average annual change in salary and bonus
Entire sample	6,523	7.8%	3,314	6.9%	3,209	8.8%
Less than -20%	639	0.4%	257	0.5%	382	0.4%
-20% to 0%	1,734	5.3%	1,002	5.5%	732	4.9%
0% to 20%	1,917	8.3%	989	7.5%	928	9.2%
20% to 40%	1,212	9.6%	538	7.1%	674	11.6%
More than 40%	1,021	13.8%	528	11.1%	493	16.6%

Note: Rates of return and percentage pay increases have been adjusted for inflation. As an example of how the rate of return is calculated, suppose that a share of stock worth $10 at the beginning of the year had increased in price to $12 by the end of the year and that the company paid cash dividends of $1 per share during the year. The holder of a share of the company's common stock would have realized a return of $3, or 30% for the year. Salary and bonus data were constructed from *Forbes* annual compensation surveys from 1975 to 1984. The sample consists of 1,948 executives in 1,191 corporations.

Chief executives in companies with returns greater than 40% received inflation-adjusted average annual increases in salary and bonus of 11.1% from 1975 to 1979 and 16.6% from 1980 to 1984....

As measured by the rate of return on common stock, a strong, positive statistical relationship exists between executive pay and company performance. These results are sharply at odds with recent studies that compare pay levels with measures of profitability and conclude that compensation is independent of performance.[3] The problem with such studies is that they look at the level of executive compensation across companies at a particular time instead of considering the extent to which compensation varies with companies' performance *over time*. This is an important distinction. Whether a company has well-paid—or low-paid—executives tells us nothing about the sensitivity of pay to performance.

To illustrate, consider two well-documented relationships—the positive relationship between company size and executive compensation and the negative one between company size and the average rate of return realized by shareholders.[4] From these it follows that a large company would have low rates of return and well-paid executives, while a small company would have high rates of return and low-paid executives. You'd conclude that pay and performance didn't correlate, and you'd be right if you took this kind of snapshot of the relationships. But if you took a moving picture—that is, looked at the results over time—you'd see that the pay of individual executives and the performance of their companies are strongly and positively related.

It is better to study how executive pay varies from year to year in a given company. *Table 1 . . .* show[s] that changes in executive pay mirror changes in shareholders' wealth. Two studies presented at the Rochester symposium corroborate this result. The first was based on a sample of 461 executives in 72 manufacturing companies over 18 years; in it I examined salary, bonus, stock options, deferred compensation, total compensation, and stock ownership. It shows that executive compensation parallels corporate performance as measured by the rate of return on common stock.[5]

Another study of 249 executives from as many companies from 1978 to 1980 reaches the same conclusion. It found a strong, positive correlation between changes in executive compensation and stock-price performance (adjusted for marketwide price changes). Ranking companies on the basis of their stock-price performance, it suggests that those in the top 10% will raise their executives' compensation by an inflation-adjusted 5.5% and those in the bottom 10% will lower pay by 4%. In addition, the study finds that chief executives in the bottom 10% of the performance ranking are almost three times more likely to leave their companies than executives in the top 10%.[6]

The Expanded Compensation Package

. . . Most studies in the financial press consider *only* salary and bonus and ignore potentially crucial variables like restricted stock, stock options, and long-term performance plans. In fact, these plans have become increasingly important. By their very nature, these plans tie executives' ultimate compensation directly to their companies' performance.

Executives' holdings of their companies' common stock constitute a large part of their wealth. The value of these stock holdings obviously goes up in good years and down in bad ones, quite independently of any relationship between performance and base pay. Suppose an executive with $4 million of stock sees the share price drop 25%. Because of his company's poor performance in the securities market, he has lost a million dollars—a loss that trivializes anything a board of directors might do to his base pay.

To assess the importance of inside stock ownership, I collected a 20-year time series of chief executive officer data from the proxy statements of 73 *Fortune* "500" manufacturing companies. Executives in this sample, which covered fiscal years 1964 through 1983, held an average (in 1984 constant dollars) of almost $7 million in their companies' common stock. Although this sample does not include shares held by family members and outside trusts, it does include a few executives with extraordinary stock holdings; the median stock holding for executives in this 20-year period is $1.5 million. That is, 50% of the chief executives in the 73 sample companies held more than $1.5 million in their companies' common stock....

Does Generosity Backfire?

Executive employment contracts are determined by the board of directors, which in turn is elected by shareholders. A cooperative relationship between executives and their directors is usually required for corporate success, and some have incorrectly interpreted this fact as evidence that executives can set their own salaries by pushing their compensation plans past "captive" directors. A friendly relationship between executives and their boards does not mean that the executives are free of constraints; rather, constraints usually operate in subtle yet powerful ways.

For example, some corporations have adopted short- and long-term compensation plans that pay off only if the executives meet a certain performance standard. Golden parachutes, which compensate executives if they leave their company after a takeover, have also grown in popularity. If, as some critics contend, these plans benefit executives and harm shareholders, you would expect stock prices to fall at the announcement of the plan. Likewise, if these plans benefit shareholders, you would expect prices to rise.

Three symposium studies examined market reaction. One found that average stock prices rise by about 11% when companies make the first public announcement of bonus and other plans that reward short-term performance.[7] Another concluded that shareholders realize a 2% return when companies adopt long-term compensation plans.[8] A third study found that, on average, stock prices increase by 3% when companies announce the adoption of a golden parachute provision.[9] This favorable reaction supports the contention that golden parachutes benefit shareholders by removing managers' incentives to block economically efficient takeovers. The price increase may also indicate that takeovers are more likely when golden parachutes are adopted but does not indicate that these provisions harm shareholders.

In each study, stock values not only increase when companies announce compensation plans but also continue to trade at the new, higher levels. The studies thus support the idea that such plans help align the interests of executives and shareholders and signal "good times ahead" to the market. They refute the view that executives "overreach" when they adopt lucrative compensation schemes.

On average, executives do not harm shareholders when they alter employment-contract provisions nor do they arbitrarily set their own salaries. If executives were truly able to set their salaries, why wouldn't they make them comparable with those of rock stars like Michael Jackson, whose income is many times that of even the highest paid executive? The only way the "set-their-own-salaries" argument works is if you assume that these salaries are somehow within some reasonable range of the competition—what other executives in similar industries are paid.

What's Out of Hand?

"Top management pay increases have gotten out of hand," warns Arch Patton, citing an apparent "explosion in top management compensation."[10] Indeed, a casual (but careless) look at compensation totals published in the business press seems to justify such concern. *Figure 1* shows the total compensation received by the nation's best paid executives from 1974 to 1984 using *Forbes* data (unadjusted for inflation). Before 1977, the fattest paycheck hovered around $1 million but then jumped to $3.4 million in 1978, $5.2 million in 1979, and $7.9 million in 1980. Warner Communications' Steven Ross shattered the eight-digit barrier with a total compensation of $22.6 million in 1981; in 1982, Frederick Smith of Federal Express received a total package of $51.5 million. The figure "plummeted" in 1983 to the mere $13.2 million received by NCR's retiring William Anderson but rebounded in 1984 to the $23 million received by Mesa's T. Boone Pickens, Jr.

A closer look at the data reveals that the apparent increase stems, in part, from a shift in the structure of compensation and has been exaggerated by changes in SEC reporting requirements. Moreover, the increase does not indicate that the conflict of interest between executives and their shareholders has worsened. Rather, the trend reflects a growing reliance on stock options and other long-term performance plans designed to link compensation more closely with shareholder wealth. The often spectacular payoffs are a once-in-a-lifetime experience.

For example, Frederick Smith's 1982 salary and bonus of $413,600 accounted for less than 1% of his $51.5 million total compensation; if the ranking had been based on salary and bonus alone, he wouldn't have made the top 300. NCR's William Anderson received only 8% of his 1983 compensation in the form of salary and bonus; his salary and bonus of $1,075,000 was only the nation's thirty-seventh highest. (Mr. Pickens's 1984 salary and bonus of $4.2 million was indeed the nation's highest but included $3 million for services provided in 1982 and 1983 when bonuses were not awarded.) In any given year, only a small percentage of executives enjoy big gains from stock options or other performance plans. The overwhelming majority get most of their compensation in the form of salaries and cash bonuses.

Even so, the great popularity of stock options and other long-term performance plans has several implications. First, an executive's pay in any given year reflects amounts actually accrued or earned over several years and tends to increase the maximum compensation observed, just as a switch from weekly to monthly pay periods will increase the maximum compensation observed in any given week (for example, the last week of the month).

Second, long-term performance plans give high rewards for excellent performance but are neutral toward poor or mediocre performance. It's the same as designing a state lottery with one grand prize of $1 million rather than a hundred prizes of $10,000 each; you increase the amount paid to the winner but not the total amount awarded. If the chief executives of ten different companies were each awarded stock options at the beginning of the year, their value at the

Figure 1

Total Compensation Received by the Nation's Highest Paid Executives
1974–1984

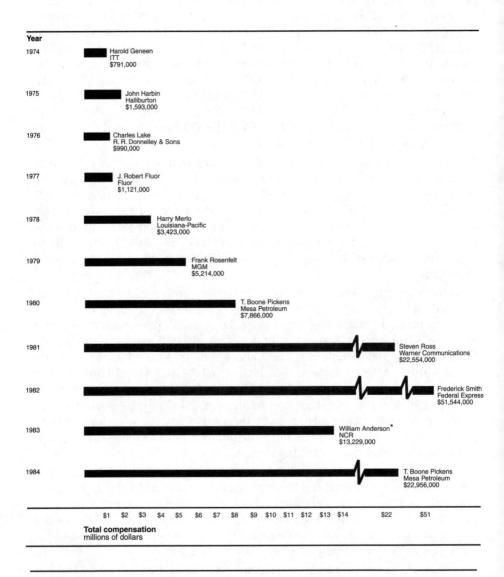

Year

1974 — Harold Geneen / ITT / $791,000

1975 — John Harbin / Halliburton / $1,593,000

1976 — Charles Lake / R. R. Donnelley & Sons / $990,000

1977 — J. Robert Fluor / Fluor / $1,121,000

1978 — Harry Merlo / Louisiana-Pacific / $3,423,000

1979 — Frank Rosenfelt / MGM / $5,214,000

1980 — T. Boone Pickens / Mesa Petroleum / $7,866,000

1981 — Steven Ross / Warner Communications / $22,554,000

1982 — Frederick Smith / Federal Express / $51,544,000

1983 — William Anderson* / NCR / $13,229,000

1984 — T. Boone Pickens / Mesa Petroleum / $22,956,000

$1 $2 $3 $4 $5 $6 $7 $8 $9 $10 $11 $12 $13 $14 $22 $51

Total compensation
millions of dollars

Note: Data are not adjusted for inflation. Total compensation before 1978 does not include gains from exercise of stock options.

Source: Forbes, various issues.
*Forbes does not include Anderson in its 1984 compensation survey since he retired just prior to the end of the 1983 fiscal year.

date of grant might be similar. By the end of the option period, however, only a few would be worth a great deal of money; the others would be worthless.

Third, most long-term performance plans are based on stock prices. The stock market boom produced high payoffs from 1981 to 1983, while the market decline in the 1970s produced low or zero payoffs. Thus an executive awarded an equal number of stock options or performance plan units each year would have realized zero gains during the stock market decline and large gains during the boom; cyclical movements produced increases in the dollar amounts realized even though the amounts granted under these plans remained relatively constant.

Finally, before 1978, the payoffs from stock options and other long-term plans were reported in a somewhat incomprehensible table at the back of corporate proxy statements. Changes in SEC reporting rules have moved these payoffs to the front of the statement, where they are much more accessible to the media. Compensation totals published in *Forbes* (see *Figure 1*) and other business periodicals before 1978 exclude option realizations; data published after 1978 include them. The editors of these compensation surveys warn against making year-to-year comparisons when the definitions have changed. Unfortunately, critics have often ignored these warnings.

Why Such Controversy?

The recent attacks on executive compensation come mainly from a few individuals and special-interest groups who use the controversy to further their own agendas. In 1984, for example, former U.S. Trade Representative William Brock assailed "excessive" auto executive bonuses to argue against Japanese import quotas. Labor unions have used the executive pay issue to bolster demands for higher wages for their members. Mark Green's condemnation of "overreaching" executives continues the general Nader-Green attack on the corporation. In each case, the executive compensation question is virtually unrelated to the ultimate objectives of the attackers.

Such highly publicized assaults cause confusion about executive compensation, a confusion exacerbated by the second-rate research conducted and reported by most media commentators. How compensation is determined is complex; current performance is only one of the many factors that affect executive pay. Thus performance cannot explain all or even most of an individual's compensation even though the relationship between pay and performance is strong, positive, and statistically significant. In any case, estimating the relationship between pay and performance is tricky and cannot be done by making simple cross-sectional comparisons....

The nation's shareholders need not fear that they are being swindled by greedy executives. Compensation policies normally make a great deal of sense. Companies are, moreover, adopting compensation plans that benefit shareholders by creating better managerial incentives.

Author's note: I am indebted to Michael Jensen and Jerold Zimmerman for their help. I gratefully acknowledge financial support from the Managerial Economics Research Center.

References

1. See, for example, Joseph E. Muckley, " 'Dear Fellow Shareowner'," HBR March–April 1984, p. 46; Mark Green and Bonnie Tenneriello, "From Pay to Perks to Parachutes: The Trouble with Executive Compensation," Democracy Project Report No. 8, March 1984.
2. Papers presented at the symposium are published in the *Journal of Accounting and Economics,* April 1985.
3. See, for example, Carol Loomis, "The Madness of Executive Compensation," *Fortune,* July 1982, p. 42.
4. The relationship between compensation and sales is reported by Harland Fox, *Top Executive Compensation,* Report No. 854 (New York: Conference Board, 1985). Evidence relating company size and shareholder return appears in the Symposium on Size and Stock Returns, published in the *Journal of Financial Economics,* June 1983.
5. Kevin J. Murphy, "Corporate Performance and Managerial Remuneration: An Empirical Analysis," *Journal of Accounting and Economics,* April 1985, p. 11.
6. Anne T. Coughlan and Ronald M. Schmidt, "Executive Compensation, Management Turnover, and Firm Performance: An Empirical Investigation," *Journal of Accounting and Economics,* April 1985, p. 43.
7. Hassan Tehranian and James Waegelein, "Market Reaction to Short-Term Executive Compensation Plan Adoption," *Journal of Accounting and Economics,* April 1985, p. 131.
8. James Brickley, Sanjai Bhagat, and Ronald C. Lease, "The Impact of Long-Range Managerial Compensation Plans on Shareholder Wealth," *Journal of Accounting and Economics,* April 1985, p. 113.
9. Richard A. Lambert and David F. Larcker, "Golden Parachutes, Executive Decision Making, and Shareholder Wealth," *Journal of Accounting and Economics,* April 1985, p. 179.
10. Arch Patton, "Those Million-Dollar-A-Year Executives," HBR January–February 1985, p. 56.

NO

Lisa H. Newton

The Care and Feeding of the Truly Greedy: CEO Salaries in World Perspective

In 1996, Jack Welch, CEO of General Electric, received $21.4 million in salary and performance bonuses (and about $18 million in stock options); Lawrence Coss of the Green Tree Financial Corporation received $102.4 million in salary and bonus (plus stock options worth at least $38 million). Michael Eisner of Disney added $196 million in stock to his previous holding, somewhere around a third of a billion. The list goes on: Intel's Andrew Grove took home $97.6 million, Traveler's Group Sanford Weill made $94.2 million, and Citicorp's John Reed got $43.6 million. (These figures from John Cassidy's piece, aptly titled "Gimme," in *The New Yorker* of April 21, 1997; See also "The Top Ten List" in *The Nation,* December 8, 1997.) According to a preliminary study of 60 companies by Pearl Meyer & Partners, the CEO of a multibillion-dollar company received an average of $4.37 million in compensation in 1995. That was a 23% increase from 1994. (That number from an anonymous squib, "Checking in on the CEO's Pay," in *HR Focus,* May 1996, p. 15.) As Cassidy points out, we're not supposed to think those figures excessive:

> But, according to *Business Week,* when you add together salary, bonuses, and options packages the typical C.E.O. at a large company saw his pay envelope grow by just fifty-four per cent—barely eighteen times the increase necessary to keep pace with the cost of living. (All told, his paycheck was only two hundred and nine times as big as the average factory employee's.)

Meanwhile, World Resource Institute figures from a few years earlier show that average annual compensation for a citizen (or Gross Domestic Product per capita, which is as close to the same thing as we can get in largely non-cash economies), in U.S. dollars, was less than $100 in Mozambique and Tanzania, less than $200 in seven other African countries (Burundi, Chad, Malawi, Rwanda, Sierra Leone, Somalia, Uganda), plus Nepal and Vietnam, under $300 in another 15 countries worldwide. (That list from *World Resources 1996–1997,* published by the World Resources Institute, p. 166.) We are not living in a rich world. But some CEO's are rich, very rich.

How, the untaught observer might ask, is this kind of disparity justified? How can it be that one of the world's inhabitants has a yearly compensation

Copyright © 2000 by Lisa H. Newton.

equal to the combined resources of 43,700 other of the world's inhabitants? We can understand that some people are lucky (born with perfect pitch) and others are not (born without arms). But the agreement to compensate an executive to the tune of tens of millions is not a matter of luck. It's a human decision if ever there was one. What on earth could make it the right human decision?

Justifications abound. Justifications are products, and like all products, are for sale for a fair market price. They are not always necessary or desirable, but become so very quickly if something not quite right—something that just doesn't *smell* very good—is happening. Having an annual compensation 209 times that of your employees, and 43,700 times that of fellow humans across the world, is one of those conditions that assaults the nostrils, so CEO's need justifications; and with that much money to spend, there's bound to be some left after the mortgage and the groceries to splurge on a justification or two. It's a perfect free market situation: a willing buyer (the CEO and his loyal staff) meets a willing seller (a well-educated and articulate wordsmith who really needs money), and a justification changes hands. A rudimentary knowledge of human psychology tells you that the wordsmith will instantly convince himself (or herself: this is an equal opportunity sellout) that CEO's really are worth the enormous amount of money they're getting, and that the CEO will instantly convince himself (never herself: equal opportunity has not yet reached this level) that the justification is sound. But it isn't. As we might expect of products turned out at such speed in such an uncritical market, the quality isn't the best. It might be worthwhile to count some of the errors.

It won't do, for instance, to claim that the CEO contributes 43,700 times as much value to the world as the shepherd in Tanzania or the farmer in Chad. Even if the movies, or software, or candy bars produced by the CEO's company are really worth that many times the wool or corn produced by the Africans, they are not made by the CEO, who never goes near the production floor, but by the minions of the company, making 1/209 their CEO's annual pay. Whatever value the company produces, in short, could equally well be produced with a CEO making half that annual compensation, or, most likely, no CEO at all. (That suggestion might be worth examining.)

Nor will it do to claim that a company simply *has* to pay that much for such rare talent, that you really *can't* get a good CEO these days for under that price, given all the competition. The reason why that rings somehow false is that these decisions are made by the Board of Directors of the company, being a very small club of similarly compensated executives (on whose Boards of Directors the CEO will also sit), and the whole decision stays within that little overpaid group. One wonders if, given another Search Committee, someone could not have been found to do the job for, say, $2,000,000 per annum. Or maybe $650,000, which will pay most of the bills that a CEO might run up in the course of a year.

Comparisons with other high-paid talent also ring false. Entertainers, to be sure, make big bucks, singing or acting or shooting baskets. But here we have direct value for money, paid by those who are entertained. The entertainers make a lot of money: but their careers come to an end as soon as *our* tastes change or attention wanders, and for the time being, they are at least fun to watch. Careers can also end in a minute with a car accident or even a badly twisted knee. But the CEO is not at all fun to watch, and he seems to be immune to the changing of consumer tastes or accidental assaults on the body; he can write his memos from a wheelchair.

Now we come to the crux of the value! He writes memos. What is he *writing*, in those memos, that makes him so valuable? For an answer to that question, a review of the incentive structures of the publicly held corporation is needed:

The Corporation From Cradle to Grave

How does the corporation get started? An investor, or a group of investors, decide that there is a good market for a good or service (i.e. a high demand coupled with the money to buy that which will fill the demand), and that the revenue from sales will exceed the cost of making the good or service available by a healthy margin (i.e. they're going to make a lot of money), so they buy the machinery and supplies and office space and talent required for the production of this good or service, and the production and marketing and advertising begin. In a magic metaphysical moment the articles of incorporation are signed, and a bouncing baby company is launched. Pretty soon the money's rolling in and the investors are very happy.

Now, it's always possible for one of these investors to decide he wants his money back, possibly to invest in some other enterprise; he can try to sell out his share in the enterprise, to one of the other investors or to a stranger. He may have problems doing that if the enterprise is not doing well or if he owns a very large share. To make a long story very short, that problem and myriads of others were solved by a common Stock Market where all such shares can be bought and sold. In the present day, if an investor decides he no longer wants to be a shareholder, an investor, in Acme Corporation, he can sell his shares on the open market and invest instead in Beter Corporation. His choice.

Why would a shareholder want to sell out? The reason he bought in was to make money, and the company he set up is doing fine. If he wants continuing income, he'll do better to hang on to the stock and continue collecting dividends. But suppose he just wants lots of cash right now: fine, he sells his shares, "liquidates" his share of the assets of the company, and he gets the cash. Now of course, if all the original investors early in the company's history decided to do that at once, the whole company would be liquidated. But that's not likely to happen. (In the contemporary stock market, it's almost impossible, just because of the huge volume of stock traded; some mutual funds turn over their entire portfolio in the course of the year, and stray stocks are likely to be picked up.)

Why is it not likely to happen, at least in the original model of shareholdership? Because a funny thing happens when you put your money into a company as an investor. You begin to think of the company as "yours," which is appropriate, because it is, in part. You become anxious for its fortunes, not only for the monetary value of your initial investment, but for its own sake, as you would be anxious for the fortunes of a nephew. You watch its coverage in the press, cheering when it is favorable, grousing when it is not. You get attached to the company. You don't call your broker and have him sell it if it goes down a few points. For one thing, by the time you got hold of your broker and he got the stock offered for sale, the whole situation would have changed; for another, his fee would wipe out any gains; but for a third, your sense of ownership has become tinged with loyalty: you don't "sell out" until something really big, college or retirement or a new house, comes along. Besides, the individual shareholder is important in the company. If you are the owner of the company, even a part owner, you are the "principal," and all the company's employees are your "agents"—they act for you and for your interests. The CEO has to please you or (in theory: it almost never happened) you can wage a proxy fight at the annual meeting, bring about the election of your own Board of Directors, and have them hire a new CEO who will represent your interests more perfectly. So the CEO wants to keep you happy. But what does the CEO of your company have to do to please you? Not much: keep the company on an even keel, no scandals, distribute profits regularly, but remember to keep some of those profits to reinvest for the long term, because the long term is what you're in for.

That was the American shareholder up into the 1960's. There were mutual funds, of course, that owned stock, effectively pooling the investment funds of small shareholders to give them a diversified portfolio. Mutual funds did not operate like individual shareholders, for their managers, under the same fiduciary obligation to *their* shareholders, were not permitted to get attached to the companies they held—their job was to increase the total amount of stock value in the fund, and they didn't care what companies they had to hold shares in, in order to do that. But the funds were not really big players at the time.

They could become big players if they were joined by the vast money salted away in huge trust funds—pension funds and the like, and the endowments of not-for-profit institutions of all kinds. But these funds always invested in bonds, for the sake of safety; they didn't buy stocks. Until the 1960's, that is. Then these huge funds decided that 1929 was a long time ago, that stocks were quite as safe as bonds, and that it was time to trade in creditorship for ownership. Slowly they moved into the market, and took it over.

Again: what a fund manager wants from the investments he makes is rapid growth, the swift increase in the total amount of money in the fund. If it is a pension fund, that money is what the workers are going to retire on, and he (or she) works for the workers. If the fund is an investment pool, the manager works for the investors; if it is the endowment fund of a University, the manager works for the University. He will keep his huge funds invested in a company for the long term only if it is pouring money into his fund at a rate unmatched anywhere else in the market, or if he really has no choice. For a long time, the customs of the market and the available technology kept the funds' money moving slowly through the market, as well-weighted decisions moved the cash from blue chip to blue chip. But in the 1980's, the established ways of the market broke down, the white-shod country clubbers were shoved aside by the new breed of traders and arbitragers, and computer technology advanced to the point of allowing program trading (programming your computer to make trades automatically, in a split second, in response to certain changes in the market) and otherwise very rapid shifts of money from one stock to another.

Then it all came together. The new breed of trader talked the managers of the huge slowmoving funds into becoming players in a new rapid-fire market, and their money funded the leveraged buyouts, the mergers and acquisitions, and the infamous hostile takeovers for which the 1980's became famous. In the process a new breed of fund manager was born, one who is acutely aware, first, that his fund (for instance, my favorite pension fund), CREF, owns very large chucks of (say) Acme Company, second, that the Acme Board of Directors had therefore better take CREF's interests seriously or he'll have them replaced (he may even demand, and get, his own Director on the Board), third, that his obligation is to increase the amount of money in CREF as rapidly as possible, fourth, that therefore the Acme Board of Directors must instruct the Acme CEO to run the company in such a way that CREF's stock position appreciates, and fifth, that if the CEO is unresponsive to that instruction, the Board must fire him and get a more responsive one. This is what we call an "active" investor: no longer does the fund manager simply sell Acme and buy Beter when Acme is not running the way he wants it to run. He gets in there and makes it do what he wants. (Oh, but doesn't CREF offer a "social responsibility" track, in which only stocks in socially responsible corporations are purchased, for conscientious investors? Yes indeed; and CREF's fund manager manages those funds just as aggressively as all the others.)

Once a CEO is on board who promises to extract money from the company's workings and move it into shareholder hands faster than ever, the Board kind of makes *sure* he doesn't forget what to do by structuring incentives to help his memory: the more the dividends flow and the price per share of the stock goes up, the greater his bonus.

That, of course, is the link between the new way of doing business and the CEO's compensation.

Now, what was on that memo? How does the CEO suddenly put lots more money into shareholder hands? We know that the size profit to be divided among the shareholders is based in part on the ratio of corporate revenue to corporate costs—best understood as a fraction with revenue as a numerator and costs as the denominator—so the CEO has to increase the numerator, the revenue stream, or cut costs, the denominator, or, preferably, both. Let me count the ways he might do that: (1) He can discover that the company's operations were rife with waste, inefficiency, theft, whatever; tighten it up, get things working the way they should, and the company saves oodles of money, squeezing down the denominator, without changing operations at all. He'll always say that's what he's doing, but it's unlikely that much savings will be got that way. (2) He can try to raise the numerator, the revenue, by raising price. In some markets he can get away with that for awhile, but in a highly competitive market that's just likely to reduce sales, theoretically to zero. (3) He can try to raise revenue by developing new products, new markets, or both. That's a good idea, but it requires more investment, therefore lower distributions of profits right now. CREF is not interested in waiting. It wants money now. (4) There aren't any other ways to raise revenue, so he has to cut costs. He can cut the paper clip budget and pick up cheaper raw materials for his manufacturing, and he'll do that, but it's not enough. The big item in any company is payroll, not only for the meager salaries and wages the workers make, but also for those infinitely expensive medical and other insurance plans the company signed on for and now can't back out of. Fire a worker, and you save all that money. Fire (lay off) lots of workers, and you save lots of money. The denominator goes way down, raising profits, and the stock price goes way up. And that was the object of the expedition.

So that's what the memo was about. The CEO was setting the ball in motion to lay off thousands of workers. CREF will see the stock price go way up, and will be happy when the Board of Directors presents the CEO with a wonderful year-end bonus. That's why CEO compensation is so high, millions of dollars for successfully pink-slipping the company.

What does CREF do next? Sells the stock, obviously. After all, the prospects for the company are not good. They've cut way back on the quality of their materials, refused to reinvest in better plant or equipment, and laid off the folks who were doing the work, all to cut costs and send the price of the stock way up. In effect, they sold off some fraction of the value of the company, "liquidated" it, for quick cash, and distributed the cash. Now the company is worth a lot less, and CREF has no intention of holding on to worthless goods. Seeing the stock go up, investors who do not know why it went up will buy into Acme now on the expectation that it will go higher. CREF will take their cash and invest in the stock of (say) Beter, and promptly insist that Beter go through the same round of liquidation—cost-cutting, laying off, and neglecting reinvestment. Then Beter's stock will go up, CREF will sell it, and repeat the process. And all other funds are doing the same thing. In theory, the process could lead to the liquidation of the entirety of American industry. The grave of the productive corporation is already prepared; we await the death rattle. However long it takes, the CEO's will be well paid throughout.

In the Public Interest

What's wrong with very high CEO compensation? Two things: First, it is bad stewardship for people to take more than they can use, and unjust that some people should be making 43,700 times what other people make, especially when at least some of those other people are starving. John Locke, high priest of private property, put the case for the morality of private property very simply: each man may take from the commons (the world resources available to all) only as much as he can use, and only as long as enough and as good is left for others. The CEO fails on both counts.

Second, this compensation system is destroying American industry. It is commonplace by now that our cost-saving schemes have cost us the economy: our products made obsolete by foreign companies that invested in R & D [research and development] when we did not, and invested in new plants when we did not, our industrial jobs lost as our obsolete plants have to be shuttered, as pink slips flutter from the corner offices in the most recent "downsizings" and "rightsizings," as the actual work is assigned to East Asian and Mexican factories and American workers are handed over to unemployment. We are moving, we are told, from an era of manufacturing to an era of information-driven service industries. These are precisely the industries for which the vast majority of the population is not prepared and from which they cannot profit. We are condemning a majority of working-age adults to temporary, underpaid, service jobs, while the tiny minority feeds off the global wealth generated by the exploitation of the rest of the world. The entire system is unjust, and cries out to heaven, and to an informed citizenry, for remedy. The compensation of the truly greedy might be a good place to start.

POSTSCRIPT

Is CEO Compensation Justified by Performance?

In 1992, when Colvin wrote the article bringing the problem of CEO compensation to public attention, he was worried about America's perception of annual outlays of $1.7 million average total CEO compensation for almost 300 large companies, with pay going up to a whopping $3.2 million annually for the really big companies. By 1995 the CEO of a multibillion-dollar company received an average of $4.37 million in compensation in 1995, up 23 percent from 1994.

The Business Section of the *New York Times* at the end of 1997 presented reports of projected bonuses of $11 billion for Wall Street in 2001. These bonuses were to be over and above salary and before stock options. In 1999 General Electric CED Jack Welch was pulling in $68 million per year. The amounts of CEO compensation quadrupled, and the amounts per individual dwarf the annual health budgets of most of the world. It seems that the situation is not correcting itself.

The political impact of CEOs' salaries may be muted for the present, but the moral dimensions of the problem have not changed since the days of the prophet Amos of the Hebrew Scriptures: What right have the rich to enjoy their warm palaces and mansions, dining plentifully on the best food from all the world, while the poor suffer from hunger and cold? But the political dimensions are volatile and dependent upon the rest of the system to provide context and opportunity. This issue will likely be with us for a while.

Suggested Readings

AP Dispatch, "Welch Defends Pay: Ratio Proposal Rejected by Shareholders," *Connecticut Post* (April 22, 1999).

John A. Byrne, "Gross Compensation?" *Business Week* (March 18, 1996).

Jack Lederer and Carl R. Weinberg, "CEO Compensation: Share the Wealth," *Chief Executive* (September 1996).

Dana Wechsler Linden and Vicki Contavespi, "Incentivize Me, Please," *Forbes* (May 27, 1991).

Mike Maharry, "AFL-CIO Launches Web Site to Expose CEO Pay Levels," *The News Tribune* (April 11, 1997).

Peter Passell, "A Theory of Capitalism: Lonely and Rich at the Top," *The New York Times* (August 27, 1995).

Frederick Schmitt, "Study Finds CEO Salaries Tracking Performance," *National Underwriter* (October 21, 1996).

Thomas A. Stewart, "CEO Pay: Mom Wouldn't Approve," *Fortune* (March 31, 1997).

Peter Truell, "Another Year, Another Bundle: Billions in Bonuses Are Expected to Fall on Wall Street," *The New York Times* (December 5, 1997).

On the Internet . . .

DUSHKIN ONLINE

Advertising World

Advertising World, maintained by the Department of Advertising at the University of Texas at Austin, links to numerous sites on marketing and advertising. Among the many indexed topics are ethics and self-regulation, consumer interest, public relations, and market research.

http://advertising.utexas.edu/world/

Overlawyered.com

Overlawyered.com explores an American legal system that too often turns litigation into a weapon against guilty and innocent alike, erodes individual responsibility, rewards sharp practice, enriches its participants at the public's expense, and resists even modest efforts at reform and accountability. This page focuses on litigation over auto safety.

http://overlawyered.com/topics/auto.html

The Pew Initiative on Food and Biotechnology

The Pew Initiative on Food and Biotechnology was established as an independent and objective source of information that encourages research and debate on agricultural biotechnology. It is the purpose of this site to provide a resource that would enable consumers as well as policymakers to make their own informed decisions on the subject.

http://pewagbiotech.org

PART 4

Consumer Issues

*W*hat does the company owe the customer? Presumably, the least *we could ask for is honesty. We expect the company to produce a good-quality product without cutting corners during production and without lying about the results of tests for safety and quality. We expect the product to be represented honestly in its advertising and marketing literature. We expect the label on the product to be truthful, as well. It all sounds so simple. But it is not. Three representative controversies follow.*

- Are Marketing and Advertising Fundamentally Exploitive?

- Was Ford to Blame in the Pinto Case?

- Should We Require Labeling for Genetically Modified Food?

ISSUE 12

Are Marketing and Advertising Fundamentally Exploitive?

YES: John P. Foley, from "Ethics in Advertising: A Look at the Report by the Pontifical Council for Social Communications," *Journal of Public Policy & Marketing* (Fall 1998)

NO: Gene R. Laczniak, from "Reflections on the 1997 Vatican Statements Regarding Ethics in Advertising," *Journal of Public Policy & Marketing* (Fall 1998)

ISSUE SUMMARY

YES: Archbishop John P. Foley summarizes and comments on the 1997 report of the Pontifical Council for Social Communications, which charges that advertising can be deceptive and improperly influential on media editorial policy and states that it often promotes a lifestyle based on unbridled consumption.

NO: Professor of marketing Gene R. Laczniak contends that many of the Pontifical Council report's conclusions are overstated, only partially true, economically naive, and socially idealistic. While sympathetic to its aims, he argues that the Church's contribution to the debate is vitiated by such errors.

In a film on Wall Street, made at the height of "merger mania" in the 1980s, investment banker Felix Rohatyn is asked his opinion of a contemporary statement by the American Bishops on the problems of capitalism and the need to share America's wealth with the poor. He was expected, apparently, to attack the Bishops as naive, ignorant, and possibly Communists—much as former secretary of the treasury William Simon did. But that was not Rohatyn's reply. Instead, he suggested that the Bishops had spoken well, they spoke out of concern for the poor, and that, he said, is what bishops are supposed to do. Who else would do it? Who else but the pastors of the beleaguered flock will recall that not every aspect of a plump American economy is good for absolutely everyone? There are many who agree that capitalism is a good system; it helps many people make a living and enjoy a prosperous life. But there are poor people, and they, too, have to be fed. The burden of speaking out on issues of social justice and of the welfare of those who have not been as fortunate as Rohatyn or Simon often falls on the Church.

The Pontifical Council for Social Communications, some say, is trying to tell advertisers how to do their business. The council seems to be worried about the possibility that advertisers may be promoting a lifestyle based on unbridled consumption. And the Council accuses advertisers of causing "people to feel and act upon cravings for items and services they do not need." Some would say that this is exactly the whole idea behind the business of advertising. According to Foley, what the Council is trying to do, however, is to direct people toward possibilities of living that do not include the pleasurable materialistic styles Americans have adopted within the capitalist system and to squire peoples energies to goals often forgotten, having to do with a communal life enjoyed for its own sake and for its potential to make us all into better people.

In many ways Gene R. Laczniak and the Council have visions of society that they do not share with each other. But the visions meet on the ground. Advertisers and marketers have to decide every day what sorts of advertising meet the moral minimal criteria of acceptable taste and adequate truth. How can one decide what violates taste (or human dignity) and what is overly untruthful unless one has some idea of the worth, basic human rights, and dignity of the audience? Can the Church and other moral advisors help to formulate sensible guidelines for advertising?

As you read the following selections bear in mind, that while Foley and Laczniak sometimes seem to be talking past each other, they present a genuine choice between views of human nature, as well as between views of what is desirable in business enterprise. As Foley suggests, even advertisers want to do the right thing and are occasionally grateful for suggestions as to how they might.

John P. Foley  **YES**

Ethics in Advertising: A Look at the Report by the Pontifical Council for Social Communications

In February 1997, the cabinet-level Pontifical Council for Social Communications at the Vatican released a report on the state of advertising worldwide. To complete its review, the council solicited materials from advertising practitioners and scholars through a variety of venues, including a plea in the trade magazine *Advertising Age....*

A Brief Summary of the Report

The report by the Pontifical Council for Social Communications (1997) is divided into five sections: introduction, benefits of advertising, harm done by advertising, ethical and moral principles, and conclusions. These sections build on one another and overlap in significant ways. A description of each follows, using quotes from the document whenever possible.

The introduction opens with the conclusion that "advertising has a profound impact on how people understand life, the world and themselves, especially in regard to their values and their ways of choosing and behaving" (p. 7). The media are described as "gifts from God" that can be employed to accomplish "his providential design, bringing people together and [to] help them to cooperate with his plan for their salvation" (p. 6). However, the council also "calls attention to moral principles and norms relevant to social communications" (p. 6) that should shape the content, target, and influence of advertising.

The next section, on advertising benefits, is divided into four segments. In the first segment, the council studies the economic benefits of advertising and notes that "advertising can be a useful tool for sustaining honest and ethically responsible competition that contributes to economic growth in the service of authentic human development" (p. 11). These benefits are accomplished in a variety of ways, including "by informing people about the availability of rationally desirable new products and services and improvements in existing ones" (pp. 11–12). The council examines the benefits of political advertising in the

From John P. Foley, "Ethics in Advertising: A Look at the Report by the Pontifical Council for Social Communications," *Journal of Public Policy & Marketing*, vol. 17, no. 2 (Fall 1998). Copyright © 1998 by American Marketing Association. Reprinted by permission.

second segment and comes to a similar conclusion. The primary benefit is educational, "informing people about the ideas and policy proposals of parties and candidates, including new candidates not previously known to the public" (p. 13). In the third segment, the council discusses the cultural benefits of advertising, which comprise "a positive influence on decisions about media content" as well as "motivating [people] to act in ways that benefit themselves and others" (p. 13). The popular culture influence also is recognized as positive because "advertising can brighten lives simply by being witty, tasteful and entertaining" (p. 13). In the fourth and final segment, the council explores the moral and religious benefits of advertising, noting that advertising can deliver "messages of faith, of patriotism, of tolerance, compassion and neighborly service" (pp. 13–14), as well as others. From this perspective, advertising is viewed as essential to effective moral suasion and "a necessary part of a comprehensive pastoral strategy" (p. 14).

Section Three is titled "The Harm Done by Advertising," and it is divided into the same four segments as the previous section. Among the economic harms of advertising, the council includes deceptive advertising, the improper use of influence on media editorial content by advertisers, and the implicit promotion of a lifestyle built on unbridled consumption. It also argues against "brand-related advertising" that drives "people to act on the basis of irrational motives ('brand loyalty,' status, fashion, 'sex appeal,' etc.) instead of presenting differences in product quality and price as bases for rational choice" (p. 16). Furthermore, advertisers are indicted for causing "people to feel and act upon cravings for items and services they do not need" (p. 17).

With regard to the harms of political advertising, the council is concerned that "the costs of advertising limit political competition to wealthy political candidates or groups, or require that office-seekers compromise their integrity and independence by over-dependence on special interests for funds" (p. 18). In addition, political advertising is an "obstruction of the democratic process" when it "seeks to distort the views and records of opponents" or "appeals more to people's emotions and base instincts" (p. 19).

According to the council, the cultural harms of advertising are multi-faceted and include "cultural injury done to those nations and their peoples by advertising whose content and methods, reflecting those prevalent in the first world, are at war with sound traditional values in indigenous cultures" (p. 19). Advertisers also are blamed for pressure on the media to "ignore the educational and social needs of certain [market] segments" in favor of editorial content that "attracts ever larger audiences" through the delivery of editorial content that "lapses into superficiality, tawdriness and moral squalor" (p. 20). Furthermore, advertising is blamed for "invidious stereotyping of particular groups that places them at a disadvantage in relation to others," especially the "exploitation of women," which often ignores "the specific gifts of feminine insight, compassion, and understanding" (pp. 20–21).

Finally, the moral and religious harms of advertising include "appeals to such motives as envy, status seeking and lust," or those that "seek to shock and titillate by exploiting content of a morbid, perverse, pornographic nature" (p. 21). The council also finds advertising unacceptable "when it involves exploiting religion or treating it flippantly," or it "is used to promote products and inculcate attitudes and forms of behavior contrary to moral norms," "for instance, with the advertising of contraceptives, abortifacients, and products harmful to health" (p. 22).

The fourth section identifies "moral principles that are particularly relevant to advertising" (p. 25), and three in particular are discussed: truthfulness, the dignity of the human person, and social responsibility. The principle of truthfulness in advertising lobbies against advertisements that are "simply and deliberately untrue" or "distort the truth by implying things that are not so or withholding relevant facts" (p. 25). The principle of the dignity of the human person condemns advertisements that violate our right "to make a responsible choice" or "exploit man's lower inclinations" (e.g., "lust, vanity, envy and greed") (pp. 26–27). This principle is particularly relevant for vulnerable groups such as "children and young people, the elderly, the poor, the culturally disadvantaged" (p. 27). Finally, the principle of advertising and social responsibility criticizes "advertising that fosters a lavish life style which wastes resources[,] despoils the environment[, and] offends against important ecological concerns" (p. 28).

The fifth and final section is the conclusion. Much of this section is consumed with who is responsible for ensuring that advertising is "ethically correct." According to the council, the "indispensable guarantors" of such behavior are advertising professionals who "may be called upon to make significant personal sacrifices to correct [unethical practices]" (p. 34). The council recommends "voluntary ethical codes" before turning to government intervention, and these codes should be updated regularly by the industry, with feedback from "ethicists and church people, as well as representatives of consumer groups" (p. 31).

When all else fails, the government should intervene, especially in areas such as the "quantity" and "content of advertising directed at groups particularly vulnerable to exploitation, such as children and old people. Political advertising also seems an appropriate area for regulation: how much may be spent, how and from whom may money for advertising be raised" (p. 32). Furthermore, "besides avoiding abuses, advertisers also should undertake to repair the harm sometimes done by advertising, insofar as that is possible: for example, by publishing corrective notices, compensating injured parties, increasing the quantity of public service advertising, and the like" (pp. 33–34).

Remarks Made by Archbishop Foley at the 1998 Public Policy Conference

First of all, I wish to express my thanks to Dean Ron Hill of the School of Business Administration of the University of Portland for having arranged this session on ethics in advertising, with a special focus on the document of the same name published last year by our Pontifical Council for Social Communications in Rome. I also wish to thank Professors Brenkert, Laczniak, and Murphy for their generally favorable comments, and also for their constructive criticisms. Such dialogue is exactly what we wanted to happen, not only within the

Catholic Church, but also in the advertising and communications industries and in the academic community.

While a number of comments seem to imply that our document will have little or no effect within the advertising community, I must confess that I have been encouraged by the reaction of the advertising community. Not only have I been invited all over the world to comment on this document in various fora of advertisers, agencies, and associations, but the document has been translated into more than a dozen languages and distributed widely, either through advertising associations or the communications committees of bishops' conferences. At a meeting in Geneva of the World Federation of Advertisers, I was even asked to have our Council begin the development of a wider study on ethics in communications, and we are trying to do just that. In fact, I already invoke such ethical norms when I represent the Holy See at the council of Europe to recall that broadcast frequencies should be considered a public trust and should be required to serve the public interest and not merely private commercial interests.

It would be unrealistic, however, to think that our document, which we strove to keep brief, readable, and practical, would result in overnight worldwide conversion. After 2000 years, the world is not yet Christian, and Jesus was (and is) God! If we can get some people all over the world thinking about ethics in advertising, however, using some of the principles which we have articulated, we will consider that some progress had been made.

There were areas into which we did not enter, but well could have entered; for example, the failure in the United States to distinguish when commercial announcements are beginning or ending, so that one can confuse the news or the entertainment program with the advertising message; the use of product placement in films and television programs; [and] the promotion of products connected with programs being shown, so that there is a temptation to use programs which have product tie-ins.

As we know, there are also endorsements of products by famous persons— sometimes apparent endorsements without the knowledge or permission of the person in question. Let me give an example: When I went to Budapest to speak on this same theme, I saw a billboard on the way from the airport showing a yawning Pope saying something in Hungarian, obviously in support of RTL, Radio-TV Luxembourg, one of the continent's largest private broadcasters. I mentioned this in my talk and said that the use of a person's image to sell a product or service without that person's authorization is at least immoral, if not illegal. The head of the Hungarian Advertising Standards Council rose to say that the billboard would be removed, the Ambassador of Hungary to the Holy See called me to apologize, and the president of the RTL later saw me at a dinner and told me that they had canceled that campaign in all of Europe. Occasionally, invoking ethical standards has dramatic results.

I am in favor of advertising, and I am in favor of commercially supported media; after all, I was editor of a newspaper which depended upon advertising for its survival. I am also in favor of ethics in advertising; after all, I was a Professor of Ethics for 17 years. I am convinced, however, that most people want to do the right thing and that they appreciate some guidance and support, preferably through industry guidelines, and even, if necessary, regulations by public authority to guarantee that they will not be victimized by their competition for being ethical.

Our point is that ethics in advertising serves the truth, the authentic development of the human person, and the healthy progress of society. If that sounds idealistic, so be it; if the Catholic Church cannot articulate an ideal, who can? What is encouraging to me is that so many seem to be hungry to hear such ideals articulated and, as advertising executives might say, in promoting our document, we are meeting a felt need. In this, we are not claiming a monopoly on truth; we are merely trying to articulate a consensus—and I hope that, in large measure, we have succeeded.

NO ⬅

Gene R. Laczniak

Reflections on the 1997 Vatican Statements Regarding Ethics in Advertising

In February 1997, the Vatican Pontifical Council for Social Communications issued a 35-page pamphlet, which provides a religion-based commentary on the ethics of advertising. This document is composed of five sections that endeavor to treat the economic, political, cultural, and moral dimensions of advertising as they affect society. Although the thematic tone of the writing is difficult to capture by excerpting a few paragraphs, the following quotations sample the rhetorical sense of the essay:

> On advertising in developing countries: "serious harm can be done them if advertising and commercial pressure becomes so irresponsible that communities seeking to rise from poverty to a reasonable standard of living are persuaded to seek this progress by satisfying wants that have been artificially created" (Section 10).

> On the relationship of advertising and the media: "In the competition to attract ever larger audiences and deliver them to advertisers, communicators can find themselves tempted—in fact pressured, subtly and not so subtly—to set aside high artistic and moral standards and lapse into superficiality, tawdriness, and moral squalor" (Section 12).

> On the morality of advertising: "Advertising can be tasteful and in conformity with high moral standards, and occasionally even morally uplifting but it can also be vulgar and morally degrading. Frequently it deliberately appeals to such motives as envy, status seeking, and lust. Today, too, some advertisers conscientiously seek to shock and titillate by exploiting content of a morbid, perverse, pornographic nature" (Section 13).

From Gene R. Laczniak, "Reflections on the 1997 Vatican Statements Regarding Ethics in Advertising," *Journal of Public Policy & Marketing*, vol. 17, no. 2 (Fall 1998). Copyright © 1998 by American Marketing Association. Reprinted by permission.

The Vatican essay concludes with the postulation of three ethical principles, which are discussed subsequently. It pointedly calls for greater responsibility on the part of those involved in the advertising industry, especially advertising practitioners. The document states (Section 14), "advertisers—that is, those who commission, prepare or disseminate advertising—are morally responsible for what they seek to move people to do." This pamphlet was distributed in its entirety by the Vatican Office to all Catholic bishops for the purposes of pastoral teaching and reflection. Its explicit target market consists of more than 600 million Catholics worldwide, as well as the global advertising community, but it also is intended for all people of goodwill.

The Statement's Fundamental Structure and Method

The Vatican essay takes the form of an analytical commentary on the social implications of advertising. The pamphlet, drawing almost exclusively on Catholic religious sources, logically moves from a statement of purpose to a final explication of principles. It is composed of four parts and 23 sections and runs approximately 35 pages in length.

The bibliographic citations made throughout the essay are scripturally and religiously rooted. The majority of references are to papal encyclicals and the *Catechism of the Catholic Church* (1994). These footnoted sources, in turn, are referenced heavily with additional biblical and doctrinal citations and can be used to examine the full scope of religious teaching that is invoked as a basis for the statements made. This approach to source authority can be expected to receive negative comment in most academic circles. That is, many will argue that, to maximize the credibility and defensibility of the observations made in this document, its tenets should be supported not by sectarian, religious documents but mainly by references to the most current and reputable social science and business literature dealing with the social outcomes of advertising. Such criticism partially misses the point.

... [M]ost of the issues raised regarding the possible economic, political, and cultural harms for which the institution of advertising might be responsible have been dissected previously by serious academic analysis (Rotzoll and Haefner 1990). But elaborate discussion of the questions previously raised by advertising should not imply a consensus resolution of the issues. In the mid-1980s, Richard Pollay authored a now-classic article that examines the ever-evolving history of advertising criticism as perceived by significant humanities and social science scholars. Pollay (1986, p. 21) writes in summation, "They see advertising as reinforcing materialism, cynicism, irrationality, selfishness, anxiety, social competitiveness, powerlessness and/or the loss of self respect." As such observations suggest, the power and visibility of advertising breeds ongoing, critical commentary in some sectors of society, but often this criticism raises more issues than solutions. For example, one recent literature review, covering the period 1987 to 1993, found 127 articles published on the topic of advertising ethics alone (Hyman, Tansey, and Clark 1994). That the Catholic Church also might weigh in on this pervasive topic should not be astounding to anyone. Thus, the systematic elaboration of religious values and accompanying citation of supporting writings should be understood as a different and possibly valuable perspective on the impact of advertising in a complex society. For example, Protestant and Jewish academics have drawn on their own religious traditions to offer commentary on addressing and improving business ethics (Camenish 1998; Pava 1998).

The Statement's Likely Impact: Ideal and Actual

The Vatican pamphlet on advertising ethics will receive a modicum of discussion, especially in Catholic circles, given its source and purpose. For example, I already am aware of several faculty, teaching at Catholic business schools, who have incorporated it into classroom discussions that pertain to the social impact of marketing activities. More than likely, it also will be used by some members of the Catholic clergy as an inspiration for homilies or a possible theme in parish programs or youth education efforts that include social reflections. The Vatican essay also can be expected to fall on some sympathetic ears among nonsectarian audiences, especially those searching for novel ideas wherever they can be found. For example, business academics interested in the questions of public policy and social issues certainly would fall into this category. On the balance, however, I believe this statement will not have much visibility or impact, at least not without a concerted effort to publicize (dare I say advertise?) it to upper-level marketing and advertising executives. According to a *New York Times* (Charry 1997) article published approximately 30 days after the Vatican essay on advertising ethics had been released, few high-profile advertising practitioners even were aware of its existence. There is little evidence to suggest that awareness levels regarding the content of the document will increase among the advertising community at any time in the future.

Perhaps more disturbing is my contention that, even if the document comes to the attention of the advertising community, the opinions of the Catholic Church on such matters will not be welcomed. On what basis do I say this? Church leaders systematically have opined on other economic issues on previous occasions (Naughton and Laczniak 1993). These observations, directed at the Catholic laity in general, but at the broader business community as well, have not been received graciously by business. For example, in 1986, the U.S. Catholic bishops published a lengthy, thoughtful pastoral letter titled *Economic Justice for All* (1986). That document attempted to articulate the implications of Catholic social teaching (CST) for the U.S. economy. Specifically, the principles of CST were explicated, and their connections to various managerial issues, such as employment, poverty, and economic development, were laid out comprehensively. In a poll of 2000 randomly selected business executives, reported in *Chicago Studies* (McMahon 1989), the majority of the executives perceived that this Catholic bishops' letter on economics was a political statement, rather than a constructive contribution to the dialogue regarding social justice. This observation was made despite the majority of executives claiming that religious values significantly influenced their business decision making....

As a business professor at a Catholic university, who teaches classes in both competitive strategy and business ethics, I have been asked by corporate executives on several occasions my opinion regarding the standing of the Catholic Church to comment intelligently on economic matters. My standard reply has been to say that Catholic Church leaders probably have at least as much useful to say about "justice" and "fairness" in the operation of the economy as business executives do about the efficient running of universities.

Observations in the Vatican Ethics Statement Likely to Be Attacked

Almost any assertion pertaining to the social role of advertising has a high likelihood of engendering debate. The Vatican statement on ethics in advertising contains several observations that are likely to serve as lightning rods for controversy. Regrettably, a few of these remarks will bolster the position of those in the business community who contend that the clergy lack economic understanding. For purposes of illustration, I focus on three such postulations from the ethics document.

First, in Section 10, the statement criticizes brand-related advertising for often accentuating irrational buying motives by consumers and causing potentially serious, supposedly ethical, problems. This condemnation is blanket and without sufficient illustration. Presumably, unstated examples, such as targeting $180 basketball shoes at the poorest urban youth, would represent such egregious abuse. In these cases, the Vatican and most of us should be outraged appropriately. But, this superficial criticism of branding and brand-related advertising as often leading to product proliferation and irrational consumer choice is also naive. Although branding, at the extreme, has been subject to some marketing exploitation, the benefits of branding are well accepted and key elements in enhancing the social value of advertising (Wilkie and Moore-Shay, in press). Even many severe critics of advertising generally are willing to grant this and admit that branding is one of the net "pluses" of complex marketing systems. Branding enables consumers to accrue a shorthand form of product identification and provides them with a longitudinally consistent indicator of price and quality across product categories. My point here is that such hypercritical analysis of possible advertising shortcomings undermines the credibility of the entire Vatican document.

Second, in Section 11, there is an unfortunate foray into the dysfunctions of political advertising. More than likely, this commentary by the Vatican Office was well intended, given that contemporary political campaigns have evolved away from interpersonal communications campaigns to ones that feature mass communications and often contain destructive negative advertising (Laczniak and Caywood 1987). Nevertheless, political advertising, at least in the United States, remains a protected class of speech that arises from constitutional guarantees. For this reason, political advertising would have best been eliminated in the Pontifical discussion. I say this because, by questioning the ethics of political speech, the church raises a frightening specter. If the Vatican is willing to delimit the sacrosanct area of paid-for political debate, advertising executives will wonder how much else church leaders would want to censor quickly. Such issues would have been better addressed in a separate document on the ethics and morality of modern political campaigns.

Third, in Section 14, the Vatican essay raises a dichotomy that, in my opinion, is far too dramatic. Referencing the media in general, and advertising in particular, the essay portrays media practitioners as facing a forked choice: "Either they help human persons to grow in their understanding and practice of what is true and good, or they are destructive forces in conflict with human well-being." Is human nature really so black and white? Does the Vatican believe that all advertising is either all good or all bad? Such simplistic analysis again undermines the credibility of other useful and valuable insights contained in the essay.

Moral Principles Relevant to Improving Advertising Ethics

The most substantive portion of the document involves the postulation of three principles that should be used to adjudicate the ethics of advertising. According to the Vatican essay, these are the following:

1. A principle of *truthfulness*. It states that, "advertising may not deliberately seek to deceive, whether it does that by what it says, by what it implies, or what it fails to say" (Section 15).
2. A principle of *human dignity*. "There is an imperative requirement" that advertising "respect the human person, his right/duty to make a responsible choice, his interior freedom; all these goods would be violated if man's lower inclinations were to be exploited, or his capacity to reflect and decide compromised" (Section 16). In the explication of this principle, promotions that appeal to lust, vanity, envy, and greed are referenced specifically. In addition, advertising that is directed exploitatively at vulnerable groups, such as children, the elderly, and the poor, is mentioned as particularly troubling.
3. A principle of *social responsibility*. "Advertising that reduces human progress to acquiring material and cultivating a lavish lifestyle expresses a false, destructive vision of the human person harmful to individuals and society alike" (Section 17). Specifically noted in this principle, by way of explanation, are advertisements that encourage lifestyles that contribute to the waste of resources or the despoiling of the natural environment.

Taken together, the worth of these principles is that they cover important, fundamental, and necessary ground. They remind advertisers of their proactive duties to avoid deception and respect persons, particularly those who are vulnerable, and of the special requirement of enlightened stewardship that managers should embrace in constructing responsible marketing campaigns.

The principles serve as noteworthy moral commentary in the long-running debate about how advertising is moderated best from a social and public policy standpoint (e.g., Preston 1994).

However, it is also fair to note that most of the issues addressed by these principles have been brought previously to the attention of the advertising community. The sentiment of nondeception covered in the first principle, at least in its basic form (i.e., "do not intentionally deceive"), is included in most existing professional codes of advertising ethics, as well as in the law. For example, "avoidance of false and misleading advertising" is a specific provision of the American Marketing Association code of ethics (Laczniak and Murphy 1993). And regarding the third ethical principle, advertisers long have espoused a high level of social responsibility. For example, the document titled *Standards of Practice of the American Association of Advertising Agencies* begins with the following language:

> We hold that a responsibility of advertising agencies is to be a constructive force in business. We hold that to discharge this responsibility, advertising agencies must recognize an obligation, not only to their clients, but to the public, the media they employ, and to each other... unethical competitive practices in the advertising agency business lead to financial waste, dilution of service, diversion of manpower, loss of prestige, and tend to weaken public confidence both in advertisements and in the institution of advertising (quoted in Laczniak and Murphy 1993).

If anything, these three Vatican principles might be faulted as too general. What may be needed more, perhaps, are midrange corollaries that address specific, documentable abuses in the advertising system.

The Professional Responsibilities of Advertising Educators and Practitioners

In the end, whether cleric, layperson, academic, or advertising practitioner, readers are left with the question: What social obligations are incumbent on advertising executives? Clearly, advertisers have some duties to contribute to the common good. The real debate comes regarding how broadly these social requirement parameters should be drawn and how aggressively practitioners should seek to fulfill their professional duties.

References

Camenish, Paul (1998), "A Presbyterian Approach to Business Ethics," in Perspectives in Business Ethics, L. P. Hartman, ed. Chicago: Irwin/McGraw-Hill, 229–38.

Catechism of the Catholic Church (1994). Chicago: Loyola University Press.

Charry, Tamer (1997), "Advertising: Roman Catholic Church Gets Mixed Review on Ads," New York Times, (March 31), Business Section, 1.

Economic Justice for All: Catholic Social Teaching and the U.S. Economy (1986). Washington, DC: National Conference of Catholic Bishops.

Hyman, Michael Richard, R. Tansey, and Jarvis W. Clark (1994), "Research on Advertising Ethics: Past, Present, and Future," Journal of Advertising, 23, 5–15.

Laczniak, Gene R. and Clarke L. Caywood (1987), "The Case For and Against Tele-
vised Political Advertising: Implications for Research and Public Policy," Journal
of Public Policy & Marketing, 6, 16–32.

—— and Patrick E. Murphy (1993), Ethical Marketing Decisions. Boston, MA: Allyn
& Bacon.

McMahon, Thomas F. (1989), "Religion and Business," Chicago Studies, 3–15.

Naughton, Michael and Gene R. Laczniak (1993), "A Theological Context of Work
from the Catholic Social Encyclical Tradition," Journal of Business Ethics, 12, 981–
94.

Pava, Moses L. (1998), "Developing a Religiously Grounded Business Ethics: A Jewish
Perspective," Business Ethics Quarterly, 8, 65–83.

Pollay, Richard W. (1986), "The Distorted Mirror: Reflections on the Unintended
Consequences of Advertising," Journal of Marketing, 50 (April), 18–36.

Pontifical Council for Social Communications (1997), Ethics in Advertising. Vatican
City: Vatican Documents.

Preston, Ivan L. (1994), The Tangled Web They Weave: Truth, Falsity, and Advertisers.
Madison, WI: University of Wisconsin Press.

Rotzoll, Kim and James Haefner (1990), Advertising in Contemporary Society. Cincin-
nati, OH: Southwestern.

Wilkie, William and Elizabeth S. Moore-Shay (in press), "Marketing's Contributions
to Society," Journal of Marketing, forthcoming.

POSTSCRIPT

Are Marketing and Advertising Fundamentally Exploitive?

We live in an age of rapid change in the communications business. Many are concerned over the directions that change is taking, and for good reason. How can one assess what proportion of the problems of society are traceable to advertising and the general marketing practices of corporations? For instance, if it turns out that ads for diet products and slim fashions, advertised by emaciated supermodels, are unduly influencing young girls to lose their self-esteem and self-confidence, ruin their health with fad diets, and sometimes even starve themselves, what, can or should be done about that? Is government regulation the answer? Is industry self-regulation the answer? As citizens and as consumers, you will be part of these serious decisions.

Suggested Readings

Stevan Alburty, "The Ad Agency to End All Agencies," *Fast Company* (December–January 1997).

George Brenkert, "Ethics in Advertising: The Good, the Bad, and the Church," *Journal of Public Policy and Marketing* (Fall 1998).

Carol Krol, "Pontifical Council Sets Guidelines for Making Ads," *Advertising Age* (vol. 68, no. 4, 1997).

James E. Liebig, *Merchants of Vision: People Bringing New Purpose and Values to Business* (Berret-Koehier, 1994).

Pontifical Council for Social Communications, *Ethics in Advertising* (Vatican Documents, 1997).

ISSUE 13

Was Ford to Blame in the Pinto Case?

YES: Mark Dowie, from "Pinto Madness," *Mother Jones* (September/October 1977)

NO: Ford Motor Company, from "Closing Argument by Mr. James Neal," Brief for the Defense, *State of Indiana v. Ford Motor Company*, U.S. District Court, South Bend, Indiana (January 15, 1980)

ISSUE SUMMARY

YES: Award-winning investigative journalist Mark Dowie alleges that Ford Motor Company deliberately put an unsafe car—the Pinto—on the road, causing hundreds of people to suffer burn deaths and horrible disfigurement. He contends that the related activities of Ford's executives, both within the company and in dealing with the public and the government, were criminal.

NO: James Neal, chief attorney for Ford Motor Company during the Pinto litigation, argues to the jury that Ford cannot be held responsible for deaths that were caused by others—such as the driver of the van that struck the victims—and that there is no proof of criminal intent or negligence on the part of Ford.

On August 10, 1978, three girls had stopped their car, a 1973 Ford Pinto, on U.S. Highway 22 near Goshen, Indiana, and were about to get under way again when they were struck from the rear at high speed by a van. The car immediately burst into flames, and the girls had no chance to escape before the flames reached them.

The blame for these girls' deaths fell not on the driver of the van but on the manufacturer of the Pinto. Questions that were asked were: What was wrong with the car? Why did it burst into flames so quickly? Mark Dowie, then–general manager of business operations of the magazine *Mother Jones,* had argued a year earlier that there was a great deal wrong with the Pinto. Dowie's argument, which is reprinted here, is based on data obtained for him by some disaffected Ford engineers. In it, he suggests that the Pinto had been rushed into production without adequate testing; that it had a vulnerable fuel system that would rupture with any rear-end collision; that even though the vulnerability was discovered before production, Ford had hurried the Pinto to the market anyway; and that successful lobbying thereafter had prevented government regulators from instituting a requirement for a safer gas tank. Most suggestive to the public was a document supplied by one of the engineers, an estimate of the probable costs of refitting valves to prevent fire in a rollover accident. It was a cost-benefit analysis that placed a dollar value on human life—among the estimates were the probability of a fatal accident, the amount of money needed to settle a lawsuit for the loss of a life, and the amount of money needed to do the refitting so that there would be less chance for that loss of life—and concluded that it was more economical to accept the higher probability of death occurring and then settle the suits as they come. The document caused serious damage to Ford Motor Company's reputation.

Ford endured two sets of court appearances as a result of Dowie's article. More common, and successful, were the civil suits, alleging culpable negligence that damaged the rights of other individuals. But the state of Indiana also brought a public prosecution for *criminal* negligence, and James Neal's brief, which also follows, was prepared for that trial.

The 1916 case *McPherson v. Buick* helps set the stage for this debate. In this case, McPherson successfully sued the Buick Motor Company for injury sustained as a direct result of a poorly manufactured product. This was the first instance of a consumer's suing a manufacturer (as opposed to the seller), and it marked the transfer of product liability cases from the form of action known as "contract" to the form of action known as "tort" (in this case, negligence). The logic is that not only is an individual agreement breached when a shoddy product injures a consumer but a general obligation on the part of a manufacturer (an implied "warrant of merchantability") to avoid putting an unsafe product on the market is not met. Given the myriad ways that people can injure themselves, that obligation seems to be very broad indeed.

With regard to the Pinto case, was Ford guilty of deliberate malfeasance? Was it a series of unlucky decisions made in good faith? Or was this just a very unfortunate accident? As you read these selections, ask yourself what conditions need to be satisifed in order to attribute "responsibility" to any person or company. Also, what kinds of risks do people assume when buying a car, a motorcycle, or a can of tuna fish? For what is the manufacturer responsible? Should we be willing to assume more risks in the enormously competitive market that prevails among small automobiles? Does the product liability suit unjustly cripple American efforts to compete in highly competitive industries? Is this something that we should be concerned about?

Mark Dowie

 **YES**

Pinto Madness

One evening in the mid-1960s, Arjay Miller was driving home from his office in Dearborn, Michigan, in the four-door Lincoln Continental that went with his job as president of the Ford Motor Company. On a crowded highway, another car struck his from the rear. The Continental spun around and burst into flames. Because he was wearing a shoulder-strap seat belt, Miller was unharmed by the crash, and because his doors didn't jam he escaped the gasoline-drenched, flaming wreck. But the accident made a vivid impression on him. Several months later, on July 15, 1965, he recounted it to a U.S. Senate subcommittee that was hearing testimony on auto safety legislation. "I still have burning in my mind the image of that gas tank on fire," Miller said. He went on to express an almost passionate interest in controlling fuel-fed fires in cars that crash or roll over. He spoke with excitement about the fabric gas tank Ford was testing at that very moment. "If it proves out," he promised the senators, "it will be a feature you will see in our standard cars."

Almost seven years after Miller's testimony, a woman, whom for legal reasons we will call Sandra Gillespie, pulled onto a Minneapolis highway in her new Ford Pinto. Riding with her was a young boy, whom we'll call Robbie Carlton. As she entered a merge lane, Sandra Gillespie's car stalled. Another car rear-ended hers at an impact speed of 28 miles per hour. The Pinto's gas tank ruptured. Vapors from it mixed quickly with the air in the passenger compartment. A spark ignited the mixture and the car exploded in a ball of fire. Sandra died in agony a few hours later in an emergency hospital. Her passenger, 13-year-old Robbie Carlton, is still alive; he has just come home from another futile operation aimed at grafting a new ear and nose from skin on the few unscarred portions of his badly burned body. (This accident is real; the details are from police reports.)

Why did Sandra Gillespie's Ford Pinto catch fire so easily, seven years after Ford's Arjay Miller made his apparently sincere pronouncements—the same seven years that brought more safety improvements to cars than any other pe-

From Mark Dowie, "Pinto Madness," *Mother Jones*, vol. 2, no. 8 (September/October 1977). Copyright © 1977 by Mark Dowie. Reprinted by permission.

riod in automotive history? An extensive investigation by *Mother Jones* over the past six months has found these answers:

• Fighting strong competition from Volkswagen for the lucrative small-car market, the Ford Motor Company rushed the Pinto into production in much less than the usual time.

• Ford engineers discovered in pre-production crash tests that rear-end collisions would rupture the Pinto's fuel system extremely easily.

• Because assembly-line machinery was already tooled when engineers found this defect, top Ford officials decided to manufacture the car anyway—exploding gas tank and all—*even though Ford owned the patent on a much safer gas tank.*

• For more than eight years afterwards, Ford successfully lobbied, with extraordinary vigor and some blatant lies, against a key government safety standard that would have forced the company to change the Pinto's fire-prone gas tank.

By conservative estimates Pinto crashes have caused 500 burn deaths to people who would not have been seriously injured if the car had not burst into flames. The figure could be as high as 900. Burning Pintos have become such an embarrassment to Ford that its advertising agency, J. Walter Thompson, dropped a line from the end of a radio spot that read "Pinto leaves you with that warm feeling."

Ford knows the Pinto is a firetrap, yet it has paid out millions to settle damage suits out of court, and it is prepared to spend millions more lobbying against safety standards. With a half million cars rolling off the assembly lines each year, Pinto is the biggest-selling subcompact in America, and the company's operating profit on the car is fantastic. Finally, in 1977, new Pinto models have incorporated a few minor alterations necessary to meet that federal standard Ford managed to hold off for eight years. Why did the company delay so long in making these minimal, inexpensive improvements?

• Ford waited eight years because its internal "cost-benefit analysis," *which places a dollar value on human life,* said it wasn't profitable to make the changes sooner.

Before we get to the question of how much Ford thinks your life is worth, let's trace the history of the death trap itself. Although this particular story is about the Pinto, the way in which Ford made its decision is typical of the U.S. auto industry generally. There are plenty of similar stories about other cars made by other companies. But this case is the worst of them all.

⋅◀◉▶⋅

The next time you drive behind a Pinto (with over two million of them on the road, you shouldn't have much trouble finding one), take a look at the rear end. That long silvery object hanging down under the bumper is the gas tank. The tank begins about six inches forward of the bumper. In late models the bumper is designed to withstand a collision of only about five miles per hour. Earlier bumpers may as well not have been on the car for all the protection they offered the gas tank.

Mother Jones has studied hundreds of reports and documents on rear-end collisions involving Pintos. These reports conclusively reveal that if you ran into that Pinto you were following at over 30 miles per hour, the rear end of the car would buckle like an accordion, right up to the back seat. The tube leading to the gas-tank cap would be ripped away from the tank itself, and gas would immediately begin sloshing onto the road around the car. The buckled gas tank would be jammed up against the differential housing (that big bulge in the middle of your rear axle), which contains four sharp, protruding bolts likely to gash holes in the tank and spill still more gas. Now all you need is a spark from a cigarette, ignition, or scraping metal, and both cars would be engulfed in flames. If you gave that Pinto a really good whack—say, at 40 mph—chances are excellent that its doors would jam and you would have to stand by and watch its trapped passengers burn to death.

This scenario is no news to Ford. Internal company documents in our possession show that Ford has crash-tested the Pinto at a top-secret site more than 40 times and that *every* test made at over 25 mph without special structural alteration of the car has resulted in a ruptured fuel tank. Despite this, Ford officials denied under oath having crash-tested the Pinto.

Eleven of these tests, averaging a 31-mph impact speed, came before Pintos started rolling out of the factories. Only three cars passed the test with unbroken fuel tanks. In one of them an inexpensive light-weight plastic baffle was placed between the front of the gas tank and the differential housing, so those four bolts would not perforate the tank. (Don't forget about that little piece of plastic, which costs one dollar and weighs one pound. It plays an important role in our story later on.) In another successful test, a piece of steel was placed between the tank and the bumper. In the third test car the gas tank was lined with a rubber bladder. But none of these protective alterations was used in the mass-produced Pinto.

In pre-production planning, engineers seriously considered using in the Pinto the same kind of gas tank Ford uses in the Capri. The Capri tank rides over the rear axle and differential housing. It has been so successful in over 50 crash tests that Ford used it in its Experimental Safety Vehicle, which withstood rear-end impacts of 60 mph. So why wasn't the Capri tank used in the Pinto? Or, why wasn't that plastic baffle placed between the tank and the axle—something that would have saved the life of Sandra Gillespie and hundreds like her? Why was a car known to be a serious fire hazard deliberately released to production in August of 1970?

⚜

Whether Ford should manufacture subcompacts at all was the subject of a bitter two-year debate at the company's Dearborn headquarters. The principals in this corporate struggle were the then-president Semon "Bunky" Knudsen, whom Henry Ford II had hired away from General Motors, and Lee Iacocca, a spunky Young Turk who had risen fast within the company on the enormous success of the Mustang. Iacocca argued forcefully that Volkswagen and the Japanese were going to capture the entire American subcompact market unless Ford put out its own alternative to the VW Beetle. Bunky Knudsen said, in effect: let them have the small-car market; Ford makes good money on medium and large models. But he lost the battle and later resigned. Iacocca became president and almost immediately began a rush program to produce the Pinto.

Like the Mustang, the Pinto became known in the company as "Lee's car." Lee Iacocca wanted that little car in the showrooms of America with the 1971 models. So he ordered his engineering vice president, Bob Alexander, to oversee what was probably the shortest production planning period in modern automotive history. The normal time span from conception to production of a new car model is about 43 months. The Pinto schedule was set at just under 25.

... Design, styling, product planning, advance engineering and quality assurance all have flexible time frames, and engineers can pretty much carry these on simultaneously. Tooling, on the other hand, has a fixed time frame of about 18 months. Normally, an auto company doesn't begin tooling until the other processes are almost over: you don't want to make the machines that stamp and press and grind metal into the shape of car parts until you know all those parts will work well together. *But Iacocca's speed-up meant Pinto tooling went on at the same time as product development.* So when crash tests revealed a serious defect in the gas tank, it was too late. The tooling was well under way.

When it was discovered the gas tank was unsafe, did anyone go to Iacocca and tell him? "Hell no," replied an engineer who worked on the Pinto, a high company official for many years, who, unlike several others at Ford, maintains a necessarily clandestine concern for safety. "That person would have been fired. Safety wasn't a popular subject around Ford in those days. With Lee it was taboo. Whenever a problem was raised that meant a delay on the Pinto, Lee would chomp on his cigar, look out the window and say 'Read the product objectives and get back to work.'"

The product objectives are clearly stated in the Pinto "green book." This is a thick, top-secret manual in green covers containing a step-by-step production plan for the model, detailing the metallurgy, weight, strength and quality of every part in the car. The product objectives for the Pinto are repeated in an article by Ford executive F. G. Olsen published by the Society of Automotive Engineers. He lists these product objectives as follows:

1. TRUE SUBCOMPACT
   - Size
   - Weight
2. LOW COST OF OWNERSHIP
   - Initial price
   - Fuel consumption
   - Reliability
   - Serviceability
3. CLEAR PRODUCT SUPERIORITY
   - Appearance
   - Comfort
   - Features

- Ride and Handling
- Performance

Safety, you will notice, is not there. It is not mentioned in the entire article. As Lee Iacocca was fond of saying, "Safety doesn't sell."

Heightening the anti-safety pressure on Pinto engineers was an important goal set by Iacocca known as "the limits of 2,000." The Pinto was not to weigh an ounce over 2,000 pounds and not to cost a cent over $2,000. "Iacocca enforced these limits with an iron hand," recalls the engineer quoted earlier. So, even when a crash test showed that that one-pound, one-dollar piece of plastic stopped the puncture of the gas tank, it was thrown out as extra cost and extra weight.

People shopping for subcompacts are watching every dollar. "You have to keep in mind," the engineer explained, "that the price elasticity on these subcompacts is extremely tight. You can price yourself right out of the market by adding $25 to the production cost of the model. And nobody understands that better than Iacocca."

Dr. Leslie Ball, the retired safety chief for the NASA manned space program and a founder of the International Society of Reliability Engineers, recently made a careful study of the Pinto. "The release to production of the Pinto was the most reprehensible decision in the history of American engineering," he said. Ball can name more than 40 European and Japanese models in the Pinto price and weight range with safer gas-tank positioning. Ironically, many of them, like the Ford Capri, contain a "saddle-type" gas tank riding over the back axle. *The patent on the saddle-type tank is owned by the Ford Motor Co.*

Los Angeles auto safety expert Byron Bloch has made an in-depth study of the Pinto fuel system. "It's a catastrophic blunder," he says. "Ford made an extremely irresponsible decision when they placed such a weak tank in such a ridiculous location in such a soft rear end. It's almost designed to blow up—premeditated."

A Ford engineer, who doesn't want his name used, comments: "This company is run by salesmen, not engineers; so the priority is styling, not safety." He goes on to tell a story about gas-tank safety at Ford.

Lou Tubben is one of the most popular engineers at Ford. He's a friendly, outgoing guy with a genuine concern for safety. By 1971 he had grown so concerned about gas-tank integrity that he asked his boss if he could prepare a presentation on safer tank design. Tubben and his boss had both worked on the Pinto and shared a concern for its safety. His boss gave him the go-ahead, scheduled a date for the presentation and invited all company engineers and key production planning personnel. When time came for the meeting, a grand total of two people showed up—Lou Tubben and his boss.

"So you see," continued the anonymous Ford engineer ironically, "there *are* a few of us here at Ford who are concerned about fire safety." He adds: "They are mostly engineers who have to study a lot of accident reports and look at pictures of burned people. But we don't talk about it much. It isn't a popular subject. I've never seen safety on the agenda of a product meeting and, except for a brief period in 1956, I can't remember seeing the word safety in an advertisement. I really don't think the company wants American consumers to start thinking too much about safety—for fear they might demand it, I suppose."

Asked about the Pinto gas tank, another Ford engineer admitted: "That's all true. But you miss the point entirely. You see, safety isn't the issue, trunk space is. You have no idea how stiff the competition is over trunk space. Do you realize that if we put a Capri-type tank in the Pinto you could only get one set of golf clubs in the trunk?"

꧁꧂

Blame for Sandra Gillespie's death, Robbie Carlton's unrecognizable face and all the other injuries and deaths in Pintos since 1970 does not rest on the shoulders of Lee Iacocca alone. For, while he and his associates fought their battle against a safer Pinto in Dearborn, a larger war against safer cars raged in Washington. One skirmish in that war involved Ford's successful eight-year lobbying effort against Federal Motor Vehicle Safety Standard 301, the rear-end provisions of which would have forced Ford to redesign the Pinto.

But first some background:

During the early '60s, auto safety legislation became the *bête-noire* of American big business. The auto industry was the last great unregulated business, and if *it* couldn't reverse the tide of government regulation, the reasoning went, no one could.

People who know him cannot remember Henry Ford II taking a stronger stand than the one he took against the regulation of safety design. He spent weeks in Washington calling on members of Congress, holding press conferences and recruiting business cronies like W. B. Murphy of Campbell's Soup to join the anti-regulation battle. Displaying the sophistication for which today's American corporate leaders will be remembered, Murphy publicly called auto safety "a hula hoop, a fad that will pass." He was speaking to a special luncheon of the Business Council, an organization of 100 chief executives who gather periodically in Washington to provide "advice" and "counsel" to government. The target of their wrath in this instance was the Motor Vehicle Safety Bills introduced in both houses of Congress, largely in response to Ralph Nader's *Unsafe at Any Speed.*

By 1965, most pundits and lobbyists saw the handwriting on the wall and prepared to accept government "meddling" in the last bastion of free enterprise. Not Henry. With bulldog tenacity, he held out for defeat of the legislation to the very end, loyal to his grandfather's invention and to the company that makes it. But the Safety Act passed the House and Senate unanimously, and was signed into law by Lyndon Johnson in 1966.

While lobbying for and against legislation is pretty much a process of high-level back-slapping, press-conferencing and speech-making, fighting a regulatory agency is a much subtler matter. Henry headed home to lick his wounds in Grosse Pointe, Michigan, and a planeload of the Ford Motor Company's best brains flew to Washington to start the "education" of the new federal auto safety bureaucrats.

Their job was to implant the official industry ideology in the minds of the new officials regulating auto safety. Briefly summarized, that ideology states that auto accidents are caused not by *cars,* but by 1) people and 2) highway conditions.

This philosophy is rather like blaming a robbery on the victim. Well, what did you expect? You were carrying money, weren't you? It is an extraordinary experience to hear automotive "safety engineers" talk for hours without ever mentioning cars. They will advocate spending billions educating youngsters, punishing drunks and redesigning street signs. Listening to them, you can momentarily begin to think that it is easier to control 100 million drivers than a handful of manufacturers. They show movies about guardrail design and advocate the clear-cutting of trees 100 feet back from every highway in the nation. If a car is unsafe, they argue, it is because its owner doesn't properly drive it. Or, perhaps, maintain it.

In light of an annual death rate approaching 50,000, they are forced to admit that driving is hazardous. But the car is, in the words of Arjay Miller, "the safest link in the safety chain."

Before the Ford experts left Washington to return to drafting tables in Dearborn they did one other thing. They managed to informally reach an agreement with the major public servants who would be making auto safety decisions. This agreement was that "cost-benefit" would be an acceptable mode of analysis by Detroit and its new regulators. And as we shall see, cost-benefit analysis quickly became the basis of Ford's argument against safer car design.

⋘⊙⋙

Cost-benefit analysis was used only occasionally in government until President Kennedy appointed Ford Motor Company President Robert McNamara to be Secretary of Defense. McNamara, originally an accountant, preached cost benefit with all the force of a Biblical zealot. Stated in its simplest terms, cost-benefit analysis says that if the cost is greater than the benefit, the project is not worth it—no matter what the benefit. Examine the cost of every action, decision, contract, part, or change, the doctrine says, then carefully evaluate the benefits (in dollars) to be certain that they exceed the cost before you begin a program or—and this is the crucial part for our story—pass a regulation.

As a management tool in a business in which profits matter over everything else, cost-benefit analysis makes a certain amount of sense. Serious problems come, however, when public officials who ought to have more than corporate profits at heart apply cost-benefit analysis to every conceivable decision. The inevitable result is that they must place a dollar value on human life.

Ever wonder what your life is worth in dollars? Perhaps $10 million? Ford has a better idea: $200,000.

Remember, Ford had gotten the federal regulators to agree to talk auto safety in terms of cost-benefit analysis. But in order to be able to argue that various safety costs were greater than their benefits, Ford needed to have a dollar value figure for the "benefit." Rather than be so uncouth as to come up

Table 1

What's Your Life Worth? Societal Cost Components for Fatalities, 1972 NHTSA Study

Component	1971 Costs
Future productivity losses	
Direct	$132,000
Indirect	41,300
Medical costs	
Hospital	700
Other	425
Property damage	1,500
Insurance administration	4,700
Legal and court	3,000
Employer losses	1,000
Victim's pain and suffering	10,000
Funeral	900
Assets (lost consumption)	5,000
Miscellaneous accident costs	200
Total per fatality: $200,725	

Here is a chart from a federal study showing how the National Highway Traffic Safety Administration has calculated the value of a human life. The estimate was arrived at under pressure from the auto industry. The Ford Motor Company has used it in cost-benefit analyses arguing why certain safety measures are not "worth" the savings in human lives. The calculation above is a breakdown of the estimated cost to society every time someone is killed in a car accident. We were not able to find anyone, either in the government or at Ford, who could explain how the $10,000 figure for "pain and suffering" had been arrived at.

with such a price tag itself, the auto industry pressured the National Highway Traffic Safety Administration to do so. And in a 1972 report the agency decided a human life was worth $200,725. (For its reasoning, see [Table 1].) Inflationary forces have recently pushed the figure up to $278,000.

Furnished with this useful tool, Ford immediately went to work using it to prove why various safety improvements were too expensive to make.

Nowhere did the company argue harder that it should make no changes than in the area of rupture-prone fuel tanks. Not long after the government arrived at the $200,725-per-life figure, it surfaced, rounded off to a cleaner $200,000, in an internal Ford memorandum. This cost-benefit analysis argued that Ford should not make an $11-per-car improvement that would prevent 180 fiery deaths a year. (This minor change would have prevented gas tanks from breaking so easily both in rear-end collisions, like Sandra Gillespie's, and in rollover accidents, where the same thing tends to happen.)

Ford's cost-benefit table [Table 2] is buried in a seven-page company memorandum entitled "Fatalities Associated with Crash-Induced Fuel Leakage and

Table 2

$11 vs. a Burn Death: Benefits and Costs Relating to Fuel Leakage Associated With the Static Rollover Test Portion of FMVSS 208

Benefits

Savings: 180 burn deaths, 180 serious burn injuries, 2,100 burned vehicles.

Unit cost: $200,000 per death, $67,000 per injury, $700 per vehicle.

Total benefit: 180 x ($200,000) + 180 x ($67,000) + 2,100 x ($700) = $49.5 million.

Costs

Sales: 11 million cars, 1.5 million light trucks.

Unit cost: $11 per car, $11 per truck.

Total cost: 11,000,000 x ($11) + 1,500,000 x ($11) = $137 million.

From Ford Motor Company internal memorandum: "Fatalities Associated with Crash-Induced Fuel Leakage and Fires."

Fires." The memo argues that there is no financial benefit in complying with proposed safety standards that would admittedly result in fewer auto fires, fewer burn deaths and fewer burn injuries. Naturally, memoranda that speak so casually of "burn deaths" and "burn injuries" are not released to the public. They are very effective, however, with Department of Transportation officials indoctrinated in McNamarian cost-benefit analysis.

All Ford had to do was convince men like John Volpe, Claude Brinegar and William Coleman (successive Secretaries of Transportation during the Nixon-Ford years) that certain safety standards would add so much to the price of cars that fewer people would buy them. This could damage the auto industry, which was still believed to be the bulwark of the American economy. "Compliance to these standards," Henry Ford II prophesied at more than one press conference, "will shut down the industry."

The Nixon Transportation Secretaries were the kind of regulatory officials big business dreams of. They understood and loved capitalism and thought like businessmen. Yet, best of all, they came into office uninformed on technical automotive matters. And you could talk "burn injuries" and "burn deaths" with these guys, and they didn't seem to envision children crying at funerals and people hiding in their homes with melted faces. Their minds appeared to have leapt right to the bottom line—more safety meant higher prices, higher prices meant lower sales and lower sales meant lower profits.

So when J. C. Echold, Director of Automotive Safety (which means chief anti-safety lobbyist) for Ford wrote to the Department of Transportation—which he still does frequently, at great length—he felt secure attaching a memorandum that in effect says it is acceptable to kill 180 people and burn another 180 every year, *even though we have the technology that could save their lives for $11 a car.*

Furthermore, Echold attached this memo, confident, evidently, that the Secretary would question neither his low death/injury statistics nor his high cost estimates. But it turns out, on closer examination, that both these findings were misleading.

First, note that Ford's table shows an equal number of burn deaths and burn injuries. This is false. All independent experts estimate that for each person who dies by an auto fire, many more are left with charred hands, faces and limbs. Andrew McGuire of the Northern California Burn Center estimates the ratio of burn injuries to deaths at ten to one instead of the one to one Ford shows here. Even though Ford values a burn at only a piddling $67,000 instead of the $200,000 price of life, the true ratio obviously throws the company's calculations way off.

The other side of the equation, the alleged $11 cost of a fire-prevention device, is also a misleading estimation. One document that was *not* sent to Washington by Ford was a "Confidential" cost analysis *Mother Jones* has managed to obtain, showing that crash fires could be largely prevented for considerably *less* than $11 a car. The cheapest method involves placing a heavy rubber bladder inside the gas tank to keep the fuel from spilling if the tank ruptures. Goodyear had developed the bladder and had demonstrated it to the automotive industry. We have in our possession crash-test reports showing that the Goodyear bladder worked well. On December 2, 1970 (*two years before* Echold sent his cost-benefit memo to Washington), Ford Motor Company ran a rear-end crash test on a car with the rubber bladder in the gas tank. The tank ruptured, but no fuel leaked. On January 15, 1971, Ford again tested the bladder and again it worked. The total purchase and installation cost of the bladder would have been $5.08 per car. That $5.08 could have saved the lives of Sandra Gillespie and several hundred others.

⋅⟨⊙⟩⋅

When a federal regulatory agency like the National Highway Traffic Safety Administration (NHTSA) decides to issue a new standard, the law usually requires it to invite all interested parties to respond before the standard is enforced—a reasonable enough custom on the surface. However, the auto industry has taken advantage of this process and has used it to delay lifesaving emission and safety standards for years. In the case of the standard that would have corrected that fragile Pinto fuel tank, the delay was for an incredible eight years.

The particular regulation involved here was Federal Motor Vehicle Safety Standard 301. Ford picked portions of Standard 301 for strong opposition back in 1968 when the Pinto was still in the blueprint stage. The intent of 301, and the 300 series that followed it, was to protect drivers and passengers *after* a crash occurs. Without question the worst postcrash hazard is fire. So Standard 301 originally proposed that all cars should be able to withstand a fixed barrier impact of 20 mph (that is, running into a wall at that speed) without losing fuel.

When the standard was proposed, Ford engineers pulled their crash-test results out of their files. The front ends of most cars were no problem—with minor alterations they could stand the impact without losing fuel. "We were already working on the front end," Ford engineer Dick Kimble admitted. "We knew we could meet the test on the front end." But with the Pinto particularly, a 20-mph rear-end standard meant redesigning the entire rear end of the car. With the Pinto scheduled for production in August of 1970, and with $200 million worth of tools in place, adoption of this standard would have created a minor financial disaster. So Standard 301 was targeted for delay, and, with some assistance from its industry associates, Ford succeeded beyond its wildest expectations: the standard was not adopted until the 1977 model year. Here is how it happened:

There are several main techniques in the art of combating a government safety standard: a) make your arguments in succession, so the feds can be working on disproving only one at a time; b) claim that the real problem is not X but Y (we already saw one instance of this in "the problem is not cars but people"); c) no matter how ridiculous each argument is, accompany it with thousands of pages of highly technical assertions it will take the government months or, preferably, years to test. Ford's large and active Washington office brought these techniques to new heights and became the envy of the lobbyists' trade.

The Ford people started arguing against Standard 301 way back in 1968 with a strong attack of technique b). Fire, they said, was not the real problem. Sure, cars catch fire and people burn occasionally. But statistically auto fires are such a minor problem that NHTSA should really concern itself with other matters.

Strange as it may seem, the Department of Transportation (NHTSA's parent agency) didn't know whether or not this was true. So it contracted with several independent research groups to study auto fires. The studies took months which was just what Ford wanted.

The completed studies, however, showed auto fires to be more of a problem than Transportation officials ever dreamed of. Robert Nathan and Associates, a Washington research firm, found that 400,000 cars were burning up every year, burning more than 3,000 people to death. Furthermore, auto fires were increasing five times as fast as building fires. Another study showed that 35 per cent of all fire deaths in the U.S. occurred in automobiles. Forty per cent of all fire department calls in the 1960s were to vehicle fires—a public cost of $350 million a year, a figure that, incidentally, never shows up in cost-benefit analyses.

Another study was done by the Highway Traffic Research Institute in Ann Arbor, Michigan, a safety think-tank funded primarily by the auto industry (the giveaway there is the words "highway traffic" rather than "automobile" in the group's name). It concluded that 40 per cent of the lives lost in fuel-fed fires could be saved if the manufacturers complied with proposed Standard 301. Finally, a third report was prepared for NHTSA by consultant Eugene Trisko entitled "A National Survey of Motor Vehicle Fires." His report indicates that the Ford Motor Company makes 24 per cent of the cars on the American road, yet these cars account for 42 per cent of the collision-ruptured fuel tanks.

Ford lobbyists then used technique a)—bringing up a new argument. Their line then became: yes, perhaps burn accidents do happen, but rear-end collisions are relatively rare (note the echo of technique b) here as well). Thus

Standard 301 was not needed. This set the NHTSA off on a new round of analyzing accident reports. The government's findings finally were that rear-end collisions were seven and a half times more likely to result in fuel spills than were front-end collisions. So much for that argument.

By now it was 1972; NHTSA had been researching and analyzing for four years to answer Ford's objections. During that time, nearly 9,000 people burned to death in flaming wrecks. Tens of thousands more were badly burned and scarred for life. And the four-year delay meant that well over 10 million new unsafe vehicles went on the road, vehicles that will be crashing, leaking fuel and incinerating people well into the 1980s.

Ford now had to enter its third round of battling the new regulations. On the "the problem is not X but Y" principle, the company had to look around for something new to get itself off the hook. One might have thought that, faced with all the latest statistics on the horrifying number of deaths in flaming accidents, Ford would find the task difficult. But the company's rhetoric was brilliant. The problem was not burns, but . . . impact! Most of the people killed in these fiery accidents, claimed Ford, would have died whether the car burned or not. They were killed by the kinetic force of the impact, not the fire.

And so once again, as in some giant underwater tennis game, the ball bounced into the government's court and the absurdly pro-industry NHTSA began another slow-motion response. Once again it began a time-consuming round of test crashes and embarked on a study of accidents. The latter, however, revealed that a large and growing number of corpses taken from burned cars involved in rear-end crashes contained no cuts, bruises or broken bones. They clearly would have survived the accident unharmed if the cars had not caught fire. This pattern was confirmed in careful rear-end crash tests performed by the Insurance Institute for Highway Safety. A University of Miami study found an inordinate number of Pintos burning on rear-end impact and concluded that this demonstrated "a clear and present hazard to all Pinto owners."

Pressure on NHTSA from Ralph Nader and consumer groups began mounting. The industry-agency collusion was so obvious that Senator Joseph Montoya (D-N.M.) introduced legislation about Standard 301. NHTSA waffled some more and again announced its intentions to promulgate a rear-end collision standard.

Waiting, as it normally does, until the last day allowed for response, Ford filed with NHTSA a gargantuan batch of letters, studies and charts now arguing that the federal testing criteria were unfair. Ford also argued that design changes required to meet the standard would take 43 months, which seemed like a rather long time in light of the fact that the entire Pinto was designed in about two years. Specifically, new complaints about the standard involved the weight of the test vehicle, whether or not the brakes should be engaged at the moment of impact and the claim that the standard should only apply to cars, not trucks or buses. Perhaps the most amusing argument was that the engine should not be idling during crash tests, the rationale being that an idling engine meant that the gas tank had to contain gasoline and that the hot lights needed to film the crash might ignite the gasoline and cause a fire.

Some of these complaints were accepted, others rejected. But they all required examination and testing by a weak-kneed NHTSA, meaning more of those 18-month studies the industry loves so much. So the complaints served their real purpose—delay; all told, an eight-year delay, while Ford manufactured more than three million profitable, dangerously incendiary Pintos. To justify this delay, Henry Ford II called more press conferences to predict the demise of American civilization. "If we can't meet the standards when they are published," he warned, "we will have to close down. And if we have to close down some production because we don't meet standards we're in for real trouble in this country."

⋯⟨◉⟩⋯

While government bureaucrats dragged their feet on lifesaving Standard 301, a different kind of expert was taking a close look at the Pinto—the "recon man." "Recon" stands for reconstruction; recon men reconstruct accidents for police departments, insurance companies and lawyers who want to know exactly who or what caused an accident. It didn't take many rear-end Pinto accidents to demonstrate the weakness of the car. Recon men began encouraging lawyers to look beyond one driver or another to the manufacturer in their search for fault, particularly in the growing number of accidents where passengers were uninjured by collision but were badly burned by fire.

Pinto lawuits began mounting fast against Ford. Says John Versace, executive safety engineer at Ford's Safety Research Center, "Ulcers are running pretty high among the engineers who worked on the Pinto. Every lawyer in the country seems to want to take their depositions." (The Safety Research Center is an impressive glass and concrete building standing by itself about a mile from Ford World Headquarters in Dearborn. Looking at it, one imagines its large staff protects consumers from burned and broken limbs. Not so. The Center is the technical support arm of Jack Echold's 14-person anti-regulatory lobbying team in World Headquarters.)

When the Pinto liability suits began, Ford strategy was to go to a jury. Confident it could hide the Pinto crash tests, Ford thought that juries of solid American registered voters would buy the industry doctrine that drivers, not cars, cause accidents. It didn't work. It seems that juries are much quicker to see the truth than bureaucracies, a fact that gives one confidence in democracy. Juries began ruling against the company, granting million-dollar awards to plaintiffs.

"We'll never go to a jury again," says Al Slechter in Ford's Washington office. "Not in a fire case. Juries are just too sentimental. They see those charred remains and forget the evidence. No sir, we'll settle."

Settlement involves less cash, smaller legal fees and less publicity, but it is an indication of the weakness of their case. Nevertheless, Ford has been settling when it is clear that the company can't pin the blame on the driver of the other car. But, since the company carries $2 million deductible product-liability insurance, these settlements have a direct impact on the bottom line. They must therefore be considered a factor in determining the net operating profit on the

Pinto. It's impossible to get a straight answer from Ford on the profitability of the Pinto and the impact of lawsuit settlements on it—even when you have a curious and mildly irate shareholder call to inquire, as we did. However, financial officer Charles Matthews did admit that the company establishes a reserve for large dollar settlements. He would not divulge the amount of the reserve and had no explanation for its absence from the annual report.

Until recently, it was clear that, whatever the cost of these settlements, it was not enough to seriously cut into the Pinto's enormous profits. The cost of retooling Pinto assembly lines and of equipping each car with a safety gadget like that $5.08 Goodyear bladder was, company accountants calculated, greater than that of paying out millions to survivors like Robbie Carlton or to widows and widowers of victims like Sandra Gillespie. The bottom line ruled, and inflammable Pintos kept rolling out of the factories.

In 1977, however, an incredibly sluggish government has at last instituted Standard 301. Now Pintos will have to have rupture-proof gas tanks. Or will they?

◦⟨◉⟩◦

To everyone's surprise, the 1977 Pinto recently passed a rear-end crash test in Phoenix, Arizona, for NHTSA. The agency was so convinced the Pinto would fail that it was the first car tested. Amazingly, it did not burst into flame.

"We have had so many Ford failures in the past," explained agency engineer Tom Grubbs, "I felt sure the Pinto would fail."

How did it pass?

Remember that one-dollar, one-pound plastic baffle that was on one of the three modified Pintos that passed the pre-production crash tests nearly ten years ago? Well, it is a standard feature on the 1977 Pinto. In the Phoenix test it protected the gas tank from being perforated by those four bolts on the differential housing.

We asked Grubbs if he noticed any other substantial alterations in the rear-end structure of the car. "No," he replied, "the [plastic baffle] seems to be the only noticeable change over the 1976 model."

But was it? What Tom Grubbs and the Department of Transportation didn't know when they tested the car was that it was manufactured in St. Thomas, Ontario. Ontario? The significance of that becomes clear when you learn that Canada has for years had extremely strict rear-end collision standards.

Tom Irwin is the business manager of Charlie Rossi Ford, the Scottsdale, Arizona, dealership that sold the Pinto to Tom Grubbs. He refused to explain why he was selling Fords made in Canada when there is a huge Pinto assembly plant much closer by in California. "I know why you're asking that question, and I'm not going to answer it," he blurted out. "You'll have to ask the company."

But Ford's regional office in Phoenix has "no explanation" for the presence of Canadian cars in their local dealerships. Farther up the line in Dearborn, Ford people claim there is absolutely no difference between American and Canadian Pintos. They say cars are shipped back and forth across the border as a matter of course. But they were hard pressed to explain why some Canadian Pintos were shipped all the way to Scottsdale, Arizona. Significantly, one engineer at the St. Thomas plant did admit that the existence of strict rear-end collision standards in Canada "might encourage us to pay a little more attention to quality control on that part of the car."

The Department of Transportation is considering buying an American Pinto and running the test again. For now, it will only say that the situation is under investigation.

⊶⊙⊷

Whether the new American Pinto fails or passes the test, Standard 301 will never force the company to test or recall the more than two million pre-1977 Pintos still on the highway. Seventy or more people will burn to death in those cars every year for many years to come. If the past is any indication, Ford will continue to accept the deaths.

According to safety expert Byron Bloch, the older cars could quite easily be retrofitted with gas tanks containing fuel cells. "These improved tanks would add at least 10 mph improved safety performance to the rear end," he estimated, "but it would cost Ford $20 to $30 a car, so they won't do it unless they are forced to." Dr. Kenneth Saczalski, safety engineer with the Office of Naval Research in Washington, agrees. "The Defense Department has developed virtually fail-safe fuel systems and retrofitted them into existing vehicles. We have shown them to the auto industry and they have ignored them."

Unfortunately, the Pinto is not an isolated case of corporate malpractice in the auto industry. Neither is Ford a lone sinner. There probably isn't a car on the road without a safety hazard known to its manufacturer. And though Ford may have the best auto lobbyists in Washington, it is not alone. The anti-emission control lobby and the anti-safety lobby usually work in chorus form, presenting a well-harmonized message from the country's richest industry, spoken through the voices of individual companies—the Motor Vehicle Manufacturers Association, the Business Council and the U.S. Chamber of Commerce.

Furthermore, cost-valuing human life is not used by Ford alone. Ford was just the only company careless enough to let such an embarrassing calculation slip into the public records. The process of willfully trading lives for profits is built into corporate capitalism. Commodore Vanderbilt publicly scorned George Westinghouse and his "foolish" air brakes while people died by the hundreds in accidents on Vanderbilt's railroads.

The original draft of the Motor Vehicle Safety Act provided for criminal sanction against a manufacturer who willfully placed an unsafe car on the market. Early in the proceedings the auto industry lobbied the provision out of the bill. Since then, there have been those damage settlements, of course, but the only government punishment meted out to auto companies for non-compliance to standards has been a minuscule fine, usually $5,000 to $10,000. One wonders how long the Ford Motor Company would continue to market lethal cars were Henry Ford II and Lee Iacocca serving 20-year terms in Leavenworth for consumer homicide.

Closing Argument by Mr. Neal

If it please the Court, Counsel, ladies and gentlemen:

Not too many years ago our broad American Industry straddled the world like a giant.

It provided us with the highest standards of living ever known to man.

It was ended, eliminated, no more. Now it is an Industry weakened by deteriorating plants and equipment, weakened by lack of products, weakened by lack of manpower, weakened by inadequate capital, weakened by massive Government controls, weakened by demands on foreign oil and reeling from competition from foreign manufacturers.

I stand here today to defend a segment of that tattered Industry.

One company that saw the influx of foreign, small-made cars in 1967 and '68 and tried to do something about it, tried to build a small car with American labor that would compete with foreign imports, that would keep Americans employed, that would keep American money in America.

As State's witness, Mr. Copp, admitted, Ford Motor Company would have made more profit sticking to the bigger cars where the profit is.

That would have been the easiest way.

It was not the way Ford Motor Company took.

It made the Ford to compete. And this is no easy effort, members of the jury.

As even Mr. Copp admitted, the Automobile Industry is extremely regulated.

It has to comply with the Clean Air Act, the Safety Act, the Emissions Control Act, the Corporate Average Fuel Economy Act, the Safety Act, and OSHA as well as a myriad of Statutes and Regulations applicable to large and small businesses generally, and, again, as Mr. Copp admitted, it now takes twice as many Engineers to make a car as it did before all the massive Government controls.

Nevertheless, Ford Motor Company undertook the effort to build a subcompact, to take on the imports, to save jobs for Americans and to make a profit for its stockholders.

This rather admirable effort has a sad ending.

On August 10, 1978, a young man gets into a van weighing over 4,000 pounds and heads towards Elkhart, Indiana, on a bad highway called "U.S. 33."

From U.S. District Court, South Bend, Indiana, *State of Indiana v. Ford Motor Company* (January 15, 1980).

He has a couple of open beer bottles in his van, together with his marijuana which he may or may not have been smoking....

As he was cruising along on an open stretch of highway in broad daylight at at least 50 to 55 miles per hour, he drops his "smoke," ignores his driving and the road, and fails to see a little Pinto with its emergency flashers on stopped on the highway ahead.

He plows into the rear of the Pinto with enormous force and three young girls are killed.

Not the young man, but Ford Motor Company is charged with reckless homicide and arraigned before you.

I stand here to defend Ford Motor Company, and to tell you that we are not killers....

Mr. Cosentino gave you the definition of "reckless homicide" as "plain, conscious and unjustifiable disregard of harm, which conduct involves substantial deviation from acceptable standards of conduct."

This case and the elements of this case, strictly speaking, involve 40 days, July 1, 1978 to August 10, 1978, and the issue is whether, during that period of time, Ford Motor Company recklessly, as that term is defined, omitted to warn of a danger and repair, and that reckless omission caused the deaths involved....

[I]n my opening statement, I asked you to remember nine points, and I asked you to judge me, my client, by how well or how poorly we supported those nine points.

Let me run through briefly and just tick them off, the nine points, with you, and then let me get down to discussing the evidence and record with respect to those nine points.

One, I said this was a badly-designed highway, with curbs so high the girls couldn't get off when they had to stop their car in an emergency.

Two, I said that the girls stopped there with their emergency flashers on, and this boy in a van weighing more than 4,000 pounds, with his eyes off the road, looking down trying to find the "smoke," rammed into the rear of that Pinto at at least 50 miles an hour, closing speed.

And by "closing speed," I mean the differential speed.

That is Points 1 and 2.

Point 3, I said the 1973 Pinto met every fuel-system integrity standard of any Federal, State or Local Government.

Point No. 4, I said, Ford Motor Company adopted a mandatory standard dealing with fuel-system integrity on rear-impact of 20 miles per hour moving-barrier, 4,000 pound moving-barrier, and I said that no other manufacturer in the world had adopted any standard, only Ford Motor Company.

Five, I said that the Pinto, it is not comparable to a Lincoln Continental, a Cadillac, a Mercedes Benz or that Ascona, or whatever that exotic car was that Mr. Bloch called—but I did say No. 5, it is comparable to other 1973 subcompacts.

No. 6, I said that... we would bring in the Engineers who designed and manufactured the Pinto, and I brought them from the stand, and they would tell you that they thought the Pinto was a good, safe car, and they bought it for themselves, their wives and their children to drive.

No. 7, I told you that we would bring in the statistics that indicated to us as to our state of mind that the Pinto performed as well or better than other subcompacts.

And, No. 8, I said we would nevertheless tell you that we decided to recall the Pinto in June of 1978, and having made that decision for the reasons that I—that I told you I would explain, we did everything in our power to recall that Pinto as quickly as possible, that there was nothing we could have done between July 1, 1978 and 8-10-1978, to recall the Pinto any faster.

And finally, No. 9, I said we would demonstrate that any car, any subcompact, any small car, and even some larger cars, sitting out there on Highway 33 in the late afternoon of August 10, 1978 and watching that van roar down that highway with the boy looking for his "smoke"—any car would have suffered the same consequences.

Those are the nine points I ask you to judge me by, and let me touch on the evidence, now, with respect to those nine points. . . .

The van driver, Duggar, took his eyes off the road and off driving to look around the floor of the van for a "smoke."

Duggar had two open beer bottles in the car and a quantity of marijuana.

Duggar was not prosecuted for reckless homicide or for possession of marijuana, even though his prior record of conviction was:

November, '73, failure to yield right-of-way;

April, '76, speeding 65 miles an hour in a 45 mile an hour zone;

July, '76, running stop sign;

June, '77, speeding 45 in a 25 zone;

August, '77, driver's license suspended;

September, '77, driving with suspended license;

December, '77, license suspended again.

Mr. Cosentino, you got up in front of this jury and you cried.

Well, I cry, too, because Mr. Duggar is driving, and you didn't do anything about him with a record like that except say, "Come in and help me convict Ford Motor Company, and I will help you get probation."

We all cry.

But crying doesn't do any good, and it doesn't help this jury.

The big disputed fact in this case regarding the accident, ladies and gentlemen, is the closing speed. The differential speed, the difference between the speed the Pinto was going, if any, and the speed the van was going.

That is the big disputed fact in regard to this accident.

And whether the Pinto was stopped or not is relevant only as it affects closing speed. . . .

Mr. Duggar testified—I guess he is great about speed, because while he's looking down there for his "smoke," he knows he is going 50 miles per hour in the van.

But he said he was going 50 miles per hour at the time of impact, and he said the Pinto was going 15.

But here is the same man who admits he was going at least 50 miles per hour and looking around down "on a clear day," trying to find the "smoke" and looked up only to see the Pinto ten feet ahead of him.

Here is a witness willing to say under oath that the Pinto was going 15 miles per hour, even though he had one-sixth of a second—one-sixth of a second to make the judgment on the speed.

Here is a witness who says he had the time to calculate the speed of the Pinto but had no time even to try to apply brakes because there were no skid marks.

And here is a witness who told Dr. Galen Miller, who testified here, that— told him right after the accident that in fact the Pinto was stopped.

And here was a witness who made a deal with the State.

And here was a witness who's not prosecuted for recklessness.

And here is a witness who is not prosecuted for possession of marijuana.

So the State's proof from Mr. Alfred Clark through Mr. Duggar is kind of a smorgasbord or a buffet—you can go in and take your choice.

You can pick 15—5 miles per hour, if you want to as to differential speed, or you can take 35 miles per hour.

And the State, with the burden of proof says, "Here," "Here," "Here. I will give you a lot of choice."

"You want choices? I will give you choices. Here. Take 5. Take 15. 10, 15, 20, 25, 30, 35."

Because, ladies and gentlemen of the jury,—and I'm sure you are—the alternatives the State offers you are closing speeds of anywhere from 5 miles—on the low side—to 35 miles on the high side as a differential speed in this accident....

Mr. Toms, the former National Highway Traffic Safety Administrator, told you that in his opinion the 20 mile per hour rear-impact moving-barrier was a reasonable and acceptable standard of conduct for 1973 vehicles.

Why didn't Ford adopt a higher standard?

Mr. MacDonald, a man even Mr. Copp—do you remember this? Mr. Mac-Donald sitting on the stand, the father of the Pinto, as Mr. Cosentino called him—and he didn't deny it.

He says, "Yes, it is my car."

Mr. MacDonald, a man even Mr. Copp—on cross examination I asked him, I said:

"Q Mr. Copp, isn't it a fact that you consider Harold MacDonald an extremely safety-conscious Engineer?"

And he said:

"A Yes, sir."

Mr. MacDonald, that extremely safety-conscious Engineer, told you he did not believe a higher standard could be met for 1973 cars without greater problems, such as handling, where more accidents and death occur.

Mr. Copp, let's take the State's witness, Copp.

Mr. Copp admitted that even today, seven years later, the Federal Government Standard is only 30 miles per hour, 10 miles higher than what Ford adopted—voluntarily adopted for itself for 1973.

And Mr. Copp further testified that a 30 mile an hour would be equivalent only to a 31.5 or 32 mile car-to-car.

So, ladies and gentlemen of the jury, Mr. Cosentino tells you about, "Oh, isn't it terrible to put these cars out there, wasn't it awful—did you know?"

Well, do you know that today, the—today, 1980 model cars are required to meet only a 30 mile an hour rear-impact moving-barrier standard? 1980 cars.

And that that is equivalent to a 32 mile an hour car-to-car, and yet Ford Motor Company, the only company in the world, imposed upon itself a standard and made a car in 1973, seven years ago, that would meet 26 to 28 miles an hour, within 5, 6 or 7 miles of what the cars are required by law to meet today.

Mr. Cosentino will tell you, frankly, the cars today, in his judgment, are defective and he will prosecute.

What a chaos would evolve if the Government set the standard for automobiles and says, "That is reasonable," and then Local Prosecutors in the fifty states around the country start saying, "I am not satisfied, and I am going to prosecute the manufacturer."

Well, Mr. Cosentino may say that the standard should be 40.

The Prosecutor in Alabama may say, "No, it should be 50."

The Prosecutor in Alaska may say, "No, it should be 60."

And the Prosecutor in Tennessee—they say—you know, "I am satisifed—I am satisfied with 30," or, "I think it should be 70."

How can our companies survive?

Point 5, the 1973 Pinto was comparable in design and manufacture to other 1973 subcompacts.

I say again, ladies and gentlemen, we don't compare the Pinto with Lincolns, Cadillacs, Mercedes Benz—we ask you to compare the Pinto with the other three subcompacts.

Let's take the State's witnesses on this point first.

Mr. Bloch—Mr. Cosentino didn't mention Mr. Bloch, but I don't want him to be forgotten.

Mr. Bloch and Mr. Copp complain about the Pinto, and that is easy.

Let's descend to the particulars. Let's see what they really said.

Well, they complain about the metal, the gage of the metal in the fuel tank; you remember that?

And then on cross examination it was brought out that the general range of metal in fuel tanks ranged between twenty-three-thousandths of an inch and forty-thousandths of an inch.

That is the general range. Twenty-three-thousandths on the low to forty-thousandths on the high, and lo and behold, what is the gage of metal in the Pinto tank?

Thirty-five-thousandths.

And Mr. Bloch admits that it is in the upper third of the general range.

And they complain about the bumper on the Pinto.

And, remember, I said we would show that the Pinto was comparable to other '73 subcompacts.

They complain about the bumper, but then they admit on cross examination the Vega, the Gremlin, the Colt, the Pinto and the Toyota had about the same bumper.

And they complain of a lack of a protective shield between the tank and the axle, but they admitted on cross examination that no other 1973 car had such a shield, and Mr. Copp admits that there was no significant puncture in the 1973—in the Ulrich accident caused by the axle, and you remember I had him get up here and say, "Point out where this protective shield would have done something, where this puncture source we are talking about—" and you remember, it is so small—I can't find it now.

So much for the protective shield.

And then they complained about the insufficient rear structure in the Pinto, but they both admit that the Pinto had a left side rail hat section and that the Vega had none, nothing on either side, that the Pinto had shear plates, these plates in the trunk, and that neither the Vega, the Gremlin or the Colt or Toyota had any of these.

And the Vega used the coil-spring suspension, when the Pinto had a leaf-spring, and that was additional structure.

I am not going through all those—well, I will mention one more thing.

They talked about puncture sources, there is a puncture source there, puncture source here, but on cross examination, they end up by admitting that the puncture sources on all subcompacts have about the same—and in about the same space....

Mr. MacDonald testified, "Yes, I thought the Pinto was a reasonably safe car. I think the '73 Pinto is still a reasonably safe car, and I bought one, I drove it for years for myself."

Mr. Olsen—you remember little Mr. Frank Olsen?

He came in here, has his little eighteen-year-old daughter—he said, "I am an Engineer responsible for the Pinto. I think it is a safe car. I bought one for my little eighteen-year-old daughter, and she drove it for several years."

And Mr. Freers, the man who Mr. Cosentino objected to going over the fact that he was from Rose-Hullman, and on the Board of Trustees there—Mr. Freers said, "I like the Pinto. I am an Engineer responsible for the Pinto, and I bought a '73 Pinto for my young son and he drove it several years."

And then Mr. Feaheny says, "I am one of the Engineers responsible for the Pinto, and I bought one for my wife, the mother of my six children, and she drove it for several years."

Now, when Mr. Cosentino tried to say there was something phoney about that—he brought out their salaries.

And I—I don't know how to deal with the salary question.

It just seems to me to be so irrelevant, like some other things I am going to talk about in a minute that I am just going to simply say, "It is irrelevant," and go on.

But he said to these people—he suggested to you, suggested to these people, "Well, you make a lot of money, you can afford better than a Pinto."

Like, "You don't really mean you had a Pinto?"

And Mr. Feaheny says, "Yes, I could afford a more expensive car, but, you know, I—all of us, we have been fighting, we come out with something we thought would fight the imports, and we were proud of it, and our families were proud of it."

Do you think, ladies and gentlemen of the jury, that Mr. MacDonald was indifferent, reckless, when he bought and drove the Pinto?

He drives on the same roads, he has the—subject to the same reckless people that Mr. Cosentino didn't prosecute.

Do you think that Mr. Olsen was reckless and indifferent when he gave a Pinto to his eighteen-year-old daughter, a '73 Pinto?

Do you think that Mr. Freers was reckless when he gave one to his young son? . . .

Finally, ladies and gentlemen—not "finally," but Point No. 8: Notwithstanding all I have said, Ford Motor Company decided on June 8th, 1978, to recall the Pintos to improve fuel systems and did everything in its power to recall it as quickly as possible.

This is really what this case, I guess, is all about, because that period of time involved is July 1, 1978 until August 10, 1978.

And the Court will charge you, as I said, the elements are whether we recklessly failed to warn and repair during that period of time.

And whether that reckless omission, if any, caused the deaths.

And you may ask—and I think it is fair to ask—why recall the Pinto, the '73 Pinto, if it is comparable to other subcompacts, if statistics say it is performing as well as other '73 subcompacts?

And if Ford had a standard for '73 that no other manufacturer had?

And Feaheny and Mr. Misch told you why.

The Federal Government started an investigation. The publicity was hurting the Company.

They thought the Government was wrong, but they said, "You can't fight City Hall."

"We could fight and fight and we could go to Court and we could fight, but it's not going to get us anywhere. If we can improve it, let's do it and let's don't fight the Federal Government."

Maybe the Company should not have recalled the '73 Pinto.

Douglas Toms did not think, as he told you on the stand under oath, that the '73 Pinto should have been recalled.

He had information that the Pinto did as well as other cars;

That Pinto fire accidents equaled the total Pinto population or equaled the percentage of Pinto population to all car population.

And Mr. Bloch, on the other hand, says, "All of them should be recalled."

He said, "The Pinto should have been recalled."

He said, "The Vega should have been recalled."

He said, "The Gremlin should be recalled."

And he didn't know about the Dodge Colt.

Nevertheless, the Company did decide to recall the Pinto. And they issued widely-disseminated Press Releases on June 9, 1978.

It was in the newspapers, TV, radio, according to the proof in this case.

And thereafter the Government regulated what they did in the recall.

That is what Mr. Misch told you.

He said, "From the time we started—June 9, 1978—to August 10, Mr.—the Federal Government regulated what we did."

Now, Mr. Cosentino is prosecuting us.

And the Federal Government has regulated us.

Mr. Misch said, "The Federal Government reviewed what kind of Press Releases we should issue, what kind of Recall Letter we should issue, what kind of a Modification Kit that they would approve."

Even so—it is undisputed, absolutely undisputed that we did everything in our power to recall as fast as possible—nights, days, weekends.

And notwithstanding all of that, the first kit—the first complete kit was assembled August 1, 1978.

And on August 9, 1978, there were only 20,000 kits available for 1,600,000 cars.

And this was not Ford's fault. Ford was pushing the suppliers, the people who were outside the Company doing work for them.

And Mr. Vasher testified that he got the names of the current owners from R. L. Polk on July 17;

That the Ulrich name was not among them;

That he sent the Recall Letter in August to the original owner because he had no Ulrich name.

Now,—and he said he couldn't have gotten the Ulrich name by August 10.

Now, Mr. Cosentino said, "Well, the Ulrich Registration was on file with the State of Indiana and it is open to the public."

Well, Ford Motor Company doesn't know where these 1,600,000 cars are. It has to use R. L. Polk because they collect the information by the VIN Numbers.

If Ford Motor Company went to each state, they would go to fifty states and they would have each of the fifty states run through its files 1,600,000 VIN Numbers.

And Mr. Vasher, who is the expert in there, said it would take months and months to do that.

And, finally, ladies and gentlemen, the Government didn't approve the Modification Kit until August 15, 1978.

But the State says that we should have warned—we should have warned 1973 Pinto owners not to drive the car.

But the Government never suggested that.

Based on our information, and confirmed by the Toms testimony, our cars were performing as well—or better than—other '73 subcompacts.

As Mr. Misch so succinctly stated, "We would have been telling the Pinto owners to park their Pintos and get into another car no safer—and perhaps even less safe—than the Pinto." ...

Well, we submit that the physical facts, the placement of the—the placement of the gasoline cap, where it is found, the testimony of Levi Woodard, and Nancy Fogo—demonstrate the closing speed in this case was at least 50 to 60 miles per hour.

Mr. Copp, the State's witness, testified that no small car made in America in 1973 would withstand 40 to 50 miles per hour—40 to 50 rear-impact. No small car made in America in 1973 would withstand a 40-plus mile per hour rear-impact.

The Dodge Colt would not have; the Vega could not have; the Gremlin would not have; and certainly even the Toyota would not have.

Mr. Habberstad told you that no small car—and some big cars—would have withstood this crash.

And he established by the crash-tests you have seen that the Vega could not withstand 50;

That the Gremlin could not withstand 50;

That the Toyota Corolla with the tank over the axle could not withstand 50;

And that even a full-sized Chevrolet Impala cannot withstand 50 miles per hour.

If it made no difference what kind of car was out there, members of the jury, how can Ford Motor Company have caused the deaths? . . .

I am not here to tell you that the 1973 Pinto was the strongest car ever built.

I'm not here to tell you it is equal to a Lincoln, a Cadillac, a Mercedes—that funny car that Mr. Bloch mentioned.

I'm not here to tell you a stronger car couldn't be built.

Most of us, however, learn early in life that there is "no Santa Claus," and, "There's no such thing as a free lunch."

If the public wanted it, and could pay for it, and we had the gasoline to drive it, Detroit could build a tank of a car—a car that would withstand practically anything, a car that would float if a careless driver drove it into the water.

A car that would be invulnerable even to the "Duggars" of the world.

But, members of the jury, only the rich could afford it and they would have to stop at every other gasoline station for a refill.

I am here to tell you that the 1973 Pinto is comparable to other '73 subcompacts, including that Toyota, that Corolla with the tank over the axle.

I am here to tell you it was not designed by some mysterious figure you have never seen.

It was designed and manufactured by Harold MacDonald, Frank Olsen and Howard Freers.

I am here to tell you these are the decent men doing an honorable job and trying to do a decent job.

I am here to tell you that Harold MacDonald, Frank Olsen, and Howard Freers are not reckless killers.

Harold MacDonald is the same man, State's witness, Copp, called an "extremely safety-conscious individual."

Frank Olsen is the same "Frank Olsen" Mr. Copp said was a "good Engineer."

And Howard Freers is the same "Howard Freers" Mr. Copp said was a "man of honesty and integrity."

I am here to tell you that these men honestly believe and honestly believed that the 1973 Pinto was—and is—a reasonably safe car—so safe they bought it for their daughters, sons and family.

Do you think that Frank Olsen believed he was acting in plain, conscious, unjustifiable disregard of harm?

When he bought a '73 Pinto for his eighteen-year-old daughter?

Or Howard Freers, when he bought one for his young son?

I am here to tell you that the design and manufacture of an automobile is not an easy task;

That it takes time to know whether a change in one part of the 14,000 parts of a car will or will not cause greater problems elsewhere in the car or its performance.

I am here to tell you that safety is a matter of degree;

That no one can say that a car that will meet a 26 to 28 mile per hour rear-impact is unsafe and one that will meet a 30 to 32 impact is safe.

I am here to tell you that if this country is to survive economically, it is really time to stop blaming Industry or Business, large or small, for our own sins.

I am here to tell you that no car is now or ever can be safe when reckless drivers are on the road.

I am here to tell you that Ford Motor Company may not be perfect, but it is not guilty of reckless homicide.

Thank you, members of the jury.

And God bless you in your deliberations.

POSTSCRIPT

Was Ford to Blame in the Pinto Case?

Was Ford guilty? The jury said no, but the larger issue remains: Who takes responsibility when many factors combine to bring about an injury?

Consider the following: Ford Motor Company obeyed the law, but the law may not have been all that it *should* have been. The reason for this is that the Ford Motor Company spent a great deal of money lobbying Congress to prevent the release of new and higher legal safety standards in order to be able to sell the Pinto for a lower price and thus increase its market share and its profits. Is the government, through its agencies, guilty for not fulfilling its role as protector of the consumer? Does government have some absolute duty in these cases, or are legislators asked only to bring about the greatest good for the greatest number?

Ford Motor Company found new structural allies when the criminal negligence case was brought against it. Under the U.S. Constitution, the legal system tends to protect the defendant in these cases. The tradition in the United States is to protect the rights of the individual against the interests of the community. In this case, the "individual" was one of the largest corporations in the world. However, legal traditions held true, and the rights of Ford were supported when the company was acquitted.

Manufacturers know how to make a safe car. They *could* build one like a tank and rig it to go no faster than 30 miles per hour, but very few people would buy it. So they make relatively unsafe cars that people will buy—lighter and faster, but more likely to crumple and burn in an accident. Is this trade-off acceptable to a nation that is used to making choices? Or should we be more diligent about eliminating threats to safety?

Suggested Readings

Lawrence A. Benningson and Arnold I. Benningson, "Product Liability: Manufacturers Beware!" *Harvard Business Review* (May–June 1974).

Richard T. DeGeorge, "Ethical Responsibilities of Engineers in Large Organizations: The Pinto Case," *Business and Professional Ethics Journal* (Fall 1981).

Richard A. Epstein, "Is Pinto a Criminal?" *Regulation* (March–April 1980).

Niles Howard and Susan Antilla, "What Price Safety? The Zero-Risk Debate," *Dun's Review* (September 1979).

ISSUE 14

Should We Require Labeling for Genetically Modified Food?

YES: Philip L. Bereano, from "The Right to Know What We Eat," *The Seattle Times* (October 11, 1998)

NO: Joseph A. Levitt, from Statement Before the Health, Education, Labor, and Pensions Committee, United States Senate (September 26, 2000)

ISSUE SUMMARY

YES: Professor of technical communication Philip L. Bereano contends that consumers have a real and important interest in knowing the processes by which their foods arrive on the table. He argues that the demand for a label for bioengineered foods is entirely legitimate.

NO: Joseph A. Levitt, director of the Center for Food Safety and Applied Nutrition, states that as far as the law is concerned, only the nutritional traits and characteristics of foods are subject to safety assessment. He notes that labeling has been required only where health risks exist or where there is danger that a product's marketing claims may mislead the consumer as to the food's characteristics.

$\mathbf{W}$e have seen a profound change in the function of the label over the course of the last century. At first labels only bore information concerning what the packages contained and the brand name (i.e., "Carter's Little Liver Pills," "Argo Cornstarch"). With advances in packaging, the labels became more attractive, brighter, and eye-catching, and they began to carry marketing claims. That was the label's purpose: to sell the product by featuring a trusted brand name (usually employing a logo or trademark) and an advertisement for the product in a design aimed at capturing attention. Poisons, of course, had to be labeled as such in order to warn consumers to use them carefully—and to warn off the vulnerable. The skull and crossbones was an effective graphic image to achieve that purpose.

The consumer movement changed the function of labels. Calling upon the police power of the state (the right and obligation of the state to protect the health, safety, and morals of the citizens), the Food and Drug Administration

(FDA) began requiring labels to fulfill serious informational functions. Now actual weights have to be listed on the package, a list of ingredients in order of weight must appear on any complex product, and the real nutritional content has to be listed in a plainly visible uniform panel on the back of the package (even for little candy bars). Nonfood items also have labeling requirements. For example, garments and bedding must state the materials from which they are made, and bedding labels must warrant that those materials are new.

Further, if there are substances that although they are not poisons may still be dangerous to certain people's health, those have to be listed on the label. For instance, if a company calls its drink "lite" when it contains some sugar, that sugar has to be mentioned. This prevents diabetics from assuming that the "lite" designation means that the drink is sugar-free and therefore safe for them to drink. If the product does not contain sugar, the sugar substitute it does contain must be listed along with any other additives as an "ingredient." Ethyl alcohol, in any quantity, must be mentioned (and if it exceeds a certain percentage, it falls under the state's alcoholic beverage laws).

Should a label carry information that has nothing to do with the actual content of the product (or instructions for the product's use)? As Philip L. Bereano argues, the property of a product to satisfy certain religious dietary requirements has long been a part of the labeling of certain foods only because the religious group that is targeted is willing to restrict purchases to those so labeled. More recently, distributors of canned tuna fish, convinced that a sufficient number of consumers would limit their tuna purchases to those certified to have been caught in a manner not to endanger dolphins, started including that information on their labels. Soon legislation forbade the importation of tuna caught any other way (or shrimp caught in such a way as to endanger sea turtles); the labeling had both raised the consciousness of the consumers and channeled the interests of the distributors to support the legislation.

Those who would like genetically modified (GM) foods to be labeled as such do not conceal their interest in the same agenda. They would like to see all GM foods (corn, for instance) and all processed foods containing GM ingredients (vegetable oil, for instance) labeled as such. They hope that consumers will be alarmed by the labels so that eventually GM foods will be taken off the market. In light of the general profitability of GM foods, it seems politically more feasible to get a labeling requirement than a prohibition. Some polls show that up to 70 percent of consumers have said that they would want to know if the product they bought was genetically modified. Who could object to full information about a product—the process by which it was produced as well as its content—being given to the consumer?

As it turns out, there are many objections. One is the sheer mass of effort required to sort out foods that contain GM products, especially processed foods like cereals and bake mixes. More important, whether or not a label designates a difference in a product, the consumer may assume it does. There was no doubt as to the intention or the effect of the requirement of labeling for tobacco products. Some assert that there is every reason to think that a required label such as "contains genetically modified products" could be read as a skull and crossbones.

Philip L. Bereano  **YES**

The Right to Know What We Eat

"I personally have no wish to eat anything produced by genetic modifica-tion, nor do I knowingly offer this sort of produce to my family or guests. There is increasing evidence that many people feel the same way."

— Prince Charles, London Telegraph, June 8, 1998.

Genetic engineering is a set of new techniques for altering the basic makeup of plants and animals. Genes from insects, animals and humans have been added to crop plants; human genes have been added to pigs and cattle.

Although genetic-engineering techniques are biologically novel, the in-dustry and government are so eager to achieve financial success that they say the products of the technologies are pretty much the same ("substantially equiva-lent") as normal crops. Despite the gene tinkering, the new products are not being tested extensively to find out how they differ and to be sure that any hazards are within acceptable limits.

These foods are now appearing in the supermarkets and on our dinner plates, but the industry and government have been vigorously resisting con-sumer attempts to label these "novel foods" in order to distinguish them from more traditional ones.

The failure of the U.S. government to require that genetically engineered foods (GEFs) be labeled presents consumers with quandaries: issues of free speech and consumers' right to know, religious rights for those with dietary restrictions, and cultural rights for people, such as vegetarians, who choose to avoid consuming foods of certain origins.

The use of antibiotic-resistant genes engineered into crop plants as "mark-ers" can contribute to the spread of antibiotic-tolerant disease bacteria; this resistance is a major public-health problem, as documented by a recent study of the National Academy of Sciences. Some genetic recombinations can lead to allergic or auto-immune reactions. The products of some genes which are used as plant pesticides have been implicated in skin diseases in farm and market workers.

The struggle over labeling is occurring because industry knows that con-sumers do not want to eat GEFs; labeled products will likely fail in the market-place. However, as the British publication The Economist noted, "if Monsanto

From Philip L. Bereano, "The Right to Know What We Eat," *The Seattle Times* (October 11, 1998). Copyright © 1998 by Philip L. Bereano. Reprinted by permission of the author.

cannot persuade us, it certainly has no right to foist its products on us." Labels would counter "foisting" and are legally justifiable.

The Government's Rationale

In 1992, the government abdicated any supervision over GEFs. Under Food and Drug Administration's rules, the agency does not even have access to industry information about a GEF unless the company decides voluntarily to submit it. Moreover, important information on risk-assessment questions is often withheld as being proprietary, "confidential business information." So "safety" cannot be judged in a precautionary way; we must await the inevitable hazardous event.

According to a former FDA official, the genetic processes used in the development of a new food are "NOT considered to be material information because there is no evidence that new biotech foods are different from other foods in ways related to safety."

James Maryanski, FDA biotechnology coordinator, claims that whether a food has been genetically engineered is not a "material fact" and FDA would not "require things to be on the label just because a consumer might want to know them."

Yet a standard law dictionary defines "material" as "important," "going to the merits," "relevant." Since labeling is a form of speech from growers and processors to purchasers, it is reasonable, therefore, to interpret "material" as comprising whatever issues a substantial portion of the consuming public defines as "important." And all the polls show that whether food is genetically engineered falls into such a category.

Last May, several religious leaders and citizen groups sued the FDA to change its position and to require that GEFs be labeled.

Process Labels

Some government officials have said that labeling should be only about the food product itself, not the process by which it is manufactured. Yet, the U.S. has many process food labels: kosher, dolphin-free, Made in America, union-made, free-range (chickens, for example), irradiated, and "green" terms such as "organic."

For many of these products, the scientific difference between an item which can carry the label and that which cannot is negligible or nonexistent. Kosher pastrami is chemically identical to non-kosher meat. Dolphin-free tuna and tuna caught by methods which result in killing of dolphins are the same, as are many products which are "made in America" when compared to those made abroad, or those made by unionized as opposed to nonunion workers.

These labeling rules recognize that consumers are interested in the processes by which their purchases are made and have a legal right to such knowledge. In none of these labeling situations has the argument been made that if the products are substantially equivalent, no label differentiation is permissible. It is constitutionally permissible for government rules to intrude slightly on the commercial speech of producers in order to expand the First Amendment rights of consumers to know what is of significant interest to them.

Substantial Equivalence

In order to provide an apparently rational basis for its refusal to exercise regulatory oversight in this regard, the U.S. government has adopted the industry's position that genetically engineered foods are "substantially equivalent" to their natural counterparts. The FDA ignores the contradictory practice of corporations in going to another government agency, the Patent Office, where they argue that a GEF is novel and different (in order to justify receiving monopoly protection).

"Substantial equivalence" is used as a basis for both eliminating regulatory assessment and failing to require labels on GEFs. However, the concept of substantial equivalence is subjective and imprecise.

Most genetic engineering is designed to meet corporate—not consumer—needs. Foods are engineered, for instance, to produce "counterfeit freshness." Consumers believe engineered characteristics such as color and texture indicate freshness, flavor and nutritional quality. Actually the produce is aging and growing stale, and nutritional value is being depleted. So much for "substantial equivalence."

The Precautionary Principle

Consumers International, a global alliance of more than 200 consumer groups, has suggested that "because the effects (of GEFs) are so difficult to predict, it is vital to have internationally agreed and enforceable rules for research protocols, field trials and post-marketing surveillance." This approach has become known as the "precautionary principle" and has entered into the regulatory processes of the European Union.

The principle reflects common-sense aphorisms such as "Better safe than sorry" and "An ounce of prevention is worth a pound of cure." It rests on the notion that parties who wish to change the social order (often while making money or gaining power and influence) should not be able to slough the costs and risks onto others. The new procedure's proponents should have to prove it is safe rather than forcing regulators or citizens to prove a lack of safety.

Look Before You Eat

For GEFs, labeling performs important functions in carrying out the precautionary principle. It places a burden on industry to show that genetic manipulations are socially beneficial and provides a financial incentive for them to do research to reduce uncertainty about the consequences of GEFs.

Democratic notions of free speech include the right to receive information as well as to disseminate it. It is fundamental to capitalist market theory that for transactions to be most efficient all parties must have "perfect informa-tion." The realities of modern food production create a tremendous imbalance of knowledge between producer and purchaser. Our society has relied on the government to redress this imbalance and make grocery shopping a fairer and more efficient—as well as safer—activity.

In an economic democracy, choice is the fundamental prerogative of the purchaser.

As some biologists have put it, "The risk associated with genetically engi-neered foods is derived from the fact that, although genetic engineers can cut and splice DNA molecules with precision in the test tube, when those altered DNA molecules are introduced into a living organism, the full range of effects on that organism cannot be predicted or known before commercialization. The introduced DNA may bring about unintended changes, some of which may be damaging to health."

Numerous opinion polls in the U.S. and abroad in the past decade have shown great skepticism about genetic alteration of foods; a large proportion of respondents, usually majorities, are reluctant to use such products. Regardless of whether they would consume GEFs, consumers feel even more strongly that they should be labeled.

In a Toronto Star poll reported on June 2, 98 percent favored labeling. Bioindustry giant Novartis surveyed U.S. consumers and found 93 percent of them wanted information about genetic engineering of food.

Alice Waters, originator of the legendary Berkeley restaurant Chez Panisse and recently selected to organize a new restaurant at the Louvre in Paris, has said, "The act of eating is very political. You buy from the right people, you support the right network of farmers and suppliers who care about the land and what they put in the food. If we don't preserve the natural resources, you aren't going to have a sustainable society."

However, the U.S. government has been resisting attempts to label GEFs. Despite the supposed environmentalist and consumer sympathies of the Clinton-Gore administration, the government believes nothing should impede the profitability of biotech as a mainstay to the future U.S. economy.

The administration's hostility to labeling may also be coupled to political contributions made to it by the interested industries.

Regulation and Free Speech

The government is constrained by the First Amendment from limiting or regu-lating the content of labels except for the historic functions of protecting health and safety and eliminating fraud or misrepresentation.

The American Civil Liberties Union has noted that "a simple distinction between noncommercial and commercial speech does not determine the ex-tent to which the guarantees of the First Amendment apply to advertising and similar communications relating to the sale or other disposition of goods and services."

Supreme Court decisions have warned against attaching "more impor-tance to the distinction between commercial and noncommercial speech than our cases warrant." Can the government prohibit certain commercial speech, such as barring a label saying "this product does not contain genetically engineered components"?

In several recent cases, the Court has restricted government regulation of commercial speech, in effect allowing more communication. The First Amendment directs us to be skeptical of regulations that seek to keep people in the dark for what the government perceives to be their own good. Thus, it would be hard to sustain the government if it tried to prohibit labeling foods as "free from genetically engineered products," if the statement were true.

In 1995, the FDA's Maryanski took the position that "the FDA is not saying that people don't have a right to know how their food is produced. But the food label is not always the most appropriate method for conveying that information." Is it acceptable for a government bureaucrat to make decisions about what are appropriate methods of information exchange among citizens?

The government and the industry suggest that labels on GEFs might amount to "misrepresentation" by implying that there is a difference between the genetically engineered and nongenetically engineered foods. It is hard, however, to understand how a truthful statement can ever amount to a "misrepresentation." (And of course, they are different, by definition.)

The first food product bearing a label "No GE Ingredients," a brand of corn chips, made its appearance this summer.

Some states have laws creating a civil cause of action against anyone who "disparages" an agricultural product unless the defendant can prove the statements were based on "reasonable and reliable scientific" evidence.

A Harvard analysis suggests that "at stake in the dispute about food-safety claims is scientific uncertainty in an uncertain and unpredictable world. Agricultural disparagement statutes are supposed to regulate the exchange of ideas in that gray area between science and the public good. The underlying approach of these statutes is to regulate speech by encouraging certain kinds of exchanges and punishing others. . . ."

According to the ACLU, "these so-called 'veggie libel' laws raise obvious First Amendment problems and threaten to chill speech on important issues of public concern." Consumers Union argues that "such laws, we believe, give the food and agriculture industry the power to choke off concerns and criticism about food quality and safety."

Such enactments did not prevail in the suit by Texas cattle ranchers against Oprah Winfrey and her guest Howard Lyman (of the Humane Society) for their on-air conversations about "mad-cow disease" possibilities in the United States. The lawsuit was widely seen as a test of the First Amendment constitutionality of such state statutes, although the case was actually resolved on much narrower grounds.

Consequences of Regulation

As Prince Charles noted in his essay, "we cannot put our principles into practice until there is effective segregation and labeling of genetically modified products. Arguments that this is either impossible or irrelevant are simply not credible."

Nonetheless, the biotech industry (and many governments, including our own) make the argument that it is impossible to keep genetically engineered foodstuffs separate from naturally produced ones. However, the same industries actually require rigorous segregation (for example, of seeds) when they are protecting their monopolies on patented food items.

Although it undoubtedly has related costs, the segregation of kosher food products from non-kosher ones, for example, has been routine in this country for decades. The only difference for GEFs appears to be one of scale, not technique, in monitoring the flow of foodstuffs, spot-testing and labeling them appropriately.

In Support of Mandatory Labeling

Can the government mandate commercial speech—for example, requiring GEFs to bear a label proclaiming their identity?

The government does require some label information which goes beyond consumer health effects; not every consumer must need mandated information in order for it to be required by law. These requirements have never been judged an infringement of producers' constitutional rights. For example:

- Very few consumers are sensitive to sulfites, although all wine must be labeled.
- The burden is put on tobacco manufacturers to carry the surgeon general's warning, even though the majority of cigarette smokers will not develop lung cancer and an intended effect of the label is to reinforce the resolve of nonconsumers to refrain from smoking.
- Labeling every processed food with its fat and calorie analysis is mandated, even though vast numbers of Americans are not overweight or suffering from heart disease.
- Irradiated foods (other than spices) must carry a specific logo.
- Finally, the source of hydrolyzed proteins in foods must be on a label to accommodate vegetarian cultural practices and certain religious beliefs.

These legal requirements are in place because many citizens want such information, and a specific fraction need it. An identifiable fraction of consumers actually need information about genetic modification—for example, as regards allergenicity—as the FDA itself has recognized in the Federal Register, and almost all want it.

Foods which are comprised, to any but a trace extent, of genetically altered components or products should be required to be labeled. This can be justified in some instances on scientific and health grounds, and for other foods on the social, cultural, religious and political interest consumers may have in the processes by which their food is produced.

Consumers' right to know is an expression of an ethical position which acknowledges individual autonomy; it is also a social approach which helps to rectify the substantial imbalance of power which exists in a modern society where commercial transactions occur between highly integrated and well-to-do corporations, on the one hand, and atomized consumers on the other.

We should let labeled GEFs run the test of the marketplace.

NO ↰

Joseph A. Levitt

Statement of Joseph A. Levitt

Introduction

Mr. Chairman and members of the Committee, thank you for giving the Food and Drug Administration (FDA or the Agency) the opportunity to testify today on its regulatory program for foods derived from plants using the tools of modern biotechnology—also known as genetically engineered, or bioengineered, foods. I am Joseph A. Levitt, Director of FDA's Center for Food Safety and Applied Nutrition (CFSAN). Within FDA, CFSAN oversees bioengineered plant products or ingredients intended for human consumption. Our Center for Veterinary Medicine oversees bioengineered plant products used as or in animal feed, as well as bioengineered products used to improve the health or productivity of animals (including fish).

We believe it is very important for the public to understand how FDA is regulating the new bioengineered foods being introduced into the marketplace and to have confidence in that process. To that end, I appreciate this opportunity to describe our policies and procedures to the Committee and to the public.

First, let me state that FDA is confident that the bioengineered plant foods on the U.S. market today are as safe as their conventionally bred counterparts. This conclusion was echoed by a report by the National Resource Council of the National Academy of Sciences which stated, "The committee is not aware of any evidence that foods on the market are unsafe to eat as a result of genetic modification." Since FDA's 1994 evaluation of the Flavr Savr tomato, the first genetically-engineered plant food to reach the U.S. market, FDA has reviewed the data on more than 45 other products, ranging from herbicide resistant soybeans to a canola plant with modified oil content. To date, there is no evidence that these plants are significantly different in terms of food safety from crops produced through traditional breeding techniques.

The topic of bioengineering has generated much controversy, particularly about whether these foods should be labeled or not. As I discuss in more detail later in my testimony, FDA held three public meetings on bioengineered foods late last year, the second one of which I chaired. We wanted to hear the views from all, and importantly, we wanted to discuss and obtain feedback on ways

From U.S. Senate. Health, Education, Labor, and Pensions Committee. *The Future of Food: Biotechnology and Consumer Confidence.* Hearing, September 26, 2000. Washington, DC: U.S. Government Printing Office, 2000.

283

in which information on bioengineered foods could be most appropriately and helpfully conveyed.

Partly in response to information gained from the public meetings and comments received by the Agency, FDA announced on May 3, 2000, that it will be taking steps to modify our current voluntary process for bioengineered foods to establish mandatory premarket notification and make the process more transparent. Further, we will be developing guidance for food manufacturers who wish voluntarily to label their products regarding whether or not they contain bioengineered ingredients. To ensure that the Agency has the best scientific advice, we also are adding experts in this field to our foods and veterinary medicine advisory committees. FDA is taking these steps to help provide consumers with continued confidence in the safety of the U.S. food supply and to ensure that the Agency's oversight procedures will meet the challenges of the future. The proposed notification rule and draft guidance are currently under development....

Legal and Regulatory Issues

FDA regulates bioengineered plant food in conjunction with the United States Department of Agriculture (USDA) and the Environmental Protection Agency (EPA). FDA has authority under the Federal Food, Drug, and Cosmetic (FD&C) Act to ensure the safety of all domestic and imported foods for man or other animals in the United States market, except meat, poultry and egg products which are regulated by USDA. (Note that the safety of animal drug residues in meat and poultry is regulated by FDA's Center for Veterinary Medicine.) Pesticides are regulated primarily by EPA, which reviews safety and sets tolerances (or establishes exemptions from tolerance) for pesticides. FDA enforces the pesticide tolerances set by EPA. USDA's Animal & Plant Health Inspection Service (APHIS) oversees the agricultural and environmental safety of planting and field testing of bioengineered plants.

Bioengineered foods and food ingredients must adhere to the same standards of safety under the FD&C Act that apply to their conventionally-bred counterparts. This means that these products must be as safe as the traditional foods in the market. FDA has broad authority to initiate regulatory action if a product fails to meet the standards of the FD&C Act.

FDA relies primarily on two sections of the FD&C Act to ensure the safety of foods and food ingredients:

(1) The adulteration provisions of section 402(a)(1). Under this postmarket authority, FDA has the power to remove a food from the market (or sanction those marketing the food) if the food poses a risk to public health. It is important to note that the FD&C Act places a legal duty on developers to ensure that the foods they market to consumers are safe and comply with all legal requirements.

(2) The food additive provisions (section 409). Under this section, a substance that is intentionally added to food is a food additive, unless the substance is generally recognized as safe (GRAS) or is otherwise exempt (e.g., a pesticide, the safety of which is overseen by EPA).

The FD&C Act requires premarket approval of any food additive—regardless of the technique used to add it to food. Thus, substances introduced into food are either (1) new food additives that require premarket approval by FDA or (2) GRAS, and are exempt from the requirement for premarket review (for example, if there is a long history of safe use in food). Generally, foods such as fruits, vegetables, and grains, are not subject to premarket approval because they have been safely consumed over many years. Other than the food additive system, there are no premarket approval requirements for foods generally.

In 1992, knowing that bioengineered products were on the horizon, FDA published a policy explaining how existing legal requirements would apply to products developed using the tools of biotechnology (57 FR 22984; May 29,1992; "Statement of Policy: Foods Derived from New Plant Varieties"). The 1992 policy was designed to answer developers' questions about these products prior to marketing to assist them in meeting their legal duty to provide safe and wholesome foods to consumers. The basic principle of the 1992 policy is that the traits and characteristics of the foods should be the focus of safety assessment for all new varieties of food crops, no matter which techniques are used to develop them.

Under FDA policy, a substance that would be a food additive if it were added during traditional food manufacturing is also treated as a food additive if it is introduced into food through bioengineering of a food crop. Our authority under section 409 permits us to require premarket approval of any food additive and thus, to require premarket review of any substance intentionally introduced via bioengineering that is not generally recognized as safe.

Generally, substances intentionally introduced into food that would be reviewed as food additives include those that have unusual chemical functions, have unknown toxicity, or would be new major dietary components of the food. For example, a novel sweetener bioengineered into food would likely require premarket approval. In our experience with bioengineered food to date, however, we have reviewed only one substance under the food additive provisions, an enzyme produced by an antibiotic resistance gene, and we approved that one. In general, substances intentionally added to food via biotechnology to date have been well-characterized proteins and fats, and are functionally very similar to other proteins and fats that are commonly and safely consumed in the diet and thus are presumptively GRAS.

In 1994, for the first bioengineered product planned for introduction into the market, FDA moved deliberately, following the 1992 policy. We conducted a comprehensive scientific review of Calgene's data on the Flavr Savr™ tomato and the use of the kanamycin resistance marker gene. FDA also held a public meeting of our Food Advisory Committee (the Committee) to examine applicability of the 1992 policy to products such as the Flavr Savr™ tomato. The Committee members agreed with FDA that the scientific approach presented in the 1992 policy was sound and that questions regarding the Flavr Savr™ had been addressed. The Committee members also suggested that we remove unnecessary reviews to provide an expedited decision process on the marketing of bioengineered foods that do not raise substantive scientific issues.

In response, that same year, FDA established a consultative process to help companies comply with the FD&C Act's requirements for any new food, including a bioengineered food, that they intend to market. Since that time, companies have used the consultative process more than 45 times as they sought to introduce genetically altered plants representing ten different crops into the U.S. market. We are not aware of any bioengineered food product on the market under FDA's jurisdiction that has not been evaluated by FDA through the current consultation process.

Typically, the consultation begins early in the product development stage, before it is ready for market. Company scientists and other officials will meet with FDA scientists to describe the product they are developing. In response, the Agency advises the company on what tests would be appropriate for the company to assess the safety of the new food.

After the studies are completed, the data and information on the safety and nutritional assessment are provided voluntarily to FDA for review. The Agency evaluates the information for all of the known hazards and also for potential unintended effects on plant composition and nutritional properties, since plants may undergo changes other than those intended by the breeders. Specifically, FDA scientists are looking to assure that the newly expressed compounds are safe for food consumption, there are no allergens new to the food, no increased levels of natural toxicants, and no reduction of important nutrients. They are also looking to see whether the food has been changed in any substantive way such that the food would need to be specially labeled to reveal the nature of the change to consumers.

Some examples of the information reviewed by FDA include: the name of the food and the crop from which it is derived; the uses of the food, including both human food and animal feed uses; the sources, identities, and functions of introduced genetic material and its stability in the plant; the purpose or intended technical effect of the modification and its expected effect on the composition or characteristic properties of the food or feed; the identity and function of any new products encoded by the introduced genetic material, including an estimate of its concentration; comparison of the composition or characteristics of the bioengineered food to that of food derived from the parental variety or other commonly consumed varieties with special emphasis on important nutrients, anti-nutrients, and toxicants that occur naturally in the food; information on whether the genetic modification altered the potential for the bioengineered food to induce an allergic response; and, other information relevant to the safety and nutritional assessment of the bioengineered food.

It should be noted that if a plant developer used a gene from a plant whose food is commonly allergenic, FDA would presume that the modified food may be allergenic unless the developer could demonstrate that the food would not cause allergic reactions in people allergic to food from the source plant. If FDA scientists have more questions about the safety data, the company either provides more detailed answers or conducts additional studies. Our experience has been that no bioengineered product has gone on the market until FDA's questions about the product have been answered.

Labeling

Labeling, either mandatory or voluntary, of bioengineered foods is a controversial issue. Section 403 of the FD&C Act sets labeling requirements for all foods. All foods, whether derived using bioengineering or not, are subject to these labeling requirements.

Under section 403(a)(1) of the FD&C Act, a food is misbranded if its labeling is false or misleading in any particular way. Section 201(n) of the FD&C Act provides additional guidance on how labeling may be misleading. It states that labeling is misleading if it fails to reveal all facts that are "material in light of such representations (made or suggested in the labeling) or material with respect to consequences which may result from the use of the article to which the labeling or advertising relates under the conditions of use prescribed in the labeling or advertising thereof or under such conditions of use as are customary or usual."

While the legislative history of section 201(n) contains little discussion of the word "material," there is precedent to guide the Agency in its decision regarding whether information on a food is in fact material within the meaning of 201(n). Historically, the Agency has generally limited the scope of the materiality concept to information about the attributes of the food itself. FDA has required special labeling on the basis of it being "material" information in cases where the absence of such information may: 1) pose special health or environmental risks (e.g., warning statement on certain protein diet products); 2) mislead the consumer in light of other statements made on the label (e.g., requirement for quantitative nutrient information when certain nutrient content claims are made about a product); or 3) in cases where a consumer may assume that a food, because of its similarity to another food, has nutritional, organoleptic, or functional characteristics of the food it resembles when in fact it does not (e.g., reduced fat margarine not suitable for frying).

FDA does not require labeling to indicate whether or not a food or food ingredient is a bioengineered product, just as it does not require labeling to indicate which breeding technique was used in developing a food plant. Rather, any significant differences in the food itself have to be disclosed in labeling. If genetic modifications do materially change the composition of a food product, these changes must be reflected in the food's labeling. This would include its nutritional content, (for example, more folic acid or greater iron content) or requirements for storage, preparation, or cooking, which might impact the food's safety characteristics or nutritional qualities. For example, one soybean variety was modified to alter the levels of oleic acid in the beans; because the oil from this soybean is significantly different when compared to conventional soybean oil, we advised the company to adopt a new name for that oil, a name that reflects the intended change.

If a bioengineered food were to contain an allergen not previously found in that food, information about the presence of the allergen would be material as to the potential consequences of consumption of the food. If FDA determined that labeling would be sufficient to enable the food to be safely marketed, the

Agency would require that the food be labeled to indicate the presence of the allergen.

FDA has received comments suggesting that foods developed through modern biotechnology should bear a label informing consumers that the food was produced using bioengineering. While we have given careful consideration to these comments, we do not have data or other information that would form a basis for concluding under the FD&C Act that the fact that a food or its ingredients was produced using bioengineering is material within the meaning of 201(n) and thus, is a fact that must be disclosed in labeling. Hence, we believe that we have neither a scientific nor legal basis to require such labeling. We are developing, however, draft guidance for those that wish voluntarily to label either the presence or absence of bioengineered food in food products.

Public Outreach

Although FDA is confident that its current science-based approach to regulating bioengineered foods is protecting the public health, we realized we had been quietly looking at and reviewing these products and making decisions related to their safety while the public was largely unaware of what we were doing. When trade issues erupted last summer with Europe—and in the World Trade Organization meetings in Seattle—it raised public concern that there might be safety issues with these foods.

New technologies typically raise complex questions—scientific, policy, and even ethical. In light of the newness of this technology and the apparent concern, FDA held the three public meetings I previously mentioned. The public meetings had three purposes: to determine whether there were any new scientific or labeling issues that the Agency should consider; to help the public understand FDA's current policy and become familiar with what we are already doing; and to explore the ways in which information on bioengineered foods could be most appropriately and helpfully conveyed.

FDA asked specific questions on both scientific and safety issues as well as about public information issues. We heard from 35 panelists and over 250 additional speakers in the three meetings. More than 50,000 written comments have been submitted.

What did we learn at these meetings?

First and foremost, no information was presented that indicates there is a safety problem with any bioengineered food or feed now in the marketplace.

In general, we heard support for strengthening FDA's premarket review process for bioengineered foods, in varying degrees. Views on labeling were very strong and much more polarized. Overall, we heard from many points of view that FDA needs to take additional steps to increase consumer confidence in these products.

As to specific concerns, there were four basic points of view:

1) One group was concerned primarily with anything that could possibly harm the environment, with food safety being a secondary concern.

2) A second group was concerned about the possibility that there might be unknown long-term food safety problems, despite the absence of any scientific information that would support the existence of such problems.

3) A third group said they were not so concerned about food safety—they would eat bioengineered foods—but still wanted to know what technologies and ingredients were involved in producing their food.

4) A fourth group speaking for developing countries, said they need this technology and do not want it limited or taken away.

New Initiatives

As I mentioned, FDA announced on May 3, as part of an Administration initiative, that we will be taking steps to strengthen the premarket notification program for bioengineered foods. We also intend to provide guidance to food manufacturers who wish voluntarily to label their products regarding whether or not they contain bioengineered ingredients. Our goal is to enhance public confidence in the way in which FDA is regulating bioengineered foods. We want the public to know, loud and clear, that FDA stands behind the safety of these products.

As part of this initiative, we will be proposing regulations to make it mandatory that developers of bioengineered plant varieties notify FDA at least 120 days before they intend to market such products. FDA will require that specific information be submitted to help determine whether the foods pose any safety or labeling concerns. The Agency will be providing further guidance to industry on the scientific data needed to ensure that foods developed through bioengineering are safe for human consumption. To help make the process more transparent, the Agency has made a commitment to ensuring that, consistent with information disclosure laws, consumers have access to information submitted to FDA as part of the notification process and to FDA's responses in a timely fashion.

The proposed rule on premarket notification and the draft labeling guidance are both high priorities for the Agency, and we intend to publish each of these later this fall. Both will provide a full opportunity for public comment before final policies are established. Let me assure you that when we come to a decision regarding these matters, FDA will operate in an open, transparent manner so that the public can understand our regulatory approach and continue to provide us with feedback about its impact. As a scientific organization we are comfortable with debate over complex scientific issues, and welcome the discussions that have occurred at public meetings to date. It is important that the public, including the scientific community, clearly understand FDA's policy on bioengineered foods.

Additional Activities

Before closing, let me briefly describe a few other activities of Agency involvement in the food biotechnology subject area. In our May 3 announcement, FDA stated our intention to augment our food and veterinary medicine advisory committees by adding scientists with agricultural biotechnology expertise. FDA will use these committees to address over-arching scientific questions pertaining to bioengineered foods and animal feed. More specifically, I am restructuring the Food Advisory Committee so that it will contain several special focus subcommittees. One of those subcommittees will have scientists with expertise in bioengineering, and will focus on issues pertaining to food biotechnology.

As I am sure you are aware, the National Academy of Sciences has formed a new standing Committee on Agricultural Biotechnology. FDA has participated in several of its meetings, including one just last week, on September 18, in which two FDA experts made presentations. We think the work of this committee is very important. We are formalizing our relationship with it, particularly with regard to exploring what the potential is for any unknown long-term health effects to result from consumption of bioengineered food.

FDA is actively participating in the work of the U.S. Codex Committee on food labeling, which is considering issues on policies for possible labeling of foods derived using bioengineering. In addition, FDA is participating in the newly formed "Ad Hoc Committee on Foods Derived from Biotechnology." This committee is especially important because its initial focus is to develop principles and guidelines for the evaluation of the safety of bioengineered foods. FDA is providing an international leadership role in this committee to develop harmonized policies for assessing the safety of bioengineered food.

Let me comment briefly on the recall announced by Kraft Foods this past Friday. FDA commends Kraft Foods for acting responsibly in light of testing showing the possibility that the products contained a bioengineered protein that had not been approved for human consumption. This reinforces the importance of FDA, EPA and other interested parties to be vigilant in assuring that the rules pertaining to bioengineered foods are being fully adhered to. FDA's investigation is continuing in this case.

Mr. Chairman, thank you again for the opportunity to address these issues. I am happy to answer any questions you might have.

POSTSCRIPT

Should We Require Labeling for Genetically Modified Food?

William Safire, a journalist often amused by popular trends in the use of the English language, titled one of his weekly essays "Franken-: A Monstrous Prefix Is Stalking Europe," *The New York Times* (August 13, 2000). His point was not that many European nations, acting in fear, have banned or restricted the import of genetically modified foods but that language had evolved to express that fear. "Franken-," from Mary Godwin Shelley's nineteenth-century book *Frankenstein,* has come to characterize the product of any human "tampering" with nature that one finds displeasing. The fact that we have modified breeds of plants and animals for centuries, in fact millennia, through selective breeding or other methods of assisting evolution, tends to get lost in the debate.

Labeling is another way to use language to affect policy. It simply is not politically neutral to attach a label to something, especially when based on our usual understandings, it should not need one. Every required addition to the labels on our food has been made in response to a public agenda, usually concerning public health but occasionally concerning public causes that have nothing to do with the quality of the food. Is it appropriate for genetically engineered products to follow that route?

Suggested Readings

Michael Fumento, "Crop Busters," *Reason* (January 2000).

Kristi Coale, "Mutant Food," *Salon* (January 12, 2000).

Jon Luoma, "Pandora's Pantry," *Mother Jones* (January/February 2000).

Frederic Golden, "Who's Afraid of Frankenfood?" *Time* (November 29, 1999).

U.S. Business Cycle Indicators Data

This site leads to the 256 data series known as the U.S. Business Cycle Indicators, which are used to track and predict U.S. business activity. The subjects of the data groups are clearly listed.

http://www.economagic.com/bci-97.htm

Voice of the Shuttle: Postindustrial Business Theory Page

This site links to a variety of resources on many subjects related to business theory, including restructuring, reengineering, downsizing, flattening, the team concept, outsourcing, business and globalism, human resources management, labor relations, statistics, and history, as well as information and resources on job searches, careers, working from home, and business start-ups.

http://vos.ucsb.edu/browse.asp?id=2727

Society, Religion, and Technology Project

This is the home page on patenting living organisms of the Society, Religion, and Technology Project (SRT) of the Church of Scotland. It provides a simple introduction to the issues involved, other SRT pages on patenting, and links to related pages.

http://www.srtp.org.uk.patent.shtml

PART 5

International Operations: Global Obligations

A merican business is increasingly carried out over distant waters and in foreign villages. The corporation of the future is a global enterprise and difficult to track, avoiding the jurisdiction of any national government. What ethical obligations attend these operations? Are there products we should not buy because of the way they were manufactured? How far does the global reach of U.S. industries extend? These questions form the core of the issues that follow.

- Are Multinational Corporations Free From Moral Obligation?

- Are Sweatshops Necessarily Evil?

- Should Patenting Life Be Forbidden?

ISSUE 15

Are Multinational Corporations Free From Moral Obligation?

YES: Manuel Velasquez, from "International Business, Morality and the Common Good," *Business Ethics Quarterly* (January 1992)

NO: John E. Fleming, from "Alternative Approaches and Assumptions: Comments on Manuel Velasquez," *Business Ethics Quarterly* (January 1992)

ISSUE SUMMARY

YES: Professor of business ethics Manuel Velasquez doubts that, in the absence of accepted enforcement agencies, any multinational corporation will suffer for violating rules that restrict business for the sake of the common good. He argues that since any business that tried to conform to moral rules in the absence of enforcement would cease to be competitive, moral strictures cannot be binding on such companies.

NO: Professor emeritus John E. Fleming asserts that multinational corporations tend to deal with long-term customers and suppliers in the goldfish bowl of international media and must therefore adhere to moral standards or lose business.

This issue is a complex one with many gray areas.

In the first selection, for example, Manuel Velasquez perceives the issue to be between the Hobbesian realists (those who adhere to the philosophies of Thomas Hobbes), who value the bottom line above all else, and those who believe that high moral thoughts influence world affairs. Velasquez concludes that a Hobbesian realist, knowing the worst about human nature, must acknowledge that moral obligations simply do not apply in the absence of moral community. John E. Fleming does not counter Velasquez's argument in the tone of lofty idealism but in that of a practitioner who has to keep an enterprise afloat from day to day. He concludes that the only way to serve the bottom line is through moral behavior.

Second, Velasquez perceives right action to be on trial. He asks, Can morality justify itself with regard to profit? Can we show that acting for the common good will not damage the profit picture or detract from the increase in shareholder wealth? If not, Velasquez suggests, then we will have to forgo morality. Fleming seems to say that right action is compatible with (in fact, necessary for) the health of the bottom line and the corporate enterprise in general. If Fleming is right, then the major premise of Hobbesian capitalism—that the sole social responsibility of business is to increase its profits—may be unworkable. Any activity that might be expected to follow from the injunction to serve the bottom line and increase profits, activity in total disregard of the moral persuasions of all others in society, may result in lost business, leaving shareholders with valueless promises.

Third, according to both Velasquez and Fleming, the dispute is over human behavior in business situations—both about the way humans *will* behave and the way they *should* behave. Both authors condition their predictions and advice on the nature of the international business community. Fleming states that the international business scene is not at all how Velasquez portrays it—strangers interacting in strange lands on a one-time basis only—but is a place of custom, regular habits, and familiar people, where memories are long, word gets around, and tolerance for being taken advantage of is very low.

As you read the following selections, consider how international dealings differ from domestic dealings. Aren't folks abroad rather like folks at home, with just a few differences in manners? What are the real controls on human behavior—enforcement of laws or the simple social expectations of peers and colleagues?

YES

International Business, Morality and the Common Good

During the last few years an increasing number of voices have urged that we pay more attention to ethics in international business, on the grounds that not only are all large corporations now internationally structured and thus engaging in international transactions, but that even the smallest domestic firm is increasingly buffeted by the pressures of international competition....

Can we say that businesses operating in a competitive international environment have any moral obligations to contribute to the international common good, particularly in light of realist objections? Unfortunately, my answer to this question will be in the negative....

International Business

... When speaking of international business, I have in mind a particular kind of organization: the multinational corporation. Multinational corporations have a number of well known features, but let me briefly summarize a few of them. First, multinational corporations are businesses and as such they are organized primarily to increase their profits within a competitive environment. Virtually all of the activities of a multinational corporation can be explained as more or less rational attempts to achieve this dominant end. Secondly, multinational corporations are bureaucratic organizations. The implication of this is that the identity, the fundamental structure, and the dominant objectives of the corporation endure while the many individual human beings who fill the various offices and positions within the corporation come and go. As a consequence, the particular values and aspirations of individual members of the corporation have a relatively minimal and transitory impact on the organization as a whole. Thirdly, and most characteristically, multinational corporations operate in several nations. This has several implications. First, because the multinational is not confined to a single nation, it can easily escape the reach of the laws of any particular nation by simply moving its resources or operations out of one nation and transferring them to another nation. Second, because the multinational is not confined to a single nation, its interests are not aligned with the interests of any single nation. The ability of the multinational to achieve its

From Manuel Velasquez, "International Business, Morality and the Common Good," *Business Ethics Quarterly* (January 1992). Copyright © 1992 by *Business Ethics Quarterly*. Reprinted by permission of The Philosophy Documentation Center, publisher of *Business Ethics Quarterly*. Notes omitted.

profit objectives does not depend upon the ability of any particular nation to achieve its own domestic objectives....

The Traditional Realist Objection in Hobbes

The realist objection, of course, is the standard objection to the view that agents —whether corporations, governments, or individuals—have moral obligations on the international level. Generally, the realist holds that it is a mistake to apply moral concepts to international activities: morality has no place in international affairs. The classical statement of this view, which I am calling the "traditional" version of realism, is generally attributed to Thomas Hobbes....

In its Hobbsian form, as traditionally interpreted, the realist objection holds that moral concepts have no meaning in the absence of an agency powerful enough to guarantee that other agents generally adhere to the tenets of morality. Hobbes held, first, that in the absence of a sovereign power capable of forcing men to behave civilly with each other, men are in "the state of nature," a state he characterizes as a "war . . . of every man, against every man." Secondly, Hobbes claimed, in such a state of war, moral concepts have no meaning:

> To this war of every man against every man, this also is consequent; that nothing can be unjust. The notions of right and wrong, justice and injustice have there no place. Where there is no common power, there is no law: where no law, no injustice.

Moral concepts are meaningless, then, when applied to state of nature situations. And, Hobbes held, the international arena is a state of nature, since there is no international sovereign that can force agents to adhere to the tenets of morality.

The Hobbsian objection to talking about morality in international affairs, then, is based on two premises: (1) an ethical premise about the applicability of moral terms and (2) an apparently empirical premise about how agents behave under certain conditions. The ethical premise, at least in its Hobbsian form, holds that there is a connection between the meaningfulness of moral terms and the extent to which agents adhere to the tenets of morality: If in a given situation agents do not adhere to the tenets of morality, then in that situation moral terms have no meaning. The apparently empirical premise holds that in the absence of a sovereign, agents will not adhere to the tenets of morality: they will be in a state of war. This appears to be an empirical generalization about the extent to which agents adhere to the tenets of morality in the absence of a third-party enforcer. Taken together, the two premises imply that in situations that lack a sovereign authority, such as one finds in many international exchanges, moral terms have no meaning and so moral obligations are nonexistent....

Revising the Realist Objection: The First Premise

... The neo-Hobbsian or realist... might want to propose this premise: When one is in a situation in which others do not adhere to certain tenets of morality, and when adhering to those tenets of morality will put one at a significant competitive disadvantage, then it is not immoral for one to like-wise fail to adhere to them. The realist might want to argue for this claim, first, by pointing out that in a world in which all are competing to secure significant benefits and avoid significant costs, and in which others do not adhere to the ordinary tenets of morality, one risks significant harm to one's interests if one continues to adhere to those tenets of morality. But no one can be morally required to take on major risks of harm to oneself. Consequently, in a competitive world in which others disregard moral constraints and take any means to advance their self-interests, no one can be morally required to take on major risks of injury by adopting the restraints of ordinary morality.

A second argument the realist might want to advance would go as follows. When one is in a situation in which others do not adhere to the ordinary tenets of morality, one is under heavy competitive pressures to do the same. And, when one is under such pressures, one cannot be blamed—i.e., one is excused —for also failing to adhere to the ordinary tenets of morality. One is excused because heavy pressures take away one's ability to control oneself, and thereby diminish one's moral culpability.

Yet a third argument advanced by the realist might go as follows. When one is in a situation in which others do not adhere to the ordinary tenets of morality it is not fair to require one to continue to adhere to those tenets, especially if doing so puts one at a significant competitive disadvantage. It is not fair because then one is laying a burden on one party that the other parties refuse to carry.

Thus, there are a number of arguments that can be given in defense of the revised Hobbsian ethical premise that when others do not adhere to the tenets of morality, it is not immoral for one to do likewise. . . .

Revising the Realist Objection: The Second Premise

Let us turn to the other premise in the Hobbsian argument, the assertion that in the absence of a sovereign, agents will be in a state of war. As I mentioned, this is an apparently empirical claim about the extent to which agents will adhere to the tenets of morality in the absence of a third-party enforcer.

Hobbes gives a little bit of empirical evidence for this claim. He cites several examples of situations in which there is no third party to enforce ci-vility and where, as a result, individuals are in a "state of war." Generalizing from these few examples, he reaches the conclusion that in the absence of a third-party enforcer, agents will always be in a "condition of war." . . .

Recently, the Hobbsian claim . . . has been defended on the basis of some of the theoretical claims of game theory, particularly of the prisoner's dilemma. Hobbes' state of nature, the defense goes, is an instance of a prisoner's dilemma, and *rational* agents in a Prisoner's Dilemma necessarily would choose not to adhere to a set of moral norms. . . .

A Prisoner's Dilemma is a situation involving at least two individuals. Each individual is faced with two choices: he can cooperate with the other individual or he can choose not to cooperate. If he cooperates and the other individual also cooperates, then he gets a certain payoff. If, however, he chooses not to cooperate, while the other individual trustingly cooperates, the noncooperator gets a larger payoff while the cooperator suffers a loss. And if both choose not to cooperate, then both get nothing.

It is a commonplace now that in a Prisoner's Dilemma situation, the most rational strategy for a participant is to choose not to cooperate. For the other party will either cooperate or not cooperate. If the other party cooperates, then it is better for one not to cooperate and thereby get the larger payoff. On the other hand, if the other party does not cooperate, then it is also better for one not to cooperate and thereby avoid a loss. In either case, it is better for one to not cooperate.

. . . In Hobbes' state of nature each individual must choose either to cooperate with others by adhering to the rules of morality (like the rule against theft), or to not cooperate by disregarding the rules of morality and attempting to take advantage of those who are adhering to the rules (e.g., by stealing from them). In such a situation it is more rational . . . to choose not to cooperate. For the other party will either cooperate or not cooperate. If the other party does not cooperate, then one puts oneself at a competitive disadvantage if one adheres to morality while the other party does not. On the other hand, if the other party chooses to cooperate, then one can take advantage of the other party by breaking the rules of morality at his expense. In either case, it is moral rational to not cooperate.

Thus, the realist can argue that in a state of nature, where there is no one to enforce compliance with the rules of morality, it is more rational from the individual's point of view to choose not to comply with morality than to choose to comply. Assuming—and this is obviously a critical assumption—that agents behave rationally, then we can conclude that agents in a state of nature will choose not to comply with the tenets of ordinary morality. . . .

Can we claim that it is clear that multinationals have a moral obligation to pursue the global common good in spite of the objections of the realist?

I do not believe that this claim can be made. We can conclude from the discussion of the realist objection that the Hobbsian claim about the pervasiveness of amorality in the international sphere is false when (1) interactions among international agents are repetitive in such a way that agents can retaliate against those who fail to cooperate, and (2) agents can determine the trustworthiness of other international agents.

But unfortunately, multinational activities often take place in a highly competitive arena in which these two conditions do not obtain. Moreover, these conditions are noticeably absent in the arena of activities that concern the global common good.

First, as I have noted, the common good consists of goods that are indivisible and accessible to all. This means that such goods are susceptible to the free rider problems. Everyone has access to such goods whether or not they do their part in maintaining such goods, so everyone is tempted to free ride on the generosity of others. Now governments can force domestic companies to do their part to maintain the national common good. Indeed, it is one of the functions of government to solve the free rider problem by forcing all to contribute to the domestic common good to which all have access. Moreover, all companies have to interact repeatedly with their host governments, and this leads them to adopt a cooperative stance toward their host government's objective of achieving the domestic common good.

But it is not clear that governments can or will do anything effective to force multinationals to do their part to maintain the global common good. For the governments of individual nations can themselves be free riders, and can join forces with willing multinationals seeking competitive advantages over others. Let me suggest an example. It is clear that a livable global environment is part of the global common good, and it is clear that the manufacture and use of chlorofluorocarbons is destroying that good. Some nations have responded by requiring their domestic companies to cease manufacturing or using chlorofluorocarbons. But other nations have refused to do the same, since they will share in any benefits that accrue from the restraint others practice, and they can also reap the benefits of continuing to manufacture and use chlorofluorocarbons. Less developed nations, in particular, have advanced the position that since their development depends heavily on exploiting the industrial benefits of chlorofluorocarbons, they cannot afford to curtail their use of these substances. Given this situation, it is open to multinationals to shift their operations to those countries that continue to allow the manufacture and use of chlorofluorocarbons. For multinationals, too, will reason that they will share in any benefits that accrue from the restraint others practice, and that they can meanwhile reap the profits of continuing to manufacture and use chlorofluorocarbons in a world where other companies are forced to use more expensive technologies. Moreover, those nations that practice restraint cannot force all such multinationals to discontinue the manufacture or use of chlorofluorocarbons because many multinationals can escape the reach of their laws. An exactly parallel, but perhaps even more compelling, set of considerations can be advanced to show that at least some multinationals will join forces with some developing countries to circumvent any global efforts made to control the global warming trends (the so-called "greenhouse effect") caused by the heavy use of fossil fuels.

The realist will conclude, of course, that in such situations, at least some multinationals will seek to gain competitive advantages by failing to contribute to the global common good (such as the good of a hospitable global environment). For multinationals and rational agents, i.e., agents bureaucratically structured to take rational means toward achieving their dominant end of increasing their profits. And in a competitive environment, contributing to the common good while others do not, will fail to achieve this dominant end. Joining this conclusion to the ethical premise that when others do not adhere to the requirements of morality it is not immoral for one to do likewise, the realist can conclude that multinationals are not morally obligated to contribute to such global common goods (such as environmental goods).

Moreover, global common goods often create interactions that are not iterated. This is particularly the case where the global environment is concerned. As I have already noted, preservation of a favorable global climate is clearly part of the global common good. Now the failure of the global climate will be a one-time affair. The breakdown of the ozone layer, for example, will happen once, with catastrophic consequences for us all; and the heating up of the global climate as a result of the infusion of carbon dioxide will happen once, with catastrophic consequences for us all. Because these environmental disasters are a one-time affair, they represent a non-iterated prisoner's dilemma for multinationals. It is irrational from an individual point of view for a multinational to choose to refrain from polluting the environment in such cases. Either others will refrain, and then one can enjoy the benefits of their refraining; or others will not refrain, and then it will be better to have also not refrained since refraining would have made little difference and would have entailed heavy losses.

Finally, we must also note that although natural persons may signal their reliability to other natural persons, it is not at all obvious that multinationals can do the same. As noted above, multinationals are bureaucratic organizations whose members are continually changing and shifting. The natural persons who make up an organization can signal their reliability to others, but such persons are soon replaced by others, and they in turn are replaced by others. What endures is each organization's single-minded pursuit of increasing its profits in a competitive environment. And an enduring commitment to the pursuit of profit in a competitive environment is not a signal of an enduring commitment to morality.

John E. Fleming

 **NO**

Alternative Approaches and Assumptions: Comments on Manuel Velasquez

Introduction

I feel that Professor Velasquez has written a very interesting and thought-provoking paper on an important topic. His initial identification with a "strong notion of the common good" raises the level of analysis to a high but very complex plane. The author introduces the interesting and, from my view, unusual *realist objection* in the Hobbsian form. After a rigorous analysis of this concept Professor Velasquez reaches what I find to be a disturbing conclusion: "It is not obvious that we can say that multinationals have an obligation to contribute to the global common good. . . ." He then finishes the paper with a strong plea for the establishment of "an international authority capable of forcing everyone to contribute toward the global good."

It would be presumptuous of me to question the fine ethical reasoning that appears in the paper. I am impressed with its elegance. However, in a topic of this complexity I would like to think that there might be alternative approaches and assumptions that would lead us to a different conclusion. The presentation of such alternatives will be the path that I will take, examining the conceptual and empirical underpinnings of the argument from a management viewpoint.

The Model of a Multinational Corporation

The profit-maximizing, rational model of a multinational corporation presented in the paper is consistent with traditional economics and serves as a useful approximation of the firm from a theoretical viewpoint. But it falls somewhat short in less than purely competitive environments and was never intended to describe the decision processes of actual managers. Empirical studies of firms can lead to a profit-sacrificing, bounded rational model. The importance of profit is still there, but the stockholder does not get all the benefits. Other stakeholders are considered and rewarded. Out of all this can come

From John E. Fleming, "Alternative Approaches and Assumptions: Comments on Manuel Velasquez," *Business Ethics Quarterly* (January 1992). Copyright © 1992 by *Business Ethics Quarterly*. Reprinted by permission of The Philosophy Documentation Center, publisher of *Business Ethics Quarterly*. Notes omitted.

the important concept of corporate social responsibility, which can include such topics as concerns for the environment and for host country governments.

I also find the faceless and interchangeable bureaucrat a poor model for business executives, particularly the chief executive officers of large corporations. Many of these individuals have a personal impact on the organization, including such areas as business ethics and corporate responsibility. There are also important behavioral aspects of management, such as pride in the firm and corporate culture, that are fertile soil for the nurture of ethics.

Most large American multinational corporations have codes of ethics and some have well-developed programs concerned with ethical behavior world-wide. A number of these firms emphasize that their one code of conduct applies everywhere that they do business. At the GTE Corporation its vision and values statements have been translated into nine different languages and distributed to all its employees to ensure this world-wide understanding of how it conducts its business. This is a far cry from the situational ethics described in the model used by Professor Velasquez.

Model of the International Business Climate

The planning and decision environment of the managers conducting international business is different from that described in the paper. There is the very real problem of a lack of an overarching global government and enforceable laws for the international arena. Nevertheless, there are other very strong restraining forces on companies that prevent the "state of nature" (or law of the jungle) described in the paper. For example, the national governments that do exist influence the ethical behavior of companies acting within their boundaries and beyond. The Foreign Corrupt Practices Act of the United States has set a new standard of behavior in the area of bribery that dictates how American companies will behave world-wide. The financial practices of large banks and securities markets have added major constraints to global corporate behavior. There are also a number of regional and functional organizations in the areas of trade and monetary issues that provide limitations to managerial decision making.

The decisions of multinational executives are also constrained by such factors as public opinion and the pressures of special interest groups. In this area the media also plays a strong role. Examples of these forces are the actions of interest groups that forced marketing changes on infant formula manufacturers and the strong "green" movement that is affecting business decisions throughout many parts of the world. My own view is that considerable progress has been made in the area of limiting the manufacture and release of chlorofluorocarbons. This is a very complex issue involving tremendous social and economic changes that are far more critical, widespread and controlling than the profits of the producing companies. Even with the existence of an enforcing government there is no guarantee that the problem would be solved speedily. An example in point is the acid rain problem of the United States.

Model of the Prisoner's Dilemma

From the standpoint of managerial decision making the Prisoner's Dilemma model does not simulate a situation that is frequently found in international business. An executive generally would not be negotiating or making mutually beneficial decisions with competitors. I would see the greatest amount of effort of multinational decision makers devoted to the development of repeat customers. Such an accomplishment comes about through solving customer problems with better product/service at a lower cost. An emphasis on efficiency and excellence is a far more effective use of executive time than questionable negotiations with a competitor. I believe that the weakness Professor Velasquez identifies in the Prisoner's Dilemma model as a one-time event with competitors applies even more to negotiations with customers.

The author also points out a major weakness of the model in the signaling of intent that goes on between individuals. He then states that this same signaling is not found to any great extent between companies. I would disagree with this thought. An important part of corporate strategic planning is analyzing market signals. United States antitrust forbids direct contact between competitors on issues relating to the market. But there is no limitation on independent analysis of competitive actions and the interpretation of actions by competitors. When Kodak introduced its instant camera, both Kodak and Polaroid watched the other's actions to determine whether it signaled detente or fight.

Conclusion

For the reasons enumerated above I tend to question the models and assumptions that Professor Velasquez has used in his ethical analysis. And, with these underpinnings in jeopardy, I also tend to question the tentative conclusion of his moral reasoning as it relates to the managerial aspects of international business. I feel that multinationals *do* have a strong obligation to contribute to the global common good.

POSTSCRIPT

Are Multinational Corporations Free From Moral Obligation?

As we write, international business has sunk into a sea of troubles: the once-booming Asian economies seem to be self-destructing, prominent public figures such as movie stars and athletes are being accused of exploitation and owning sweatshops, and trade in securities has gone global and is running wild. What are the possibilities for the comprehensive set of international laws, guidelines, and the committees to enforce them, as suggested by Velasquez?

Is national sovereignty an idea whose time has come, gone, and gone south? While national boundaries between peoples are in violent dispute worldwide, and while the economy goes global with blinding speed, does the concept of national boundaries make any sense at all? How else would we know what each central government controls? What is the reason for the centrality of national sovereignty?

Suggested Readings

Corporate Ethics: A Prime Business Asset, Report of the Business Roundtable (1988).

Ashay B. Desai and Terri Rittenburg, "Global Ethics: An Integrative Framework for MNEs," *Journal of Business Ethics* (June 1997), pp. 791–800.

Thomas Donaldson, *The Ethics of International Business* (Oxford University Press, 1989).

Thomas L. Friedman, *The Lexus and the Olive Tree: Understanding Globalization* (Farrar, Straus & Giroux, 2000).

W. Michael Hoffman, Ann E. Lange, and David A. Fedo, eds., *Ethics and the Multinational Enterprise* (University Press of America, 1986).

Kevin T. Jackson, "Globalizing Corporate Ethics Programs: Perils and Prospects," *Journal of Business Ethics* (September 1997), pp. 1227–1235.

ISSUE 16

Are Sweatshops Necessarily Evil?

YES: Susan S. Black, from "Ante Up," *Bobbin* (September 19, 1996)

NO: Allen R. Myerson, from "In Principle, a Case for More 'Sweat-shops,'" *The New York Times* (June 22, 1997)

ISSUE SUMMARY

YES: Susan S. Black, publisher of *Bobbin*, argues that customers will not tolerate goods made by slave labor, children, or women working in inhumane conditions. She maintains that customers are willing to pay more to make sure that the goods they buy were not made in sweatshops.

NO: Allen R. Myerson, a writer for the *New York Times*, looks at the economies of less developed countries and finds that allowing their citizens to work in sweatshops may be the only option these nations have to accumulate capital.

T he Scottish economist Adam Smith's recommendation regarding government regulation of the terms of commercial contracts was to let every player in the market make his or her own best bargain, and in the end everyone would be better off.

Consider the conditions for the "voluntary exchange": there must be no fraud or misrepresentation on either side—both parties must know what they are getting into—and there must be no coercion. Simply put, this means that there must be no gun held to the head of either party. Less obviously, there must be no economic coercion: one party may not be under absolute economic coercion to sign. For example, if someone takes a job for the money to buy a new car, that decision seems to be perfectly free. But if the person needs the job immediately just to feed his or her family, it could be argued that the individual is not "free" to turn it down—the offer of a job is impossible to refuse. When one party has enormous economic power, and the other has none, there cannot be a free or voluntary agreement—there must be a certain degree of economic equality between the contracting parties, not absolute but not nonexistent, or there is no voluntariness.

Smith probably never imagined that this situation could arise. In a society with many employers in competition with each other for labor and other resources, not one of which is large enough to dominate the market, the laborer can simply withhold his or her services until he or she finds the employer that is willing to pay the most. There was a time when independent craftspeople made their contracts with individual buyers and when many small farmers needed help at harvest time. Then perhaps the economic power of the contracting parties was approximately equal and all exchanges were voluntary. But in the day of the huge factory that dominates the town and of the replaceable unskilled worker, one side seems to hold all the chips, and the other side holds none.

It could be argued that sweatshops—huge mass-production facilities where hundreds work in barbaric conditions for subsistence wages—built the United States. Workers rendered vulnerable by their immigrant status, disorientation in unfamiliar urban settings, and irremediable poverty were forced to take whatever jobs were available; entrepreneurs with access to capital threw up factories, and so the sweatshop was born. The union movement in the United States is all about the abolition of the sweatshop and the development of the modern factory—clean, safe, pleasant, and paying its workers adequate wages and benefits.

Clean, safe, pleasant, and losing money, modern entrepreneurs might say. In many industries, like the garment industry, the major cost of manufacture is labor. As long as there is no alternative, consumers seem willing to pay whatever they have to for their merchandise. But as soon as less expensive products become available—and with the growth of Asian competition, they certainly have become available—consumers buy them instead. Some say that only by continuing to manufacture offshore, in the sweatshops of Asia, can America remain competitive.

Meanwhile, the nations in which America is building these sweatshops do not seem to be complaining. On the contrary, they complain when U.S. multinational corporations shut down the sweatshops in response to American protests against them. Because so many of these nations' people can obtain jobs in American sweatshops, these shops are considered by some to be the only way the nations can grow.

As you read the following selections by Susan S. Black and Allen R. Myerson, ask yourself whether or not the outrage over sweatshop conditions in the developing world is justified. Are we importing standards appropriate to the early-twenty-first-century United States rather than putting these manufactures against a backdrop of the lives lived by the workers before the factory came? Should a country be allowed to oppress or exploit its people in an effort to get its economy started?

 **YES**

Ante Up

Another chapter in the U.S. Labor Department's self-proclaimed war on apparel industry sweatshops was played out in mid-July when Secretary of Labor Robert Reich hosted a group of some 300, including *Bobbin*, to discuss what could be done about the problem.

The "Fashion Industry Forum," held at Marymount University just outside of Washington, D.C., drew manufacturers and retailers, union leaders, industry association representatives and such celebrity endorsers at Kathie Lee Gifford and Cheryl Tiegs, many of whom participated in panel presentations.

While Reich said he didn't expect "major headlines" to result from the forum, he did say that he hoped it would be a "turning point" and that he expected it to foster a "renewed commitment" to battle sweatshops and child labor. Of course, the fact that such major players as Wal-Mart Stores, Kmart Corp., Nordstrom, Liz Claiborne, Patagonia Inc. and Levi Strauss & Co. participated in the forum is evidence in itself that Reich has managed to focus industry's attention on the subject of sweatshops. And whether one agrees with Reich's tactics or not—I don't—it seems almost certain that his momentum-gaining antisweatshop campaign is going to result in changes for our industry, namely that both retailers and manufacturers are going to have to incur additional expenses to prove to consumers that their goods are made under fair and legal labor conditions.

Among the options put on the table at the forum were "no-sweat" labeling programs, independent third-party monitoring of factories and increasing the duties of quality assurance personnel to encompass monitoring responsibilities —each of which undoubtedly comes with a price tag and such possible complex concerns as, "Who monitors the monitors?" If additional monitoring and labeling programs do come to fruition, the key question is who will pay the price. Opinions on the level of cost and who should bear responsibility for that cost varied at the forum, but my bet is that ultimately it will be the entire soft goods chain—and the consumer—that pays.

"The customer can't have its cake and eat it too," said Tiegs, who first licensed her name for an apparel line in the 1980s. "They must pay the price."

John Ermatinger, senior vice president of operations and sourcing for Levi Strauss North America, said it's time to stop placing blame and time to start

From Susan S. Black, "Ante Up," *Bobbin* (September 1996). Copyright © 1996 by *Bobbin*. Reprinted by permission. Notes omitted.

finding solutions. "I would like to spend more time working on this issue and less time talking about it," he said. "It's unfair to focus on the retailer. It's a supply chain challenge and we will have to find flexible, non-mandated solutions. It's not a one-size-fits-all solution."

Levi's success in producing no-sweat goods (it first established standards for monitoring contractors in 1991) is a result of making monitoring an integral part of the business. "This is how we do business," Ermatinger said. "It's part of how we measure performance."

As part of its reengineering, Levi's also has cut its supplier base by 50 percent, said Ermatinger, "enabling us to focus more efficiently on our remaining base."

Roberta Karp, vice president of corporate affairs and general counsel for Liz Claiborne, agreed that there is no "recipe to follow" when it comes to monitoring. She said Claiborne has its own internal monitoring program, but might consider expanding it. "We must reach out to partnerships [in monitoring]," she said.

Warren Flick, president of merchandising for Kmart, said for its part, the merchant is "rebuilding" its entire buying organization. He said Kmart will have fewer vendors, and longer-term relationships with those vendors.

Flick also said Kmart has created a new executive position, based in Hong Kong, to oversee Kmart's global monitoring efforts. "Our eyes and ears are wide open," he added. "We know what products and regions where our focus needs to be."

Gale Cottle, executive vice president for Nordstrom who said that Nordstrom will not tolerate vendors who use illegal practices, also pointed to some of the challenges a retailer has in monitoring the conditions under which its goods are made. For starters, she said Nordstrom has 13,000 U.S. vendors, and 870 decentralized buyers who buy on a customized level according to changing fashion needs. She said: "A buyer cannot identify cost in a showroom... and even the right price doesn't guarantee the right conditions."

Also bringing a practical slant to the forum was Tracy Mullin, president of the National Retail Federation (NRF), who observed that while retailers cannot afford to jeopardize their reputations and want to take "aggressive steps forward," there are a myriad of considerations in handling sweatshop accusations. Noting that the problem of sweatshops often involves organized crime and immigration violations, she recommended coordinated efforts among the Internal Revenue Service, the Immigration and Naturalization Service and the Justice Department.

The granddaddy retailer of them all, Wal-Mart—around which much media attention has been generated after it was discovered that Kathie Lee Gifford apparel was being produced in a New York, NY, sweatshop—said at the forum that it never had inspected U.S. factories with whom it does business, but is doing so now. It also will be recertifying the overseas factories with whom it does business, and has studied an independent monitoring program used by The Gap, said Lee Scott, executive vice president of merchandise and sales for Wal-Mart.

Still, Scott cautioned that there could be a tendency to migrate toward using only large, well-established vendors, which would "keep out the young, innovative companies."

If the Fashion Industry Forum means that some companies will adopt more careful monitoring practices with their contractors and subcontractors, there's no question the results will be positive. After all, good manufacturing practices logically should result in better quality and higher profits. But it's important to note that behind the publicly spoken words at the forum were many forces at play, several with distinctly different motives. Government, unions, retailers, manufacturers, contractors—each has its own self-interests.

Let's just hope that as many of the already law-abiding businesses in our industry commit themselves to more thorough documentation of how their goods are made, the illicit businesses and sweatshops will fall by the wayside in greater numbers. Because the last thing this industry needs is more bad publicity based on the actions of a few.

One last thought. Did you know that the members of the American Apparel Manufacturers Association (AAMA)—which represent about two-thirds of the garments made in the United States—manufacture 85 percent of their goods in their own plants? And that the average U.S. apparel worker makes double the minimum wage, plus another 30 percent in benefits?

Those statistics came from AAMA president Larry Martin at the forum. I think they're worth remembering—and repeating.

NO ⬅

Allen R. Myerson

In Principle, a Case for More "Sweatshops"

CAMBRIDGE, MASS.

For more than a century, accounts of sweatshops have provoked outrage. From the works of Charles Dickens and Lincoln Steffens to today's television reports, the image of workers hunched over their machines for meager rewards has been a banner of reform.

Last year, companies like Nike and Wal-Mart and celebrities like Kathie Lee Gifford struggled to defend themselves after reports of the torturous hours and low pay of the workers who produce their upscale footwear or downmarket fashions. Anxious corporate spokesmen sought to explain the plants as a step up for workers in poor countries. A weeping Mrs. Gifford denied knowing about the conditions.

Now some of the nation's leading economists, with solid liberal and academic credentials, are offering a much broader, more principled rationale. Economists like Jeffrey D. Sachs of Harvard and Paul Krugman of the Massachusetts Institute of Technology say that low-wage plants making clothing and shoes for foreign markets are an essential first step toward modern prosperity in developing countries.

Mr. Sachs, a leading adviser and shock therapist to nations like Bolivia, Russia and Poland, is now working on the toughest cases of all, the economies of sub-Saharan Africa. He is just back from Malawi, where malaria afflicts almost all its 13 million people and AIDS affects 1 in 10; the lake that provided much of the country's nourishment is fished out.

When asked during a recent Harvard panel discussion whether there were too many sweatshops in such places, Mr. Sachs answered facetiously, "My concern is not that there are too many sweatshops but that there are too few," he said.

Mr. Sachs, who has visited low-wage factories around the world, is opposed to child or prisoner labor and other outright abuses. But many nations, he says, have no better hope than plants paying mere subsistence wages. "Those are precisely the jobs that were the steppingstone for Singapore and Hong Kong,"

From Allen R. Myerson, "In Principle, a Case for More 'Sweatshops,'" *The New York Times* (June 22, 1997). Copyright © 1997 by The New York Times Company, Inc. Reprinted by permission.

he said, "and those are the jobs that have to come to Africa to get them out of their backbreaking rural poverty."

Rising Stakes

The stakes in the battle over sweatshops are high and rising. Clinton Administration officials say commerce with the major developing nations like China, Indonesia and Mexico is crucial for America's own continued prosperity. Corporate America's manufacturing investments in developing nations more than tripled in 15 years to $56 billion in 1995—not including the vast numbers of plants there that contract with American companies.

In matters of trade and commerce, economists like Mr. Sachs, who has also worked with several Government agencies, are influential. A consensus among economists helped persuade President Clinton, who had campaigned against President Bush's plan of lowered restrictions, to ram global and North American trade pacts through Congress.

Paradoxically, economists' support of sweatshops represents a sort of optimism. Until the mid-1980's, few thought that third world nations could graduate to first world status in a lifetime, if ever. "When I went to graduate school in the early to mid-1970's," Mr. Krugman said, "it looked like being a developed country was really a closed club." Only Japan had made a convincing jump within the past century.

Those economists who believed that developing nations could advance often prescribed self-reliance and socialism, warning against foreign investment as a form of imperialism. Advanced nations invested in the developing world largely to extract oil, coffee, bananas and other resources but created few new jobs or industries. Developing nations, trying to lessen their reliance on manufactured imports, tried to bolster domestic industries for the home market. But these protected businesses were often inefficient and the local markets too small to sustain them.

From Wigs to Cars

Then the Four Tigers—Hong Kong, Singapore, South Korea and Taiwan—began to roar. They made apparel, toys, shoes and, at least in South Korea's case, wigs and false teeth, mostly for export. Within a generation, their national incomes climbed from about 10 percent to 40 percent of American incomes. Singapore welcomed foreign plant owners while South Korea shunned them, building industrial conglomerates of its own. But the first stage of development had one constant. "It's always sweatshops," Mr. Krugman said.

These same nations now export cars and computers, and the economists have revised their views of sweatshops. "The overwhelming mainstream view among economists is that the growth of this kind of employment is tremendous good news for the world's poor," Mr. Krugman said.

Unlike the corporate apologists, economists make no attempt to prettify the sweatshop picture. Mr. Krugman, who writes a column for Slate magazine called "The Dismal Scientist," describes sweatshop owners as "soulless multinationals and rapacious local entrepreneurs, whose only concern was to take advantage of the profit opportunities offered by cheap labor." But even in a nation as corrupt as Indonesia, he says, industrialization has reduced the portion of malnourished children from more than half in 1975 to a third today.

In judging the issue of child labor also, Mr. Krugman is a pragmatist, asking what else is available. It often isn't education. In India, for example, destitute parents sometimes sell their children to Persian Gulf begging syndicates whose bosses mutilate them for a higher take, he says. "If that is the alternative, it is not so easy to say that children should not be working in factories," Mr. Krugman said.

Not that most economists argue for sweatshops at home. The United States, they say, can afford to set much higher labor standards than poor countries—though Europe's are so high, some say, that high unemployment results.

Labor leaders and politicians who challenge sweatshops abroad say that they harm American workers as well, stealing jobs and lowering wages—a point that some economists dispute. "It is especially galling when American workers lose jobs to places where workers are really being exploited," said Mark Levinson, chief economist at the Union of Needletrades, Industrial and Textile Employees, who argues for trade sanctions to enforce global labor rules.

Yet when corporations voluntarily cut their ties to sweatshops, the victims can be the very same people sweatshop opponents say they want to help. In Honduras, where the legal working age is 14, girls toiled 75 hours a week for the 31-cent hourly minimum to make the Kathie Lee Gifford clothing line for Wal-Mart. When Wal-Mart canceled its contract, the girls lost their jobs and blamed Mrs. Gifford.

No Jobs in Practice

Mr. Krugman blames American self-righteousness or guilt over Indonesian women and children sewing sneakers at 60 cents an hour. "A policy of good jobs in principle, but no jobs in practice, might assuage our consciences," he said, "but it is no favor to its alleged beneficiaries."

POSTSCRIPT

Are Sweatshops Necessarily Evil?

As the troubles now afflicting Asia remind us, no economic powerhouse is forever. Before the current crumbling of Asian economies, Americans had watched in fascination while the once-invulnerable Japan went through a "miniature U.S. history": workers clamoring for better conditions, people spending more on consumer goods and saving less, and wages rising steadily. Then, of course, manufacture shifted to Thailand and other places where labor was very inexpensive.

An article by Barry Bearak entitled "Lives Held Cheap in Bangladesh Sweatshops," *The New York Times* (April 15, 2001) demonstrates the dilemma faced when making efforts to stop the use of underage labor in sweatshops. After a bad fire in a factory in Bangladesh that killed many of the children working there, a powerful outcry emerged from the United States and other countries to boycott all goods produced from child labor. The factory in Bangladesh responded by firing all underage workers. However, since the children in many cases were the sole income earners for their families, they were forced to turn to selling tobacco and prostitution to earn money.

What are the true consequences of closing down sweatshops in developing countries? Is it worse to close them or to keep them open? This is an issue that is highly debated.

Suggested Readings

"Watching the Sweatshops," *The New York Times* (August 20, 1997).

David R. Henderson, "The Case for Sweatshops," *Fortune* (October 28, 1996), pp. 48–52.

Mark Henricks, "Labor Says No Sweat," *Apparel Industry Magazine* (January 1996), pp. 68–70.

James Mamarella, "Decent Labor Standards Should Be the Standard," *Discount Store News* (April 1, 1996), p. 2.

Jack A. Raisner, "Using the 'Ethical Environment' Paradigm to Teach Business Ethics: The Case of the Maquiladoras," *Journal of Business Ethics* (September 1997), pp. 1331–1346.

ISSUE 17

Should Patenting Life Be Forbidden?

YES: Jeremy Rifkin, from "Should We Patent Life?" *Business Ethics* (March/April 1998)

NO: William Domnarski, from "Dire New World," *Intellectual Property Magazine* (January 1999)

ISSUE SUMMARY

YES: Jeremy Rifkin, president of the Foundation on Economic Trends, fears that genetic engineering extends human power over the rest of nature in ways that are unprecedented and whose consequences cannot be known. He urges a halt to such research, especially research whose aim is profit for the company that "owns" the results.

NO: William Domnarski, an intellectual property lawyer, finds the patenting of genes or genetic discoveries no different than patenting any other ideas. The purpose of patents is to reward and encourage useful invention, he argues, and there is no doubt that the modifications we introduce to the genetic material of plants and animals are useful to feed a starving world.

There is an apocryphal story that at a meeting of the gentlemanly Scientific Society of the seventeenth century, one of the members proposed a toast to the next scientific discovery, to which another of the members immediately added a fervent wish "that it may be of no use to anyone." The story illustrates well the ambivalence of scientific research that informs this issue.

Why do we seek knowledge? Some answer this question by saying that the Lord created our minds, and a fascinating world to study, and that in seeking wisdom and insight into the ways of Nature we honor our creator and raise our minds closer to the Divine mind.

But Francis Bacon, an early seventeenth-century philosopher of science, suggested another reason: "The end of our foundation is the knowledge of causes, and secret motions of things; and the enlarging of the bounds of human empire, to the effecting of all things possible." Knowledge is power, and the reason we pursue knowledge, some argue, is to increase the power of human beings. It is the mission of science to expand the domain of human understanding precisely so that in knowing all things, we might do all things.

Shall we pursue knowledge of the genetic factors in animal and plant life, including knowledge of the human genome? As one reflects on the problem, Monsanto Inc. is going forward with genetically engineered agricultural plant germ lines for export. Europe has firmly said that no genetically modified organisms (GMOs) shall appear on its tables, and in many places farmers have refused to grow them. Already a controversy has exploded in the grocery market: may GMOs grown without fertilizers or pesticides be labeled "organic"? Enthusiasts point out that GMOs, because they are better plants, often do not need any fertilizers or pesticides, so that should make organic farmers and their customers very happy. Critics point out that the reason they do not need chemical fertilizers or pesticides is that they have the bug repellent and who knows what other chemicals engineered into their skins. For example, Monsanto came up with a "terminator gene," a genetic modification that sets only sterile seeds and cannot naturally reproduce. Why do this? Monsanto explained that it did not want genetically inserted bug repellent spreading to the natural weeds, which would make it harder to keep them under control; opponents of Monsanto suggested that the technique made it impossible for farmers to collect and set their own seed from the harvest, so ensuring that the farmers would have to come back to Monsanto year after year for refills.

Why is Monsanto investing so much time and money to develop new lines of plants? One obvious reason is to make money. But if the company is going to make money, there have to be patents on the new seeds it develops, or they will immediately be outflanked and undersold by similar firms, which can duplicate their seeds without all of the expensive investment. So patents are necessary in order to protect the enterprise. Meanwhile, Monsanto maintains that all it wants to do is provide more food for a hungry world, a goal that we can only applaud, and that it needs the protection of patents to keep up the good work.

Where is technology taking us in this case? Can we separate out the genuine altruism from the scientific curiosity and from the selfish desire to make a very large amount of money very quickly?

As you read the following selections, bear in mind that you are looking at a real cutting-edge issue. For most of biotechnology, no one knows the empirical consequences 10 years down the road—that is how recent the science is. Should we calculate costs versus benefits, as far as they may be known? Or, should we adopt the precautionary principle and put off all introduction of this technology? Shall we allow the entrepreneur inventor to reap the fortunes associated with a good patent or two on the most recent developments? Or, shall we decide that life in all its forms is sacred and not open to private claim or profit?

Jeremy Rifkin

Should We Patent Life?

A handful of companies are engaged in a race to patent all 100,000 human genes. In less than a decade, the race will be over. The genetic legacy of our species will be held in the form of private intellectual property. The genes inside your cells will belong not to you, but to global corporations. Welcome to the world of the biotech revolution.

While the 20th century was shaped by breakthroughs in physics and chemistry, the 21st century will belong to the biological sciences. Scientists are deciphering the genetic code, unlocking the mystery of millions of years of evolution. Global life science companies, in turn, are beginning to exploit these new advances. The raw resources of the new economic epoch are genes—already being used in businesses ranging from agriculture and bioremediation to energy and pharmaceuticals.

By 2025, we may be living in a world remade by a revolution unmatched in history. The biotech revolution raises unprecedented ethical questions we've barely begun to discuss. Will the artificial creation of cloned and transgenic animals mean the end of nature and the substitution of a bio-industrial world? Will the release of genetically engineered life forms into the biosphere cause catastrophic genetic pollution? What will it mean to live in a world where babies are customized in the womb—and where people are stereotyped and discriminated against on the basis of their genotype? What risks do we take in attempting to design more "perfect" human beings?

At the heart of this new commercial revolution is a chilling question of great ethical impact, whose resolution will affect civilization for centuries to come: *Should we patent life?* The practice has already gotten a green light, through a controversial Supreme Court decision and a subsequent ruling by the Patent and Trademark Office in the 1980s. But if the question were put directly to the American people, would they agree? If you alter one gene in a chimpanzee, does that make the animal a human "invention"? If you isolate the gene for breast cancer, does that give you the right to "own" it? Should a handful of global corporations be allowed to patent all human genes?

On the eve of the Biotech Century, we do still have an opportunity to raise ethical issues like these—although the window is rapidly closing.

From Jeremy Rifkin, "Should We Patent Life?" *Business Ethics* (March/April 1998), pp. 15–17. Copyright © 1998 by *Business Ethics*. Reprinted by permission of *Business Ethics*, P.O. Box 8439, Minneapolis, MN 55408.

We've only completed the first decade of a revolution that may span several centuries. But already there are 1,400 biotech companies in the U.S., with a total of nearly $13 billion in annual revenues and more than 100,000 employees. Development is proceeding in an astonishing number of areas:

At Harvard University, scientists have grown human bladders and kidneys in laboratory jars. Monsanto hopes to have a plastic-producing plant on the market by the year 2003—following up on the work of Chris Sommerville at the Carnegie Institution of Washington, who inserted a plastic-making gene into a mustard plant. Another biotech company, the Institute of Genomic Research, has successfully sequenced a microbe that can absorb large amounts of radioactivity and be used to dispose of deadly radioactive waste. The first genetically engineered insect, a predator mite, was released in 1996 by researchers at the University of Florida, who hope it will eat other mites that damage strawberries and similar crops.

At the University of Wisconsin, scientists have genetically altered brooding turkey hens to increase their productivity, by eliminating the "brooding" instinct: the desire to sit on and hatch eggs. Other researchers are experimenting with the creation of sterile salmon who will not have the suicidal urge to spawn, but will remain in the open sea, to be commercially harvested. Michigan State University scientists say that by breaking the spawning cycle of chinook salmon, they can produce seventy-pound salmon, compared to less than eighteen pounds for a fish returning to spawn. In short, the mothering instinct and the mating instinct are being bred out of animals.

With genetic engineering, humanity is extending its reach over the forces of nature far beyond the scope of any previous technology—with the possible exception of the nuclear bomb. At the same time, corporations are assuming ownership and control over the hereditary blueprints of life itself. Can any reasonable person believe such power is without risk?

❧◉❧

Genes are the "green gold" of the biotech century, and companies that control them will exercise tremendous power over the world economy. Multinational corporations are already scouting the continents in search of this new precious resource, hoping to locate microbes, plants, animals, and humans with rare genetic traits that might have future market potential. Having located the desired traits, biotech companies are modifying them and seeking patent protection for their new "inventions."

The worldwide race to patent the gene pool is the culmination of a 500-year-odyssey to enclose the ecosystems of the Earth. That journey began in feudal England in the 1500s, with the passage of the great "enclosure acts," which privatized the village commons—transforming the land from a community trust to private real estate. Today, virtually every square foot of landmass on the planet is under private ownership or government control.

But enclosure of the land was just the beginning. Today, the ocean's coastal waters are commercially leased, the air has been converted into commercial airline corridors, and even the electromagnetic spectrum is considered commercial property—leased for use by radio, TV, and telephone companies. Now the most intimate commons of all—the gene pool—is being enclosed and reduced to private commercial property.

The enclosure of the genetic commons began in 1971, when an Indian microbiologist and General Electric employee, Ananda Chakrabarty, applied to the U.S. Patents and Trademark Office (PTO) for a patent on a genetically engineered microorganism designed to consume oil spills. The PTO rejected the request, arguing that living things are not patentable. The case was appealed all the way to the Supreme Court, which in 1980—by a slim margin of five to four —ruled in favor of Chakrabarty. Speaking for the majority, Chief Justice Warren Burger argued that "the relevant distinction was not between living and inanimate things," but whether or not Chakrabarty's microbe was a "human-made invention."

In the aftermath of that historic decision, bioengineering technology shed its pristine academic garb and bounded into the marketplace. On Oct. 13, 1980 —just months after the court's ruling—Genentech publicly offered one million shares of stock at $35 per share. By the time the trading bell had rung that first day, the stock was selling at over $500 per share. And Genentech had yet to introduce a single product.

Chemical, pharmaceutical, argribusiness, and biotech startups everywhere sped up their research—mindful that the granting of patent protection meant the possibility of harnessing the genetic commons for vast commercial gain. Some observers, however, were not so enthused. Ethicist Leon Kass asked:

> "What is the principled limit to this beginning extension of the domain of private ownership and dominion over living nature . . . ? The principle used in Chakrabarty says that there is nothing in the nature of being, not even in the patentor himself, that makes him immune to being patented."

While the Supreme Court decision lent an air of legal legitimacy to the emerging biotech industry, a Patent Office decision in 1987 opened the floodgates. In a complete about-face, the PTO ruled that all genetically engineered multicellular living organisms—including animals—are potentially patentable. The Commissioner of Patents and Trademarks at the time, Donald J. Quigg, attempted to calm a shocked public by asserting that the decision covered every creature except human beings—because the Thirteenth Amendment to the Constitution forbids human slavery. On the other hand, human embryos and fetuses as well as human genes, tissues, and organs were now potentially patentable.

What makes the Supreme Court decision and Patent Office ruling suspect, from a legal point of view, is that they defy previous patent rulings that say one cannot claim a "discovery of nature" as an invention. No one would suggest that scientists who isolated, classified, and described the properties of chemical elements in the periodic table—such as oxygen and helium—ought to be granted a patent on them. Yet someone who isolates and classifies the properties of human genes can patent them.

The European Patent Office, for example, awarded a patent to the U.S. company Biocyte, giving it ownership of all human blood cells which have come from the umbilical cord of a newborn child and are being used for any therapeutic purposes. The patent is so broad that it allows this one company to refuse the use of any blood cells from the umbilical cord to any individual unwilling to pay the patent fee. Blood cells from the umbilical cord are particularly important for marrow transplants, making it a valuable commercial asset. It should be emphasized that this patent was awarded simply because Biocyte was able to isolate the blood cells and deep-freeze them. The company made no change in the blood itself.

A similarly broad patent was awarded to Systemix Inc. of Palo Alto, Calif., by the U.S. Patent Office, covering all human bone marrow stem cells. This extraordinary patent on a human body part was awarded despite the fact that Systemix had done nothing whatsoever to alter or engineer the cells. Dr. Peter Quisenberry, the medical affairs vice chairman of the Leukemia Society of America, quipped, "Where do you draw the line? Can you patent a hand?"

❦

The life patents race is gearing up in the wake of government and commercial efforts to map the approximately 100,000 human genes that make up the human genome—a project with enormous commercial potential. As soon as a gene is tagged its "discoverer" is likely to apply for a patent, often before knowing the function of the gene. In 1991, J. Craig Venter, then head of the National Institute of Health Genome Mapping Research Team, resigned his government post to head up a genomics company funded with more than $70 million in venture capital. At the same time, Venter and his colleagues filed for patents on more than 2,000 human brain genes. Many researchers on the Human Genome Project were shocked and angry, charging Venter with attempting to profit off research paid for by American taxpayers.

Nobel laureate James Watson, co-discoverer of the DNA double helix, called the Venter patent claims "sheer lunacy." Still, it's likely that within less than ten years, all 100,000 or so genes that comprise the genetic legacy of our species will be patented—making them the exclusive intellectual property of global corporations.

The patenting of life is creating a firestorm of controversy. Several years ago, an Alaskan businessman named John Moore found his own body parts had been patented, without his knowledge, by the University of California at Los Angeles (UCLA), and licensed to the Sandoz Pharmaceutical Corp. Moore had been diagnosed with a rare cancer and underwent treatment at UCLA. A researcher there discovered that Moore's spleen tissue produced a blood protein that facilitates the growth of white blood cells valuable as anti-cancer agents. The university created a cell line from Moore's spleen tissue and obtained a patent on the "invention." The cell line is estimated to be worth more than $3 billion.

Moore subsequently sued, claiming a property right over his own tissue. But in 1990, the California Supreme Court ruled against him, saying Moore had no such ownership right. Human body parts, the court argued, could not be bartered as a commodity in the marketplace.

The irony of the decision was captured by Judge Broussard, in his dissenting opinion. The ruling "does *not* mean that body parts may not be bought or sold," he wrote. "[T]he majority's holding simply bars *plantiff*, the source of the cells, from obtaining the benefit of the cell's value, but permits *defendants*, who allegedly obtained the cells from plaintiff by improper means, to retain and exploit the full economic value of their ill-gotten gains."

꒰◦꒱

A battle of historic proportions has also emerged between the high-technology nations of the North and the developing nations of the South, over ownership of the planet's genetic treasures. Some Third World leaders say the North is attempting to seize the biological commons, most of which is in the rich tropical regions of the Southern Hemisphere, and that their nations should be compensated for use of genetic resources. Corporate and governmental leaders in the North maintain that the genes increase in value only when manipulated using sophisticated gene-splicing techniques, so there's no obligation to compensate the South.

To ease growing tensions, a number of companies have proposed sharing a portion of their gains. Merck & Co., the pharmaceutical giant (often considered a leader in social responsibility), entered into an agreement recently with a research organization in Costa Rica, the National Biodiversity Institute, to pay the organization a paltry $1 million to secure the group's plant, microorganism, and insect samples. Critics liken the deal to European settlers giving American Indians trinkets in return for the island of Manhattan. The recipient organization, on the other hand, is granting a right to bio-prospect on land it has no historic claim to in the first place—while indigenous peoples are locked out of the agreement.

Such agreements are beginning to meet with resistance from countries and non-governmental organizations (NGOs) in the Southern Hemisphere. They claim that what Northern companies are calling "discoveries" are really the pirating of the indigenous knowledge of native peoples and cultures. To defuse opposition, biotech corporations are seeking to impose a uniform intellectual property regime worldwide. And they've gone a long way toward achieving that with the passage of the Trade Related Aspects of Intellectual Property Agreements (TRIPS) at the Uruguay Round of the General Agreement on Tariffs and Trade (GATT). Sculpted by companies like Bristol Myers, Merck, Pfizer, Dupont, and Monsanto, the TRIPS agreement makes no allowance for indigenous knowledge, and grants companies free access to genetic material from around the world.

Suman Sahai, director of the Gene Campaign—an NGO in New Delhi—makes the point, "God didn't give us 'rice' or 'wheat' or 'potato.'" These were once wild plants that were domesticated over eons of time and patiently bred by generations of farmers. Sahai asks, "Who did all of that work?" Groups like his argue that Southern countries should be compensated for their contribution to biotech.

Still others take a third position: that neither corporations nor indigenous peoples should claim ownership, because the gene pool ought not to be for sale, at any price. It should remain an open commons and continue to be used freely by present and future generations. They cite precedent in the recent historic decision by the nations of the world to maintain the continent of Antarctica as a global commons free from commercial exploitation.

· ✿ ·

The idea of private companies laying claim to human genes as their exclusive intellectual property has resulted in growing protests worldwide. In May of 1994, a coalition of hundreds of women's organizations from more than forty nations announced opposition to Myriad Genetics's attempt to patent the gene that causes breast cancer in some women. The coalition was assembled by The Foundation on Economic Trends. While the women did not oppose the screening test Myriad developed, they opposed the claim to the gene itself. They argued that the breast cancer gene was a product of nature and not a human invention, and should not be patentable. Myriad's exclusive rights to such a gene could make screening more expensive, and might impede research by making access to the gene too expensive.

The central question in these cases—Can you patent life?—is one of the most important issues ever to face the human family. Life patenting strikes at the core of our beliefs about the very nature of life and whether it is to be conceived as having sacred and intrinsic value, or merely utility value. Surely such a fundamental question deserves to be widely discussed by the public before such patents become a ubiquitous part of our daily lives.

The biotech revolution will force each of us to put a mirror to our most deeply held values, making us ponder the ultimate question of the purpose and meaning of existence. This may turn out to be its most important contribution. The rest is up to us.

Dire New World

With an authorial voice that only a conspiracy maven such as Oliver Stone could love, Jeremy Rifkin is back, this time to warn us about the dangers inherent in our idea of so-called "progress," as Rifkin puts it.

Rifkin—the president of the Foundation of Economic Trends and the author of many books on economic trends relating to science, technology, and culture—is especially worried about the implications of the biotech century that will not wait two years to begin. It's here now, and unless we heed Rifkin's warnings and keep ourselves from temptation by agreeing with him that progress is too fraught for mischief to be acceptable, we'll end up in a genetically polluted world in which genetic discrimination reigns—though you will be able to go down to your local laboratory when the time comes to be fitted with that new vital organ you've had cloned in the expectation that you might need it.

The advances in genetic engineering in medicine—to say nothing of the advances in plant genetics—have been staggering. Now knowing most of the code, we can identify and even act on various types of diseases and disabilities before birth. We have added a range of new treatments in which genetically engineered cells are introduced into the body to take hold and combat disease. Alzheimer's disease and Parkinson's disease are not on the verge of being conquered, but we are closer to victory than ever because of genetic research.

But where some see the advances that genetic engineering has produced, Rifkin sees a new wave of eugenic zealots eager to use our genetic makeup as even more revealing of our true nature than the SAT.

Ripped From the Headlines

Rifkin relies primarily on national news magazines and newspapers to sketch both the developments in and the predictions for various aspects of this scientific revolution, and, in that sense, his story is one ripped from the headlines. His persistent complaint is that journalists fail to present balanced coverage because of a delight in describing the often dazzling possible uses of the technology at issue. What's left out, he argues, are the myriad ethical issues that coalesce around the question of whether progress, by itself, is a good thing.

From William Domnarski, "Dire New World," *Intellectual Property Magazine* (January 1999). Copyright © 1999 by NLP IP Company. Reprinted by permission of American Lawyer Media.

Trying to interpret the scientific breakthroughs that are changing the way we think of both ourselves as individuals and the dominant species on the planet, Rifkin details seven strands of what he calls the new operational matrix of the biotech century. It's not the evil that men do that outlives them; it's the mischief that computers and genetic research can get us into when they are spliced together that we need to worry about.

Four strands of the biotech century's matrix encompass recombinant DNA techniques; the wholesale reseeding of the planet with genetically enhanced and devised plants; gene mapping; and computers that can probe and manage the vast genetic resources of our bodies and our planet. The other strands include the ideological, philosophical, and cultural structures supporting the new research and its application.

In Rifkin's view, the courts are primarily to blame for this state of affairs because they have allowed for the patenting of genetically altered cells, thus creating a slippery slope that we will be unable to negotiate. Going further, however, he argues that a new cultural context has emerged that favors the new biotechnologies. Underpinning all of this is a new cosmological narrative that sees evolution as an improvement in information processing, rather than as a random process of selection winnowing its way through passive natural elements.

They Know Not What They Do

Rifkin complains that the scientists know not what they do, unwittingly creating Frankensteins at every turn. He objects that their sheer ability to do something seems to them justification enough to just do it. They are too little concerned with the collateral effects of genetic engineering.

It's clear that Rifkin is writing for an audience already persuaded by his general thesis and by his credentials as a prophet of doom. And he wants us to know that he was right in all the predictions on genetic engineering that he began making 20 years ago. But the world still hasn't caught on to the issue as he has framed it—that progress is generally bad—so he's back for more hectoring. What Rifkin does not want to accept is that as a culture we desire and embrace progress.

The press does not seem guilty of the one-sided reporting that Rifkin ascribes to it. Recently, for example, *The New York Times* featured two reports on a new technique in genetic engineering that allows scientists to take embryonic human stem cells before they have distinguished themselves as the type of cell they will be, such as a brain cell or heart cell; the technique then coaxes those cells to morph into the type of cell that is needed. The result is that heart cells can be grown and then used to heal the heart when it fails—all rather heady—or should I say hearty—stuff.

The use of such new cell technology has been condemned by some because it comes perilously close to infringing on our notion of what constitutes an individual. As opponents see it, there is a great difference between using stem cells from miscarried fetuses, which a spokesperson for the Catholic

Church finds acceptable, and using cells derived from pre-implantation embryos that were created in fertility clinics. To use the latter cells is to use humans for research, the opponents stress.

Annoying Disingenuousness

One senses, however, that Rifkin would not have been satisfied with the coverage that the ethical issues received, because the heart of the story emphasizes that scientists are all but dancing with excitement over this new technology. There is, at the core of Rifkin's book, an annoying disingenuousness. He poses himself in a neutral posture that pretends to provide us with the information we need to decide if this biotech century is for us; at the same time, Rifkin urges us to think that the problems created by the new technologies outweigh the possible benefits.

Two lines of reasoning in particular show how, despite his good intentions, Rifkin seems out of touch with reality, at least as it is defined by law. The first is the supposed exploitation of indigenous peoples by agribusiness and pharmaceutical companies that search the world, especially the world in the southern hemisphere, for new plants that yield new drugs or new strains of foodstuffs. The indigenous peoples, the argument goes, have done all the work in cultivating the plants over time, which makes the genetic manipulations of the big companies a negligible contribution at best, certainly not one entitling them to patent protection and profits. What Rifkin does not want to acknowledge is that patents are hard earned and necessary for research to continue. Rifkin wants a world that does not privilege the capacity of science to make productive what otherwise wouldn't be. His is a politically correct world, blissfully ignorant of law's contribution to society.

The second and perhaps more revealing line of misguided reasoning is Rifkin's unwillingness to accept patent law for what it is. The Supreme Court has recognized that the distinction is not between living and inanimate things, but between products of nature, whether living or not, and human-made inventions. Rifkin's argument is that scientists cannot be said to create anything patentable because the life they manipulate was already there. That is a narrow and misguided view of both the law and of what scientists do. The law sides with progress; Rifkin sides against it. What Rifkin cannot accept is what Justice William O. Douglas wrote in *The Great A&P Tea Co. v. Supermarket Corp.*, 340 U.S. 147 (1950)—30 years before the celebrated oil-eating bacteria case of 1980: That the inventions that most benefit mankind are those that "push back the frontiers of chemistry, physics and the like."

As his book makes all too clear, Rifkin does not want to explore the frontier. He wants to circle the wagons and hold off, through the pouting in his book, that which cannot be held back. Those concerned with the ethical implications of genetic research are with us and are heard. That we as a society want to search the frontier should not be dismissed, as Rifkin so keenly wants to dismiss them, as ignorant, selfish or misguided.

POSTSCRIPT

Should Patenting Life Be Forbidden?

In general, the United States has adopted the "cost-benefit approach" to problems with new products. If Americans cannot foresee the consequences of a new technology, they tend to make educated guesses about the benefits of all kinds and the probable costs, and balance the one against the other. Engineered seeds seem to have the potential to increase crop yields, cut labor costs, and not, inconsequentially, lower the use of fertilizers and pesticides. Those are benefits. Costs may be negligible. Is this a good argument for going ahead with the new life forms and allowing the companies the patents they need to make them profitable?

In Europe, on the other hand, the custom is to use the "precautionary approach" toward new technology. Europe's strategy is if the costs are unknown, then try the seeds in a small controlled area for a long time and see what develops. Only after the seeds are proven safe over generations will Europeans make them publicly available. Which approach do you think is the best for such new technologies?

Suggested Readings

Lester R. Brown, "Struggling to Raise Cropland Productivity," *State of the World 1998* (W. W. Norton, 1998).

Charles C. Mann, "The Brave New World of Science and Business," *Foreign Policy* (December 1998).

Ho Mae-Wan, *Genetic Engineering: Dream or Nightmare?* (Gateways Books, 1998).

G. Tyler Miller, *Living in the Environment,* 11th ed. (Brooks/Cole Publishing, 2000).

FAQs About Free-Market Environmentalism

Sponsored by the Thoreau Institute, this site lists and answers frequently asked questions about free-market environmentalism. It is the institute's position that a free-market system can solve many environmental problems better than more government regulation can.

http://ti.org/faqs.html

Pennsylvania Department of Environmental Protection

This home page of the Pennsylvania Department of Environmental Protection monitors environmental responsibility.

http://www.dep.state.pa.us

Rainforest Facts

This Rainforest Facts site contains statistics on the rain forest as well as information on rain forest products, worldwide rain forest protection efforts, the tropical timber industry, and more.

http://www.pbs.org/tal/costa_rica/rainfacts.html

PART 6

Environmental Policy and Corporate Responsibility

T *he dilemmas that surround the preservation of the environment are the most serious that this generation will have to face. We are accustomed to letting business enterprise lead us into any area that promises jobs, goods for the market, new tax bases, and general prosperity. However, those days are coming to an end. The environment is suffering badly and may cease to support us before the next century is over. Business will have to suffer restrictions; but with some creative thinking, business may be the catalyst that will lead to new solutions. The final debates in this book consider both possibilities.*

- Do Environmental Restrictions Violate Basic Economic Freedoms?

- Can Rain Forest Products Save the Tropical Rain Forest?

ISSUE 18

Do Environmental Restrictions Violate Basic Economic Freedoms?

YES: John Shanahan, from "Environment," in Stuart M. Butler and Kim R. Holmes, eds., *Issues '96: The Candidate's Briefing Book* (Heritage Foundation, 1996)

NO: Paul R. Ehrlich and Anne H. Ehrlich, from "Brownlash: The New Environmental Anti-Science," *The Humanist* (November/ December 1996)

ISSUE SUMMARY

YES: John Shanahan, vice president of the Alexis de Tocqueville Institution in Arlington, Virginia, argues that many government environmental policies are unreasonable and infringe on basic economic freedoms. He concedes that environmental problems exist but denies that there is any environmental "crisis."

NO: Environmental scientists Paul R. Ehrlich and Anne H. Ehrlich, whose 1974 book *The End of Affluence* first outlined the consequences of environmental mismanagement, contend that many objections to environmental protections are self-serving and based on bad or misused science.

If you had to choose, which would you think is more important: profitability in the corporation; yielding return on investment to the shareholder; good products reliably supplied for the customer; a tax base for the public sector; jobs for the workers; and, in short, the fundamentals of American life? Or, would you choose the protection of the natural environment and our fragile ecosystems for the generations to follow us? This is not an easy choice to make, and it is a choice that confronts governments on a daily basis.

Take pesticides, for example. They form a profitable part of the chemicals manufacturing industry all by themselves, precisely because they greatly increase agricultural production wherever they are used. Pesticides have been the difference between crop success and crop failure. Pesticide use means wealth for the shareholders of chemical companies, jobs for the companies' workers, income for the farmers, and food for the people of the world. The use of pesticides, among other developments of the twentieth century agricultural revolution, has made it possible for more than enough food to be grown for the country with a fraction of the labor that used to be required by agriculture.

On the other hand, as Rachel Carson argued in her 1962 book *Silent Spring* (Houghton Mifflin), pesticides don't know enough to poison only crop-eating insects; they poison every living thing that consumes them. They poison the insects that eat the crops, the predator insects that used to keep the crop-eaters' numbers under control, the birds that eat the insects that fall to earth, the fish that eat the insects that land in the water, and the people who eat the fish. When pesticides poison the birds, their eggs are no longer viable, and the species starts to die out. Which is more important: the present profits of the industry and the current low prices in the vegetable aisle or the future of the birds? What do you say? What might your grandchildren say?

Since the 1960s, successive administrations in America have attempted, with more or less enthusiasm, to adopt regulations that will limit economic freedoms in order to protect the environment. As our knowledge of ecology has increased, so have the regulations, and predictably, so have the objections to them. It seems that every plant manager, every developer, and even every homeowner bump into environmental regulations every time they turn around or try to get something done to improve the value of their property or enterprise. Given that America was founded on freedom, all this regulation rankles many people.

Are there ways that humans can live harmoniously with nature, profiting from relationships that mimic those prior to the industrial revolution? The Rocky Mountain Institute has published a powerful argument that such relationships are entirely possible—and even more economical than the business arrangements we have now. See *Natural Capitalism,* by Amory Lovins, Hunter Lovins, and Paul Hawken (Rocky Mountain Institute, 1999).

Ask yourself, as you read the following selections, which orientation toward the environment is likely to result in a stronger world in the next generation. John Shanahan states that the environment has been improving overall and that the economy will suffer as a result of overly stringent environmental restrictions. Paul R. Ehrlich and Anne H. Ehrlich insist that the environmental crisis is very real and that the "brownlash" opponents of environmentalism are peddling worthless ideology in the face of the facts.

John Shanahan  **YES**

Environment

The Issues

Americans want a clean, healthy environment. They also want a strong economy. But environmental protection is enormously expensive, costs jobs, and stifles economic opportunity. On the other hand, before government stepped in, robust economic activity such as manufacturing led to a deteriorating and unhealthy environment. The challenge is how to achieve both a strong economy and a healthy environment. After all, what Americans actually want is a high overall quality of life.

Three decades ago, as people perceived that their quality of life was beginning to deteriorate, they began to support aggressive policies to reduce pollution. These policies frequently failed to live up to their sponsors' claims; they also became increasingly and unnecessarily expensive. But the environment did improve, especially in the early years. Now, however, Americans are becoming aware that many of these policies are unreasonable and that, even when they work, they result only in small improvements at a heavy cost in jobs and freedom. Americans also are beginning to recognize that there often is no sound scientific basis for assertions of environmental harm or risk to the public. The pendulum finally has begun to swing the other way.

Conservatives, like Americans generally, have no wish to return to the days of black smoke billowing out of smokestacks. But they do believe common sense can be brought to bear in dealing with the environment: that it is possible to protect the environment without sacrificing the freedoms for which America stands. Conservative candidates and legislators therefore should stress the following themes:

Examples of regulatory abuse   It is important to show that "good intentions" often are accompanied by oppressive, senseless regulations.

An ethic of conservation   Candidates need to explain that conserving or efficiently using natural resources is not in dispute. The debate is over how best to do this: through markets or through government controls.

From John Shanahan, "Environment," in Stuart M. Butler and Kim R. Holmes, eds., *Issues '96: The Candidate's Briefing Book* (Heritage Foundation, 1996). Copyright © 1996 by The Heritage Foundation. Reprinted by permission. Notes omitted.

Economic freedom   Candidates need to point out that many government "solutions" to environment problems conflict with basic economic freedoms.

Property-based solutions   Candidates need to explain that environmental objectives can be achieved best not by issuing thousands of pages of rules that people will try to circumvent, but by capitalizing on the incentives associated with owning property.

Sound science   Candidates need to argue that we need policies based on sound science, not "tabloid science."

Priority setting   Candidates must explain that not all problems are of the same importance or urgency, and that regulating all risks equally means fewer lives are saved for the dollars spent than would be saved if priorities were set.

The Facts

While pollution levels have fallen dramatically since 1970, most reductions were achieved early and at relatively low cost. From 1970 to 1990, total emission levels fell 33.8 percent. Over the same period, lead levels in the air fell 96.5 percent, and carbon monoxide levels in the air fell 40.7 percent. But reductions have slowed dramatically. . . .

Unworkable Regulations

Environmental regulation does more than just cost too much. Candidates also should use the growing litany of horror stories to demonstrate how ill-conceived environmental regulations, while delivering little benefit, lead to unintended consequences for businesses especially small businesses, which are disproportionately minority-owned and minority-run.

- Larry Mason's family owned a sawmill employing 40 workers in Beaver, Washington. In the mid-1980s, based on harvest assurances from the U.S. Forest Service and loan guarantees from the Small Business Administration, the family invested $1 million in its business. Then, says Mason, "in 1990, the spotted owl injunctions closed our mill, made my equipment worthless, and my expertise obsolete. The same government that encouraged me to take on business debt then took away my ability to repay."
- While the Clean Water Act (CWA) requires a waste treatment facility to submit a simple form stating that a fence restricts access by the public, the Resource Conservation and Recovery Act (RCRA) requires an additional 25 pages detailing the fence design, the location of the posts and gates, a cross section of the wire mesh, and other minor technical matters. RCRA is so wasteful that one plant, whose CWA permit application was only 17 pages long, had to file a seven-foot stack of supporting documents with its applications.

- Ronald Cahill, a disabled Wilmington, Massachusetts, dry cleaner, purchased expensive dry-cleaning equipment to comply with EPA regulations governing the use of trichlorotrifluoroethane (CFC-113). But the EPA levied a tax on all chlorofluorocarbons (CFCs), making CFC-113 hard to find and extremely expensive. In 1995, Cahill's business went under. Washington, says Cahill, "has put me out of business with excessive taxes and regulations."

Regulatory abuses like these usually are a direct result of the way government bureaucracies attack environmental problems. Typically, these agencies regulate without regard to the cost imposed on individuals and businesses. Yet it makes no sense to issue a regulation for which the burden far outweighs any benefit that might be conferred. In fact, it often is unclear whether there will be any benefit at all because the science on which many regulations are based is so poor.

Also, instead of setting realistic performance standards and giving businesses the freedom to develop innovative ways of meeting them, agencies typically rely on inflexible command-and-control regulations that, for example, specify what technologies companies must use. Since businesses differ in their operating structures, this one-size-fits-all approach rarely leads to cost-effective solutions compared to more flexible and dependable performance standards. Moreover, by eliminating the incentive for companies to seek out these cost-effective solutions, it stifles innovative technologies or techniques that reduce costs. In the end, of course, the consumer is the one who pays.

Perhaps the most troublesome aspect of current environmental policy is the fact that bureaucrats and liberal lawmakers generally consider regulation the only option. Creative solutions shown to be less expensive, more effective, and more respectful of human liberty are rejected out of hand. Instead of setting up a system of incentives to lure businesses into operating with environmental impact in mind, the system relies on punishment regardless of whether this accomplishes the desired goal or creates unintended consequences.

Rejecting Property Rights

Regulations have become increasingly unfair. The Environmental Protection Agency (EPA), Department of the Interior (DOI), Army Corps of Engineers, and other federal agencies operate on the premise that property should be used to satisfy government's needs and objectives without regard to who owns the property or the financial burden imposed on them. It is this mentality that leads government reflexively to reject the creative solutions advanced by free-market advocates, including incentive-based approaches to protecting endangered species. By ignoring property rights, establishment environmentalists, bureaucrats, and liberal legislators also ignore the benefits to be derived from free trade and free markets.

The most unfair and burdensome hardship inflicted by government "regulatory takings" is that property owners are not compensated for their losses. For instance, if an elderly husband and wife spend a large portion of their retirement savings to buy land on which to build their dream home and that land subsequently is designated a wetland, they lose the value of their property as well as their savings. They are stuck with property they cannot use and the government does nothing to reimburse them for their loss. Unfortunately, tales of financial hardship caused by government designation of land as wetland or endangered-species habitat have become common. For instance:

- Bill Stamp's family in Exeter, Rhode Island, has been blocked from farming or developing its 70 acres of land for 11 years, yet has been assessed taxes at rates determined by the land's industrial value up to $72,000 annually. As a result, this fifth-generation farm family may lose its life savings. The government, however, appears unmoved. Stamp relates what one Army Corps of Engineers enforcement officer told him: "We know that this is rape, pillage, and plunder of your farm, but this is our job."
- A small church in Waldorf, Maryland, was told by the Army Corps of Engineers that one-third of its land, on which it planned to build a parking lot, was a wetland and could not be used. Part of this so-called wetland is a bone-dry hillside which almost never collects water. Says Reverend Murray Southwell of the Freewill Baptists, "this obvious misinterpretation of wetland law made it necessary for us to purchase an additional lot [for $45,000, which] has been a heavy financial burden on this small missions church."
- Developer Buzz Oates wants to develop less than 4 percent of the Sutter Basin in Sacramento, California, where an estimated 1,000 giant garter snakes live. But the federal government mandated that he pay a "mitigation" fee of nearly $3.8 million for the 40 or fewer snakes he might disturb: $93,950 per snake. Says Oates, in an age of "depleted [fiscal] resources and deteriorating school infrastructure, this is a very tough pill to swallow."

Hundreds of such stories have surfaced over the past few years, and many analysts suspect that far more are never made public. According to Bob Adams, Project Director for Environmental and Regulatory Affairs at the National Center for Public Policy Research, "the stories we have compiled are just the tip of the iceberg, but many people are simply too scared to come forward or feel powerless against the government."

Ironically, federal agencies and the Clinton Administration argue that it would cost too much money to compensate landowners. Leon Panetta, then Director of the Office of Management and Budget, told the House Committee on Public Works and Transportation's Subcommittee on Water Resources and the Environment on May 26, 1994, that paying compensation for wetlands regulation would be "an unnecessary and unwise use of taxpayer dollars" and a drain on the federal budget.

Property owners counter that regulatory takings are a drain on the family budget. Nancie Marzulla, President of Defenders of Property Rights, points out that "what people don't realize is that these landowners typically are not wealthy and powerful corporations, but normal Americans schoolteachers and elderly couples whose lives are destroyed by stretched interpretations of a single environmental law." Moreover, the federal government already owns about one out of every three acres in the country (with even more owned by state and local governments). If the federal government can afford to maintain one-third of the nation's land, it should be able to pay landowners for regulatory confiscation of their property. If not, maybe it should consider selling the least ecologically sensitive land from its vast holdings to pay for the land it wants.

Lost Opportunities, Lost Lives

Ask the average American how much a human life is worth, and the answer likely will be that "no amount is too much." This is how Congress and federal agencies justify imposing sometimes staggering costs on businesses to reduce the risks of death by infinitesimal amounts. What policymakers fail to understand is that wasting resources in this way means not being able to use them in other ways that might well produce better results and save even more lives.

If lawmakers ever did consider which environmental policies actually save the most lives, they would scrap many existing rules, freeing up resources to be used in other ways. This commonsense approach would lead to regulation that is very different, in its scope and fundamental assumptions, from that which burdens America today....

What America Thinks About the Environment

When asked by the media, pollsters, or politicians, Americans routinely answer that they want a clean and healthy environment. Indeed, the majority of Americans consider themselves "environmentalists." This does not translate, however, into automatic acceptance of the environmental lobby's agenda. Conservative candidates need to make this clear to discourage voters from supporting policies they do not believe in simply because they are portrayed as "pro-environment."

The dichotomy in public opinion shows up in polling data. When respondents are asked general or theoretical questions that involve little personal sacrifice, or that do not identify those burdened, government intervention fares well. In one poll, for instance, 60 percent of respondents agreed that we must protect the environment even if it costs jobs in the community. In another, 72 percent of respondents said they would pay somewhat higher taxes if the money was used to protect the environment and prevent water and air pollution.

On the other hand, when respondents are asked questions that are more specific, that involve greater sacrifice, or that identify the people losing jobs, government intervention is less popular. When respondents are asked to pay much higher taxes to protect the environment, support drops by almost half. By the same token, only one-third would be willing to accept cuts in their standard of living. When asked to pick between spotted owls and Northwest workers who stand to lose their jobs because of efforts to protect the owls, respondents choose jobs by a margin of 3 to 2....

Perhaps the most refreshing change in attitudes in recent years is the recognition that the country can have economic growth and environmental protection simultaneously. Vice President Al Gore has made the point that economic growth and environmental protection are not incompatible. This is true, but only if America's environmental laws are structured correctly to encourage responsible behavior as part of the business decision-making process. Gore advocates stringent command-and-control regulations that are inconsistent with growth and lead to little real gains in environmental protection.

Whenever this question comes up, Americans must be told that the way to promote both environmental protection and economic growth is to allow them to work hand in hand. The government must stop regarding them as mutually exclusive and stop pitting economic freedom against the environment. Laws must be based on, and work with, a free market. Only then can Americans maximize their economic and environmental quality of life.

The Need for Common Sense

Given Americans' ambivalence on the question of environmental protection, it is all the more important for conservatives to approach the issue in a commonsense way. People must understand that environmental protection need not come at the expense of jobs, but will cost jobs if the socialist model of centralized control for protecting the environment is not set aside. It doesn't work. Rather, the country should adopt a reasonable, commonsense approach to environmental protection that is based on:

Freedom with responsibility   Conservatives traditionally have stressed economic growth while ignoring the importance of environmental problems. Thus, they have fought environmentalists step by step and have lost step by step. The reason, while unpleasant, is not complicated. Environmentalists have had the moral high ground, even though they typically have not provided the most beneficial solutions. In short, conservatives have been on the wrong side of an emotional issue.

Two lessons demonstrate why:

- **First,** leftists and the public at large understand that publicly owned goods, free of constraints on usage, will be depleted over time. Garrett Hardin, Professor Emeritus of Human Ecology at the University of California, in his seminal 1968 work *The Tragedy of the Commons* showed that when a good is publicly owned, or "owned" in common, no one has an incentive to conserve or to manage it. In fact, there is a perverse incentive to use the good inefficiently to deplete it. This fact is at the heart of most environmental problems, such as air and water pollution and species extinction.
- **Second,** if there are incentives to conserve resources, people will conserve out of self-interest. People with a vested interest in providing environmental benefits through property ownership or other positive incentives will provide them voluntarily, without coercion.

... "Freedom with responsibility for one's actions" should be the conservative message. Responsibility restrains wasteful behavior. Ironically, the old environmentalist slogan "Make the polluter pay" is consistent with this message. But when they say this, conservatives and liberals mean different things. As Al Cobb, then Director of Environment and Energy at the National Policy Forum, has said, "What the environmental lobby means by that phrase is that corporate polluters should be punished severely for any pollution whatsoever. What conservatives mean, however, is that polluters should bear the full cost of environmental degradation, but no more." At the same time, individuals and corporations also should be rewarded for conservation and other environmentally sound practices.

Conservation through property rights   The free market reflects the conservation ethic better than any command-and-control regulation from Washington. A free market can occur, however, only when private citizens engage in trade, and people can trade only what they own: some form of property. Thus, property is the cornerstone of a free market. If property rights are insecure or publicly owned, a market cannot function effectively. Some critics misleadingly call this "market failure," but it is really a failure to use markets and their main engine: property rights. As a result, both environmental protection and personal liberty suffer. A resource that is not owned will deteriorate or be depleted because neither protection of nor damage to that resource is part of the individual's usual decision-making process. Others, however, are still forced to bear the consequences.

Conservative candidates should concentrate on explaining the innovative ways in which property rights can be used to protect the environment. The most efficient method and the most protective of individual rights and freedoms is to enlist self-interest in the service of environmental protection.

Consider [two] examples of how the principle of property rights-based environmentalism works: ...

- In Scotland and England, the popularity of fishing has burgeoned in recent decades. Property rights to fishing sites have developed as the building block for markets to provide access to prime fishing spots. As a result, many private, voluntary associations have been formed to purchase fishing rights access. In Scotland, "virtually every inch of every major river and most minor ones is privately owned or leased...." Owners of fishing rights on various stretches of the rivers charge others for the right to fish. These rivers are not overfished because it is not in the owner's best interest to allow the fish population to be depleted. Because he wants to continue charging fishermen for the foreseeable future, the owner conserves his fish stock, allowing them to reproduce, and prevents pollution from entering his stretch of the river. If a municipality pollutes the water upstream, the owner of the fishing rights can sue for an injunction. Everyone wins, including fishermen looking for quality fishing with some privacy.

- One group's approach to wetland protection has shown the power of property rights to achieve environmental goals. Ducks Unlimited, a group consisting of hunters and non-hunters alike, is dedicated to enhancing duck populations. To do this, it has purchased property or conservation easements with privately raised funds. Unlike other groups (for example, the National Wildlife Federation) that began as organizations of hunters and outdoorsmen but later lost much of their original focus and joined forces with the more extreme elements of the environmental lobby, Ducks Unlimited still focuses on protecting duck habitat. In the last 58 years, it has raised and invested $750 million to conserve 17 million acres in Canada alone, an effort which benefits other wildlife as well as ducks. In 1994, it restored or created about 50,000 acres of wetlands. Since Ducks Unlimited itself pays for the habitat it protects, in many ways it embodies the essence of the conservative message: that the market should be allowed to determine the best and highest use of a good or resource in this case, duck habitat.

Unfortunately, property rights are under attack from the environmental lobby. The Fifth Amendment to the U.S. Constitution states, "nor shall private property be taken for public use, without just compensation," but this has been interpreted as protection primarily against the physical taking of property. Most infringements, however, involve federal decrees that deny owners the right to use their property as they see fit, for example, to continue farming. Since the courts have been unclear on the degree of protection property owners should have from such intrusions, legislative protection is needed.

Sound science, not tabloid science   Before issuing regulations to protect health, regulators should ask whether the science behind a measure justifies the often enormous expenditures involved. Unfortunately, however, the federal government often acts in response to strong environmentalist-generated public pressure without adequate scientific justification. . . .

- In 1992, the National Aeronautics and Space Administration (NASA) reported that [the] hole in the Earth's protective ozone layer might open up over North America that spring. This hypothetical hole, which would have been in addition to the annual Antarctic hole, would be caused by chlorofluourocarbons (CFCs), a refrigerant. After widespread media coverage on the threat of CFCs, the White House moved a production ban, scheduled for the year 2000, up to 1996, raising the cost of the ban by tens of billions of dollars. Unfortunately, NASA held its press conference before it had finished the study or subjected it to even cursory peer review. The hypothesized ozone hole over North America never materialized. Nor could it have. According to Patrick Michaels of the Climatology Department at the University of Virginia, "The only way you could produce an ozone hole in the high latitudes of the Northern Hemisphere that resembles what occurs in the Southern Hemisphere (where the ozone hole occurs) would be to flatten our mountains and submerge our continents. Then you would have airflow patterns similar to those that occur in the Southern Hemisphere, and are the ones that are required to create an ozone hole." One would think NASA would know this as well. Now, although no information other than a thoroughly discredited hypothesis justifies dramatically stepping up the phaseout, the country is redirecting its limited economic resources at an extra cost of hundreds of dollars per household because of the ban, which is now in place.

Instead of merely responding to tabloid claims or politically motivated studies by federal agencies and environmental organizations trying to justify their budgets, regulations should be based on credible scientific findings open to public scrutiny. For instance, agencies should use consistent methodologies to determine risks. Currently, they use different methods. Thus, for example, risk assessments by different agencies may turn up different answers as to whether a chemical at a particular dose level causes cancer. Theoretically, exposure to some level of a chemical could be found to be both deadly and perfectly safe.

Government assessments also should reveal the assumptions and uncertainties in their analyses. Typically, because of missing data, most studies use certain assumptions to estimate these uncertainties. These assumptions, sometimes unreasonably gloomy, usually determine the conclusion reached. For instance, sometimes an estimate of the likely risk from some chemical is multiplied thousands, or even millions, of times just to be "conservative." Yet the analyses used to justify these enormously expensive regulations often are obscure as to their assumptions. Moreover, the reports rarely reveal the level of uncertainty involved in arriving at their conclusions.

Whenever regulations that address risks are considered, each agency should be required to conduct risk assessments if only to aid in intelligent decision-making that are consistent, that are transparent to public scrutiny, and that fully detail their assumptions and levels of uncertainty. Moreover, each study should be reviewed before a regulation is published to ensure that scientific guidelines are strictly followed. If federal agencies cannot meet even this very limited standard, it is unconscionable for them to impose costly standards on others.

The need to set priorities   The economy has a limited capacity to absorb environmental regulations. Simply put, the country cannot afford to eliminate every risk. Thus, there is a trade-off: Attempting to regulate one risk out of existence may mean that another risk (or other risks) will have to be tolerated. In most cases, the cure is worse than the disease. Misguided and excessive regulation can cost lives, so it is critical that regulators recognize the costs of their actions. Spending enormous amounts of money to eradicate small or even hypothetical risks means that those dollars cannot be used in other productive ways public or private that might be of greater benefit to the nation.

... [I]t is essential that policymakers develop a priority list of environmental problems, based on the extent of the possible risk each appears to pose and the cost of reducing that risk to acceptable levels. With such a list, policymakers can know just how much protection is being bought for every dollar spent. Americans finally will get the maximum environmental "bang for the buck." Conversely, the federal government will be able to achieve environmental objectives at the lowest cost, and thus with the fewest "pink slips" for American workers.

Is There an Environmental Crisis?

Is there an environmental crisis? The answer is a resounding "No." Certainly the country and planet have environmental problems that need to be addressed. But overall, the environment has been improving. Unfortunately, the public is subjected only to the "Chicken Little" version of the situation, and reports of environmental progress and refutations of environmental alarmists are rarely covered in the press.

In his 1995 book *A Moment on the Earth,* which details many of the improvements that have taken place in the last three decades, *Newsweek* editor Gregg Easterbrook notes that reports of positive environmental developments, such as significantly lower air pollution in major U.S. cities, are buried inside the newspapers. Negative news, meanwhile, gets front-page attention, and the news that is reported often contains numerous misleading "facts."

The truth is that threats to the environment have lessened considerably. Lead has been almost eliminated. Even in Los Angeles, the most polluted city in the country, levels of Volatile Organic Compounds (VOCs) have fallen by more than half since 1970. In other formerly polluted cities, such as Atlanta, the air is now considered relatively clean as VOCs are down by almost two-thirds and Nitrous Oxide is down 15 percent.

In area after area so-called global warming, endangered species, wetlands, pesticides, hazardous waste, and automotive fuel economy, for example, the problem is the same: only rarely are the facts heard by the American people.

Paul R. Ehrlich and Anne H. Ehrlich ↰ **NO**

Brownlash: The New Environmental Anti-Science

Humanity is now facing a sort of slow-motion environmental Dunkirk. It remains to be seen whether civilization can avoid the perilous trap it has set for itself. Unlike the troops crowding the beach at Dunkirk, civilization's fate is in its own hands; no miraculous last-minute rescue is in the cards. Although progress has certainly been made in addressing the human predicament, far more is needed. Even if humanity manages to extricate itself, it is likely that environmental events will be defining ones for our grandchildren's generation —and those events could dwarf World War II in magnitude.

Sadly, much of the progress that has been made in defining, understanding, and seeking solutions to the human predicament over the past 30 years is now being undermined by an environmental backlash. We call these attempts to minimize the seriousness of environmental problems the *brownlash* because they help to fuel a backlash against "green" policies. While it assumes a variety of forms, the brownlash appears most clearly as an outpouring of seemingly authoritative opinions in books, articles, and media appearances that greatly distort what is or isn't known by environmental scientists. Taken together, despite the variety of its forms, sources, and issues addressed, the brownlash has produced what amounts to a body of anti-science—a twisting of the findings of empirical science—to bolster a predetermined worldview and to support a political agenda. By virtue of relentless repetition, this flood of anti-environmental sentiment has acquired an unfortunate aura of credibility.

It should be noted that the brownlash is not by any means a coordinated effort. Rather, it seems to be generated by a diversity of individuals and organizations. Some of its promoters have links to right-wing ideology and political groups. And some are well-intentioned individuals, including writers and public figures, who for one reason or another have bought into the notion that environmental regulation has become oppressive and needs to be severely weakened. But the most extreme—and most dangerous—elements are those who, while claiming to represent a scientific viewpoint, misstate scientific findings to support their view that the U.S. government has gone overboard with regulation, especially (but not exclusively) for environmental protection, and that subtle, long-term problems like global warming are nothing to worry about.

From Paul R. Ehrlich and Anne H. Ehrlich, "Brownlash: The New Environmental Anti-Science," *The Humanist* (November/December 1996). Copyright © 1996 by Paul R. Ehrlich and Anne H. Ehrlich. Reprinted by permission.

The words and sentiments of the brownlash are profoundly troubling to us and many of our colleagues. Not only are the underlying agendas seldom revealed but, more important, the confusion and distraction created among the public and policymakers by brownlash pronouncements interfere with and prolong the already difficult search for realistic and equitable solutions to the human predicament.

Anti-science as promoted by the brownlash is not a unique phenomenon in our society; the largely successful efforts of creationists to keep Americans ignorant of evolution is another example, which is perhaps not entirely unrelated. Both feature a denial of facts and circumstances that don't fit religious or other traditional beliefs; policies built on either could lead our society into serious trouble.

Fortunately, in the case of environmental science, most of the public is fairly well informed about environmental problems and remains committed to environmental protection. When polled, 65 percent of Americans today say they are willing to pay good money for environmental quality. But support for environmental quality is sometimes said to be superficial; while almost everyone is in favor of a sound environment—clean air, clean water, toxic site cleanups, national parks, and so on—many don't feel that environmental deterioration, especially on a regional or global level, is a crucial issue in their own lives. In part this is testimony to the success of environmental protection in the United States. But it is also the case that most people lack an appreciation of the deeper but generally less visible, slowly developing global problems. Thus they don't perceive population growth, global warming, the loss of biodiversity, depletion of groundwater, or exposure to chemicals in plastics and pesticides as a personal threat at the same level as crime in their neighborhood, loss of a job, or a substantial rise in taxes.

So anti-science rhetoric has been particularly effective in promoting a series of erroneous notions, including:

- Environmental scientists ignore the abundant good news about the environment.
- Population growth does not cause environmental damage and may even be beneficial.
- Humanity is on the verge of abolishing hunger; food scarcity is a local or regional problem and not indicative of overpopulation.
- Natural resources are superabundant, if not infinite.
- There is no extinction crisis, and so most efforts to preserve species are both uneconomic and unnecessary.
- Global warming and acid rain are not serious threats to humanity.
- Stratospheric ozone depletion is a hoax.
- The risks posed by toxic substances are vastly exaggerated.
- Environmental regulation is wrecking the economy.

How has the brownlash managed to persuade a significant segment of the public that the state of the environment and the directions and rates in which it is changing are not causes for great concern? Even many individuals who are sensitive to local environmental problems have found brownlash distortions of global issues convincing. Part of the answer lies in the overall lack of scientific knowledge among United States citizens. Most Americans readily grasp the issues surrounding something familiar and tangible like a local dump site, but they have considerably more difficulty with issues involving genetic variation or the dynamics of the atmosphere. Thus it is relatively easy to rally support against a proposed landfill and infinitely more difficult to impose a carbon tax that might help offset global warming.

Also, individuals not trained to recognize the hallmarks of change have difficulty perceiving and appreciating the gradual deterioration of civilization's life-support systems. This is why record-breaking temperatures and violent storms receive so much attention while a gradual increase in annual global temperatures—measured in fractions of a degree over decades—is not considered newsworthy. Threatened pandas are featured on television, while the constant and critical losses of insect populations, which are key elements of our life-support systems, pass unnoticed. People who have no meaningful way to grasp regional and global environmental problems cannot easily tell what information is distorted, when, and to what degree.

Decision-makers, too, have a tendency to focus mostly on the more obvious and immediate environmental problems—usually described as "pollution" —rather than on the deterioration of natural ecosystems upon whose continued functioning global civilization depends. Indeed, most people still don't realize that humanity has become a truly global force, interfering in a very real and direct way in many of the planet's natural cycles.

For example, human activity puts ten times as much oil into the oceans as comes from natural seeps, has multiplied the natural flow of cadmium into the atmosphere eightfold, has doubled the rate of nitrogen fixation, and is responsible for about half the concentration of methane (a potent greenhouse gas) and more than a quarter of the carbon dioxide (also a greenhouse gas) in the atmosphere today—all added since the industrial revolution, most notably in the past half-century. Human beings now use or co-opt some 40 percent of the food available to all land animals and about 45 percent of the available freshwater flows.

Another factor that plays into brownlash thinking is the not uncommon belief that environmental quality is improving, not declining. In some ways it is, but the claim of uniform improvement simply does not stand up to close scientific scrutiny. Nor does the claim that the human condition in general is improving everywhere. The degradation of ecosystem services (the conditions and processes through which natural ecosystems support and fulfill human life) is a crucial issue that is largely ignored by the brownlash. Unfortunately, the superficial progress achieved to date has made it easy to label ecologists doomsayers for continuing to press for change. At the same time, the public often seems unaware of the success of actions taken at the instigation of the environmental movement. People can easily see the disadvantages of environmental regulations but not the despoliation that would exist without them. Especially resentful are those whose personal or corporate ox is being gored when they are forced to sustain financial losses because of a sensible (or occasionally senseless) application of regulations.

Of course, it is natural for many people to feel personally threatened by efforts to preserve a healthy environment. Consider a car salesperson who makes a bigger commission selling a large car than a small one, an executive of a petrochemical company that is liable for damage done by toxic chemicals released into the environment, a logger whose job is jeopardized by enforcement of the Endangered Species Act, a rancher whose way of life may be threatened by higher grazing fees on public lands, a farmer about to lose the farm because of environmentalists' attacks on subsidies for irrigation water, or a developer who wants to continue building subdivisions and is sick and tired of dealing with inconsistent building codes or U.S. Fish and Wildlife Service bureaucrats. In such situations, resentment of some of the rules, regulations, and recommendations designed to enhance human well-being and protect life-support systems is understandable.

Unfortunately, many of these dissatisfied individuals and companies have been recruited into the self-styled "wise-use" movement, which has attracted a surprisingly diverse coalition of people, including representatives of extractive and polluting industries who are motivated by corporate interests as well as private property rights activists and right-wing ideologues. Although some of these individuals simply believe that environmental regulations unfairly distribute the costs of environmental protection, some others are doubtless motivated more by a greedy desire for unrestrained economic expansion.

At a minimum, the wise-use movement firmly opposes most government efforts to maintain environmental quality in the belief that environmental regulation creates unnecessary and burdensome bureaucratic hurdles which stifle economic growth. Wise-use advocates see little or no need for constraints on the exploitation of resources for short-term economic benefits and argue that such exploitation can be accelerated with no adverse long-term consequences. Thus they espouse unrestricted drilling in the Arctic National Wildlife Refuge, logging in national forests, mining in protected areas or next door to national parks, and full compensation for any loss of actual or potential property value resulting from environmental restrictions.

In promoting the view that immediate economic interests are best served by continuing business as usual, the wise-use movement works to stir up discontent among everyday citizens who, rightly or wrongly, feel abused by environmental regulations. This tactic is described in detail in David Helvarg's book, *The War Against the Greens:*

> To date the Wise Use/Property Rights backlash has been a bracing if dangerous reminder to environmentalists that power concedes nothing without a demand and that no social movement, be it ethnic, civil, or environmental, can rest on its past laurels.... If the anti-enviros' links to the Farm Bureau, Heritage Foundation, NRA, logging companies, resource trade associations, multinational gold-mining companies, [and] ORV manufacturers... proves anything, it's that large industrial lobbies and transnational corporations have learned to play the grassroots game.

Wise-use proponents are not always candid about their motivations and intentions. Many of the organizations representing them masquerade as groups seemingly attentive to environmental quality. Adopting a strategy biologists call "aggressive mimicry," they often give themselves names resembling those of genuine environmental or scientific public-interest groups: National Wetland Coalition, Friends of Eagle Mountain, the Sahara Club, the Alliance for Environment and Resources, the Abundant Wildlife Society of North America, the Global Climate Coalition, the National Wilderness Institute, and the American Council on Science and Health. In keeping with aggressive mimicry, these organizations often actively work *against* the interests implied in their names—a practice sometimes called *greenscamming*.

One such group, calling itself Northwesterners for More Fish, seeks to limit federal protection of endangered fish species so the activities of utilities, aluminum companies, and timber outfits utilizing the region's rivers are not hindered. Armed with a $2.6 million budget, the group aims to discredit environmentalists who say industry is destroying the fish habitats of the Columbia and other rivers, threatening the Northwest's valuable salmon fishery, among others.

Representative George Miller, referring to the wise-use movement's support of welfare ranching, overlogging, and government giveaways of mining rights, stated: "What you have . . . is a lot of special interests who are trying to generate some ideological movement to try and disguise what it is individually they want in the name of their own profits, their own greed in terms of the use and abuse of federal lands."

Wise-use sentiments have been adopted by a number of deeply conservative legislators, many of whom have received campaign contributions from these organizations. One member of the House of Representatives recently succeeded in gaining passage of a bill that limited the annual budget for the Mojave National Preserve, the newest addition to the National Parks System, to one dollar—thus guaranteeing that the park would have no money for upkeep or for enforcement of park regulations.

These same conservative legislators are determined to slash funding for scientific research, especially on such subjects as endangered species, ozone depletion, and global warming, and have legislated for substantial cutbacks in funds for the National Science Foundation, the U.S. Geological Survey, the National Aeronautics and Space Administration, and the Environmental Protection Agency. Many of them and their supporters see science as self-indulgent, at odds with economic interests, and inextricably linked to regulatory excesses.

The scientific justifications and philosophical underpinnings for the positions of the wise-use movement are largely provided by the brownlash. Prominent promoters of the wise-use viewpoint on a number of issues include such conservative think tanks as the Cato Institute and the Heritage Foundation. Both organizations help generate and disseminate erroneous brownlash ideas and information. Adam Myerson, editor of the Heritage Foundation's journal *Policy Review*, pretty much summed up the brownlash perspective by saying: "Leading scientists have done major work disputing the current henny-pennyism about global warming, acid rain, and other purported environmental catastrophes." In reality, however, most "leading" scientists support what Myerson calls henny-pennyism; the scientists he refers to are a small group largely outside the mainstream of scientific thinking.

In recent years, a flood of books and articles has advanced the notion that all is well with the environment, giving credence to this anti-scientific "What, me worry?" outlook. Brownlash writers often pepper their works with code phrases such as *sound science* and *balance*—words that suggest objectivity while in fact having little connection to what is presented. *Sound science* usually means science that is interpreted to support the brownlash view. *Balance* generally means giving undue prominence to the opinions of one or a handful of contrarian scientists who are at odds with the consensus of the scientific community at large.

Of course, while pro-environmental groups and environmental scientists in general may sometimes be dead wrong (as can anybody confronting environmental complexity), they ordinarily are not acting on behalf of narrow economic interests. Yet one of the remarkable triumphs of the wise-use movement and its allies in the past decade has been their ability to define public-interest organizations, in the eyes of many legislators, as "special interests"—not different in kind from the American Tobacco Institute, the Western Fuels Association, or other organizations that represent business groups.

But we believe there is a very real difference in kind. Most environmental organizations are funded mainly by membership donations; corporate funding is at most a minor factor for public-interest advocacy groups. There are no monetary profits to be gained other than attracting a bigger membership. Environmental scientists have even less to gain; they usually are dependent upon university or research institute salaries and research funds from peer-reviewed government grants or sometimes (especially in new or controversial areas where government funds are largely unavailable) from private foundations.

One reason the brownlash messages hold so much appeal to many people, we think, is the fear of further change. Even though the American frontier closed a century ago, many Americans seem to believe they still live in what the great economist Kenneth Boulding once called a "cowboy economy." They still think they can figuratively throw their garbage over the backyard fence with impunity. They regard the environmentally protected public land as "wasted" and think it should be available for their self-beneficial appropriation. They believe that private property rights are absolute (despite a rich economic and legal literature showing they never have been). They do not understand, as Pace University law professor John Humbach wrote in 1993, that "the Constitution does not guarantee that land speculators will win their bets."

The anti-science brownlash provides a rationalization for the short-term economic interests of these groups: old-growth forests are decadent and should be harvested; extinction is natural, so there's no harm in overharvesting economically important animals; there is abundant undisturbed habitat, so human beings have a right to develop land anywhere and in any way they choose; global warming is a hoax or even will benefit agriculture, so there's no need to limit the burning of fossil fuels; and so on. Anti-science basically claims we can keep the good old days by doing business as usual. But the problem is we can't.

Thus the brownlash helps create public confusion about the character and magnitude of environmental problems, taking advantage of the lack of consensus among individuals and social groups on the urgency of enhancing environmental protection. A widely shared social consensus, such as the United States saw during World War II, will be essential if we are to maintain environmental quality while meeting the nation's other needs. By emphasizing dissent, the brownlash works against the formation of any such consensus; instead it has helped thwart the development of a spirit of cooperation mixed with concern for society as a whole. In our opinion, the brownlash fuels conflict by claiming the environmental problems are overblown or nonexistent and that unbridled economic development will propel the world to new levels of prosperity with little or no risk to the natural systems that support society. As a result, environmental groups and wise-use proponents are increasingly polarized.

Unfortunately, some of that polarization has led to ugly confrontations and activities that are not condoned by the brownlash or by most environmentalists, including us. As David Helvarg stated, "Along with the growth of Wise Use/Property Rights, the last six years have seen a startling increase in intimidation, vandalism, and violence directed against grassroots environmental activists." And while confrontations and threats have been generated by both sides—most notably (but by no means exclusively) over the northern spotted owl protection plan—the level of intimidation engaged in by wise-use proponents is disturbing, to say the least....

Fortunately, despite all the efforts of the brownlash to discourage it, environmental concern in the United States is widespread. Thus a public-opinion survey in 1995 indicated that slightly over half of all Americans felt that environmental problems in the United States were "very serious." Indeed, 85 percent were concerned "a fair amount" and 38 percent "a great deal" about the environment. Fifty-eight percent would choose protecting the environment over economic growth, and 65 percent said they would be willing to pay higher prices so that industry could protect the environment better. Responses in other rich nations have been similar, and people in developing nations have shown, if anything, even greater environmental concerns. These responses suggest that the notion that caring about the environment is a luxury of the rich is a myth. Furthermore, our impression is that young people care especially strongly about environmental quality—a good omen if true.

Nor is environmental concern exclusive to Democrats and "liberals." There is a strong Republican and conservative tradition of environmental protection dating back to Teddy Roosevelt and even earlier. Many of our most important environmental laws were passed with bipartisan support during the Nixon and Ford administrations. Recently, some conservative environmentalists have been speaking out against brownlash rhetoric. And public concern is rising about the efforts to cripple environmental laws and regulations posed by right-wing leaders in Congress, thinly disguised as "deregulation" and "necessary budget-cutting." In January 1996, a Republican pollster, Linda Divall, warned that "our party is out of sync with mainstream American opinion when it comes to the environment."

Indeed, some interests that might be expected to sympathize with the wise-use movement have moved beyond such reactionary views. Many leaders in corporations such as paper companies and chemical manufacturers, whose activities are directly harmful to the environment, are concerned about their firms' environmental impacts and are shifting to less damaging practices. Our friends in the ranching community in western Colorado indicate their concern to us every summer. They want to preserve a way of life and a high-quality environment—and are as worried about the progressive suburbanization of the area as are the scientists at the Rocky Mountain Biological Laboratory. Indeed, they have actively participated in discussions with environmentalists and officials of the Department of the Interior to set grazing fees at levels that wouldn't force them out of business but also wouldn't subsidize overgrazing and land abuse.

Loggers, ranchers, miners, petrochemical workers, fishers, and professors all live on the same planet, and all of us must cooperate to preserve a sound environment for our descendants. The environmental problems of the planet can be solved only in a spirit of cooperation, not one of conflict. Ways must be found to allocate fairly both the benefits and the costs of environmental quality.

POSTSCRIPT

Do Environmental Restrictions Violate Basic Economic Freedoms?

The dilemmas that face us as we attempt to adjust our lifestyles to the needs of a suddenly threatened environment may be some of the hardest that this generation will know. It is not just that we are being asked to refrain in the future from certain profitable activities in order to preserve some part of the environment—like building hotels on barrier beaches, for instance. We will likely be required to cut back on portions of our lives that we have taken for granted. We may be told to stop driving our cars except in direst emergency, cancel travel plans, forget the vacation house, and pay astronomical prices for goods and services that have always been reasonable. We may be told to separate our trash more scrupulously—into plastics, glass, metals, paper, and organic waste—and to take it to five different receiving stations for recycling and reusing. The quality of daily life will likely be poorer and will take up much more of our time and labor. Most of these burdens will be chosen by us, through democratically conducted elections and legislation. But there will be no real choice, for the alternative may be the death of the biosphere, including its human component.

These scenarios may sound terrible to many. But it does not have to be. Some believe that we have the technology on board now to save the planet and provide Americans and the rest of the world with a very pleasant lifestyle.

Suggested Readings

J. Baird Callicott and Michael Nelson, eds., *The Great, New, Wilderness Debate* (University of Georgia Press, 1998).

Joan Iverson Nassauer, ed., *Placing Nature: Culture and Landscape Ecology* (Island Press, 1997).

Ernest Callenbach, Fritjof Capra, Lenore Goldman, Rudiger Lutz, and Sandra Marburg, *EcoManagement: The Elmwood Guide to Ecological Auditing and Sustainable Business* (Berritt-Koehler Publishers, 1993).

Christopher Flavin, "The Legacy of Rio," *State of the World 1997* (W. W. Norton, 1997).

ISSUE 19

Can Rain Forest Products Save the Tropical Rain Forest?

YES: Thomas A. Carr, Heather L. Pedersen, and Sunder Ramaswamy, from "Rain Forest Entrepreneurs: Cashing in on Conservation," *Environment* (September 1993)

NO: Jon Entine, from "Let Them Eat Brazil Nuts: The 'Rainforest Harvest' and Other Myths of Green Marketing," *Dollars and Sense* (March/April 1996)

ISSUE SUMMARY

YES: Economics professors Thomas A. Carr and Sunder Ramaswamy and mathematics teacher Heather L. Pedersen describe three projects to promote sustainable use of rain forest products, which they argue help to preserve the forest and support the local economy.

NO: Investigative reporter Jon Entine asserts that most green marketing programs do nothing to slow forest destruction and, moreover, frequently result in the mistreatment of employees, vendors, and customers.

T he tropical rain forests of the world, spread in rapidly decreasing pockets over South America (especially in Brazil's Amazon region), Africa, and Malaysia, are the home of most of the species in the world. Due to the favorable climate and stability over many centuries, the speciation of the dominant varieties of life has progressed to degrees only imaginable elsewhere. Some whole species of insect, for instance, live on *only one tree* in the Amazonian forest. Each species —or rather, the DNA of each species—is a parcel of information that may be irreplaceably valuable in the human scheme of things. (The rosy periwinkle of Madagascar, for instance, found nowhere else, is the source of methetrexate and vincristine, two very effective cancer therapies.) There is no way we could invent for ourselves the variety of effective chemicals that are supplied free of charge by the rain forest.

More than that, the tropical rain forest, a huge green canopy spread under the hottest sun, is the lungs of the world. Every leaf in the canopy carries on the endless task of absorbing carbon from the air (in the form of the most problematic "greenhouse gas," CO_2, or carbon dioxide) and releasing oxygen. That huge canopy supplies a significant amount of the oxygen for the world's air-breathers.

With all these functions for our good, how can it be that the rain forest would be destroyed? Tragically, the interests of a few people, in the absence of worldwide concerted action to protect it, conspire to cut down the trees of the rain forest. Tropical rain forests once covered 14 percent of the planet. Less than half remain, most of the loss occurring in the last 50 years; an area the size of Germany is lost every year.

As much as one-third of the annual contribution to the increase in atmospheric carbon dioxide, which contributes to global warming, comes from deforestation. The global warming connection comes from the fact that the cutting and combustion of trees release carbon dioxide that can only be balanced by an equal number of new trees removing that same amount of carbon dioxide as they grow. Not only do we lose the canopy that breathes for us, but we contribute to the greenhouse gases by allowing the forest to be cut. On the other hand, since global warming is an issue of concern to many, there is hope among environmentalists that it will serve to mobilize the enormous number of people needed to save the forests.

Tropical forests supply many useful commercial products and are the source of a wide variety of chemicals, including natural products that are used in the pharmaceutical industry. Among the serious consequences of rain forest destruction would be the loss of a principal source of organic chemicals used in medical research.

Designing and implementing appropriate and effective strategies for reducing or reversing rain forest decimation has produced heated controversy, both within the tropical nations where the destruction is occurring and in the international community. Among the proposals that have been advanced, along with the "debt for nature" swaps that would allow debtor nations to get rid of their national debt by promising to preserve forests, are many "green marketing" strategies whose goal is to enhance the economic worth of goods that can be produced from the forests in a sustainable manner. This is a means of motivating entrepreneurs to favor forest preservation over using forest land for profit.

In the following selections, Thomas A. Carr, Heather L. Pedersen, and Sunder Ramaswamy describe two projects involving the use of forest products and one ecotourism initiative, which they argue are the types of endeavors that "may be key to preserving the vital and fragile resources of the tropical rain forests." Jon Entine discusses green marketing "schemes," such as Ben and Jerry's promotion of Rainforest Crunch ice cream and Body Shop International's tropical skin and hair care products. He argues that, while encouraging consumers to "shop for a better world," these enterprises frequently mistreat employees, vendors, and customers, and do little or nothing to help preserve the forests or support the indigenous peoples.

Thomas A. Carr, Heather L. Pedersen, and Sunder Ramaswamy

 **YES**

Rain Forest Entrepreneurs: Cashing in on Conservation

Each year, nearly 17 million hectares of rain forest—an area roughly equal to that of Wisconsin—are lost world-wide as a result of deforestation. Because more than half of all species on the planet are found in rain forests, this destruction portends serious environmental consequences, including the decimation of biological diversity. Another threat lies in the fact that rain forests serve as an important sink for carbon dioxide, a greenhouse gas that contributes to global warming. The Amazon region alone stores at least 75 billion tons of carbon in its trees. Furthermore, when stripped of its trees, rain forest land soon becomes inhospitable and nonarable because the soil is nutrient-poor and ill-suited to agriculture. Under current practices, therefore, the forests are being destroyed permanently.

Economic forces result in exploitation of the rain forest to extract hardwood timber and fuel and in clearcutting the land for agriculture and cattle ranching, which are primary causes of the devastation. Mounting evidence shows that these conventional commercial and industrial uses of the rain forest (see Table 1) are not only ecologically devastating but also economically unsound. These findings have inspired an innovative approach to save the rain forest. Environmental groups are now targeting their efforts toward developing commercially viable and sustainable uses of the rain forest. Their strategy is to create economic incentives that encourage local inhabitants to practice efficient stewardship over the standing forests. These environmental entrepreneurs no longer view the market as their nemesis but as an instrument to bring about constructive social and environmental change. In theory, the strategy promotes win-win solutions: Environmentalists gain by preserving the rain forests, and local inhabitants gain from an improved standard of living that is generated by enlightened, sustainable development. In practice, the challenge lies in implementing such programs.

Three applications of environmental entrepreneurship in the rain forests have been particularly successful. Conservation International's "The Tagua Initiative," Shaman Pharmaceutical's search for useful drugs in the rain forest, and the management of ecotourism in Costa Rica are three projects that together

From Thomas A. Carr, Heather L. Pedersen, and Sunder Ramaswamy, "Rain Forest Entrepreneurs: Cashing in on Conservation," *Environment* (September 1993), pp. 12–15, 33–37. Copyright © 1993 by Heldref Publications, 1319 Eighteenth St., NW, Washington, DC 20036-1802. Reprinted by permission of The Helen Dwight Reid Educational Foundation. Notes omitted.

Table 1

Commercial and Industrial Products Derived From Tropical Rain Forests

Product	Value of imports by region (millions of U.S. dollars)	Marketshare of rain forest products (percent)	Region receiving imports	Year of estimate
Commercial Products				
Fruit and vegetable juices	4,000	100	World	1988
Cut flowers	2,500	100	World	1985
Food additives	750	100	United States, European Community	1991
Spices	439	small	United States	1987
Nuts	216	100	World	1988
Food colorings	140	10	World	1987
Vitamins	67	small	United States	1990
Fiber	54	100	United States	1983/4
Industrial Products				
Fuel	60,000	<1	United States	1984
Pesticides	16,000	1	World	1987
Natural rubber	666	100	United States	1978
Tannins	170	large	United States	1980
Construction material	12	1	United States	1984
Natural waxes	9.3	100	United States	1985

Note: James Duke, an economic botanist at the U.S. Department of Agriculture, has been compiling estimates of the economic value of hundreds of key commercial and industrial rain forest products. Some of the important estimates are summarized here. Although not all of the imported products are derived from tropical rain forest countries, Duke claims that they all have the potential to be sustainably harvested from these regions.

Source: James Duke, "Tropical Botanical Extractives" (Unpublished manuscript, U.S. Department of Agriculture, Washington, D.C., April 1989).

provide an interesting cross section of the efforts under way to promote sustainable use of rain forest products. A number of common issues and challenges confront these environmental entrepreneurs.

Responding to Deforestation

Although people everywhere may benefit from preserving the rain forest, the costs of preservation are borne mainly by the local inhabitants. Usually, the inhabitants' immediate financial needs far outweigh the long-term benefit gained by forgoing the traditional extractive methods of forestry or land conversion for agriculture. In many of these countries, high levels of poverty, rapid population growth, and unequal distribution of land encourage migration into the forest regions. Local inhabitants, confronted with the tasks of daily survival, cannot be expected to respond to appeals for altruistic self-sacrifice. Consequently, forests are cut and burned for short-term economic gains. This problem is often exacerbated by misguided government policies in many countries, such as government-sponsored timber concessions that promote inefficient harvest levels, tree selection, and reforestation levels. Governments may charge a royalty far below the true economic value of the standing forest. Such low royalties and special tax breaks raise the profits of logging companies, which thereby stimulate timber booms. In addition, some governments provide special land tenure rules or tax benefits to individuals who "improve" the land by clearing the forest. These rules encourage development in the rain forest region because they impel poor settlers to seek land for agriculture and wealthy landowners to look for new investments.

Environmental entrepreneurs can create commercial alternatives to the traditional damaging uses of rain forest resources, but several factors must first be taken into consideration. For example, commercial development cannot be allowed to harm the ecological integrity of the ecosystem. This can be a difficult challenge as the scale of production increases for many projects. Also, if existing firms are profitable, new firms will be attracted into the industry, thus placing additional pressure on the fragile ecosystem. Of course, the product must also pass the test of the market; consumers must be willing to pay a price that covers the full cost of production. Some environmentally conscious consumers may be willing to pay a premium for sustainably harvested rain forest products. The size of this "green premium" would depend upon these consumers' willingness and ability to pay, as well as on the prices of other products competing with the rain forest products. To maintain the green premium over time, environmental entrepreneurs need to devise a strategy that differentiates their products from others through advertising and some type of institutionalized labeling system. These entrepreneurs must also anticipate the effect of expanding output on market prices. Previous studies have examined the market value of sustainable products from a single hectare. One study in the Amazonian rain forest in Peru found that sustainably harvested products such as fruit, nuts, rubber latex, and selectively logged timber yield more net value than do plantation forestry and cattle ranching. If harvests are expanded, however, market prices may be pushed down, and the profitability of the program reduced. Another consideration is that entrepreneurs may be able to avoid the expense of developing extensive distribution networks and other marketing costs by forming alliances with established commercial firms. These firms typically have retail outlets and experienced business personnel that can assist the small entrepreneur.

Finally, the environmental entrepreneur must channel income back to the effective owners of the rain forests—the local indigenous people. This return raises the issue of rain forest property rights. The property rights over rain forest resources are not well defined or enforced. Rain forest land is often held collectively, and government-owned land marked as a reserve is not always protected. Even private landowners have a difficult time preventing landless squatters from using their property. Without the enforcement of property rights, rain forests become an open-access resource that is overexploited. This result is not inevitable, however. History suggests that, when the benefits of establishing new property rights exceed the costs, societies often devise new ways to define property rights and improve the allocation of resources.

In addition to the question of physical property rights, there is the problem of defining intellectual property rights. Indigenous people possess a wealth of esoteric knowledge about local plants and animals and their usages. Conservation groups argue that the wisdom of the local inhabitants must be given an economic value or else that knowledge will disappear amidst the destruction of the forest. At the same time, scientists and entrepreneurs also contribute value to rain forest products by discovering useful medicinal compounds in the plants. If these interests are not protected, there will not be sufficient economic incentive to develop new products. During the Earth Summit in Rio de Janeiro [in June 1992], the Bush administration refused to sign an international treaty on biodiversity on the grounds that it would harm the interests of biotechnology firms. (The Clinton administration signed the biodiversity treaty on 4 June 1993.) A key challenge is to develop an institutional mechanism that recognizes the value of both the natives' knowledge and the scientists' and entrepreneurs' contributions, and therefore rewards both types of intellectual property rights in the development of rain forest products.

The Tagua Initiative

Conservation International is an environmental organization based in Washington, D.C., that works to conserve biodiversity by supporting local rain forest communities world-wide. Through a project entitled "The Tagua Initiative," Conservation International is attempting to synthesize "the approaches of business, community development, and applied science to promote conservation through the marketing of non-timber forest products." The tagua nut is an ivory-like seed that is harvested from tropical palm trees to make buttons, jewelry, chess pieces, carvings, and other arts and crafts. Conservation International links button manufacturers in the United States and other countries with rural tagua harvesters in the endangered rain forests of Esmeraldas in Ecuador. The organization works independently with participating companies to design unique marketing strategies tailored to those companies' individual images, product offerings, and marketing campaigns.

In 1990, Conservation International began expanding the market for tagua products and developing a local industry around tagua. Today, tagua buttons are being used by 24 clothing companies, including such major manufacturers as Smith & Hawken, Esprit, J. Crew, and L. L. Bean. The current distribution network links the Ecuadorian tagua producers to the clothing companies through four wholesale button manufacturers. Conservation International collects a royalty based on a percentage of sales to wholesale button manufacturers and uses the proceeds to support local conservation and community development programs in the rain forest. It has also focused its efforts on developing a viable local tagua industry that includes harvesting and manufacturing. A primary objective of The Tagua Initiative is to provide the 1,200 local harvesters with an attractive price for tagua so that they have an economic incentive to protect the standing forest. Recent figures indicate that the price paid to tagua collectors has risen 92 percent since the program began (a 32 percent real price increase after adjusting for the estimated inflation rate). To increase the flow of income to the native economy, Conservation International encourages the development of new tagua products that can be manufactured locally. Currently, the tagua production line has expanded to include eight manufacturers of jewelry, arts and crafts, and other items.

The Tagua Initiative provides a tremendously successful example, at least in the initial stages of development. Since February 1990, 850 tons of tagua have been delivered directly to factories, and the program has generated approximately $2 million in button sales to manufacturers in North America, Europe, and Japan. According to Robin Frank, tagua product manager at Conservation International, the organization is collaborating with about 50 companies worldwide, and many others have expressed interest. Moreover, The Tagua Initiative in Ecuador has become a role model for new projects in Colombia, Guatemala, Peru, the Philippines, and a number of other countries. In all of these cases, Conservation International is working with local organizations to identify and develop sustainable commercial products in a manner that protects sensitive ecosystems. These projects are expanding the rain forest product line to Brazil nuts and pecans from Peru, fibers for textiles, and waxes and oils for the personal health and hygiene market.

In addition to creating marketable rain forest products, Conservation International cooperates with conservation and community development programs, such as the Corporacion de Investigaciones para el Desarrollo Socio/ Ambiental (CIDESA) in Ecuador. Ecologists, economic botanists, and conservation planners affiliated with Conservation International help CIDESA to identify critical rain forest sites and monitor harvesting practices to ensure their sustainability, among other things. The province of Esmeraldas in Ecuador is considered a critical "hot spot" because it contains some of the highest levels of biodiversity in Latin America and harbors some of Ecuador's last remaining pristine tracts of western Andean rain forest. Coincidentally, it is one of Ecuador's poorest communities, with a meager annual average per-capita income of $600, about one-half of the national average. The community of Comuna Rio Santiago in Esmeraldas has a population of 70,000, which grows dramatically at an annual rate of 3.7 percent. Four out of every 10 children suffer from malnutrition, and the infant mortality rate is 60 per 1,000 births. There is a high level of alcoholism, and drug addiction is a growing problem. Life expectancy is just 50 years, and the illiteracy level is near 50 percent. All of these actualities indicate an urgent need to protect the natural resources found in this region, not only to maintain biodiversity but also to ensure the economic welfare of the local inhabitants. If these needs are addressed, the program will have the potential to change the current low standard of living in Ecuador by promoting both conservation and economic development.

Over the next 10 years, Conservation International plans to increase the use of numerous rain forest products, such as medicines, furniture, and baskets. These efforts can serve as a role model for firms in the industrial world that seek to create rain forest products and improve the well-being of rain forest inhabitants.

Shaman Pharmaceuticals

Shaman Pharmaceuticals, Inc., draws its name from rain forest *shamans*, traditional medicine men who possess a vast amount of knowledge about the use of plants for medicinal purposes. The shamans' ability to cure a variety of illnesses is founded on centuries of practice and an intimate association with, and dependence upon, indigenous plants. By tapping the knowledge of the shamans, scientists hope to reduce the research costs of identifying plants with beneficial medicinal properties. Furthermore, investigating plant species already known to possess healing characteristics yields a much higher chance of success in the screening process. This ethnobotanical approach—which combines the skills of anthropology and botany to study how native peoples utilize plants—is the basic premise by which Shaman Pharmaceuticals functions. By innovatively combining the disciplines of ethnobotany, isolation chemistry, and pharmacology with a keen market-driven strategy, the company hopes to create a more efficient drug-discovery program.

Shaman has formed strategic alliances with the pharmaceutical industry to enhance its prospects of turning a pharmaceutical discovery into a financial gain. "Shaman feels it is in a strong position to strike such alliances because the company is not only formed around a handful of products, but also around an efficient, ongoing process for generating compounds with a greater likelihood of being active in humans." The company has two main objectives in building these alliances: generating research funds through cooperative arrangements and gaining access to a larger marketing network. Three major pharmaceutical manufacturers have entered into agreements with Shaman: Inverni della Beffa, an Italian manufacturer of plant-derived pharmaceuticals, has signed licensing and marketing agreements and invested $500,000 in Shaman; Eli Lilly committed $4 million to Shaman and collaborates in developing drugs for fungal infections; and Merck & Company is working with Shaman on projects targeting analgesics and medicines for diabetes. (For more on this topic, see "Making Biodiversity Conservation Profitable: A Case Study of the Merck/INBio Agreement," by Elissa Blum, in the May 1993 issue of *Environment*.)

To address the question of intellectual property rights and needs of the indigenous population, Shaman Pharmaceuticals created a nonprofit conservation organization called "The Healing Forest Conservancy" to protect global plant biodiversity and promote sustainable development. The company initially donated 13,333 shares of its own stock to the conservancy and plans to channel future product profits into projects that benefit the people of the source country. The first conservancy project provided health care benefits for the indigenous peoples of Amazonian Ecuador, a region that supplies valuable medicinal plants to Shaman. In return for information about these plants, physician Charles Limbach extended his medical services to three communities and treated 30 children during a whooping cough epidemic. Additionally, the conservancy seeks to create sustainable harvesting techniques for plants with commercial medicinal value. These programs have the task of reconciling the ecological constraints on plant extraction with the economic realities of producing a marketable product. This strategy reflects Shaman's concern that both the physical and intellectual property rights of the indigenous population are protected and that the inhabitants benefit from the research on these products.

As a result of its research efforts over the past few years, Shaman Pharmaceuticals has a pipeline full of active plant leads. Two antiviral products are currently being tested in clinical trials and are expected to reach the market in 1996: Provir is an oral treatment for respiratory viral infections that are common in young children; Virend is a topical treatment for the herpes simplex virus. Both products use the ingredient known as SP-303, a compound that was derived from a medicinal plant that grows in South America and was isolated by the company's discovery process. Patents have been filed on both the pure compounds and the methods of use for these products, which have a target market greater than $1 billion worldwide. Another consequential find is an antifungal agent found in an African plant that is traditionally ingested to treat infections. Shaman is using this compound to make a product that treats thrush, a fungal infection of the mouth, esophagus, and gastrointestinal tract. Given this discovery, the company hopes to find new treatments for other types of fungal infection. Shaman has strategically targeted its product development to address problems for which few effective treatments exist, such as viral and fungal infections. Moreover, there is a growing demand to find treatment for herpes and thrush because the increasing population of immunocompromised patients (including AIDS, chemotherapy, and transplant patients) is particularly vulnerable to these ailments. A third promising line of product development is in the area of analgesics. Shaman has found two plants exhibiting special binding properties that raise the prospect of creating a nonaddictive pain-relief drug. The company is conducting laboratory tests to identify the pure compounds responsible for this analgesic activity and is expanding its screening process by collaborating with Merck.

The raw materials for the screening all come from plants that are either presently harvested or sustainably collected. This discovery process has been quite successful at identifying plants with potential medicinal properties. Based on thousands of field samples collected by ethnobotanical field researchers and on reviews by a scientific strategy team, the company has screened 262 plants and found 192 to be active—a "hit rate" of 73 percent in the discovery process. Future products will be developed from some of these "hits."

According to company president Lisa Conte, "Shaman's well-defined strategic focus and outstanding, dedicated scientists will create a successful business by uniquely combining the newest in technology with the oldest of tribal lore." As a leader in ethnobotanical investigations, Shaman hopes that its initial success will translate into the development of a market for plant-based drugs from rain forest countries. The goal here is to use the revenue generated by these medicines as an economic incentive to preserve the forests and the wisdom of the native healers.

Ecotourism in Costa Rica

Ecotourism has been defined as "purposeful travel that creates an understanding of cultural and natural history, while safeguarding the integrity of the ecosystem and producing economic benefits that encourage conservation." Successful ecotourism creates economic opportunities in terms of both employment and income for the local people. These benefits furnish the local community with a strong incentive to practice good stewardship over their natural resources.

In Costa Rica, ecotourism has become a large and growing industry. In 1986, tourism generated $132.7 million and ranked as Costa Rica's third largest source of foreign exchange. In 1989, more than 375,000 tourists visited Costa Rica, 36 percent of whom were motivated by ecotourism. Tourism to Costa Rica's parks increased 80 percent between 1987 and 1990 and surged another 25 percent in 1991. Costa Rica offers the ecotourist diverse rain forests, abundant biodiversity, and breathtaking scenery. To protect these valuable resources, a national park system was established in 1970, which now comprises 34 parks and covers 11 percent of the total Costa Rican land area. Some of the most popular sites for ecotourism in Costa Rica, such as the Monteverde Cloud Forest Reserve and the La Selva Biological Station, are also centers for important biological research. Recently, these areas have attracted thousands of visitors each year, primarily because of the rich flora (more than 2,000 plant species) and fauna (some 300 animal species).

During the mid 1980s, the Costa Rican government sought to reconcile conservation and development interests by pursuing a strategy of sustainable development. Ecotourism was viewed as a clean source of development that might facilitate the preservation of the natural resource base. The actual implementation of this strategy was left to the private sector. The early environmental entrepreneurs in Costa Rica's ecotourism industry included Costa Rica Expeditions, Tikal, Horizontes, and the Organization for Tropical Studies. The growth of the ecotourism industry has since put strains on the fragile resource base. For example, the large number of visitors at popular parks is causing such problems as erosion and water pollution. Given the attraction of tourist revenues and the danger of overcrowding, environmental entrepreneurs are finding it difficult to create ecotourism programs that are consistent with the principles of sustainable development. Efforts to control ecotourism in Costa Rica are still in the early stages, and more research is needed soon if the industry is to serve its original purpose.

One firm that is striving to attain this balance is International Expeditions. This 11-year-old, Alabama-based company operates 30 travel programs on 6 continents. Company president Richard Ryel and Tom Grasse, the director of marketing and public relations, contend that the ecotourism industry needs to forgo short-run profits and adopt a four-part conservation ethic that includes increasing public awareness about the environment, maximizing economic benefits for local people, encouraging cultural sensitivity, and minimizing the negative impacts on the environment. International Expeditions applies these principles to business practices: For example, to create a flow of money into the local economy, the company uses the host country's airline when possible, employs local tour operators, and uses other services within the rain forest community. The company's tour of Costa Rica begins in San Jose and proceeds through the country's national parks. The tour organizers hire

Costa Rican guides who are familiar with the local habitat, and both guides and tourists stay at accommodations close to the parks whenever possible. These steps are designed to prevent tourist revenue from leaking outside the local communities that live near the parks.

To minimize detrimental impacts on the ecosystem and to promote respect for the rain forests, International Expeditions arranges small, manageable groups, educates participants about the ecosystem, avoids fragile habitats, and minimizes disruptions to the wildlife. In keeping with its objective of promoting natural history and conservation education, International Expeditions has designed a series of workshops in Costa Rica. The workshops are led by some of the world's leading experts on life in the rain forest, including Alwyn Gentry of the Missouri Botanical Garden, Donald Wilson of the National Museum of Natural History, and James Duke of the U.S. Department of Agriculture. Participants join in small group sessions to engage in hands-on field experience, such as nature walks, boat trips, and bird watching, and visit such sites as the Monteverde Cloud Forest and Tortuguero National Park on the Caribbean coast. Various sites feature canopied walkways up to 125 feet off the forest floor, which allow participants to walk among the treetops and closely observe the flora and fauna. The local guides also educate tourists about the history, culture, and socioeconomic conditions of indigenous peoples.

During the 1992 season, the cost of the 10-day, general nature tour throughout Costa Rica was $1,998 per person, and the 8-day workshop cost $1,498 per person. Because roughly 50 percent of these expenditures go to Costa Rica, these trips create the dual benefits of educating the nature traveler and generating income for the local economy.

A Key to Preservation

Clearly, sustainable development of rain forest products has the potential to bring about positive change, preserve biodiversity, and improve the welfare of local communities. Because deforestation is spiraling out of control, the efforts of organizations like Conservation International, Shaman Pharmaceuticals, Inc., and International Expeditions have become imperative. E. O. Wilson of the Museum of Comparative Zoology at Harvard University calculates that deforestation of the rain forest is responsible for the loss of 4,000 to 6,000 species a year—an extinction rate 10,000 times higher than the natural extinction rate before the emergence of humans on Earth. Furthermore, the unwritten knowledge of forest peoples is rapidly disappearing. Thomas Lovejoy, assistant secretary for external affairs at the Smithsonian Institution, asserts that the rain forest "is a library for life sciences, the world's greatest pharmaceutical laboratory, and a flywheel of climate. It's a matter of global destiny." The need to develop methods to deal with the issue is urgent, and environmental entrepreneurs may be key to preserving the vital and fragile resources of the tropical rain forests.

NO

Jon Entine

Let Them Eat Brazil Nuts: The "Rainforest Harvest" and Other Myths of Green Marketing

Business is our new universal community," says the speaker, and there is an immediate murmur of agreement. With eyes closed, the scene echoes of a Rotary Club luncheon in a genial, Midwestern town. There is an air of optimism that everyone seems to share.

"Religion and government no longer work as forces for community and change. We are in the era of business, it defines our relationships and values, and it doesn't have to be driven by the bottom line." The burly, ruby-faced speaker is clearly taken by his own message. The all-white, well-heeled crowd is entranced. "We are the leaders who can turn business into a positive social force."

The audience rises from its seats and breaks into applause. Although the words ring of Des Moines, the audience is forty-something L.A. Aging baby boomers in khaki sportcoats and designer jeans mix with business executives in Ann Taylor power suits. One man with stylishly long hair, a black silk shirt, black pants and sunglasses whispers into a cellular phone. Judging by the cars in the parking lot, this crowd long since traded in its Beetles for BMWs and Broncos.

This was a June celebration to open the Los Angeles chapter of Business for Social Responsibility, a trade group that promotes itself as environmentally and socially progressive, and they have come to hear their hero. The slightly rumpled, three-time college dropout holds the audience spellbound with his prescription for 'saving the world through business.' Their affection, indeed the adulation, is tangible.

The object of their rapt attention is Ben Cohen, who, in the late 1970s, started mixing batches of ice cream at an abandoned gas station in Burlington, Vermont, with his high school buddy Jerry Greenfield. Today, Ben & Jerry's Rainforest Crunch, Chunky Monkey, and Cherry Garcia are indulgences of choice for baby boomers. Although he no longer runs the company day-to-day, Cohen, 44, remains Chairman and eccentric corporate symbol of Ben & Jerry's Homemade, the 18-year-old, $160 million publicly traded company.

From Jon Entine, "Let Them Eat Brazil Nuts: The 'Rainforest Harvest' and Other Myths of Green Marketing," *Dollars and Sense* (March/April 1996). Copyright © 1996 by Jon Entine. Reprinted by permission. You can reach the author at runjonrun@earthlink.net.

363

Ben & Jerry's is the best known of the "good guy" entrepreneurs with quixotic corporate personas and New Age social philosophies. Skin-and-hair-care franchiser The Body Shop International (BSI), eco-friendly apparel makers Patagonia and Esprit, Tom's of Maine natural toothpaste and personal-care wholesaler, and Reebok athletic shoes are a few of the companies which have sliced a sizable niche out of the retail pie by turning "green" issues—such as the rainforest, "natural" ingredients and an opposition to animal testing—into their points-of-difference in a fickle, ultra-competitive consumer market. Many of these companies started with non-existent advertising budgets but were run by executives with an intuitive understanding of how to play the media dominated by baby boomers like themselves. And no company has benefited more from friendly press coverage than Ben & Jerry's.

In Los Angeles, Cohen rails on about the greedy, soulless character of Corporate America, and then boasts about his special flavor of New Age business. "Rainforest Crunch," he says, "shows that harvesting Brazil nuts is a profitable alternative for Amazon natives who have seen their lands ravaged to create grazing areas or for mining." The crowd is on its feet.

Yet, Ben & Jerry's own annual report carries the not-so-socially responsible details of what some anthropologists now call the rainforest fiasco. Despite Cohen's rhetoric that buying Rainforest Crunch helps preserve the fragile Amazon environment and the aboriginals who live there—a theme repeated uncritically by most of the media—his Third World project offers a lesson in the dangers of paternalistic capitalism. In fact, many anthropologists believe the rainforest harvest has led to the worst possible scenario: an increase in clear-cutting and mining, and a greater dependence among Amazon natives on selling land for subsistence income.

Green Marketing or Green Washing?

Cohen & Company preach an oxymoronic message: the generation that wanted to change the world now encourages consumers to "shop for a better world," the title of a best-selling "green" consumer guide. It's a two-for-one sale that rings up big profits: 'buy our not-tested-on-animals Brazil nut hair rinse or ice cream and get social justice for free.'

U.S. consumers spend upwards of $110 billion on products from companies they perceive as socially or environmentally progressive. According to a study last summer by the Social Investment Forum, $150 billion in teacher, union, church and other pension funds is held by investment managers using social screens; another $12 billion is invested in mutual funds which follow various "ethical" or "green" formulas. More than 45 funds in the U.S. alone screen out companies for manufacturing "sin" products such as cigarettes, while they include firms that promote social policies such as making "cruelty-free" products.

For years, The Body Shop was the favorite of the ethical investing community. Its founder, Anita Roddick, is the most visible and outspoken of the green marketing executives. Since opening a tiny shop in 1976 offering "one-stop ear piercing" and a range of natural-sounding lotions, Roddick has grown

BSI into an $800 million multinational company with 1300 mostly-franchised stores in 45 countries. She has cultivated a reputation for promoting the latest politically-correct social campaign: saving the whales, recycling, animal rights, AIDS research, and most prominently, preserving the environment and indigenous cultures by sourcing ingredients from the Third World. Roddick dubbed these micro-projects "Trade Not Aid," popularizing the eco-liberal concept of using capitalism instead of aid projects to reduce Third World dependency.

Despite rhetoric of good intentions, BSI has had a string of fair trade fiascos. For instance, over a year ago in Ghana, The Body Shop bought $20,000 worth of shea-butter from 10 villages for use in its creams. According to a front-page article in the *Toronto Globe & Mail*, the creams didn't sell, and today, the project is abandoned and the local economy is in tatters. BSI made no follow-up orders and left villages with thousands of dollars of unsold butter and no buyers.

The Body Shop's fair trade program has been plagued with problems. Richard Adams, who has founded two fair trade organizations, remembers seeing leaflets at BSI's stores in 1987 promoting its first import, foot massagers made by orphan boys in India. As director of Traidcraft in the early 1980s, Adams had briefly carried wood carvings made by the same group of orphans, who lived in a home called The Boys' Town. "Joe Homan, its director, was sourcing carvings from child labor sweat shops," he recalls discovering after poor quality shipments prompted an investigation. Worse, the local community said boys were being molested. Adams immediately sent the Roddicks a letter. "I never heard back," he says. Homan, it turns out, had been kicked out of a Christian Brothers sect. Two alarmed members of the Jesuit order visited the Roddicks after getting wind of the project. Still, nothing was done.

"Gordon [Roddick] was aware of his reputation," says Anne Downer, former head BSI franchisee for much of Asia. Downer, who attended the christening of The Boys' Town with the Roddicks in 1987, remembers Gordon saying that he had heard the rumors but didn't believe them. "He didn't seem unduly concerned and didn't seem to take it seriously."

Over the next few years, as Homan went about stealing charity funds and molesting orphan boys, the Roddicks sent out glowing reports to their franchisees. "Joe's work in The Boys' Town is ceaseless, he cares for the boys and girls and they really appreciate what he is doing for them," gushed one account in 1989. The roof caved in the next year when the English and Indian press ran exposes of Homan's escapades. The Roddicks first tried to suppress the scandal and then attempted to turn it into a public relations advantage by claiming credit for exposing him. "This story has not hit the Canadian Press yet but could erupt at any time," read one memo. "It is important that you know your facts. Anita... blew the whistle on Joe." A similar bulletin went to all of its American franchisees.

Not one of The Body Shop's dozen "Trade Not Aid" projects has been accurately promoted. And by its own statistics, they represented just 0.165% of the company's business as recently as 1993, at the height of its self-promoting rhetoric. Yet, despite their tiny size and frequent problems, these projects have generated overwhelmingly favorable media coverage—including much of the 10,000 positive mentions the company says it averages each year.

Rainforest Fiasco

Over the past decade, the "rainforest harvest," as it has come to be called, has been the most publicized international fair trade program and a defining symbol of social activism. The marketing of the rainforest blends three cultural trends: the environmentalist struggle to protect the forest against clear-cutting, the movement to preserve indigenous peoples, and baby boom narcissism.

The rainforest movement gathered momentum after the annual Brazilian Peoples Conference in 1989. Roddick and various journalists, environmentalists and eco-celebrities, from Jane Fonda to Sting, gathered in Altamira for the event, which garnered headlines around the world. Not long after, BSI introduced rainforest bath beads made with babassu nut oil, and hair conditioner from nuts harvested and processed by two Kayapo villages in the eastern Amazon.

BSI attached a bright Trade Not Aid sticker to its rainforest bead display, although babassu nuts are not grown in the Amazon, and the beads were made mostly from super-refined oil sourced from the Croda Chemical company—tested on animals in 1986. The hair conditioner uses a tiny fraction of Brazil nut oil at what cosmetic experts say are ineffective levels. According to a study by UK-based Survival International, BSI pays the workers $1.33 per kilo of nuts collected—an average of $500 for a five month harvesting season. Yet in its public relations hand-outs, BSI has claimed that workers in its projects are paid "first world wages." Little money trickles down to the villages. The young Kayapo leaders ("socios") who run the project continue to sell off land rights to profiteers cutting down mahogany trees. The village has been nicknamed Kayapo, Inc. for cashing in their timber dollars for cars, Western-style homes and even an airplane.

Harvest Moonshine

Ben & Jerry's rainforest project, which was more ambitious, has a serendipitous history. In 1988, at a party after a Grateful Dead rainforest fundraising concert, Ben Cohen casually mentioned that he was developing a new brittle for an ice cream using something more exotic than peanuts. According to those present, Jason Clay, an ambitious anthropologist with the Cambridge indigenous rights group Cultural Survival, lit up like a video game. He regaled Cohen with his pet project to market renewable non-timber rainforest products such as fruits, nuts and flowers. A few days after the concert, Cohen's new friend headed to Vermont carrying a 50-pound bag of rainforest nuts. "We mixed up the first batch of Brazil nut crunch in Ben Cohen's kitchen and served it to the board of directors that night," recalled Clay, "and we were off."

Within months, Cohen founded and became half-owner of Community Products Inc. CPI was set up to source Brazil nuts from Cultural Survival (CS) and turn them into brittle for ice cream, and cosmetic products and candy made by other companies. His intentions were no doubt benevolent; CPI promised to pay harvesters a 5% "environmental premium" and give 60% of any profits to charity, a third of that to Cultural Survival.

Ben & Jerry's has long been a favorite of both green-oriented consumers and investors. It does set an impressive standard of ethical innovation: it has published state-of-the-art social audits, gives an astonishing 7.5% of pre-tax profits to charity and buys local dairy products to help preserve the family farm. But the company is most readily identified with its flagship Rainforest ice cream.

Ben & Jerry's launched Rainforest Crunch early in 1990. "Money from these nuts," read the label, "helps to show that rainforests are more profitable when cultivated for traditional harvest than when their trees are cut and burned for short-term gain." The Third World ice cream was an overwhelming, overnight success—for Ben & Jerry's, which reaped tens of millions of dollars in profits and free publicity. But the view from Amazonia was not nearly so sanguine.

Critics found little evidence to support the central premise of the harvest—that foraging for nuts could ever approximate the income natives collect by selling off land rights to miners and foresters. "Marketing the rainforest... perpetuates the process of leaving to the forest dwellers the resources of the least interest to the broader society," wrote anthropologist Michael Dove for the East-West Center in Honolulu, in a typical critique.

Outside of Cultural Survival, where founder David Maybury-Lewis and Jason Clay were positioned to reap fame and perhaps fortune as consultants if the harvest took off, anthropologists quietly urged a go-slow strategy on Ben & Jerry's and BSI, but were ignored.

The worst case scenario was soon realized. There was no established supply chain for Amazon nuts. Most natives such as the Kayapo, long since corrupted by Western interests and fighting a losing battle to alcoholism, were not about to stop selling land rights to meet the expectations of social activists in London and Cambridge. Ben & Jerry's anticipated source for the nuts, the Xapuri cooperative (which had no native workers but was comprised of white rubber tappers, mostly of Portuguese ancestry) in western Brazil, never could meet the quality standards or quantity demands of the fad product.

To meet the sudden explosion in demand, market forces took hold and agri-businesses were drawn in to meet it. The harvest proved to be a windfall for landowners, who have long monopolized trade in this region. "That first year, we had to source all of our nuts from commercial suppliers," concedes Michelle McKinley, the former general manager of CS who left in November after reassembling the pieces of an organization nearly bankrupted by the ill-conceived harvest. Agri-barons elbowed out native suppliers and flooded the market. Nut prices, already soft, plummeted, cutting the incomes of tribes who did collect nuts. Amanakáa, a Brazilian peoples rights group, took Ben & Jerry's to task for sourcing directly from the Mutran family, a notorious Latin American agri-business convicted of killing labor organizers.

While the project was spinning out of control, harvest hype developed into a New Age business mantra. Sting set up the now-defunct Rainforest Foundation and began singing the praises of the free market. Usually-vigilant social critic Alexander Cockburn even became a convert; he attacked the UK-based indigenous rights organization Survival International after its director, Stephen Corry, published "Harvest Moonshine," a meticulously documented critique of the project which criticized Cockburn's friends at Cultural Survival.

Based in large measure on Roddick's self-promotion as a fair trade leader, Ralph Nader dubbed her "the most progressive business person I know," *Mother Jones* invited her onto its board, *USA Today* called her "The Mother Teresa of Capitalism," and the yuppie business magazine *Inc.* put Roddick on its cover with the headline, "This Woman Has Changed Business Forever."

The Brazilian and Bolivian governments took advantage of the harvest hype to justify cutting expensive, politically unpopular financial aid to native populations. A confidential report by the Alliance of Forest Peoples (a coalition including the Xapuri) attacked Cultural Survival for its "minimal" concrete support. "Their negative repercussions have been enormous," read the report. "We have not seen any return." Brazilian peoples groups, cowed at first by the Cohen-Roddick marketing barrage, gradually became more vocal. "A thriving market in forest products," said Julia Barbosa, president of the national Rubber Tappers Council which represented the Xapuri workers, "is no substitute for a political program that protects the forests and people who live in it."

To cover the economic shortfall, some native communities even sold off more land rights. In the end, the celebrated harvest has created a Brazil nut business dominated by some of Latin America's most notorious capitalists. Over the years, more than 95% of Ben & Jerry's Brazil nuts have been purchased on agribusiness dominated markets; today, almost 100% are commercially sourced. According to Cultural Survival's McKinley, the so-called progressive retailers had been increasingly unwilling to pay the 5% environmental premium; last year only $22,000 was collected. "We rushed into this project recklessly," she now says. "We created a fad market overnight and the hard sell promotions have contributed to a lot of confusion. The harvest just didn't work."

In retrospect, early optimistic projections by rainforest capitalists seem almost ridiculous. Clay had estimated a $20–25 million market by 1996 with the benefits flowing to the rubber tappers and native communities. The business peaked in 1991 at $1.3 million, dropped to $250,000 in 1995, and has nearly sunk Cultural Survival. Clay was forced out. By the spring of '94, the Xapuri had cut off all supplies to CS. The project has run in the red for four years, generating no profits for Community Products and no charity.

No Whales Have Been Killed by My Company

Ironically, despite Ben Cohen's attempts to brush off the fiasco, his company did release an independent social audit documenting it. Paul Hawken, the environmentalist, author and businessman, published his analysis as part of Ben & Jerry's annual report released last summer. "It is a legitimate question," wrote Hawken, "whether representations made on Ben & Jerry's Rainforest Crunch package give an accurate impression to the customer." He quoted sharp criticism from Amazon rights groups, then concluded: "There have been undesirable consequences which some say were predictable and avoidable."

So, why have social activists, academics and journalists been caught off guard by the ethical contradictions of socially responsible business and New Age adventures such as the rainforest fiasco? Does buying ice cream or hair rinse with Brazil nuts promote progressive social change or merely inure the public to the profligacy, and elitism, that has gradually coopted the green consumer movement?

The Sixties did inspire a new morality-based social philosophy that emphasizes the individual's responsibility to speak out against injustice and corruption. It drew its social vision from the civil rights movement, anti-Vietnam activism, environmental consciousness and feminism, and it continues to inspire social and environmental reforms. But there is an underside to the legacy of the counterculture: narcissism, arrogance and self-indulgence.

Baby boomers—people born from the mid-1940s to 1960—are beginning to dominate the business and political landscape. Since 1990, their share of national leadership—Congress and governorships—has more than doubled from 21% to 45%, and will reach more than 70% within the decade. They are gradually becoming the American political and business establishment.

Yet, many conspicuous baby boom business leaders seem convinced of their socially responsible credentials, in large measure because they came of age in the Sixties. The visionaries at the vanguard of this movement—from Cohen and Roddick to Mo Siegel at Celestial Seasonings and Paul Fireman at Reebok—are loath to admit that "social responsibility" is in part a margin game. When profits are rolling in, as they were in the 1980s, progressive gestures are painless.

But facing growing pains and intense worldwide competition, many are firing workers, closing inner city stores, cutting back on charity projects, and making their products in overseas sweatshops. Just last November, Reebok received reams of positive press when it gave a Human Rights Award, an annual event. Yet, it was curiously silent a few days later when reports surfaced that its workers in Thailand make 25 cents an hour for 18 hour days. Asked about the contradiction, Reebok's Paul Fireman told the UK newspaper *The Observer* that he will not "impose U.S. culture on other countries... 'when in Rome, do as the Romans.'" In other words, Reebok, BSI and other New Age entrepreneurs frequently act much like any business with bottom line challenges.

The not-so-pristine consequences of green consumerism have been largely absent from business reporting, since many journalists who have so slavishly profiled these successful entrepreneurs share with them common cultural pretensions. Many have convinced themselves that growing up protesting Vietnam and supporting Earth Day forever marks them as progressives, though today their closest brush with social responsibility may consist of little more than enjoying a Ben & Jerry's Peace Pop.

On close scrutiny, progressive business is often a land of alchemy where promises are easy to make, workers are frequently treated with indifference, and environmental reforms are superficially attempted. At best, the relatively small number of consumers with a high tolerance for high-priced goods—most of the products in question command a hefty premium over ordinary brands—play a modest role in raising awareness of social problems. (And even so, it's just a prosperous sliver of baby boomers affected.) At worse, cause-related marketing, as it is called, is little more than baby boom agitprop, masking serious ethical lapses. "Many socially responsible companies have noble corporate philosophies," observes Jon Lickerman, a social researcher with the Calvert Group of socially responsible mutual funds, "but mistreat their own employees, vendors, and customers."

They've also inspired a wave of green marketing by mainstream firms. Guardians of free speech and public health such as Philip Morris take out full-page ads decrying the sale of cigarettes to minors while railing against Big Government; Chevron brags that its sunken oil rigs are havens for Gulf fisheries; oil drillers, developers and natural gas companies band together to form the National Wetlands Coalition, complete with a logo featuring a duck flying over marshes, to front their attacks on environmental reform. Madison Avenue has embraced greenwashing with a vengeance, and the green business movement, with its facile posturing on complex issues, must bear some of the responsibility.

Ice Cream Politics

"It's really a disingenuous marketing strategy to say if you spend $2.99, you'll help save the rainforest," warns Michelle McKinley, formerly of Cultural Survival, which no longer sources Brazil nuts for Ben & Jerry's. But her criticism hasn't dampened Ben Cohen's enthusiasm for hawking Rainforest Crunch. Today, Cohen and co-founder Jerry Greenfield spend little time running the company that has grown far beyond their managerial expertise. They can be found on a college ice cream tour. At the Wharton Business School in Philadelphia, Ben and Jerry sermonized on their usual topics: the crazy fun of starting a business, corporate ethics and of course Rainforest Crunch. "After the speech, I talked with both Ben and Jerry personally," wrote Ritu Kalra, an MBA graduate, in a recent e-mail discussion about the controversy. "Neither of them knew much about the harvest. When it came down to it, they didn't want to comment on it and didn't feel responsible at all for any misleading labeling or for telling half-truths to about 300 college students."

In the case of the rainforest, Cohen still seems oblivious to or afraid to admit the real impact of his now-collapsed pet project. "We have created demand for rainforest products," he boasted at the annual meeting of Business for Social Responsibility in San Francisco in November. There was no mention of the rapacious agri-businesses that supply most of his nuts.

The BSR members—many personal friends of Cohen and part of an informal intelligentsia of the "progressive" business community—were reluctant to press their wounded hero. They were far more eager to munch on Ben & Jerry's Rainforest Crunch donated for the event. "It's so inspiring," one BSR member was heard to say as she licked her spoon clean, "to know that business can make money and still do so much good."

POSTSCRIPT

Can Rain Forest Products Save the Tropical Rain Forest?

It could be argued that this issue's antagonists, the professors and the journalist, are arguing past each other. On the one hand, optimistic innovation, both scientific and economic, will be required to cut through the political barriers protecting the destroyers of the rain forests, so Carr, Pedersen, and Ramaswamy should be encouraged to continue their work. On the other hand, hope does not justify hype, nor do good intentions justify false promises. The journalistic skepticism of Entine is helpful in sorting out the self-serving environmental promotion from solid efforts to use the tremendous potential of the free enterprise system to save a precious global resource.

The rain forest issue is not one of government (and the environmentalists) versus the market (the ranchers). The opinion of many is that the long-term economic opportunity in preserving and harvesting the rain forests easily surpasses any economic gain to be realized in cutting it down. It can be argued that the difficulty in preserving the forest arises because the political powers in place at this time would prefer to use the forest in nonproductive ways for the stabilization of their regimes (through homesteading of the urban poor) and the benefit of political cronies. For centuries, the only means of overwhelming personal political interests has been the higher force of personal economic interests. When we can convince the rulers of the forest that they have more to gain from joining the world in the preservation of the forest than from their present destructive course, optimism on the ultimate fate of the forests will be justified.

Suggested Readings

Erik Eckholm, "Secrets of the Rainforest," *The New York Times Magazine* (November 17, 1988), p. 20.

Sandra Hackman, "After Rio—Our Forests, Ourselves," *Technology Review* (October 1992).

Andrew Revkin, *The Burning Season* (Houghton Mifflin, 1990).

Alex Shoumatoff, *The World Is Burning* (Little, Brown, 1990).

Contributors to This Volume

EDITORS

LISA H. NEWTON is a professor of philosophy and director of the Program in Applied Ethics at Fairfield University in Fairfield, Connecticut. She is coauthor, with Catherine K. Dillingham, of *Watersheds 3: Ten Cases in Environmental Ethics,* 3rd ed. (Wadsworth, 2001) and coauthor, with David A. Schmidt, of *Wake-up Calls: Classic Cases in Business Ethics* (Wadsworth, 1996). She is also the author of numerous articles in journals of business and health care ethics.

MAUREEN M. FORD is an associate for the Program in Applied Ethics at Fairfield University in Fairfield, Connecticut. She received a B.S. in business management and applied ethics from Fairfield University. Active as a consultant to community agencies, Mrs. Ford is a former president of the YWCA in Bridgeport, Connecticut, and was for several years vice president–secretary for JHLF, Inc., a marketing and consulting firm in Westport, Connecticut.

STAFF

Jeffrey L. Hahn   Vice President/Publisher
Theodore Knight   Managing Editor
David Brackley   Senior Developmental Editor
Juliana Gribbins   Developmental Editor
Rose Gleich   Permissions Assistant
Brenda S. Filley   Director of Production/Manufacturing
Julie Marsh   Project Editor
Juliana Arbo   Typesetting Supervisor
Richard Tietjen   Publishing Systems Manager
Charlie Vitelli   Designer

AUTHORS

PHILIP L. BEREANO is a professor of technical communication at the University of Washington. He is active in the American Civil Liberties Union, the Council for Responsible Genetics, and the Washington Biotechnology Action Council. For the past seven years he has been representing public interest organizations in the negotiations of the United Nations' Biosafety Protocol.

SUSAN S. BLACK is publisher of *Bobbin* magazine.

SISSELA BOK is a faculty member of the Center for Advanced Study in the Behavioral Sciences in Stanford, California, and a former associate professor of philosophy at Brandeis University in Waltham, Massachusetts. Her publications include *Lying: Moral Choice in Public and Private Life* (Random House, 1979); *Secrets: On the Ethics of Concealment and Revelation* (Vintage Books, 1983); and *A Strategy for Peace: Human Values and the Threat of War* (Pantheon Books, 1989).

THOMAS A. CARR is an assistant professor in the economics department at Middlebury College in Middlebury, Vermont.

CHRISTOPHER L. CULP is adjunct professor of finance at the Graduate School of Business at the University of Chicago, a principal at Chicago Partners LLC, and senior fellow in financial regulation at the Competitive Enterprise Institute.

WILLIAM DOMNARSKI is an attorney in private practice in Minneapolis, Minnesota. His articles have appeared in such journals as *American Scholar* and *Virginia Quarterly,* and he is the author of *In the Opinion of the Court* (University of Illinois Press, 1995).

MARK DOWIE is an investigative journalist and a former editor of *Mother Jones* magazine. He is the author of *Losing Ground: American Environmentalism at the Close of the Twentieth Century* (MIT Press, 1996) and coauthor, with David T. Hanson and Wendell Berry, of *Waste Land: Meditations on a Ravaged Landscape* (Aperture Foundation, 1997).

WILLIAM R. EADINGTON is a professor of economics and director of the Institute for the Study of Gambling and Commercial Gaming at the University of Nevada, Reno.

ANNE H. EHRLICH is a senior research associate in biological sciences at Stanford University. She is coauthor, with Paul R. Ehrlich, of *Betrayal of Science and Reason: How Anti-Environmental Rhetoric Threatens Our Future* (Island Press, 1996). Ehrlich is coeditor, with John Birks, of *Hidden Dangers: Environmental Consequences of Preparing for War* (Sierra Club Books, 1991).

PAUL R. EHRLICH is the Bing Professor of Population Studies and a professor of biological sciences at Stanford University. He is the author of *The Population Bomb* (Ballantine Books, 1971), which launched a major sector of the environmental movement. He is coauthor, with Anne H. Ehrlich, of *Healing the Planet: Strategies for Resolving the Environmental Crisis* (Addison-Wesley, 1991).

FRIEDRICH ENGELS (1820–1895), a German socialist, was the closest collaborator of Karl Marx in the foundation of modern communism. The "official" Marxism of the Soviet Union relied heavily on Engels's contribution to Marxist theory. After the death of Marx in 1883, Engels served as the foremost authority on Marx and Marxism, and he edited volumes 2 and 3 of *Das Kapital* on the basis of Marx's incomplete manuscripts and notes. Two major works by Engels are *Anti-Duhring* and *Dialectics of Nature.*

JON ENTINE is a journalist specializing in business ethics, journalism ethics, sports, and society. His reporting over 20 years has earned him many awards, including two Emmys. He has served as adjunct professor of journalism at New York University, and he has lectured at Columbia University.

JOHN E. FLEMING is a professor emeritus at the University of Southern California, where he taught for 24 years and where he served as director of the doctoral program and chairman of the Department of Management. His research focuses on strategy and business ethics, and he has been published in the *Academy of Management Journal,* the *California Management Review,* and the *Journal of Business Ethics.*

JOHN P. FOLEY, an archbishop, is president of the Pontifical Council for Social Communications and Vatican media director for Pope John Paul II.

MILTON FRIEDMAN, a U.S. laissez-faire economist, emeritus professor at the University of Chicago, and senior research fellow at the Hoover Institution, is one of the leading modern exponents of liberalism in the nineteenth-century European sense. He is the author of *Capitalism and Freedom* (University of Chicago Press, 1962) and coauthor, with Anna Jacobson Schwartz, of *A Monetary History of the United States 1867–1960* (Princeton University Press, 1963) and, with Rose Friedman, of *Free to Choose: A Personal Statement* (Harcourt Brace Jovanovich, 1980). He was awarded the Nobel Prize for Economics in 1976.

WILLIAM A. GALSTON is a professor in the School of Public Affairs at the University of Maryland at College Park and director of the university's Institute for Philosophy and Public Policy. A political participant as well as an academic, he is executive director of the National Commission on Civic Renewal, and he served as deputy assistant to President Bill Clinton for domestic policy from January 1993 through May 1995. He is coauthor, with Karen J. Baehler, of *Rural Development in the United States: Connecting Theory, Practice, and Possibilities* (Island Press, 1995).

ROBERT GOLDBERG is a senior fellow at the Manhattan Institute. He writes for the *National Review.*

EDMUND R. GRAY is professor and chair of the Department of Management at Loyola Marymount University. He has authored or coauthored five books and over 70 articles and other scholarly publications.

STEVE H. HANKE is a professor of applied economics at the Johns Hopkins University, a principal at Chicago Partners LLC, and a senior fellow at the Cato Institute.

GILBERT HARMAN is Stuart Professor of Philosophy at Princeton University. He has been codirector (with George Miller) of the Princeton University Cognitive Science Laboratory and is chair of the Faculty Committee for Cognitive Studies. He is the author of *Explaining Values and Other Essays in Moral Philosophy* (Oxford University Press, 2000) and *Reasoning, Meaning, and Mind* (Oxford University Press, 1999).

ROBERT D. HAY is a professor of management at the University of Arkansas. He retired in 1990 after 41 years of teaching, research, and service. He is the author of 11 books as well as numerous articles and cases.

GENE R. LACZNIAK is the Wayne R. and Kathleen E. Sanders Professor in Marketing in the School of Business Administration at Marquette University in Milwaukee, Wisconsin. His research interests include marketing strategy, business ethics, and marketing and society. He has taught executive development classes in Europe and Asia, as well as in the United States. He is coauthor, with Patrick E. Murphy, of *Ethical Marketing Decisions* (Allyn & Bacon, 1992).

ROBERT A. LARMER is an associate professor of philosophy at the University of New Brunswick in Fredericton, New Brunswick, Canada. His research interests focus on the philosophy of religion, the philosophy of the mind, and business ethics. He has written numerous articles in these fields, and he is the author of *Water Into Wine? An Investigation of the Concept of Miracle* (McGill-Queen's University Press, 1996). He received his Ph.D. from the University of Ottawa.

JOSEPH A. LEVITT is director of the Food and Drug Administration's Center for Food Safety and Applied Nutrition (CFSAN).

IAN MAITLAND is a professor of business ethics and international business at the University of Minnesota. He is the author of *The Causes of Industrial Disorder: A Comparison of a British and a German Factory* (Routledge, 1983). He has been published in many sources, including the *Journal of Business Ethics, Journal of Politics, Academy of Management Review, British Journal of Industrial Relations, California Management Review,* and *Business and the Contemporary World.*

KARL MARX (1818–1883) was the revolutionist, sociologist, and economist from whom the movement known as Marxism derives its name and many of its ideas. Together with Friedrich Engels he published *Manifest der Kommunistischen Partei* (1848), commonly known as *The Communist Manifesto.* His most important theoretical work is *Das Kapital,* an analysis of the economics of capitalism. He also became the leading spirit of the International Working Men's Association, later known as the First International. His works became the intellectual basis of European socialism in the late nineteenth century.

MERTON H. MILLER is the Robert R. McCormick Distinguished Service Professor Emeritus of Finance in the Graduate School of Business at the University of Chicago in Chicago, Illinois. He and William F. Sharpe were awarded the

Nobel Prize in Economics in 1990 for their pioneering work in the theory of financial economics. He is the author of *Merton Miller on Derivatives* (John Wiley, 1997) and *Financial Innovations and Market Volatility* (Blackwell, 1991).

JENNIFER MOORE, a former assistant professor of philosophy at the University of Delaware in Newark, Delaware, has done teaching and research in business ethics and business law. She is the author of *Math Bridge* (Rainbow Bridge, 1999) and coauthor, with Karen Musalo and Richard A. Boswell, of *Refugee Law and Policy: Selected Statutes, Regulations and International Materials* (Carolina Academic Press, 1998).

KEVIN J. MURPHY is a professor of finance and business economics in the Marshall School of Business at the University of Southern California. He has also taught at the Harvard Business School and the University of Rochester. He is chairman of the Academic Research Committee of the American Compensation Association and associate editor of the *Journal of Financial Economics,* the *Journal of Accounting and Economics,* and the *Journal of Corporate Finance.* His publications include *Ecosystems,* coauthored with Gordon Dickinson (Routledge, 1997).

ALLEN R. MYERSON is a contributing journalist for the *New York Times.*

FRANK PARTNOY is an assistant professor of law at the University of San Diego Law School, where he teaches in the areas of corporations, Latin American finance, and white-collar offenses. He is the author of *Fiasco: The Inside Story of a Wall Street Trader* (Viking Penguin, 1999) and *F.I.A.S.C.O.: Blood in the Water on Wall Street* (W. W. Norton, 1997).

HEATHER L. PEDERSEN is a mathematics teacher at the Colorado Springs School in Colorado.

SUNDER RAMASWAMY is chairman of the economics department at Middlebury College in Middlebury, Vermont. He received his Ph.D. from Purdue University. He is coauthor, with John H. Sanders and Barry I. Shapiro, of *The Economics of Agricultural Technology in Semiarid Sub-Saharan Africa* (Johns Hopkins University Press, 1996).

JEREMY RIFKIN is president of the Foundation on Economic Trends. His publications include *The End of Work: The Decline of the Global Labor Force and the Dawn of the Post-Market Era* (Jeremy P. Tarcher, 1996) and *The Biotech Century: Harnessing the Gene and Remaking the World* (Putnam, 1998).

RICHARD ROSEN is a writer for *The American Prospect.*

JOHN SHANAHAN is vice president of The Alexis de Tocqueville Institution in Arlington, Virginia.

ADAM SMITH (1723–1790) was a Scottish philosopher and economist and the author of *An Inquiry Into the Nature and Causes of the Wealth of Nations,* 2 vols. (1776).

ROBERT C. SOLOMON is Quincy Lee Centennial Professor of Business and Philosophy at the University of Texas in Austin. He authored six books on business ethics, including, with Kristine R. Hanson, *It's Good Business*

(Atheneum, 1985); *Ethics and Excellence: Cooperation and Integrity in Business* (Oxford University Press, 1992); *The New World of Business: Ethics and Free Enterprise in the Global 1990s* (Rowman & Littlefield, 1994); and *A Better Way to Think About Business: How Personal Integrity Leads to Corporate Success* (Oxford University, 1999).

MANUEL VELASQUEZ is the Charles Dirksen Professor of Business Ethics at Santa Clara University, where he teaches courses in the legal, political, and social environment of the firm; in business strategy; and in business ethics. He has published numerous articles in journals such as the *Academy of Management Review,* the *Business Ethics Quarterly, Social Justice Research,* and the *Business and Professional Ethics Journal,* and he is the author of *Business Ethics: Concepts and Cases,* 4th ed. (Prentice Hall, 1998). He received his B.A. from Gonzaga University and his Ph.D. from the University of California at Berkeley.

MICHAEL A. VERESPEJ is a writer for *Industry Week.*

DAVID WASSERMAN is a research scholar at the Institute for Philosophy and Public Policy in the School of Public Affairs at the University of Maryland at College Park. He has written about legal evidence and statistical inference, the moral underpinnings of criminal law and legal practice, the concept of discrimination, and various issues in procedural and distributive justice. His present research focuses on ethical and policy issues in genetic research and technology and on justice for people with disabilities. He is coauthor, with Anita Silvers and Mary Mahowald, of *Disability, Difference, Discrimination: Perspectives on Justice in Bioethics and Public Policy* (Rowman & Littlefield, 1998).

DEBRA WATSON is a writer for the World Socialist Web site at http://www.wsws.org.

JOSEF WIELAND is director of the Centre for Business Ethics, which is associated with the German Business Ethics Network. He is also professor of economic and business ethics at the University of Hohenheim.

Index